Examining Philosophy Itself

♨METAPHILOSOPHY

METAPHILOSOPHY SERIES IN PHILOSOPHY

Series Editors Armen T. Marsoobian and Eric Cavallero

Examining Philosophy Itself

Edited by
Yafeng Shan

This edition first published 2023
Chapters and book compilation © 2023 Metaphilosophy LLC and John Wiley & Sons Ltd,

First published as *Metaphilosophy* volume 53, nos. 2-3 (April 2022).

Registered Office
John Wiley & Sons Ltd, The Atrium, Southern Gate, Chichester, West Sussex, PO19 8SQ, UK

Editorial Offices
350 Main Street, Malden, MA 02148-5020, USA
9600 Garsington Road, Oxford, OX4 2DQ, UK
The Atrium, Southern Gate, Chichester, West Sussex, PO19 8SQ, UK

For details of our global editorial offices, for customer services, and for information about how to apply
for permission to reuse the copyright material in this book please see our website at www.wiley.com.

The rights of Yafeng Shan to be identified as the author of the editorial material in this work have been
asserted in accordance with the UK Copyright, Designs and Patents Act 1988.

Library of Congress Cataloging-in-Publication Data has been applied for.
9781394160716 (paperback)

A catalogue record for this book is available from the British Library.

Cover image: © James Warwick/Getty Images
Cover design by Wiley

Set in 10/11pt Times New Roman MTStd by Straive, Chennai, India
Printed and bound by CPI Group (UK) Ltd, Croydon, CR0 4YY

C9781394160716_270223

CONTENTS

NOTES ON CONTRIBUTORS

Amanda Bryant is an independent scholar with an interest in metaphilosophy, metametaphysics, the epistemology of metaphysics, and the metaphysics of science and scientific metaphysics, as well as naturalism and scientism. She received her Ph.D. in philosophy from the City University of New York Graduate Center in 2017, after which she held a fixed-term assistant professorship at Trent University and a postdoctoral research fellowship at the University of Lisbon.

Herman Cappelen is professor of philosophy at the University of Hong Kong, director of the AI&Humanity Lab, and the author of eleven monographs and more than fifty articles across a range of philosophical topics. He is currently working on the philosophy of AI and engineering of political discourse. His most recent books are *Making AI Intelligible*, cowritten with Josh Dever (OUP, 2021), and *The Concept of Democracy: An Essay on Conceptual Engineering and Abandonment*.

Chris Daly is a professor of philosophy at the University of Manchester. His research interests are in philosophy of science and philosophy of language, and he is the author of *Introduction to Philosophical Methods* (Broadview Press, 2010) and *Philosophy of Language* (Bloomsbury, 2012).

Zack Garrett teaches logic and philosophy at Excelsior Classical Academy in Durham, North Carolina. He received his Ph.D. from the University of Nebraska—Lincoln in 2020, and his research interests include topics that lie at the intersections between metaphysics, philosophy of language, and logic. He is particularly interested in nonclassical logics and argues in his dissertation that a many-valued logic is the best way to handle the phenomenon of vagueness.

Eve Kitsik is a visiting researcher at the University of Cologne in Germany. She has published mainly on metametaphysics and conceptual engineering, in such journals as *Erkenntnis, Synthese,* and *Philosophia*. Her current research interests include epistemic value and the ethics of attention. Before Cologne, she was a junior research fellow at the University of Tartu in Estonia.

Ben Martin is an assistant professor of philosophy at the University of Padua. Before that, he was a Marie Skłodowska-Curie Fellow at the University of Bergen and the principal investigator for the European Union Horizon 2020–funded project *The Unknown Science: Understanding the Epistemology of Logic Through Practice*. He works mainly in the philosophy of logic and epistemology, and has published in such journals as the *Australasian Journal of Philosophy*, the *Journal of Philosophical Logic*, and *Synthese*.

Matthew McKeever is postdoctoral research fellow in the AI&Humanity Lab at the University of Hong Kong. His recent publications include work on social and political philosophy of language and philosophy of technology, and his research interests include philosophy of language and metaphilosophy broadly construed, particularly their applicability to contemporary AI and other novel technologies.

Charles H. Pence is chargé de cours at the Université catholique de Louvain, in Louvainla-Neuve, Belgium, where he directs the Center for Philosophy of Science and Societies (CEFISES). His work centers on the philosophy and history of biology, with a focus on the introduction and contemporary use of chance and statistics in evolution. His lab also heavily utilizes methods from the digital humanities and is increasingly engaged in the ethical implications of biological science and technology.

Jack Ritchie is an associate professor in the Department of Philosophy at the University of Cape Town. He mainly works on issues in the philosophy of science, metaphysics, and metaphilosophy and is the author of *Understanding Naturalism* (Routledge, 2008) and several journal articles.

Yafeng Shan is a research fellow in epistemology in the Department of Philosophy at the University of Cologne, Germany. He received his Ph.D. from University College London, and his main research interests are philosophy of science, epistemology, and metaphysics. He is the author of *Doing Integrated History and Philosophy of Science: A Case Study of the Origin of Genetics* (Springer, 2020) and has published research articles in such journals as *Synthese*, *Philosophy of Science*, and *Philosophy Compass*.

Karen Simecek is an associate professor of philosophy at the University of Warwick. Her research focuses on the philosophy of poetry, philosophy of voice, and the emotions. She has published articles on poetry in the *British*

Journal of Aesthetics, Estetika: European Journal of Aesthetics, the *Journal of Aesthetic Education, Philosophy Compass*, and *Philosophy and Literature*. She is currently writing a monograph on poetry entitled *Philosophy of Lyric Voice* (forthcoming from Bloomsbury Academic).

Jon Williamson is a professor of reasoning, inference, and scientific method at the University of Kent. He works on the philosophy of science and medicine, causality, formal epistemology, and logic. His books include *Evaluating Evidence of Mechanisms in Medicine* (Springer, 2018); *Lectures on Inductive Logic* (Oxford, 2017); *Probabilistic Logics and Probabilistic Networks* (Springer, 2011); *In Defence of Objective Bayesianism* (Oxford, 2010); and *Bayesian Nets and Causality* (Oxford, 2005).

Timothy Wiliiamson has been the Wykeham Professor of Logic at the University of Oxford since 2000. He is also the Whitney Griswold Visiting Professor at Yale University. His books include *Identity and Discrimination, Vagueness, Knowledge and Its Limits, The Philosophy of Philosophy, Modal Logic as Metaphysics, Tetralogue: I'm Right, You're Wrong, Suppose and Tell: The Semantics and Heuristics of Conditionals, Philosophical Method: A Very Short Introduction,* and (with Paul Boghossian) *Debating the A Priori.*

Zachariah Wrublewski is a Ph.D. student in philosophy at the University of Nebraska—Lincoln. He is currently working on a thesis examining the nature of rational requirements, the property of rationality, and the connections between rationality and reasons. His research interests include philosophy of modality (especially modal epistemology), metaethics (especially theories of reasons and rationality), and philosophy of action.

INTRODUCTION: THE UNEXAMINED PHILOSOPHY IS NOT WORTH DOING

YAFENG SHAN

ὁ δὲ ἀνεξέταστος βίος οὐ βιωτὸς ἀνθρώπῳ (... and that the unexamined life is not worth living).

—Plato, *Apology,* 38a5–6

Introduction

One of the most distinctive features of philosophy is self-reflection. Philosophers are not only concerned with metaphysical, epistemological, conceptual, ethical, and aesthetic issues of things around us, they also pay serious attention to the nature, value, methods, and development of philosophy itself. This kind of study of philosophy is often called metaphilosophy.[1] For the past two decades, there has been an increasing interest in metaphilosophical issues. The aim of philosophy has been examined. For example, Paul Horwich (2012) develops a Wittgensteinian approach to criticising the traditional conception of theoretical philosophy (or in his term "T-Philosophy") with the aim of construction and defence of important philosophical theories, while Helen Beebee argues that the view that philosophy aims at knowledge should be abandoned and replaced

---

[1] It is also sometimes called "philosophy of philosophy" (Williamson 2007), "philosophical methods" (Daly 2015), and "philosophical methodology" (D'Oro and Overgaard 2017). It should be noted that these terminological variances to some extent reflect the different views on the nature of metaphilosophical inquiries. For example, Williamson rejects the word "metaphilosophy," because he contends that "the investigation of philosophical methodology cannot and should not be philosophically neutral" (2007, 5).

Examining Philosophy Itself. Edited by Yafeng Shan.
Chapters and book compilation © 2023 Metaphilosophy LLC and John Wiley & Sons Ltd.
Published 2023 by John Wiley & Sons Ltd.

with a more modest aim: that of finding "equilibria" that "can withstand examination" (2018, 1). The development of philosophy has also been scrutinised. In particular, whether philosophy makes progress has been widely debated (e.g., Williamson 2006; Dietrich 2011; Chalmers 2015; Stoljar 2017). In addition, new problems arise with the development of new approaches and methods. Should analytic metaphysics be replaced by naturalised metaphysics (Ladyman et al. 2007)? What is the prospect of digital philosophy of science (Pence and Ramsey 2018)? Is conceptual engineering a worthwhile philosophical method (Deutsch 2022)? The present collection of essays revisits some of these metaphilosophical debates and examines and explores new philosophical methods and their prospects.

Defending Philosophy

The value of philosophy as an academic discipline or a way of inquiry has been persistently challenged in history, from ancient Greece to today. A recent example is that a well-known Cambridge physicist publicly declared: "Philosophy is dead." For him, "philosophers have not kept up with modern developments in science, particularly, physics. Scientists have become the bearers of the torch of discovery in our quest for knowledge" (Hawking and Mlodinow 2010, 5). Such a naïve argument against philosophy is not difficult to demolish, from a philosopher's point of view. That said, there are nonetheless some serious objections to philosophy.

A persistent objection to philosophy focuses on one of its central branches: metaphysics. Metaphysics has faced serious challenges throughout its history. Rudolf Carnap (1931), for example, famously argued that statements of metaphysics are meaningless and thus metaphysics should be eliminated. In this collection, Timothy Williamson in "Metametaphysics and Semantics" defends metaphysics against a challenge from intensional semantics, which can be traced back to Wittgenstein's *Tractatus Logico-Philosophicus*. The problem, in a nutshell, is that metaphysical claims are either trivially true or trivially false, in so far as metaphysics is concerned with the necessary nature and structure of reality. If this is so, it seems incompatible with the stated aim of metaphysics—to find out how the world is. Williamson argues that neither the attempt to solve Wittgenstein's problem by reinterpreting non-contingent claims as contingent metalinguistic claims nor the attempt to solve Wittgenstein's problem by invoking Fregean semantics works. He points out that the nature of the problem is about necessarily equivalent propositions rather than necessary or impossible propositions. Thus, Williamson suggests that in order to solve the problem, we must recognise that the form of our representations plays an ineliminable cognitive role that is reducible to their content.

Another typical objection to philosophy arises from a widespread view that philosophy makes little progress. Sceptics often contrast philosophy with science. Few would doubt that science has in general been progressing for the past few centuries, though it is still under debate whether scientific progress should be characterised as accumulation of knowledge (Bird 2007), approximation of truth (Niiniluoto 2014), increased usefulness of practice (Shan 2019), or better understanding (Dellsén 2021). By contrast, it is not an easy task to defend the view that philosophy has progressed greatly. To many, the significance and value of philosophy is undermined if little progress in philosophy has been made in history. In "Philosophy Doesn't Need a Concept of Progress," I defend philosophy by revisiting the notion of philosophical progress. First, I identify two criteria of an ideal concept of philosophical progress: "philosophical" progress should be a comparative notion and a useful tool to help us have a good understanding of the history of philosophy. I then argue that our accounts of philosophical progress fail to provide such an ideal concept. Furthermore, I argue that not only do we not have a good concept of philosophical progress, we do not need a concept of philosophical progress. That said, I highlight that the elimination of the concept of philosophical progress does not undermine the significance or value of philosophy. I maintain that there have been many philosophical successes in history. Accordingly, I argue that an important task for philosophers is to develop a good account of philosophical success.

In "T-Philosophy," Chris Daly addresses an objection to the aim of philosophy by arguing against Horwich's criticism of T-Philosophy. Following the late Wittgenstein, Horwich identifies four defective ingredients of T-Philosophy: (1) the illusion that theoretical progress can be made by disambiguating what appear to be unified concepts; (2) irrational distortions that arise from transferring considerations of simplicity from science to philosophy; (3) the absence of epistemic constraints needed to deliver knowledge (of theoretical philosophy); and (4) the questionable value of believing philosophical theories (Horwich 2012, 34–35). Daly argues that these claims are ill grounded. He also critically examines, as a case study, Horwich's contention that the problem of our knowledge of numbers can be dissolved on the grounds that the problem is based on a misguided analogy with our knowledge of physical objects. Daly concludes that T-Philosophy (or the traditional conception of philosophy as a theoretical enterprise) is viable.

How to Do Philosophy

Philosophical methods have been another focus of metaphilosophy. Since the first half of the twentieth century, there has been a tendency to ally philosophy more closely with science. For example, W. V. Quine famously argues that epistemology should be naturalised in the way that it is "contained in natural science, as a chapter of psychology" (1969, 83). Recently there have also been various attempts to naturalise metaphysics. Although there is a consensus that naturalised metaphysics differs from traditional analytic metaphysics in its scientific input, it is far from clear in what way science informs metaphysical inquiry (e.g., Ney 2012; Chakravartty 2013; Morganti and Tahko 2017). In "On the Continuity of Metaphysics with Science: Some Scepticism and Some Suggestions," Jack Ritchie identifies three broad (possibly overlapping) ways of naturalising metaphysics: (1) metaphysics and science use the same methods; (2) metaphysics is an attempt to synthesise theories of the natural sciences and commonsense knowledge; and (3) fundamental physics provides the best way to purpose metaphysics. Ritchie argues that a reflective metaphysician ought to reject all these three ways of doing naturalized metaphysics if metaphysics is regarded as a truth-seeking enterprise. He argues for a call to reconstruct the aim of metaphysics. By our doing so, all three ways of naturalised metaphysics can be worthwhile for the purpose of exploring scientific theories, articulating the connections between concepts, or metaphor mongering.

Ordinary language, the once popular method that uses features of certain words in ordinary or non-philosophical contexts as an aid to doing philosophy, is no longer fashionable. But in "In Defence of Ordinary Language Philosophy," Herman Cappelen and Matthew McKeever argue that ordinary concepts are central to much of philosophy. They respond to some anti-ordinary language arguments put forward by David Chalmers and contrast their view with Williamson's instrumentalist view on ordinary language. Cappelen and McKeever conclude that ordinary language is not only a tool for seeing the world better but also determines what it is we look at and tells us things about what we look at.

Under the influence of digital humanities, a digital approach to the philosophy of science has recently been developed (Pence and Ramsey 2018; Lean, Rivelli, and Pence forthcoming). Typically, it is argued that digital methods can be used for testing philosophical hypotheses and discovering new philosophical hypotheses. There is, however, an obvious tension between these two. One cannot simultaneously use the same data to propose a hypothesis and test the same hypothesis. In "Testing and Discovery: Responding to Challenges to Digital Philosophy of Science," Charles Pence tries to resolve this tension. He argues that if we focus exclusively either on hypothesis formation or on hypothesis testing, then we undermine some of the real power of digital philosophy. Instead, Pence argues for a more nuanced way to keep hold of the advantages of both hypothesis testing and hypothesis discovery. Illustrated by two interdisciplinary case studies, his argument is that we should reject the binary view of mutually exclusive testing and discovery and should instead investigate the relationship between our background data or philosophical views and the empirical generalizations that we might draw from the data. Finally, Pence identifies three challenges for philosophers and considers avenues for future work that will allow us to better justify our use of these methods.

Conceptual engineering is another new method, and it has attracted much recent attention in philosophy. Nevertheless, there are also doubts about the significance of conceptual engineering; some argue that it is unjustified that conceptual engineering is getting so much attention. In "Attentional Progress by Conceptual Engineering," however, Eve Kitsik defends conceptual engineering as a worthwhile philosophical method. She argues that conceptual engineering can contribute to philosophical progress by shifting philosophers' attention to more important questions or by making salient the phenomena that are relevant for addressing the old umbrella philosophical questions.

Inspired by the practice turn in the philosophy of science, Ben Martin argues in "The Philosophy of Logical Practice" for the need to embrace a new practice-based approach to the epistemology of logic, which aims to rectify the failures of past accounts. According to this approach, we should begin by looking in detail at the actual practice of logicians and then extract methodological principles from this practice, gradually building up a detailed account of logic's epistemology. Martin argues that there are two main benefits of his philosophy of logical practice: making progress on established questions and exploring new fruitful areas. He concludes that philosophers of logic ought to recognise the significance of building this understanding of the field of logicians' actual practice.

In "One Philosopher's Modus Ponens Is Another's Modus Tollens: Pantomemes and Nisowir," Jon Williamson revisits two widely used rules of inferences: *modus ponens* and *modus tollens*. He begins with introducing a serious problem for argumentation: one person's *modus ponens* is often another's *modus tollens*. He argues that appeals to intuition, evidence, or truth fail to solve such a problem. Williamson develops two new strategies: an appeal to normal informal standards of what is reasonable and an argument by interpretation. The method of explication features prominently in both strategies. By illustrating the problem and the two strategies with examples of arguments in formal epistemology, Williamson suggests that at least one of the strategies can help to defend against philosophical scepticism by shifting the burden of proof to the sceptic.

In "Linking Perspectives: A Role for Poetry in Philosophical Inquiry," Karen Simecek explores a new way of doing philosophy. She argues that reading lyric poetry can play a substantive role in philosophy by helping the philosopher understand how to forge connections with the perspectives of others. Simecek indicates that the rejection of the thesis that poetry can play an important role in philosophical inquiry is based on a limited understanding of the practice of philosophy, which construes philosophy as merely a truth-seeking enterprise. Following Robert Nozick, David Lewis, and Helen Beebee, she argues for a broad conception of the aim of philosophy. Through her discussion of Lucretius's *De rerum natura* (*On the Nature of Things*) and Robert Gray's "The Drift of Things," she shows how poetry cultivates the intellectual virtues essential to a philosophy that aims not at truth but at uncovering equilibria and collective understanding.

Doing Philosophy

The ultimate aim of metaphilosophy is to help philosophers to do good philosophy rather than bad philosophy. Thus, following my practical spirit (Shan 2020, 5), I contend that the best way to defend philosophy is not only to show how to do good philosophy methodologically but also to do it in practice. Accordingly, in metaphilosophy, not only should we examine philosophy from a general methodological point of view, we should also examine the use of philosophical methods in concrete cases. Two essays in this part are examples of such an approach.

In "Grounding Interventionism: Conceptual and Epistemological Challenges," Amanda Bryant examines the prospect of importing conceptual and formal resources of causal interventionism into the metaphysics of grounding. Bryant critically examines several formulations of grounding interventionism. She argues that the available epistemological options for causal interventionism and grounding interventionism are insufficiently powerful, and so concludes that grounding interventionism requires firmer epistemological foundations.

In "Impossible Worlds and the Safety of Philosophical Beliefs," Zack Garrett and Zach-ariah Wrublewski examine the modal conditions of knowledge. They identify a serious problem regarding beliefs that are necessarily true: if necessary truths are truth in all possible worlds, then such beliefs can be safe even when the bases for the beliefs are epistemically problematic. Garrett and Wrublewski argue that incorporating impossible worlds into the evaluation of beliefs solves the problem. They also highlight an implication of making reference to impossible worlds: that some philosophical beliefs are unsafe. That said, they still maintain that philosophical progress (in terms of the accumulation of safe beliefs or the achievement of reflective equilibrium) is possible.

Summary

In sum, this collection consists of three parts. The essays in the first part defend the significance and value of philosophy. In my essay, I suggest that the value of philosophy does not have to be assessed in terms of progress. Williamson defends metaphysics against a challenge from semantic intensionalism. Daly argues against Horwich's criticisms of T-Philosophy and defends the view that philosophy can devise theories that unify and explain puzzling phenomena. The essays in the second part examine and explore a variety of philosophical methods: naturalistic metaphysics, ordinary language philosophy, digital philosophy of science, conceptual engineering, the practice-based approach to logic, and the role of poetry in philosophical inquiries. The essays in the third part examine two particular approaches to the issues of grounding and the safety of philosophical beliefs, respectively. These essays thus shed new light on some important metaphilosophical issues. It is clear, however, that the topics covered in this collection are just the tip of the iceberg in the realm of metaphilosophy. Much more work is left to be done.

Acknowledgments

Most of the essays in this collection emerged from the *New Directions in Metaphilosophy* conference held virtually at the Centre for Reasoning, University of Kent, on 13 and 14 May 2021. The conference was financially supported by the Aristotelian Society and the Analysis Trust. All the essays went through a double-blind reviewing process. I am grateful to all the external referees for their time and effort. I would also like to thank Armen T. Marsoobian and Otto Bohlmann for their help in every phase of the preparation of the collection. Finally, I would like to thank Jon Williamson and Sam Taylor for reading an early draft of this introduction.

References

Beebee, Helen. 2018. "Philosophical Scepticism and the Aim of Philosophy." *Proceedings of the Aristotelian Society* 118, no. 1: 1–24.
Bird, Alexander. 2007. "What Is Scientific Progress?" *Noûs* 41, no. 1: 64–89.
Carnap, Rudolf. 1931. "Überwindung der Metaphysik durch logische Analyse der Sprache." *Erkenntnis* 2: 219–41.
Chakravartty, Anjan. 2013. "On the Prospects of Naturalized Metaphysics." In *Scientific Metaphysics*, edited by Don Ross, James Ladyman, and Harold Kincaid, 27–50. Oxford: Oxford University Press.
Chalmers, David J. 2015. "Why Isn't There More Progress in Philosophy?" *Philosophy* 90, no. 1: 3–31.
Daly, Chris, ed. 2015. *The Palgrave Handbook of Philosophical Methods.* New York: Palgrave Macmillan.
Dellsén, Finnur. 2021. "Understanding Scientific Progress: The Noetic Account." *Synthese* 199: 11249–78.
Deutsch, Max. 2022. "Trivializing Conceptual Engineering." *Inquiry.* https://doi.org/10.1080/0020174X.2020.1853343.
Dietrich, Eric. 2011. "There Is No Progress in Philosophy." *Essays in Philosophy* 12: 329–44.
D'Oro, Giuseppina, and Søren Overgaard, eds. 2017. *The Cambridge Companion to Philosophical Methodology.* Cambridge: Cambridge University Press.
Hawking, Stephen, and Leonard Mlodinow. 2010. *The Grand Design.* London: Transworld.

Horwich, Paul. 2012. *Wittgenstein's Metaphilosophy*. Oxford: Oxford University Press.

Ladyman, James, Don Ross, David Spurrett, and John Collier. 2007. *Everything Must Go: Metaphysics Naturalized*. Oxford: Oxford University Press.

Lean, Oliver M., Luca Rivelli, and Charles H. Pence. Forthcoming. "Digital Literature Analysis for Empirical Philosophy of Science." *British Journal for the Philosophy of Science.* https://doi.org/10.1086/715049.

Morganti, Matteo, and Tuomas E. Tahko. 2017. "Moderately Naturalistic Metaphysics." *Synthese* 194, no. 7: 2557–80.

Ney, Alyssa. 2012. "Neo-Positivist Metaphysics." *Philosophical Studies* 160, no. 1: 53–78.

Niiniluoto, Ilkka. 2014. "Scientific Progress as Increasing Verisimilitude." *Studies in History and Philosophy of Science Part A* 46: 73–77.

Pence, Charles H., and Grant Ramsey. 2018. "How to Do Digital Philosophy of Science." *Philosophy of Science* 85, no. 5: 930–41.

Quine, Willard V. 1969. "Epistemology Naturalized." In *Ontological Relativity and Other Essays*, 69–90. New York: Columbia University Press.

Shan, Yafeng. 2019. "A New Functional Approach to Scientific Progress." *Philosophy of Science* 86, no. 4: 739–58. https://doi.org/https://doi.org/10.1086/704980.

Shan, Yafeng. 2020. *Doing Integrated History and Philosophy of Science: A Case Study of the Origin of Genetics*. Cham: Springer.

Stoljar, Daniel. 2017. *Philosophical Progress: In Defence of a Reasonable Optimism*. Oxford: Oxford University Press.

Williamson, Timothy. 2006. "Must Do Better." In *Truth and Realism*, edited by Patrick Greenough and Michael P. Lynch, 177–87. Oxford: Oxford University Press.

Williamson, Timothy. 2007. *The Philosophy of Philosophy*. Malden, Mass.: Blackwell.

PART 1

DEFENDING PHILOSOPHY

CHAPTER 1

METAMETAPHYSICS AND SEMANTICS

TIMOTHY WILLIAMSON

Of all branches of philosophy, metaphysics has probably attracted the most opprobrium. It is the one most easily represented as a lazy, dogmatic, obsolete rival of natural science. It is also the most discursively abstract branch. Predictably, it is the one most often accused of being *nonsense*.[1]

When meaning is understood in epistemic terms, the charge of meaninglessness turns into the charge that metaphysics is epistemically inadequate: it lacks proper methods for achieving knowledge, or even reasonable belief, in its domain. The logical positivists gave a salient version of such a critique, wielding their verification principle as a blunt instrument. Since putative truths of metaphysics are neither analytic nor empirically verifiable, they are meaningless by logical empiricist standards. Of course, such an accusation is largely bluff without an adequate verificationist theory of meaning in the background, and the logical positivists made very little progress towards developing such a theory. Nevertheless, the logical empiricist dichotomy of all cognition into "empirical" and "conceptual" aspects continues to have its adherents: for example, the work of Amie Thomasson (2015; 2020) is in the tradition of Rudolf Carnap (1950), and more distantly of David Hume's dichotomy of "relations of ideas" and "matters of fact," though she has more interest than Carnap in non-scientific language. Between the conceptual and the empirical, no room seems left for substantive unconfused metaphysical theorizing.

Unfortunately, like "analytic" and "synthetic," the terms "conceptual" and "empirical" are far more problematic than they first appear. There is

---

[1] I use the term "metaphysics" as it is standardly used in contemporary philosophy, with a standard view of what counts as metaphysics. The arguments of this essay are robust to minor variations in that respect.

Examining Philosophy Itself. Edited by Yafeng Shan.
Chapters and book compilation © 2023 Metaphilosophy LLC and John Wiley & Sons Ltd.
Published 2023 by John Wiley & Sons Ltd.

a crude stereotype of the conceptual, and a crude stereotype of the empirical, but the assumptions built into those stereotypes are unclear. What is clear is that both stereotypes, separately and together, are utterly inadequate for making sense of logic and mathematics, let alone of metaphysics. I have explained the difficulties elsewhere (most recently, Williamson 2007; forthcoming *a*) and will not repeat those considerations here.

This essay addresses a different challenge to metaphysics. It is more urgent, because its starting point is less hostile. The new challenge is semantic, like the logical empiricist critique, but unlike the latter it does not depend on an epistemic conception of semantics. Instead, one might even say, it depends on a *metaphysical* conception of semantics. But that does not make the new challenge self-defeating. For if metaphysics is already in tension with a metaphysics-friendly approach to semantics, that is bad news for metaphysics.

Uncompromising metaphysics, both ancient and modern, aspires to discover the necessary nature and structure of reality. Its primary interest is in the world, not in our thought or talk about the world—of course, our thought and talk are part of the world, but (except under extreme forms of idealism) only a very small part. Thus a worldly approach to semantics, on which the semantic value of a linguistic expression in a context is a worldly item, looks like a good fit with metaphysics. For example, such a theory may identify the semantic value of a declarative sentence in a context with a proposition, understood as the set of possible worlds at which the sentence is true, or as a complex of the objects, properties, and relations the sentence is about (in both cases, relative to that context). In brief, such semantics correlates metaphysicians' words with the very metaphysical entities they wish to discuss (if there are such entities). That suggests a fully cooperative attitude of semantics to metaphysics. Any tension between the two is therefore all the more disturbing—as though semantics, with the best will in the world, still leaves no room for metaphysics.

1. Intensional Semantics

The problem arises in an especially stark form within a standard framework for intensional semantics, the mainstream of contemporary formal semantics as a branch of linguistics. The approach is referential and truth conditional. We consider it first in its simplest form. It has been elaborated and modified in various ways, but they turn out to make no essential difference to the problem.

Each expression of the language is assigned a *content* (henceforth, relativization to a context of utterance will be left implicit). The assignment is compositional: the content of a complex expression is determined by the contents of its constituent expressions and how those constituents are put together. This determination is implemented within a framework of *worlds*, treated as parameters of semantic evaluation. The semantics is *intensional* because, for many central types of expression, including predicates and (declarative) sentences, the content of an expression is its intension, a function mapping each world to its extension at that world. In particular, since the extension of a sentence at a world is its truth-value at that world, its intension is a function from worlds to truth-values (truth or falsity). We may call such sentential intensions *propositions*. Thus the sentence "There is a god" expresses the proposition that there is a god, the function mapping each world in which there is a god to truth and each world in which there is no god to falsity.

Any such intensional framework determines a *distinguished modality*, characterized by the condition that, for any sentence "A," "Necessarily A" is true at a world w if and only if "A" is true at every world, while "Possibly A" is true at w if and only if "A" is true at some world. In what follows, the words "possible" and "necessary" are used for that modality. Thus the worlds in the framework are all and only the *possible* worlds. On the compositional semantics, the logical connectives behave classically at each world, so any truth of classical propositional logic is true at every world. It is then easily shown that every theorem of the well-known modal system S5 is true at every world on this interpretation. In particular, it validates the distinctive theses that whatever is necessary is necessarily necessary (the S4 axiom) and whatever is possible is necessarily possible (the S5 axiom): matters of necessity or possibility are not themselves contingent.

Since our interest is in metaphysically oriented semantic theories, we should interpret this distinguished modality as broadly objective rather than merely epistemic in nature. Indeed, we may conceive it as the broadest kind of objective possibility, since it excludes no worlds in the framework. An attractive hypothesis is that such a maximal objective modality is just what is usually called "metaphysical modality" (Williamson 2016). But that is far from uncontroversial. For instance, the S4 axiom has been denied for metaphysical modality (Salmon 1989), and the S5 axiom has been denied for the broadest modality (Bacon 2018). A further complication is that a deeper understanding of modality may well not treat possible worlds as basic but instead start from the distinction between the possible and the impossible itself, perhaps in the setting of higher-order logic (Williamson 2013). Such alternatives, however, are all compatible with some version of intensional semantics; none of them avoids the problems discussed below. For present purposes, we can ignore the differences between them.

An immediate corollary of this approach is that propositions are very coarse grained. *Necessarily equivalent propositions are identical*: they output the same truth-value for any given world as input, and so are the same function. Thus, in particular, there is only one necessary proposition and only one impossible proposition. If you know one necessary truth, you know them all. For instance, reading "god" in a strong sense, on which being a god is a necessary property: whatever has it in a world has it in any other world too (it may also entail other standard attributes, such as omniscience, omnipotence, omnipresence, omnibenevolence, and eternity; for present purposes we omit ineffability, since it might cause distinctively semantic problems). Thus it is either necessary or impossible that there is a god. If it is necessary, the proposition that there is a god is just the proposition that all cats are cats. If it is impossible, the proposition that there is a god is just the proposition that some cats are not cats. So, on this view, when atheists argue with theists, the two propositions in dispute are that all cats are cats and that some cats are not cats, one way round or the other. Surely such a dispute is a waste of time. The moral seems to be: in so far as metaphysics concerns the non-contingent, intensionalism *trivializes* metaphysics.

Unlike empiricist and logical positivist critiques of metaphysics, the argument from intensionalism has no epistemological premises, and its conclusion is not distinctively epistemological; the argument is just semantic. Nevertheless, it reaches a similar conclusion: there is nothing non-trivial for metaphysical claims to mean. Such arguments have had significant influence. They can be traced back to Wittgenstein's *Tractatus Logico-Philosophicus*, where ultimately every declarative sentence is to be analysed as a truth-function of atomic sentences expressing simple, mutually independent states of affairs. If it is true on every assignment of truth-values to those atomic sentences, it is merely tautologous. If it is false on every assignment, it is merely contradictory. If it is true on some assignments and false on others, it is merely contingent. This taxonomy leaves nowhere for metaphysics to hide. A conception of impossibilities as trivially false may explain the claim, widespread even amongst contemporary Wittgensteinians, that it is meaningless to assert an impossibility. In contemporary philosophy, Robert Stalnaker (1984; 1999) has been a leader in pressing the radical consequences of intensionalism, though with a scaffolding of possible worlds rather than simple, mutually independent states of affairs.[2] Such intensionalist sympathies can also be found in the works of David Lewis (1970; 1996) and, in less committed form, Saul Kripke (1979), despite their major contributions to metaphysics. More recently, Eli Hirsch (2021) has extended his nuanced semantic critique of (some) metaphysics by connecting it with the kinds of coarse-grained, worldly, semantics, including intensionalism, that look friendly to out-and-out metaphysics.

Of course, intensionalist trivialization threatens more than metaphysics. It concerns any inquiry into the non-contingent. Logic and mathematics are salient examples. They can hardly be dismissed as trivial. If the proof of Fermat's Last Theorem was just a proof that all cats are cats, why did it

---

[2] For an exchange on the Wittgensteinian claim about impossibility, see Marconi 2011 and Williamson 2011b. For an exchange on Stalnaker's view, see Stalnaker 2011 and Williamson 2011a. For a view that combines ideas from Wittgenstein and Stalnaker, see Rayo 2013. For repercussions in metaethics see Williamson forthcoming *b*.

take centuries to find? Many philosophers, however, find less difficulty in convincing themselves that logic and mathematics are somehow purely formal, not really concerned with *how the world is*, so not in need of non-trivial content. By contrast, traditional metaphysics stubbornly inquires into the necessary nature of the world; for it, the threat that only triviality that way lies is existential. In what follows, the focus is on metaphysics, not on logic and mathematics as such, but the conclusions apply to the latter too, providing a way for them to be as worldly as metaphysics, with which they indeed overlap (Williamson 2013).

2. Generalizing the Problem

How robust are the trivializing consequences of intensionalism? Do they survive motivated generalizations of the intensional framework?

First indications offer metaphysics little hope. For instance, many versions of intensional semantics add a parameter for *times* to that for *worlds* in semantic evaluation, to handle tense. Then sentences express the same content if and only if they have the same truth-value at every world-time pair. But that makes no significant difference to the problem. On the operative reading of the word "god," we may assume, the property of being a god is eternal as well as necessary: something is a god at a world and time if and only if it is a god at *every* world and time. Hence either there is a god at every world and time or there is a god at no world and time. Thus, as before, "There is a god" has the same content as either "All cats are cats" or "Some cats are not cats."

A more far-reaching modification of the framework is to work with *possible situations* instead of *possible worlds*, to handle the locality of much discourse (for instance, Elbourne 2005). Situations are something like parts of worlds. A sentence is neither true nor false in situations that include too little to determine its truth-value. Presumably, then, sentences express the same content if and only if they have the same truth-value (if any) in every situation. But that still makes no crucial difference to the problem. For on the operative reading of the word "god," we may assume, something is a god in a situation if and only if it is a god in *every* situation (a form of necessary omnipresence). Hence either there is a god in every situation or there is a god in no situation. If a situation s has a god in it, "There is a god" is true in s. If s has no god in it, there must be no god, so "There is a god" is false in s. Thus if "All cats are cats" is true and "Some cats are not cats" false in every situation, "There is a god" still has the same content as either "All cats are cats" or "Some cats are not cats." There is a slight complication: some versions of situation semantics may determine no truth-value for those "cat" sentences in situations that exclude some cats. By contrast, "There is a god" is true or false in such situations, as just explained. In that case, "There is a god" *differs* in content from both "All cats are cats" and "Some cats are not cats." But this technicality will not solve the problem.

For we can introduce a logically constant sentence ⊥ for absurdity, governed by the stipulation that ⊥ is false, and so its negation ¬ ⊥ true, in each situation. Then "There is a god" has the same content as either the trivially false ⊥ or the trivially true ¬ ⊥.

A more radical strategy is to allow *impossible worlds*, understood in an ontologically harmless way as arbitrary sets of sentences of the object language. A sentence is evaluated as true at such a world if and only if it is a member of that world. To use this apparatus to individuate content more finely, we can stipulate that sentences express the same content if and only if they are true at the same worlds, possible and impossible. Then "There is a god" differs in content from any other sentence S, for the simple reason that "There is a god" is true at the world {"There is a god"}, while S is not true at that world. But this strategy trivializes sameness of content by reducing it to sameness of sentence. For even if the words "god" and "deity" are *synonyms* by normal standards, the sentences "There is a god" and "There is a deity" still count as differing in content, for the reason just given (let S = "There is a deity"). No such verbal manoeuvre will rescue the ambitions of traditional metaphysics.

A more hopeful-looking move is to abandon the identification of sentential contents with (perhaps partial) functions from circumstances of evaluation to truth-values and to adopt a more structured conception instead. In particular, one might identify the content of a declarative sentence with a *Russellian proposition*, a complex built out of the objects, properties, and relations the sentence is about, and structured according to the structure of the sentence. For example, the proposition that there is a god might be something like <∃, divinity>, the ordered pair of the second-order property ∃ of being instantiated and the first-order property "divinity," of being a god. Then a proposition p is the proposition that there is a god only if p has divinity as a constituent.

An immediate concern is that the individuation of Russellian propositions is itself hostage to the individuation of properties and relations. In particular, suppose that properties are identical if and only if they are necessarily coextensive. Then if it is in fact impossible to be a god, the property of being a god is necessarily coextensive, and so identical, with the property of being a round square; thus the proposition <∃, divinity> is just the proposition <∃, round-squarehood>, and the threat of trivialization returns. So far, this is just an isolated case; there is no such elementary argument on the alternative hypothesis that it is possible to be a god.

We can, however, develop a much more general threat of trivialization for Russellian propositions. We keep "There is a god" as our sample sentence of metaphysics but without exploiting its specific details. We introduce a new singular term "D," governed by this stipulation:

If there is a god, "D" names 1.

If there is no god, "D" names 0.

The stipulation is to be understood as belonging to the metasemantics of "D," not to its semantics, in Kripkean terms, to *fix the reference* of "D," not to *give its meaning* (Kripke 1980). Thus "D" is not to be understood as abbreviating a definite description like "the number n such that either there is a god and $n = 1$ or there is no god and $n = 0$." Rather, "D" is simply a name of a natural number; the stipulation specifies which number. Consequently, the Russellian proposition semantically expressed by the equation "$D = 1$" has none of the complex structure of the definite description but is simply something like <identity, <D, 1>>. Obviously, the sentences "There is a god" and "There is no god" have the same truth-values as the equations "$D = 1$" and "$D = 0$," respectively. If we want to argue about whether there is a god, we can argue about whether $D = 1$; it makes no dialectical difference.

Of course, whichever side is wrong about the metaphysics also has a false belief about the reference of "D," given that they have been introduced to the name by the stipulation above. If there is a god, atheists falsely believe that "D" names 0; if there is no god, theists falsely believe that "D" names 1. But that does not mean that one side or the other *misunderstands* the name "D." It is like the name "Jack the Ripper," introduced by the description "whoever committed the grisly Whitechapel murders." Some people may still falsely believe the wild theory that Edward VII committed the grisly Whitechapel murders, so that Jack the Ripper was Edward VII; familiar with the name "Jack the Ripper" in the usual way, they falsely believe that it names Edward VII but they do not thereby *misunderstand* the name "Jack the Ripper."[3]

On the Russellian view, if there is a god, the sentence "$D = 1$" expresses the same proposition as the trivially true sentence "$1 = 1$"; if there is no god, the sentence "$D = 0$" expresses the same proposition as the trivially true sentence "$0 = 0$" (on the intensional view, the corresponding necessary propositions are identical too).

The threat of trivialization has returned in completely general form. One could substitute any other sentence for "There is a god" in the preceding argument. Nothing here depends even on the non-contingency of "There is a god." The argument works in the same way if one substitutes "There is intelligent life in other galaxies" for "There is a god":

If there is intelligent life in other galaxies, "G" names 1.

If there is no intelligent life in other galaxies, "G" names 0.

Everything proceeds as with "D." In particular, since "G" is a proper name, it is a rigid designator, even though it is contingent whether there

---

[3] For relevant discussion of what counts as understanding, see Williamson 2007, 97–98, and the exchange between Stalnaker 2011 and Williamson 2011a. More generally, the discussion of analyticity in Williamson 2007 supports the arguments of this section.

is intelligent life in other galaxies. Thus, if there is intelligent life in other galaxies, we use "G" to designate 1 even with respect to counterfactual possibilities in which there is no intelligent life in other galaxies. Equally, if there is no intelligent life in other galaxies, we use "G" to designate 0 even with respect to counterfactual possibilities in which there is intelligent life in other galaxies. Thus, we are in an epistemic position to assert both "There is intelligent life in other galaxies if and only if $G = 1$" and "Either there could have been no intelligent life on other planets while G was 1 or there could have been intelligent life on other planets while G was 0." The biconditional is similar to proposed examples of contingent *a priori* truths (Kripke 1980). If we want to argue about whether there is intelligent life in other galaxies, we can argue about whether $G = 1$; it makes no dialectical difference. If there is intelligent life in other galaxies, the sentence "$G = 1$" expresses the same Russellian proposition as the trivially true sentence "$1 = 1$." If there is no intelligent life in other galaxies, the sentence "$G = 0$" expresses the same Russellian proposition as the trivially true sentence "$0 = 0$." Again, in both cases, the corresponding necessary propositions in the intensional framework are identical too.

Such examples cast doubt on any attempt to interpret the semantic considerations as revealing some pathology of metaphysics, for the question whether there is intelligent life in other galaxies is uncontentiously non-pathological.

Related examples occur quite naturally, with no need of artificial stipulations. For instance, the terms "furze" and "gorse" are simply two natural kind terms for the very same genus of thorny shrub (the example is in Kripke 1979). There is no semantic difference between them in English. Yet by normal standards someone could understand both terms without recognizing that they co-refer. Perhaps at one time in one place you were shown a green bush with yellow flowers and told "That's furze," while at another time in another place you were shown a brown bush with no flowers and told "That's gorse." Those are both adequate ostensive definitions by normal standards. You might well not realize that the differences were largely seasonal, and that you had been introduced to the same genus twice. Of course, *you* think of "furze" as green with yellow flowers and "gorse" as brown with no flowers, but that is purely idiosyncratic. Someone else may think of "furze" as brown with no flowers and "gorse" as green with yellow flowers. As words of English, they are synonyms. On the Russellian approach (if not that of the historical Russell), the English sentence "Furze is gorse" expresses the Russellian proposition <identity, <furze, gorse≫, which just is the obviously true Russellian proposition <identity, <furze, furze≫. Yet you could sensibly ask yourself "Is furze gorse?" out of simple non-pathological botanical interest. A similar issue arises on a natural implementation of the intensional approach, since "furze" and "gorse" are

rigid designators of the same genus, so "Furze is gorse" is true at all possible worlds.[4]

The evidence so far supports at least two conclusions. First, for the problem of trivialization, it makes little difference whether we adopt intensionalism or some sort of Russellian hyperintensionalism. Second, the problem is generic; it shows nothing distinctive about specific forms of inquiry. In particular, it shows nothing pathological about metaphysics. Nor does it show anything special about logic or mathematics.

3. The Metalinguistic Strategy[5]

Some philosophers are still tempted by the idea that the ignorance or at least non-triviality displayed in the cases described is fundamentally semantic, that there are serious obstacles to knowing the semantic values of some of the words or sentences in play. For instance, it is hard to know *which* numbers the names "D" and "G" designate. This ignorance would be of a familiar, unpuzzling kind, and pose no threat to the favoured semantic framework.

Consider "furze" and "gorse." The obvious line for proponents of the metalinguistic strategy is to insist that anyone—such as an expert botanist—with full, non-deferential understanding of both "furze" and "gorse" *is* in a position to know that they co-refer. Everyone else has at most partial understanding of at least one of the two terms. Thus the problem is fundamentally one of semantic ignorance.

Such an account may apply to this particular case, though what the "full understanding" might be with which "partial understanding" is implicitly contrasted is far from clear. In any case, we can vary the example. In one variant, set many centuries ago, the shrub in question is rare and grows only in remote places. It has been seen only occasionally but never studied scientifically, and no specimens have been observed over extended periods. The term "furze" was introduced by travellers who saw green bushes with yellow flowers, and in practice only bushes in that condition are recognized as "furze." Similarly, the term "gorse" was introduced by travellers who saw brown bushes with no flowers, and in practice only bushes in that condition are recognized as "gorse." Not even the best botanists in our community realize that "furze" and "gorse" co-refer; they may regard it

---

[4] The semantics works most smoothly with the stipulation that a rigid designator for *x* designates *x* even with respect to worlds at which *x* is not concretely present. After all, the semantics characterizes how *we* use words, speaking in our world *about* actual and counterfactual worlds, not how those words *would have been used* in those counterfactual worlds.

[5] The leading defender of intensionalism about content is Robert Stalnaker (1984; 1999). Since I have engaged in detail with his application of intensionalism to content in philosophy elsewhere (Stalnaker 2011 and Williamson 2011a), I will not do so here. In effect, Stalnaker's approach is a version of the metalinguistic strategy; my concern in this section is with the general strategy.

as an open question. Nevertheless, despite the community-wide difference between "furze" and "gorse" in associated recognitional capacities, there is no strictly *semantic* difference between the two words. They are both simply natural kind terms for what is in fact the very same natural kind. In that sense, they are synonyms. In these circumstances, a fully non-deferential understanding of both terms does not put one in a position to recognize their co-reference. To resolve our ignorance, our primary need is to know more botany, not more semantics.

In another variant, everything is like the original case, but without deference, since the community does not recognize the status of scientific expertise. Instead, natural kind terms are treated more as words like "if" and "know" are actually treated. Although some people devote themselves to studying conditionals or knowledge, they play no privileged role in the social practice of using the corresponding words, because the community has no tendency to defer to them in applying the words. Similarly, in the imagined case, even if some people devote themselves to studying shrubs, they play no privileged role in the social practice of using the words "furze" and "gorse," because the community has no tendency to defer to them in applying the words. At least for those who have been introduced to them ostensively, the ethos in applying them is that everyone is entitled to their own opinion. For that large, at least minimally competent, group there is no deferential partial understanding, because there is no deference to a higher level of competence. "Furze" and "gorse" are still treated as natural kind terms, but in an unscientific spirit. Many speakers fully competent by communal standards with both terms cannot recognize that they co-refer. Unlike the previous case, there is no community-wide difference between "furze" and "gorse" in associated recognitional capacities; such differences obtain only at the level of individual speakers. There is also no strictly semantic difference between the two words. They are both simply natural kind terms for what is in fact the very same natural kind. They are synonyms. In these circumstances too, a fully non-deferential understanding of both terms does not always put one in a position to recognize their co-reference. To resolve one's ignorance, one's primary need is to know more botany, not more semantics.

At first sight, the artificially introduced names "D" and "G" look more promising as candidates for semantic ignorance. The associated stipulation might plausibly be denied by itself to enable one to know *which* number "D" or "G" designates. Currently, someone familiar with the stipulation may be uncertain whether "D" co-refers with "1" or with "0." But that is because they are uncertain whether there is a god: the semantic ignorance seems to depend on prior metaphysical ignorance, contrary to the metalinguistic strategy. Proponents of the strategy may respond, however, that the relevant semantic ignorance is at the level of the *sentence*, not the singular terms: the underlying uncertainty is as to *which proposition* the sentence "There is a god" expresses. This may seem more promising.

Semantic ignorance of individual words in the sentence would be mere linguistic incompetence, which is an implausible diagnosis of the problems of metaphysics. Of course, the word "god" is hardly straightforward, but for present purposes we may assume that it has been stipulatively defined in terms of a list of attributes. The picture is that we know the semantic values of the atomic constituents of the sentence but cannot work out which proposition results from composing them in the relevant way.

Such an account makes more sense for intensional than for Russellian propositions. For the latter, if we know that a sentence is composed of a constituent expressing the second-order property ∃ predicated of a constituent expressing the first-order property of divinity, we can easily work out that the sentence as a whole expresses the Russellian proposition <∃, divinity>: there is no mystery as to which proposition that is, because the notation is already so perspicuous.[6] By contrast, if the proposition is a function from worlds to truth-values, but one is uncertain whether it maps all worlds to truth or all to falsity, one might well be counted uncertain as to which function the sentence expresses. If sentences are individuated syntactically, not semantically, it is contingent which proposition a sentence expresses, so the apparent metaphysical uncertainty has finally been traced to uncertainty about something contingent.

The proposal does not, however, withstand further scrutiny. Let "S" abbreviate whichever is false of the quotations "There is a god" and "There is no god." Thus S is the false one of those two sentences. Whatever proposition S semantically expresses is impossible. Consider a metaphysician uncertain whether S expresses a true proposition. Of course, that uncertainty is uninteresting if it results from lack of native speaker knowledge of English. We must assume our metaphysician to know what the words and modes of composition in S mean. Thus we assume that she knows that S has semantic features F, fully characterizing the semantics of S's atomic constituents and modes of composition. Consequently, since our metaphysician is rational, she is also uncertain over the conjunction that S both has F and expresses a true proposition. But the conjunction is itself impossible, for since the semantics is compositional, a necessary consequence of the first conjunct (that S has F) is that the proposition S expresses is impossible, which is incompatible with the second conjunct. Each conjunct is possible, but they are not compossible. Thus our metaphysician's uncertainty extends to something impossible, contrary to the metalinguistic strategy of confining the relevant uncertainty, ignorance, or error to contingent linguistic matters.

---

[6] The notation is perspicuous because <X, Y> = <X*, Y*> just when X = X* and Y = Y*, so one can individuate the whole by individuating its constituents. This justifies the ordered pair notation, though Russellian propositions need not literally *be* ordered n-tuples. But this fineness of grain also generates the Russell-Myhill paradox, which makes a pure Russellian account inconsistent. See Dorr 2016 for discussion.

A back-up tactic for the metalinguistic strategy is to divide an agent's beliefs into separate subsystems, individually possible but jointly incompossible (Stalnaker 1984). In the present case, however, separating the metaphysician's belief that S expresses a truth from her belief that S has F misses the depth of the problem. She does not have to *ignore* her understanding of S in order to believe that it expresses a truth; she believes that S is true *in the light of* her understanding of S. Positing a cognitive wall between her belief that S expresses a truth and her belief that it has the semantics F makes no sense of the example.

Although one could develop other ways of implementing the metalinguistic strategy, they are all vulnerable to the sort of problem just explained (to the best of my knowledge, first pointed out by Kripke in an unpublished lecture). Thus the metalinguistic strategy fails.

4. Reconceiving the Problem[7]

In order to make progress, what one must take to heart is that the underlying problem is not about necessary or impossible propositions. It is about necessarily equivalent propositions, whether they are contingent or not. For instance, the sentences "There is furze in Edinburgh" and "There is gorse in Edinburgh" express the same contingent proposition, on the worldly approach to semantics under discussion, even though a speaker who understands both sentences need not be in a position to know that they have the same truth-value.

Of course, this is just a variant on the problem of cognitive significance, which Frege introduced his distinction between sense and reference to solve. One might therefore hope that switching to a Fregean framework would help, by building modes of presentation into the semantics. But the present context makes two worries for Fregeanism salient.

The first worry concerns the big picture for metaphysics. Fregean thoughts—the senses of declarative sentences—are *perspectival* in a sense in which worldly intensional or Russellian propositions are not. A Fregean thought is a *mode of presentation* of a truth-value, presumably to a notional subject. By contrast, functions from worlds to truth-values and structured complexes of objects, properties, and relations are normally presentation independent and subject independent.[8] Thus Fregean thoughts seem less apt than such worldly propositions for being *what is objectively at stake* in an out-and-out metaphysical dispute, as traditionally conceived (in a way

---

[7] The approach in this section builds on the proposal in Williamson 2007, 66ff.

[8] David Lewis (1979) turned the intensional framework perspectival by reworking it in terms of *centred* worlds, with a distinguished agent and time, although he did not build in other aspects of modes of presentation. For criticism of such hybrid approaches, see Cappelen and Dever 2013 and Magidor 2015.

Kantians might describe as pre-Kantian). For thoughts can differ while the relevant non-presentational objects, properties, and relations stay the same. In such cases, one might think, what is objectively at stake stays the same, while Fregean thoughts vary, so what is objectively at stake is no Fregean thought. Of course, Frege himself did not treat mathematics as lacking in objectivity; his approach was explicitly, indeed prototypically, anti-psychologistic. The commitments inherent in a Fregean semantic framework are unclear. Nevertheless, those engaged in a dispute over what they understand as a purely objective metaphysical question may be suspicious of treating what is at stake as a Fregean thought.

The second worry concerns the detailed implementation of Fregean semantics. Recall the potential cognitive differences between "There is furze in Edinburgh" and "There is gorse in Edinburgh" for an individual speaker. As explained in section 3, these differences do not depend on any community-wide cognitive difference between the two sentences. They can arise for normal speakers through accidental features of the process by which they acquire the words "furze" and "gorse." In such cases, the cognitive difference for the individual speaker is not explained by any difference between the senses attached to the two words at the level of the community. One might therefore be tempted to apply Fregean semantics at the level of the individual speaker, to a family of more or less similar idiolects. But that brings back problems of its own. It ignores the lessons of social externalism and the division of linguistic labour (Putnam 1975). In particular, for purposes of metaphysics as a shared enterprise, we want to work in a common language. Frege himself insisted that thoughts (such as mathematical theorems) must be capable of forming part of the common heritage of humankind. Moreover, an individualistic account of senses has difficulty explaining their role in the inter-personal ascription of thoughts. When I say "Mary thinks there is gorse in Edinburgh," do I attribute a thought involving *my* individual sense of "gorse" to Mary? But I know that her individual sense of "gorse" probably differs from mine. Or do I attribute a thought involving *her* individual sense of "gorse" to Mary? But how can I do that when I do not know what her individual sense of "gorse" is? And how do you understand me when your individual sense of "gorse" may be different from both mine and Mary's? It looks as though a Fregean account of the inter-personal ascription of thoughts in natural language may be forced back into working with minimal community-wide senses after all, and so back to its failure to discriminate in sense between "furze" and "gorse." Historically, it is no accident that Fregean semantics has largely dropped out of discussions of propositional attitude ascriptions in natural languages, despite the apparent head start it gained from the sense-reference description: that is just not how natural languages work, or even *could* work. Fregean semantics does not solve our problem.

The moral to draw from "furze" and "gorse" and similar cases is not that semantic properties are Fregean. It is that cognitive significance does not supervene on semantic properties. At both the individual and the community levels, two sentences may have all the same semantic properties yet differ in cognitive significance. Tracking cognitive significance is not just a semantic exercise. We must track the vehicles of semantic content too, the very sentences that have semantic content and their contexts. For example, we can distinguish between believing the proposition that there is furze in Edinburgh under the guise of the sentence "There is furze in Edinburgh" and believing the same proposition under the guise of the sentence "There is gorse in Edinburgh" (in the terminology of Salmon 1986). To believe a proposition *simpliciter* is to believe it under some guise or other, where the believing-under relation has an extra argument-place for a guise. Similarly, to *know* a truth *simpliciter* is to know it under some guise or other. By treating the sentential guise as an extra parameter, we liberate semantics itself from pressure to make cognitive distinctions it is ill suited to making; we thereby avoid distorting the semantic framework. Even the quasi-syntactic structure of Russellian propositions may reflect such inappropriate pressure on the semantics, by contrast with a purely intensional approach (Salmon 1986 works within a broadly Russellian framework). Just as we should not project the difference between "furze" and "gorse" onto their worldly semantic values, so we should not project differences in syntactic structure between sentences onto *their* worldly semantic values.

In short, guises are not *what* we think, and not normally what we think *of*; they are what we think *with*. Similarly, in speech, when you make an assertion, a guise is not *what* you assert, and not normally what you assert it *of*; it is more like what you assert it *with* (though the hearer may receive it under a different guise). We must keep track of linguistic or, more generally, representational differences, without confusing them with differences at the level of reference.

Often, more than the linguistic expression type must be put into the guise to capture cognitive significance. This is clear for demonstratives: in the same context, someone may wonder "Is that gull that gull?" where the first occurrence of "that gull" refers to a seagull as she sees it in the distance, while the second refers to the same bird as she hears its cry. The case of someone who does not realize that the politician Paderewski and the pianist Paderewski are the same man also calls for such further differentiation of guises (Kripke 1979). Since full guises are not normally what need to be communicated, individuating them very finely carries little cost. Nor need guises always include something linguistic: the guise of a spatial thought might be more like a picture, seen or imagined.[9]

---

[9] What sort of Russellian proposition would correspond to a picture?

This separation of content from guise is not transparent to normal language users in producing and comprehending ascriptions of propositional attitudes. As Kripke (1979) has emphasized, our ordinary practice can easily run into trouble with tricky cases. That does not mean that ordinary practice is somehow "conceptually incoherent." As with many cognitive challenges, we may be relying on *heuristics*, tests that are quick and easy to apply, and work well enough in most normal cases, but are not perfectly reliable. Indeed, the very disquotational principles that Kripke identifies as getting us into trouble may be just such helpful heuristics: for instance, "*A normal English speaker who is not reticent will be disposed to sincere reflective assent to 'p' if and only if he believes that p.*" In using such rules of thumb, one may have no privileged access to their status as mere fallible heuristics, just as we have no privileged access to the heuristics on which we rely in making ordinary perceptual judgments (Williamson 2020; 2021b). We rely naively on our heuristics, getting things mostly right, sometimes wrong, until philosophers force us to consider the inconsistencies into which we have been led, and even then the nature of the problem remains opaque to us, though some mix of philosophical, linguistic, and psychological investigation may eventually get us to the solution.

In any case, we can provisionally use the approach of ascribing acceptance or rejection of coarse-grained intensional propositions under guises to track what is going on in inquiries into non-contingent matters, such as logic, mathematics, and metaphysics. In those inquiries, propositions usually come under sentential guises, but not always: in geometry, for example, a proposition may come under the guise of a diagram. The trap not to fall into is that of thinking that the need for tracking sentential guises shows anything distinctive about those fields—for instance, that they are somehow partly linguistic inquiries in some sense in which more "empirical" inquiries are not.

Admittedly, fields may differ in how far we can use differences in proposition expressed as convenient proxies for cognitive differences between sentences—doing so works much better in history than it does in mathematics—but in principle the two levels are *never* equivalent, and in practice the inequivalence will sometimes obtrude in every field, though more frequently in some than in others. For example, in ancient history, doubt is not uncommon as to whether the same name in different documents refers to one person or two.

Of course, this separation of semantic value from cognitive significance forms a coherent picture only if there are systematic connections between the two levels. Compositional semantics provides such connections. Although the semantic structure of a sentence is not even roughly similar to any structure intrinsic to the proposition it expresses, the former determines the latter in more or less principled ways, described by a compositional semantic theory for the language. Even in discourse where the only propositions are the necessary truth and its contradictory, a multitude of properties and relations are normally in play as the semantic values of predicates. Thus a standard first-order language for arithmetic can express infinitely many distinct monadic properties (intensions) of natural numbers. The case of metaphysics is analogous. When things go well, we learn *how* the properties and relations of interest are necessarily interconnected.

We may still feel puzzled. For when we learn how those properties and relations are necessarily interconnected, *what* we learn are necessary truths, which by intensionalist lights are all one. Indeed, if metaphysical truths are all necessary, how do we learn anything in metaphysics, since presumably we already knew the trivial necessary truth before we started doing metaphysics? In response, a first point is that calling the necessarily true proposition "trivial" already confuses the issue, because the distinction between "trivial" and "non-trivial," like that between "obvious" and "non-obvious," arises primarily at the cognitive level: the trivial is the very easily known. The necessarily true proposition is trivial under the guise of the equation "$2 + 2 = 4$" but highly non-trivial under the guise of a statement of Fermat's Last Theorem. Similarly, in such cases, learning and discovery must themselves be understood with respect to guises: mathematicians who already knew the necessary truth under one guise came to know it under another. The novelty was in the guise, not in the proposition known. Again, the same points apply to logic and metaphysics.

But if you know a truth under one guise, why bother to learn it under another? That would be a good question if knowledge were valued as a miser's hoard of true propositions. But not even true propositions have intrinsic value: the value is in how we are cognitively related to them. We can bear dramatically different cognitive relations to the same proposition under different guises. In learning an old truth under a new guise, we acquire a potentially valuable new cognitive relation to the old truth.

None of this involves a return to the discredited metalinguistic view. The latter makes the mistake of trying to get the content to do all the cognitive work, forgetting that even a metalinguistic content can be presented to the subject under different guises. The point is rather that *any* content is *present* to a subject at a time only in some form or other; that form is its guise. Even physical aspects of linguistic form are cognitively significant, because they facilitate or impede cognitive manipulation. Mathematicians know this well; metaphysicians would be well advised to know it too. As Bertrand Russell observed, "[A] good notation has a subtlety and suggestiveness which at times make it seem almost like a live teacher"; "Notational irregularities are often the first sign of philosophical errors" (1922, xix). That is why definitions matter in metaphysics, even though they merely abbreviate longer forms of words: a good definition makes salient and handy a distinction that cuts at the joints. In that respect, even metaphysics is a kind of embodied cognition.

Acknowledgments

Thanks to participants in the 2021 "New Directions in Metaphilosophy" conference at the University of Kent and a Lugano Philosophy Colloquium (both virtual), to Daniel Kodsi and Luis Rosa (in correspondence), and to two anonymous referees for helpful comments on earlier versions of this material.

References

Bacon, A. 2018. "The Broadest Necessity." *Journal of Philosophical Logic* 47: 733–83.

Cappelen, H., and J. Dever. 2013. *The Inessential Indexical: On the Philosophical Insignificance of Perspective and the First Person*. Oxford: Oxford University Press.

Carnap, R. 1950. "Empiricism, Semantics, and Ontology." *Revue internationale de philosophie* 4: 20–40.

Dorr, C. 2016. "To Be F Is to Be G." *Philosophical Perspectives* 30: 39–134.

Elbourne, P. 2005. *Situations and Individuals*. Cambridge, Mass.: MIT Press.

Hirsch, E. 2021. "Ontology by Stipulation." In *The Language of Ontology*, edited by J. T. M. Miller, 7–22. Oxford: Oxford University Press.

Kripke, S. 1979. "A Puzzle About Belief." In *Meaning and Use*, edited by Avishai Margalit, 239–83. Dordrecht: Reidel.

Kripke, S. 1980. *Naming and Necessity*. Oxford: Blackwell.

Lewis, D. 1970. "General Semantics." *Synthese* 22: 18–67.

Lewis, D. 1979. "Attitudes *De Dicto* and *De Se*." *Philosophical Review* 88: 513–43.

Lewis, D. 1996. "Elusive Knowledge." *Australasian Journal of Philosophy* 74: 549–67.

Magidor, O. 2015. "The Myth of the De Se." *Philosophical Perspectives* 29: 249–83.

Marconi, D. 2011. "Wittgenstein and Williamson on Conceptual Analysis." In *Analisi: Annuario e bollettino della Società italiana analitica (SIFA) 2011*, edited by R. Davies, 91–102. Milan: Mimesis.

Putnam, H. 1975. *Mind, Language and Reality*, vol. 2 of *Philosophical Papers*. Cambridge: Cambridge University Press.

Rayo, A. 2013. *The Construction of Logical Space*. Oxford: Oxford University Press.

Russell, B. 1922. "Introduction." In *Tractatus Logico-Philosophicus*, edited by L. Wittgenstein (trans. C. K. Ogden), ix–xxv. London: Routledge and Kegan Paul.

Salmon, N. 1986. *Frege's Puzzle*. Cambridge, Mass.: MIT Press.

Salmon, N. 1989. "The Logic of What Might Have Been." *Philosophical Review* 98: 3–34.

Stalnaker, R. 1984. *Inquiry*. Cambridge, Mass.: MIT Press.

Stalnaker, R. 1999. *Context and Content*. Oxford: Oxford University Press.
Stalnaker, R. 2011. "The Metaphysical Conception of Analyticity." *Philosophy and Phenomenological Research* 82: 507–14.
Thomasson, A. 2015. *Ontology Made Easy*. New York: Oxford University Press.
Thomasson, A. 2020. *Norms and Necessity*. Oxford: Oxford University Press.
Williamson, T. 2007. *The Philosophy of Philosophy*. Oxford: Wiley-Blackwell.
Williamson, T. 2011a. "Reply to Stalnaker." *Philosophy and Phenomenological Research* 82: 515–23. (Reprinted in Williamson 2021a, 471–80.)
Williamson, T. 2011b. "Three Wittgensteinians and a Naturalist on *The Philosophy of Philosophy*." In *Analisi: Annuario e bollettino della Società italiana analitica (SIFA) 2011*, edited by R. Davies, 127–37. Milan: Mimesis. (Reprinted in Williamson 2021a, 481–83 and 553–62.)
Williamson, T. 2013. *Modal Logic as Metaphysics*. Oxford: Oxford University Press.
Williamson, T. 2016. "Modal Science." *Canadian Journal of Philosophy* 46: 453–92.
Williamson, T. 2020. *Suppose and Tell: The Semantics and Heuristics of Conditionals*. Oxford: Oxford University Press.
Williamson, T. 2021a. *The Philosophy of Philosophy*. Second edition. Oxford: Wiley-Blackwell.
Williamson, T. 2021b. "Epistemological Consequences of Frege Puzzles." *Philosophical Topics* 49: 287–319.
Williamson, T. forthcoming *a*. "Disagreement in Metaphysics." In *The Routledge Handbook of the Philosophy of Disagreement*, edited by M. Baghramian, J. A. Carter, and R. Rowland. London: Routledge.
Williamson, T. forthcoming *b*. "Moral Anti-Exceptionalism." In *The Oxford Handbook of Moral Realism*, edited by P. Bloomfield and D. Copp. Oxford: Oxford University Press.

CHAPTER 2

PHILOSOPHY DOESN'T NEED A CONCEPT OF PROGRESS

YAFENG SHAN

1. Introduction

Philosophical progress is one of the most controversial topics in metaphilosophy. It has been widely debated whether philosophy makes any progress in history.[1] Pessimism about progress seems prevailing within and outside the philosophy community. The modest pessimist (e.g., Dietrich 2011) denies that there has been any progress in the history of philosophy. The radical pessimist (e.g., McGinn 1993) even challenges the possibility of philosophical progress in the future. In contrast, there is still some optimism about progress, though for different reasons. The global optimist contends that philosophy is making progress generally by answering big questions (for example, the problem of the external world). The selective optimist (e.g., Williamson 2006; Stoljar 2017) argues that philosophy has been progressive by solving certain types of problems or by improving our methods to solve problems. The pluralist optimist (e.g., Rescher 2014; Chalmers 2015; Brake 2017) argues that philosophy makes progress by achieving different goals (for example, the creative development of philosophical tools and broadening philosophical topics). The instrumental optimist (e.g., Koertge 2017) suggests that philosophical progress is secondary in the manner of contributing to progress in a broader context, say, scientific progress. The purpose of this essay is not to examine whether philosophy has made any progress in history or will make any progress in the future. Rather, it aims to revisit the concept of

---

[1] Philosophical progress here refers to the progress in philosophy as advance in the intellectual realm, which is contrasted with the progress of philosophy as the improvement in the professional or institutionalised realm. For a more detailed discussion, see Rescher (2014, 1–2).

Examining Philosophy Itself. Edited by Yafeng Shan.
Chapters and book compilation © 2023 Metaphilosophy LLC and John Wiley & Sons Ltd.
Published 2023 by John Wiley & Sons Ltd.

philosophical progress itself: What is an ideal concept of philosophical progress? Do we have such a concept? Does philosophy need a concept of philosophical progress?

The essay is structured as follows. Section 2 begins with an examination of the concept of philosophical progress and introduces two criteria for an ideal concept of philosophical progress. Section 3 argues that our accounts of philosophical progress fail to provide such an ideal concept. Section 4 argues that progress is not a useful conceptual tool to assess the contributions made in the history of philosophy, and thus philosophy does not need a concept of progress. Section 5 addresses two objections to my argument.

2. An Ideal Concept of Philosophical Progress: What Would Philosophical Progress Ideally Be?

First of all, I would like to disentangle three different concepts: the aim of philosophy, philosophical success, and philosophical progress. From a conceptual point of view, these three things are somehow related. Suppose the aim of philosophy is X. Philosophical success is typically defined as the achievement of X. Accordingly, philosophical progress is construed as a better achievement of X.[2] Thus, it is not unusual for philosophers to discuss these three concepts together. In particular, it seems to be quite common to discuss the aim of philosophy in order to examine philosophical progress (e.g., Chalmers 2015; Brake 2017; Beebee 2018). As Daniel Stoljar puts it, the question of philosophical progress "is pointless unless we specify [the aim of philosophy]" (2017, 21).

In this essay, however, I would keep the issue of the aim of philosophy aside. By doing so, I am not rejecting the relation of the aim of philosophy to philosophical progress. I am sympathetic to the view that philosophical progress should reflect a good development of philosophy towards its aim, if there is such a thing. But I still argue that philosophical progress and the aim of philosophy can be construed as two separate issues. There are some subtle differences between the use of the concept of philosophical progress and that of the concept of the aim of philosophy. For example, philosophical progress is typically applied to analyse the history of philosophy, while the aim of philosophy suggests a direction towards a better future for philosophy. And a given account of the aim of philosophy does imply a particular account of philosophical progress, but not vice versa. There can be an account of philosophical progress that is not defined in a teleological way. For example, one may argue that philosophy progresses if philosophy solves more problems, while it regards the aim of philosophy as an open

---

[2] Alternatively, philosophical progress can also be defined as getting closer to achieving X than before but not actually achieving it.

question.[3] In this essay, I would like to focus on the issue of philosophical progress, without making a commitment to any explicit account of the aim of philosophy.

Secondly, I would like to highlight the difference between philosophical success and philosophical progress. I argue that philosophical success should be a non-comparative notion, while philosophical progress should be a comparative notion. Typically, philosophical success refers to achievements made in philosophy, while philosophical progress is marked by greater achievements.[4] Such a clear difference is, however, sometimes overlooked. For example, Stoljar conflates success with progress when he claims "when I say that there is progress *on the questions of philosophy*—that is, on questions of that kind—I mean to assert something that is true if questions of philosophy have been solved in the past and it is reasonable to expect that they will be solved in the future—for short, that there is progress in philosophy if we are answering philosophical questions" (2017, 20–21). If Stoljar is right that philosophy is about problem-solving, then I argue that the fact that philosophy answers questions does not imply that there is philosophical progress. In this case, philosophical progress should rather be defined in the way that philosophy answers more questions or philosophy answers the same questions in a better way, whereas the fact philosophy answers questions is just a case of philosophical success. Thus, an essential feature of an ideal concept of philosophical progress is comparativeness.

Thirdly, I would maintain that philosophical progress is an evaluative concept. It suggests in what ways philosophy is better than before. Thus, if we have a good concept of philosophical progress, we may use it to assess the development of philosophy in a given period. We may also use it to evaluate the historical significance of a particular philosophical theory or argument. On the other hand, if a concept of philosophical progress is helpful for us to make sense of the trends in the history of philosophy in which philosophy is doing better than before, such a concept of progress is a good one. Accordingly, I propose that *a concept of philosophical progress is useful if and only if it helps us to have a good understanding of the development of philosophy in history*. Therefore, philosophy needs a concept of progress if and only if it is a useful conceptual tool to understand the history of philosophy.

In sum, there are two criteria of an ideal concept of philosophical progress. One is the comparative criterion: *An ideal concept of philosophical progress should be a comparative notion*. The other is the useful

---

[3] Philip Kitcher (2015) distinguishes between teleological progress and pragmatic progress. The former is defined as the decrease of our distance to a goal, while the latter consists in overcoming some problems of the current state. Kitcher's "pragmatic progress" is a good example of how philosophical progress can be examined without discussing the aim of philosophy.

[4] My "philosophical success" is different from Nathan Hanna's "philosophical success" (2015), which refers to the success of a philosophical argument.

criterion: *An ideal concept of philosophical progress ought to help us to have a good understanding of the history of philosophy.* In the next section, I examine two main accounts of philosophical progress and argue that we do not have an ideal concept of philosophical progress.

3. Two Approaches to Philosophical Progress

Contemporary accounts of philosophical progress can be classified into two groups: the consensus-based approach and the novelty-based approach. The consensus-based approach defines philosophical progress in terms of collective agreement or convergence. One of the most influential accounts of philosophical progress, namely, the problem-solving account of progress, is such a case.[5] According to it, philosophical progress is determined by problem-solving effectiveness. Whether a philosophical problem is solved or not is clearly a case of a consensus. Therefore, in order to account for progress in the history of philosophy, one has to identify the consensus on resolutions to philosophical problems. In short, philosophical progress is fundamentally a process of replacing one consensus with another, in which the new consensus is better than the old one in some sense.

There is, however, a difficulty with the consensus-based approach. History tells us that it is much easier to find disagreements than agreements among philosophers (Daly 2017). For example, in the literature on causation, there are various theories, including the regularity theory, the probabilistic theory, the counterfactual theory, the interventionist theory, the mechanistic theory, and the epistemic theory. No consensus has ever been reached. I have to note that causation is not an exceptional case in philosophy. According to the 2009 PhilPapers Survey, there is no consensus at all on twenty-three important philosophical questions (Bourget and Chalmers 2014). As David Chalmers summarises it, "There has not been large collective convergence to the truth on the big questions of philosophy" (2015, 7). Thus, if we try to assess the history of philosophy in terms

---

[5] To a great extent, most of the recent discussions on philosophical progress are situated in the problem-solving framework: Has philosophy ever solved any "big" or "core" problems (e.g., McGinn 1993; Dietrich 2011)? If not, has philosophy successfully resolved some "boundary" or "marginal" problems (e.g., Brake 2017; Stoljar 2017)? Is there a plausible way of defending the view that philosophy progresses in terms of problem-solving (e.g., Golding 2011; Kamber 2011, 2017)? Moreover, some accounts of philosophical progress that are not defined in terms of problem-solving are still fundamentally problem-solving in nature. For example, Timothy Williamson (2006) argues for a method-based account: philosophy progresses if it develops a better mathematics-informed method to articulate the problems, concepts, and arguments. That said, it is worth noting that for Williamson a better method is ultimately for the purpose of problem-solving. In this sense, I argue that Williamson's account is a problem-solving account. Helen Beebee's equilibrium-based account (2018) is another example of the consensus-based approach to philosophical progress. Other examples include the knowledge-based account and the truth-based account.

of problem-solving, it seems that we may probably end with the conclusion that philosophy does not succeed or progress. *The problem here is not that the conclusion is disappointing but that the concept of philosophical progress does not improve our understanding of the development of philosophy in history.* If few consensuses can be found in the history of philosophy, it would be even more difficult to find the shift from one consensus to another. Thus, it is pointless to understand philosophical progress in terms of consensus. In other words, the consensus-based approach to philosophical progress is useless for evaluating and understanding the historical development of philosophy. As Nicholas Rescher indicates, "[E]volving consensus simply is not the appropriate standard of progress [in philosophy]" (2014, 12).

Some challenge the view that philosophers do not have consensus. It has been argued that though philosophers seldom reach agreement on answers to "big," "central," or "core" problems, philosophy has successfully resolved many "boundary" (or "marginal") problems (e.g., Williamson 2006, 178; Frances 2017, 47–53; Stoljar 2017, 39–60). Thus, there are many philosophical consensuses on boundary problem solutions. Nevertheless, showing that there have been many philosophical consensuses in history is not a complete defence of the consensus-based account. As I argued in section 2, an ideal of philosophical progress should be comparative, referring to greater philosophical achievements. Accordingly, a minimal defence of the consensus-based approach to philosophical progress has to show (1) that there are many philosophical consensuses and (2) that these consensuses are often replaced with newer consensuses. It seems to me that (2) is really difficult to maintain. It is not unusual in the history of philosophy that a consensus is abandoned without being replaced by another. For example, in the first half of the twentieth century, the logical empiricist approach dominated many issues in the philosophy of science, such as the theory/ observation distinction (e.g., Carnap 1966), the discovery/justification distinction (e.g., Reichenbach 1938), and the pattern of theory change (e.g., Nagel 1961).[6] Under attack from outsiders (e.g., Quine 1951; Hanson 1958; Popper 1959; Kuhn 1962) and insiders (e.g., Hempel 1950; 1952), it was eventually abandoned. Nevertheless, no new consensus was reached on these issues. Some issues (for example, the theory/observation distinction) are not as important as before, while some issues (for example, the pattern of theory change) have become highly controversial. Thus, even if there were some philosophical consensuses on some boundary problems in history, it is still insufficient to show that philosophy progresses by way of replacing one consensus with another. The historical development is not a series of consensus changes. Again, the problem here is not that applying the consensus-based notion of progress to the history of philosophy leads to a disappointing conclusion about

---

[6] The logical empiricist accounts of these issues were typically called "the received views."

philosophical progress. Rather the consensus-based notion is not useful in providing us with a good understanding of the historical development of philosophical success. Therefore, I argue that the consensus-based approach is insufficient to provide an ideal concept of philosophical progress.

Let me now turn to the novelty-based approach. The novelty-based approach construes philosophical progress in terms of novel contribution. For example, Elizabeth Brake (2017) defines philosophical progress as the creative development of new models and tools to think about the world and the introduction of new problems.[7] The novelty-based approach is fundamentally different from the consensus-based approach in the sense that the consensus-based approach requires that philosophical progress be judged in terms of consensus, while the novelty-based account does not. Consider Brake's account. As long as there are new philosophical models or tools, philosophy progresses, even if these new models or tools are not widely accepted.

At first glance, the novelty-based notion of progress seems more useful than the consensus-based notion, when applied to understanding the history of philosophy. As Brake (2017) suggests, philosophers have been creatively developing new models and tools and proposing new questions for thinking about the world. In other words, the novelty account does reflect achievements in philosophy to some extent. Nevertheless, developing new models and tools and raising new questions do not fit the comparative criterion. Recall the distinction between philosophical success and philosophical progress. Developing new models and tools and raising new questions are better interpreted as instances of philosophical success than instances of philosophical progress.

Some may suggest that there is a way to understand the novelty-based notion comparatively: We have more new models, tools, and questions than we did previously. In other words, progress amounts to increasing our stock of models/tools/questions. Such an interpretation, however, is insufficient to defend the novelty-based approach. An account of philosophical progress defined by more new models/tools/questions is not a novelty-based notion. The basic feature of the novelty-based notion is novelty, which is contrasted with the consensus-based notion. According to the novelty-based approach, philosophical progress is about something new rather than about something acknowledged by the philosophical community. In other words, philosophy can be progressive as long as there is something new, regardless of whether the community acknowledges the new dimension or not. Whether we have more new models, tools, and questions depends, however, on whether we agree that we have more new models, tools, and questions. Thus, in this way, such a concept of progress

---

[7] Examples of the creative development of new models and tools include the introduction of new thought experiments (e.g., Descartes's evil demon).

is not characterised in terms of novelty. A genuine novelty-based approach to philosophical progress provides a non-comparative notion. Therefore, I argue that the novelty-based approach does not provide an ideal concept of philosophical progress, because it fails to fulfil the comparative criterion.

4. The Need for a Concept of Philosophical Progress Reconsidered

In section 3, I argued that neither the consensus-based approach nor the novelty-based approach provides us with a useful and comparative concept of philosophical progress. Thus, we do not have an ideal concept of philosophical progress of the kind elaborated by section 2. In the present section, I argue that we do not even need such a concept of progress in philosophy.

When talking of philosophical progress, philosophers typically tend to contrast it with scientific progress (e.g., Dietrich 2011; Rescher 2014; Frances 2017). The implicit assumption behind this approach is that a good concept of progress in science should be applicable or useful to philosophy.[8] I really doubt this. Despite their intimate historical relation, there are some differences between philosophical practice and scientific practice.[9] First, unlike science, philosophy values disagreement to a greater extent. It is not unusual in the history of philosophy that the introduction of a counterexample to a theory is celebrated as a great success. Edmund Gettier's three-page article "Is Justified True Belief Knowledge?" (1963) is such a clear case. All that Gettier does in the article is to suggest two counterexamples to the JTB account of knowledge, but the article has become a must-read in epistemology. In contrast, the discovery of an anomaly in science is seldom regarded as important a contribution as the introduction of a counterexample is in philosophy. Few scientists are credited merely for the work of challenging a received theory. Rather scientists are more often acclaimed for their work that earns a new consensus by replacing a once received consensus.[10]

Second, unlike science, philosophy values old ideas to a greater extent. It has been more than two thousand years since Plato wrote his dialogues,

---

[8] It should be noted that science in this context (that is, the literature on scientific progress) refers to empirical sciences, such as physics, biology, and chemistry. Mathematics and statistics are not under consideration.

[9] Philosophy in this context does not include logic.

[10] It should be noted that here I am not dismissing the significance of disagreement in scientific practice or denying the fact that there are disagreements in the history of the sciences. Disagreement plays an important role in scientific practice, and scientists do disagree with each other on many issues. Nevertheless, there is a crucial difference between scientists and philosophers. Scientists are more eager to look for a new consensus to replace the old one in order to end disagreement, while philosophers are more comfortable about keeping disagreement ongoing. To a great extent scientific disagreements are the means to scientific consensus.

but his dialogues are still widely read and discussed today. It is difficult to imagine that first-year philosophy undergraduates would not be required to read the works of Plato, Descartes, and Hume. It is not a big surprise for philosophers to develop a historically motivated approach to contemporary issues. For example, the Humean approach is still popular in the discussion on causation (see Lewis 1973; Beebee 2007), while the Kantian approach to philosophy of science is developing (see Massimi 2008). Old philosophical ideas still matter. In contrast, old ideas or theories in science are not as important today as old ones in philosophy. Chemistry students do not have to learn the phlogiston theory, and physics students are not taught about Aristotelian physics. In scientific practice, old ideas or theories are just dead. Few scientists read or discuss the works of scientists of the seventeenth century. Old scientific ideas or theories are not so relevant to contemporary practice.

I argue, moreover, that these seeming differences between philosophy and science are rooted in a crucial difference between them. Science is essentially a collective enterprise. Scientific knowledge is now widely accepted as a product of collective effort (e.g., Wray 2007; Bird 2010; de Ridder 2014).[11] As Thomas Kuhn (1962) insightfully indicates, the unit of scientific development is a community-based consensus. There are many major shifts of consensus in the history of science (for example, the Copernican revolution and the chemical revolution). Accordingly, the typical unit of analysis in the examination of the development of science is a community-based consensus (e.g., Kuhn 1962; Lakatos 1978; Laudan 1977; Chang 2012; Shan 2020). Therefore, a concept of progress is useful in examining major scientific changes. We need a concept of progress to make sense of the shifts of scientific consensus in history. In addition, we need a concept of progress to guide our choice of the most promising line of inquiry for further investigation. When a group of scientists have multiple lines of inquiry and limited resources, it is not unusual that they have to choose and focus on one of them. Thus, a concept of progress is helpful for evaluating different lines of inquiry.

In contrast, philosophy is not fundamentally a collective enterprise. Philosophers are more used to working individually. The division of labour in philosophy is not as necessary as it is in science. Thus, as I have indicated, there are fewer consensuses in philosophy and even fewer consensus shifts in the history of philosophy. Therefore, a concept of philosophical progress is not as necessary as a concept of scientific progress is.

Some may object to this by arguing that there have been quite a few consensus changes in the history of philosophy. Consider again the case of logical empiricism. Philosophers of science now agree that the logical empiricist approach to the problem of a pattern of scientific change is not plausible. It seems that there is a consensus shift from a widely accepted

---

[11] This is why agreement is more important than disagreement for scientists.

view that the logical empiricist approach is good to a view that the logical empiricist approach is problematic. That said, I have to emphasise that this is not a case of consensus shift. A consensus shift should be a process of replacing one consensus with another, where two consensuses refer to something constructive. The Copernican revolution is a good example of a positive consensus shift, a process of replacing the Ptolemaic theory with the Copernican, where both theories provide astronomical models for representing the motion of celestial bodies. The elimination of logical empiricism in the philosophy of science, however, is not a positive consensus shift, because no new approach or theory is widely adopted in the same field. And most major shifts in the history of philosophy are more akin to the elimination of logical empiricism than to the Copernican revolution.

Therefore, given that the history of philosophy lacks positive consensus changes, it is not necessary to have a concept of progress to analyse and evaluate the historical development of philosophy. In other words, a concept of philosophical progress is not very helpful to us in reaching a better understanding of the history of philosophy.

5. Objections and Responses

Regarding my argument in the last section, two worries might arise. First, some may argue that a good concept of philosophical progress should not only be retrospectively useful but also be prospectively useful in the sense that it helps us to decide how to do better philosophy. If so, my argument still fails to show that philosophy does not need a concept of progress. Second, if philosophy does not need a concept of progress, does it imply some scepticism about philosophy? Does it undermine the value or the significance of philosophy?

In response to the first worry, that a good concept of philosophical progress should be both retrospectively and prospectively useful, I argue that philosophy does need a prescriptive concept to assess and judge what philosophy to do and how to do it. I do find a concept of philosophical success necessary. A good concept of philosophical success will be helpful to assess and judge philosophical work. It is still unclear, however, whether philosophy needs a concept of progress, if there is a good concept of success.

In response to the second worry, whether not needing a concept of progress implies scepticism, I would say no: that philosophy does not need a concept of progress does not suggest or imply any scepticism about philosophy. Bryan Frances concludes his defence of philosophical progress with the following remarks.

Like many philosophers, I have long thought that philosophy has some genuine accomplishments. For instance, we have been successful at pointing out that there are certain notions that are of fundamental importance to our lives, how we interact with each other, how we interact with the world, and the world itself: justice, freedom, consciousness, perception, reason, beauty, truth, evidence, time, knowledge, intentionality, suffering, change, moral goodness, and so forth. We are also superb at generating fascinating questions, ones that are central to understanding the notions just mentioned. We are excellent at discovering certain problems or even paradoxes involving those notions. We are probably too good at crafting potential answers to the questions. We are creative and profligate at making a great many highly sophisticated arguments for and against those answers. Finally, over the millennia we have been good at generating new fields of investigation, such as special sciences. That's an impressive list: notions, questions, problems, answers, arguments, and fields. What I'm claiming is that we are also good at generating actual results, claims that can be handed down from generation to generation as things almost all of us accept. (2017, 56)

I completely agree with Frances on his observation: there have been many great philosophical achievements in history, although these philosophical achievements should be interpreted as instances of philosophical success rather than of philosophical progress. By abandoning a concept of philosophical progress, we would not end up with scepticism about philosophy. Without a concept of philosophical progress, philosophy can still do well. Contra Timothy Williamson's claim that philosophy "must do better," I argue that philosophy "must do well." Thus, for philosophers, the urgent task is to look for a good concept of success rather than a good concept of progress.[12]

6. Conclusion

In this essay, I have identified two criteria of an ideal concept of philosophical progress: philosophical progress should be a comparative notion and be useful for understanding the historical development of philosophy. I have argued that we do not have such an ideal concept. Two main approaches to philosophical progress do not provide us with a comparative or a useful notion. I have further argued that we do not need a concept of philosophical progress. In short, my central argument in this essay is to reject the concept of philosophical progress and its use in the historical analysis of philosophy. That said, rejection of the concept of philosophical progress should

---

[12] Even if a concept of progress in philosophy is necessary, it has to be articulated based on a good concept of success. As I have argued, philosophical progress, as a comparative notion, means greater philosophical success.

not be confused with the rejection of philosophical success. I am not trying to deny that there have been philosophical successes in history. Like most philosophers, I think that there are many great philosophical works. I have been learning and benefitting from these works. Nevertheless, I do not think that we need a concept of progress to compare and judge these works in order to reach a good understanding of the history of philosophy. How to develop a better account of philosophical success is a far more important task for anyone who is interested in metaphilosophy.

Acknowledgments

I would like to thank Christopher Daly, Alan Millar, and Jon Williamson for their helpful comments. I would also thank audiences at the "Philosophical Method(s)" workshop held in Zagreb in 2019 and at the "New Directions in Metaphilosophy" online conference in 2021, especially Martin Kusch, Jack Ritchie, and Timothy Williamson. The work is financially supported by the Leverhulme Trust (RPG-2019-059) and the British Academy (SRG1920\101076).

References

Beebee, Helen. 2007. "Hume on Causation: The Projectivist Interpretation." In *Causation, Physics, and the Constitution of Reality: Russell's Republic Revisited*, edited by Huw Price and Richard Corry, 224–49. Oxford: Clarendon Press.

Beebee, Helen. 2018. "Philosophical Scepticism and the Aim of Philosophy." *Proceedings of the Aristotelian Society* 118, no. 1: 1–24.

Bird, Alexander. 2010. "Social Knowing: The Social Sense of 'Scientific Knowledge'." *Philosophical Perspectives* 24: 23–56.

Bourget, David, and David J. Chalmers. 2014. "What Do Philosophers Believe?" *Philosophical Studies* 170, no. 3: 450–500.

Brake, Elizabeth. 2017. "Making Philosophical Progress: The Big Questions, Applied Philosophy, and the Profession." *Social Philosophy and Policy* 34, no. 2: 23–45.

Carnap, Rudolf. 1966. *Philosophical Foundations of Physics: An Introduction to the Philosophy of Science*. New York: Basic Books.

Chalmers, David J. 2015. "Why Isn't There More Progress in Philosophy?" *Philosophy* 90, no. 1: 3–31.

Chang, Hasok. 2012. *Is Water H_2O? Evidence, Realism and Pluralism*. Dordrecht: Springer.

Daly, Chris. 2017. "Persistent Philosophical Disagreement." *Proceedings of the Aristotelian Society* CXVII, no. 1: 23–40.

Dietrich, Eric. 2011. "There Is No Progress in Philosophy." *Essays in Philosophy* 12: 329–44.

Frances, Bryan. 2017. "Extensive Philosophical Agreeement and Progress." *Metaphilosophy* 48, nos. 1–2: 47–57.

Gettier, Edmund. 1963. "Is Justified True Belief Knowledge?" *Analysis* 23, no. 6: 121–23.

Golding, Clinton. 2011. "A Conception of Philosophical Progress." *Essays in Philosophy* 12, no. 2: 200–223.

Hanna, Nathan. 2015. "Philosophical Success." *Philosophical Studies* 172: 2109–21.

Hanson, Norwood Russell. 1958. *Patterns of Discovery*. Cambridge: Cambridge University Press.

Hempel, Carl Gustav. 1950. "Problems and Changes in the Empiricist Criterion of Meaning." *Revue internationale de philosophie* 41, no. 11: 41–63.

Hempel, Carl Gustav. 1952. *Fundamentals of Concept Formation in Empirical Science*. Chicago: University of Chicago Press.

Kamber, Richard. 2011. "Philosophy's Future as a Problem-Solving Discipline: The Promise of Experimental Philosophy." *Essays in Philosophy* 12, no. 2: 291–311.

Kamber, Richard. 2017. "Does Philosophical Progress Matter?" In *Philosophy's Future*, edited by Russell Blackford and Damien Broderick, 133–43. Hoboken, N.J.: Wiley-Blackwell.

Kitcher, Philip. 2015. "Pragmatism and Progress." *Transactions of the Charles S. Peirce Society* 51, no. 4: 475–94.

Koertge, Noretta. 2017. "Progress and Philosophy." In *Philosophy's Future*, edited by Russell Blackford and Damien Broderick, 41–49. Hoboken, N.J.: Wiley-Blackwell.

Kuhn, Thomas Samuel. 1962. *The Structure of Scientific Revolutions*. 1st ed. Chicago: University of Chicago Press.

Lakatos, Imre. 1978. "Falsification and the Methodology of Scientific Research Programmes." In *The Methodology of Scientific Research Programmes*, edited by John Worrall and Gregory Currie, 8–101. Cambridge: Cambridge University Press.

Laudan, Larry. 1977. *Progress and Its Problems: Toward a Theory of Scientific Growth*. Berkeley: University of California Press.

Lewis, David. 1973. "Causation." *Journal of Philosophy* 70: 556–67.

Massimi, Michela, ed. 2008. *Kant and Philosophy of Science Today*. Cambridge: Cambridge University Press.

McGinn, Colin. 1993. *Problems in Philosophy*. Oxford: Blackwell.

Nagel, Ernest. 1961. *The Structure of Science: Problems in the Logic of Scientific Explanation*. New York: Harcourt, Brace and World.

Popper, Karl. 1959. *The Logic of Scientific Discovery*. 1st ed. London: Hutchinson.

Quine, Willard V. O. 1951. "Two Dogmas of Empiricism." *Philosophical Review* 60, no. 1: 20–43.

Reichenbach, Hans. 1938. *Experience and Prediction: An Analysis of the Foundations and the Structure of Knowledge*. Chicago: University of Chicago Press.

Rescher, Nicholas. 2014. *Philosophical Progress: And Other Philosophical Studies*. Boston: de Gruyter.

Ridder, Jeroen de. 2014. "Epistemic Dependence and Collective Scientific Knowledge." *Synthese* 191, no. 1: 37–53. https://doi.org/10.1007/s11229-013-0283-3

Shan, Yafeng. 2020. "Kuhn's 'Wrong Turning' and Legacy Today." *Synthese* 197, no. 1: 381–406. https://doi.org/10.1007/s11229-018-1740-9.

Stoljar, Daniel. 2017. *Philosophical Progress: In Defence of a Reasonable Optimism*. Oxford: Oxford University Press.

Williamson, Timothy. 2006. "Must Do Better." In *Truth and Realism*, edited by Patrick Greenough and Michael P. Lynch, 177–87. Oxford: Oxford University Press.

Wray, K. Brad. 2007. "Who Has Scientific Knowledge?" *Social Epistemology* 21, no. 3: 337–47.

CHAPTER 3

T-PHILOSOPHY

CHRIS DALY

1. General and Special Cases Against Metaphilosophy

Criticism of metaphilosophy may take one of two forms: general or special. The general form involves a root and branch rejection of metaphilosophy as misconceived, pointless, or inimical to good thinking. A special form targets a particular conception of metaphilosophy, a particular way of thinking about what philosophy is and how it should be done. The later Wittgenstein sought to displace what he saw as the prevailing conception of philosophy as a theoretical, fact-discovering, and problem-solving enterprise in favour of his conception of philosophy as a form of therapy that frees us from the perplexities induced by a muddled understanding of language. Wittgenstein's case has recently been taken up and refurbished by Paul Horwich. To reply to Horwich, it would not be to the point simply to offer a new initiative in theoretical philosophy. Any such attempt would automatically be undercut by his objections to the enterprise of theoretical philosophy. What needs to be done is to meet those objections and to show how the enterprise is viable. To this end, sections 2 to 4 of this chapter rebut Horwich's objections. Section 5 takes as a case study Horwich's attempted dissolution of the philosophical problem of our knowledge of numbers. Section 6 draws conclusions.

2. Wittgenstein's Special Case Against Metaphilosophy

The later Wittgenstein dismissed theoretical philosophy, taking it to be permeated by linguistic confusions and driven by a misguided effort to emulate science. In Horwich's book *Wittgenstein's Metaphilosophy* (2012) these radical contentions receive explicit and sustained argumentative

Examining Philosophy Itself. Edited by Yafeng Shan.
Chapters and book compilation © 2023 Metaphilosophy LLC and John Wiley & Sons Ltd.
Published 2023 by John Wiley & Sons Ltd.

support. Horwich claims that theoretical philosophy has four "defective ingredients":

1. the illusion that theoretical progress can be made by disambiguating what appear to be unified concepts,
2. the distortions that arise from transferring considerations of simplicity from science to philosophy,
3. the absence of epistemic constraints needed to deliver knowledge of theoretical philosophy, and
4. the questionable value of believing philosophical theories. (2012, 34–35)

I intend to show that the arguments offered on behalf of (1) to (4) fail. Following the publication of his book, Horwich has addressed various replies by Timothy Williamson (Williamson 2013; Horwich 2013). I assess Horwich's counter-replies when they bear on my objections.

3. The Indictment of T-philosophy

Horwich's principal target is what he calls "T-philosophy." "T" is to suggest both "traditional" and "theoretical" philosophy (Horwich 2012, 21). The aim of T-philosophy is the "construction and defence of important philosophical theories" (21). As a first approximation, a theory of this kind consists of *a priori* principles that together provide "a complete, systematic, precise, and basic account of some pervasive yet puzzling phenomena" (21). Wittgenstein indicted such an account: "Our craving for generality has [as one source] ... our preoccupation with the method of science. I mean the method of reducing the explanation of natural phenomena to the smallest possible number of primitive natural laws; and, in mathematics, of unifying the treatment of different topics using a generalization" (1958, 18). Horwich endorses this charge: "The goals and methods that lie behind [T-philosophy] are inspired by, and modelled upon, those of the empirical sciences. The objective, as in science, is deep truth, profound understanding—fundamental principles that will explain relatively superficial facts and will have the authority to modify our naïve pre-theoretical convictions" (2012, 24).

Horwich offers as examples of T-philosophical theories Kripke's theory of truth, Lewis's theory of modality, the *Tractatus* theory of language and metaphysics, Tarski's theory of truth, Frege's theory of arithmetic, and Kant's metaethical theory. Note that there seems to be a mismatch between these examples and the claim that T-philosophical theories are scientistic, as Horwich understands this term. T-philosophical theories are said to be scientistic because they set goals and methods following those set by empirical science. None of the examples, however, closely emulates the methods of empirical science. The theories in question do not gain confirmation by using (say) a Bayesian framework. Kant, Frege, and the early Wittgenstein repudiated the intrusion of empirical considerations into their philosophical projects. Some contemporary philosophers appeal to abductive methods in their theorising (e.g., Swoyer 1999), but it is implausible that Kant, Frege, and the early Wittgenstein took themselves to be following such methods.

Suppose we take a goal of empirical science to be the formulation of the fewest principles needed to explain as many phenomena as possible in a systematic fashion. By that reckoning, philosophical theories, including the above examples, do share the goal of science. Yet it would be misleading to emphasise any parallel between philosophical theories and empirical science. The goal of achieving a simple and systematic unification of apparently disparate phenomena is equally a goal of the formal sciences, namely, mathematics and logic. In axiomatisation one seeks as small a body of principles from which to deduce as many interesting results as one can. By Horwich's lights, Euclid and Gauss would also stand guilty of scientism. But now any distinction between scientistic theories and non-scientistic theories has collapsed.

There is a general point. Philosophical theories are accused of being scientistic because they are (supposedly) modelled upon the empirical sciences. How detailed, though, are the description of the goals and methods of science required to be? On the one hand, the more detailed the descriptions, the less plausible it is that philosophical theories are scientistic—that they are modelled upon the goals and methods of science. On the other hand, the less detailed the descriptions, the less substantial the charge of being scientistic is. On this second option, it turns out, for instance, that mathematics is as scientistic as T-philosophy. But if these disciplines are in the same boat, Horwich's criticism of T-philosophy is much less troubling.

Horwich writes: "T-philosophers are committed to there being an important distinction between the methodology of science and the 'a priori' or 'armchair' forms of investigation to which they confine themselves. It seems to me that this is a *superficial* distinction, i.e. non-theoretical. It corresponds pretty well to the distinction we draw between beliefs whose justification requires sensory experience to play an *evidential* role and beliefs whose justification does not" (2013, e26, n. 1).

But I don't see why T-philosophers need to take the distinction in question to be an especially important one. Moreover, since T-philosophers are supposed to be modelling philosophy on science, one would expect them to think that the number and importance of similarities between science and philosophy together outweigh any combination of dissimilarities. In fact, it turns out that the parallel with empirical science is a red herring. Horwich's complaint is fundamentally about philosophical theorising itself. To theorise in philosophy is to seek to explain many things in terms of relatively few. It is that goal which Horwich takes issue with. He seeks to put an end to philosophical theorising and to replace it with "mere description," humdrum reminders of what we say and of how our language works (2012, 63–69). For the same reason Horwich's characterisation of T-philosophy as seeking *a priori* principles is not to the point. The epistemic status of these principles as *a priori* knowable or otherwise is of less concern to him than whether there can be philosophical principles that explain anything. It seems that Horwich characterises T-philosophy in terms of *a priori* principles only because it enables him to distinguish scientific theories from philosophical ones, Quine's scepticism about the *a priori* notwithstanding (2012, 21–23). Still, let's grant Horwich's way of framing matters and consider next his multi-pronged case against T-philosophy.

4. The Case Against T-philosophy

Horwich objects to the idea that we can take methodology that has been successful in science and apply it in philosophy. His objection is that this idea has not paid off. The history of T-philosophy, we are told, is a history of dismal failure: "Our subject is notorious for its perennial controversies and lack of decisive progress—for its embarrassing failure, after two thousand years, to settle any of its central results" (Horwich 2012, 34).

Here we have an alleged historical phenomenon—the fact that there is precious little philosophical knowledge—and a lesson—that philosophical theorising is hopeless. Let's grant that the historical phenomenon is as bleak as it is presented here.[1] Horwich's recommendation is that we should abandon theorising in this area and that there are no genuine problems to be found here, only linguistic muddles. That seems to be an over-reaction. What seems to be called for is better theorising, not the cessation of theorising. For example, although economics has not been around for more than two hundred years, it is dogged by long-standing controversies (for example, about the proper roles of government financial policy and the free market) and a lack of decisive progress (Krugman 2011). At any rate, the kind of progress it enjoys is the "negative progress" found in philosophy: over time we have found out what flaws bedevil certain kinds of theory, what problem cases face them, and so on. Nevertheless, it would be a mistake to draw the lesson that we should stop theorising in economics and deny that there are genuine economic problems.[2]

Horwich says that his lesson is warranted if we can expose "the patently defective ingredients" in T-philosophy I noted in section 2. He thinks that

---

[1] A query: the history of philosophy may be in excess of two thousand years old, but the history of science is only a few hundred years old. So, T-philosophy—understood as the modelling of philosophy on the methods of science—cannot have had a history of two and a half thousand years, and T-philosophy cannot be identified with Western philosophy.

[2] A referee rejected my claim on the ground that, in mainstream economics, formalization and mathematical sophistication have increased. I say that if that is sufficient for progress, then T-philosophy progresses: witness the burgeoning of formal epistemology. It has all the features of formalization and mathematical sophistication that the referee applauds.

certain facts about concepts are relevant to each of these ingredients (2012, 35). Our quotidian concepts have developed to serve various practical purposes besides that of understanding the world, and they do so in the light of a great variety of contingent facts about our nature, culture, and environment. Moreover, explicitly definable concepts are rare. Most concepts are too vague, open-textured, family-resemblance-like, or paradoxical to have explicit definitions.

The facts Horwich cites are familiar, but they bear only upon conceptions of T-philosophy that are concerned with conceptual analysis. So they seem to be relevant only to ingredient (1). The other ingredients do not specifically concern *a priori* investigations into the structure of concepts. Furthermore, even on conceptions of T-philosophy according to which it is an *a priori* discipline, it does not follow that T-philosophy is matter of conceptual analysis. This is evident in Kant's conception of T-philosophy as consisting of the articulation of synthetic *a priori* claims. (See also Linsky and Zalta [1995], who defend the view that mathematical truths are synthetic *a priori*.) And on conceptions of T-philosophy that see it as concerned with worldly phenomena, the facts about concepts that Horwich points out are no more damaging to T-philosophy's prospects than they are to science's. Consider folk biological concepts. They have developed to serve practical purposes, such as concerns with health or with farming, in the light of facts about us, our culture, and our environment. These concepts also lack explicit definitions, because they are vague, open-textured, or family-resemblance-like. Nevertheless, these facts do not comprehensively frustrate scientific efforts to theorise about biological phenomena. The folk concepts provide an initial and provisional means of accessing these phenomena. In the light of empirical discoveries about these phenomena and the on-going development of theories about them, the concepts in biology's repertoire may be revised (as with the concepts of fish and tomato) or even abandoned (as with the concept of a bug) (Dupré 1981).[3] Likewise, conceptions of T-philosophy that are primarily concerned with worldly phenomena rather with than our concepts of them (e.g., Stalnaker 2001; Williamson 2007) are not hobbled by the shortcomings of our stock of pre-philosophical concepts. Lastly, even conceptions of T-philosophy that champion conceptual analysis are not vitiated by facts about the vagueness and open-endedness of many of our concepts. Supporting reasons have been given by Chalmers (1996, 53–54), although Horwich does not address them.

---

[3] A referee responded that, in biology, there is explicit agreement that biologists study life and that this provides them with constraints that let them fix and clarify their terms (in whatever way), whereas in philosophy, according to Horwich, there are no such constraints, and so my analogy fails. That conclusion, I think, is too swift. For instance, since there is explicit agreement in epistemology that epistemologists study knowledge, then, by the same reckoning, that would provide them with "constraints that let them fix and clarify their terms (in whatever way)." (Kornblith 2002 takes just such a strategy).

A referee has suggested that all this misses the issue that Horwich raises: namely, that progress requires standards for assessment, and these are not found in T-philosophy. I doubt this interpretation is tenable. Horwich makes it clear he takes T-philosophy to fail by its own standards, writing, as we saw above, of "its embarrassing failure, after two thousand years, to settle any of its central results." If Horwich took there to be no standards of assessment at play, he would not be placed to make an informed judgement about the degree to which T-philosophy has failed to progress.

Let's assess each of the allegedly defective ingredients (1) to (4) that Horwich believes undermine T-philosophy. The first is:

(1) The illusion that theoretical progress can be made by disambiguating what appear to be unified concepts.

What is at issue here is the practice of seeking to understand a phenomenon by factoring it into different kinds and then accounting for each of the kinds in question. For instance, Aristotle (*Metaphysics* V 2) distinguished four different kinds of cause, David Lewis (1983) distinguished between different kinds of property (sparse and abundant), and pluralists about truth distinguish different kinds of truth (Lynch 1998). Horwich objects that "it is hard to see how any genuine gain in overall simplicity can be accomplished by drawing such distinctions. When the 'special' kind is defined by means of explicit criteria, we can easily see that the simplicity of our theory of it is purely stipulative and has been bought at the expense of sweeping all the original messiness over to the other side. Moreover, such explicit criteria are rarely agreed upon. ... [None] can yield an *overall* gain in simplicity and thereby constitute a great discovery" (2012, 35–36).

There seem to be two objections here to the tactic of factoring out concepts. The first is that the simplicity of any philosophical theory is "purely stipulative." This seems to misdescribe matters. It seems more accurate to say that a simple theory (that is, a theory that is at least simpler than any of its current rivals) is devised and then put to the test. Whether or not matters are as simple as the theory says they are isn't a matter of stipulation; it's a factual claim to be examined. Note also that nothing in this differentiates the role of simplicity in philosophy from that in science. It is not clear, then, why the charge of "sweeping all the original messiness over to the other side" is an objection facing only (or especially) T-philosophy's use of simplicity. Finally, note that Horwich's charge just assumes that the introduction of a simple theory has *no* benefit, that it *fails* to reveal any underlying systematic patterns, and *fails* to unify apparently disparate phenomena. Yet that is what is at issue between Horwich and T-philosophy; Horwich assumes what was needed to be shown.

The second objection is that there is little agreement about the criteria by which such distinctions should be drawn. This invites several responses.

First, the objection does not tell specifically against philosophy's use of these criteria as opposed to science's. Both disciplines appeal to criteria of simplicity, fertility, explanatoriness, and the like while lacking well-established informative accounts of what these theoretical virtues are and how they are to be measured. (But we shouldn't overlook the fact that valuable positive work has been done in this field: see, e.g., Schindler 2018 for a recent book-length treatment.) This is a form of procedure endemic to intellectual inquiry: we use various notions (of, say, mass, entailment, causation, species) and, in using them, develop our understanding of them. Otherwise we'd never get to use them in the first place. Also, the fact, if it is a fact, that theoretical virtues are vague and context dependent does not deprive them of content or show that no standards govern their use. (Compare Lewis 1973, chap. 4, § 4.2, on how these issues also face the notion of comparative similarity.) Note too that the same challenge faces Wittgensteinians and their apparatus of philosophical grammar, criteria, forms of life, and the rest. These notions are no less contentious and opaque than those in the T-philosopher's armoury.

Now, if our understanding of the theoretical virtues were particularly deficient, that would tell against their use in philosophy. So too would the view that the theoretical virtues have a pragmatic but not an epistemic role; that they inform what makes a theory useful to us but not how probable those theories are (as per the fictionalism of van Fraassen 1980, chap. 4, § 4).[4] But each of these options would equally tell against science's use of the theoretical virtues as a means for discovering what the world is like. Yet that is not a step that Horwich would want to take, since he endorses scientific realism. The puzzle, then, is how Horwich can secure a restricted scepticism about the theoretical virtues, a scepticism that targets only their role in T-philosophy.

At this point a referee presented the following trilemma. For my rebuttals to work, they need some set of standards to assess T-philosophical theories. These can be secured in one of three ways. (i) Tacitly assume some standards (for example, those of contemporary analytic philosophy) and thereby beg the question against Horwich. (ii) Argue for the standards and thereby prove Horwich is correct, as such arguments will lead to more arguments about standards, and so on. (iii) Dogmatically assert that some standards are the "best" ones for assessment, thereby refusing to engage with alternatives and, again, proving Horwich's contention that T-philosophy is irrational.

Each limb is dubious. The inference marked by "thereby" in (i) is questionable. We might assume standards whilst also defending them. The charge of begging the question against Horwich would arise only if

---

[4] A referee queried whether van Fraassen is a fictionalist, reporting that he is an empiricist. This is a false contrast: van Fraassen is both. For his self-identification as a fictionalist, see van Fraassen 1976, 335.

a given assumption ought to have a defence but none was forthcoming. The inference marked by "thereby" in (ii) is also questionable. I fail to see how arguing for standards would prove Horwich's view just because those arguments would invite responses and further responses. Nothing in philosophy (including Wittgensteinian views and the referee's trilemma) fails to generate responses and further arguments. But that familiar fact is inconclusive, since it prescinds from consideration how good or bad those responses or arguments might be. The puzzle is how the referee supposes that any of this lends support to Horwich's view, let alone proves it. Lastly, limb (iii) conflates a view's lacking justification with its being irrational. A view that lacked evidential support would be unjustified. It does not follow that it is irrational (cf. Clendinnen 1998, 130–31). Nor does it follow that it is dogmatic: that would mean that it ignored counterevidence. There might be no evidence for a view but also none against it.

Let's turn to the second ingredient in Horwich's case against T-philosophy:

(2) The distortions that arise from transferring considerations of simplicity from science to T-philosophy.

Horwich amplifies his claim by contrasting the role of simplicity in science with its supposed role in T-philosophy:

> [T]here is no less messiness in the *sensorily perceived* phenomena that provide the data for *scientific* theorization projects. ... [A] scientist looks for ... simplicity at some deeper level (such as the individualistic or microscopic). The superficial facts are then explained as the causal products of simple underlying laws in combination with a messily varied spatio-temporal array of particular circumstances. But no such strategy can be successfully employed in T-philosophy. For its application requires phenomena that (a) are arranged in space and time, (b) stand in causal relations to one another, and (c) are assessed via inference to the best explanation. But *a priori* reality (that is, what can be known *a priori*) does not exhibit these features. Therefore, there is no prospect of accounting for the messy data of T-philosophy via simple theories of some more fundamental level. (2012, 36–37)

One group of philosophers, self-styled naturalists, claim both that what exists cannot be known *a priori* and that all phenomena are in space-time and stand in causal relations (e.g., Armstrong 1978, chap. 12). Horwich's admonitions about *a priori* knowable reality have no bearing on their conception of T-philosophy. Suppose, though, that we restrict our attention to those philosophers who are concerned with *a priori* knowable reality. Even so, Horwich's objection is debatable. Non-deductive plausibility considerations are not confined to theorising about things in space-time that are causally active. For instance, Euler used enumerative induction from the results of a series of computations to reach his law of quadratic reciprocity (see Tappenden 2008b, 290, n. 8, and the references therein). More generally, plausibility considerations of simplicity, fruitfulness, and unification (such as with the introduction of the Legendre symbol) play an important role in mathematics, a paradigmatically *a priori* discipline (Tappenden 1995; 2008a; and 2008b).

Horwich regards the task of identifying axioms not as part of mathematics but as part of philosophy of mathematics. Its failure as fruitless T-philosophy would not, he says, affect the continued success of mathematics itself (2013, e24). This seems to misclassify a recognised task in mathematics: identifying axioms is something that working mathematicians do and that they publish in the same journals that publish standard mathematical results. In fact, when working on the independence of the Axiom of Choice from the other axioms of ZF set theory, Paul Cohen *contrasted* philosophical with mathematical approaches to the issue: "What made it so exciting to me was how ideas which at first seemed merely philosophical could actually be made into precise mathematics" (qtd. Kanamori 2008, 360; see also 356–57).

Horwich has more recently claimed that revising our concept of knowledge in the interests of theoretical simplicity might have undue consequences. That concept was formed and maintained under a "variety of shifting and often conflicting constraints imposed by our nature, our needs, our culture, and our environment" (Horwich 2020, 5228). A revision of the concept that simplified it, Horwich warns, might run counter to our interests.

Perhaps we do not have a list of all the interests that the concept of knowledge serves us or that a proposed revision of that concept would have to examine (though see Craig 1990 for an important start). Still, suppose that a proposed revision of the concept had some of the consequences Horwich warns against. Even so, I do not think this would be a reason to forego making the revision. If some interests that were served by the concept of knowledge prior to the revision were not served by the concept following the revision, I can't see what would prevent us devising a fresh concept (or concepts) to supplement the revised concept of knowledge by addressing those otherwise neglected interests. And I can't see why a single concept would have to be called upon to do all the work that the concept of knowledge did prior to the revision. This is a piece with the above point of the utility of drawing conceptual distinctions in philosophy.

A referee raised the concern that "the point of the utility of drawing conceptual distinctions in philosophy" is precisely what Horwich is targeting. For how do we determine if a revision increases utility without prior standards that, according to Horwich, T-philosophy lacks? It seems to me, however, that such a complaint is not open to Horwich. The later Wittgenstein himself drew a host of conceptual distinctions—between following a rule and merely acting in accordance with it, between sentences having the grammatical form of declaratives and their being genuine declaratives, between ordinary language and putatively private language, and the like (cf. Dummett 2010, 13–14)—and the question would arise by which standards these distinctions have utility and what kind of utility this is. Note also that Horwich evidently takes the concept of knowledge to have utility by the standards we currently employ, otherwise revising the concept would not threaten to have "undue consequences." Nor do I think that Horwich supposes that T-philosophy has been silent about the standards governing conceptual revision. For instance, Carnap's standards of explication are well known (Carnap 1950, chap. 1), and there continues to be significant work (e.g., Chalmers 2011) inspired by Carnap's project of explication.

Let's resume our survey of Horwich's arguments. His third ingredient is:

(3) The absence of epistemic constraints needed to deliver knowledge of theoretical philosophy.

Horwich writes: "Any achievable level of simplicity will be insufficiently constraining. ... [O]ur body of data—no matter how substantial it is—can always be accommodated by infinitely many competing general hypotheses. Simplicity must be brought in to help us decide between them. But the lower the degree of simplicity demanded, the greater the number of competing hypotheses that will exemplify them. The upshot ... is that our norms of theory choice will not usually be strong enough to issue in determinate results. So the truth of a philosophical theory will typically be impossible to know (2012, 38–39).

Let's grant that evidence underdetermines theory choice and that the lower the degree of simplicity invoked in selecting between theories, the fewer theories are weeded out. Yet simplicity is the only norm of theory choice that Horwich considers. To warrant the conclusion that it is "typically" impossible to know that a philosophical theory is true, Horwich needs to address the bearing of other theoretical virtues—scope, unifying power, consistency with background theory, fruitfulness, and the like—on theory selection and to show that philosophical theory underdetermination remains widespread even then. Horwich writes: "[I]n T-philosophy intuitive data are commonly dismissed ... solely on the grounds that not doing so would spoil the party" (2013, e19). Suppose that this sociological point is true. (Horwich admits that not all T-philosophers make this mistake [2013, e20]). Nevertheless, such a mistake does not reveal an inherent defect in T-philosophical theorising. In fact, I take it that another of T-philosophy's norms would be flouted by such a practice: the norm that, other things being equal, intuitive data are to be respected, not dismissed.

Horwich warns that competing philosophical theories in various fields can face ties (2013, e20), but this is an endemic problem in theory choice. (Horwich has elsewhere discussed whether there can be distinct but empirically equivalent theories: see Horwich 1982. I follow Earman 1993 in taking there to be empirically equivalent theories that significantly differ in their theoretical structure.) When Williamson raises this problem, Horwich's reply to him seems to miss the point. Horwich replies: "[S]ciences often can and should deal with their messy superficial data by postulating theoretical entities and simple laws at a more basic level," and he suggests that linguistics, psychology, and biology follow this route (2013, e24). Yet the issue was not about the propriety of postulating theoretical structures and simple laws; it was that different structures and laws can explain the same scientific phenomena. Which structures and laws should we then accept?

In closing his discussion of the third ingredient, Horwich asks us to "[l]ook at the character of the 'progress' in our attempts to discover the correct accounts of right and wrong, of truth (in the face of the liar paradox), of knowledge. ... What we tend to find are increasingly elaborate refinements of alternative approaches, with no prospect for rational convergence" (2012, 39).

Horwich's conclusion is overstated. Although Horwich officially eschews philosophical theories, he would presumably acknowledge that he is representing a certain *approach* in philosophy. Does he think that there is any prospect of rational convergence on that approach, one that counsels Wittgensteinian dissolutions of philosophical problems? If not, how is an approach of that kind in better standing than T-philosophical theories? Furthermore, it would not be open for Horwich to claim that the reason there is no prospect of convergence is that philosophers are mostly too irrational or muddled to converge on the Wittgensteinian approach. This same reason, whatever it is worth, would also be available to T-philosophers as a reply to Horwich's quoted objection.

The fourth ingredient Horwich lists is:

(4) The questionable value of believing philosophical theories to be true.

Horwich reports that "none of the explanations of the objective value of true belief available elsewhere appears to carry over to philosophy" (2012, 39). But, first, he faces an ad hominem. He says that true empirical beliefs generate successful actions, whereas believing philosophical theories lacks instrumental payoff. Fair enough, but Horwich does not make an exact contrast here. The proper contrast here is that between true empirical beliefs and true philosophical beliefs. Yet if there is a challenge to the value of believing philosophical theories to be true, there is a more general challenge to the value of having true philosophical beliefs. Such beliefs do not have value because they lead to successful actions. That challenge faces Horwich as much as his opponents—what is the value of having the true belief (as he sees it) that philosophical problems are pseudo-problems? In fact, the challenge faces the humanities and the social sciences quite generally. If it is valuable to have a true belief about who wrote Shakespeare's plays or what role economics had in the fall of the Soviet Union, it is not because those beliefs put bread on the table.[5] (A different response to Horwich would be to appropriate certain replies to van Fraassen about the value of philosophical theories both intrinsically and to science: Ladyman 2004, 135–36, and Cruse 2007, 495–96.)

Second, Horwich says that true scientific theories have the value of understanding; they describe basic explanatory principles. He thinks, however, that there is no "genuine explanatory depth" in philosophy. His reason is that "in the *a priori* domain we cannot reasonably deploy the picture of increasingly profound layers of reality—the lower-level facts explaining the higher-level ones" (Horwich 2012, 39). This contention is surprising, since earlier in his book Horwich acknowledges that the class of philosophical theories includes what he calls "foundational" theories (2012, 25). I take examples of these to include Frege's reduction of arithmetic to logic, Quine's reduction of arithmetic to set theory, and Lewis's reduction of the modal to the non-modal. Whatever the deficiencies of these theories might be, they enable us to see how philosophical theories can stratify reality into the derivative and the foundational. These examples of foundational theories concern subject matters that are knowable *a priori* (arithmetic, logic, set theory, modality), but the class of relevant foundational theories is wider than that. Cases where it is knowable *a priori* that supervenience or other dependence relations obtain are also cases that fall within the remit of foundational philosophical theories that descry *a priori* reality (Rosen 2010; Bennett 2017). And, even if each foundational philosophical theory faces problems of its own, it is unclear why we cannot use them at least to make sense of the idea of some things being more fundamental than others—why we cannot, as Horwich puts it, deploy the "picture" of "increasingly profound layers of reality."[6]

---

[5] A referee complained that my example is "empirically wrong": that the Soviet economic system and the mass famine it caused in Ukraine affected bread on the table; and that there are real-world implications in deciding if a command economy or attempts to regulate the market had deleterious effects that caused the collapse of the USSR. This badly misses the point: my claim wasn't that the mismanaged Soviet economy didn't affect food availability; the claim was that the true beliefs of a history buff about the Soviet system do not have a pay-off any more than do the true beliefs of a philosopher. And if it's allowed that a history buff could get their hands on political power and make positive real-world changes that way, then the same could be said of Nozick or Abimael Guzmán or whichever philosopher has the correct political theory—in which case Horwich's claim would have gone by the board.

[6] A referee complained that I do not address "the fundamental point" in Horwich's account: it is not the nuts and bolts of any T-philosophical theory that is at issue but "the urge to do theory in the first place that causes the issue." I agree that Wittgensteinians seek to do away with all theorising and all explanation in philosophy (Horwich 2012, 44–50). But an urge is not an argument, and I took the central interest of Horwich's book to be that he offers a series of arguments ("ingredients," as he calls them) to support the Wittgensteinian denunciation.

5. Case Study: The Problem of Our Knowledge of Numbers

Our having sought to rebut Horwich's arguments for his anti-theoretical metaphilosophy, it is also useful to evaluate his metaphilosophy by focusing on a particular case. In this section let us consider his attempted dissolution of the problem of our knowledge of numbers.

To anticipate, Horwich claims that this problem is dissolved once we see that it is brought about by our temptation to draw analogies between our knowledge of ordinary physical objects and our knowledge of numbers. My intent is to show, first, that Horwich's treatment proves too much and, second, that no such analogies need be in play in generating this problem.

Horwich says that a philosophical problem arises in the following way. We have some "perfectly familiar, ordinarily unproblematic phenomenon" (2012, 5) such as time, causation, or meaning, and then some *a priori* argument is made that the alleged phenomenon is impossible. (This characterisation seems inexact. In the case of numbers, the issue under discussion is not whether numbers are impossible but whether knowledge of them is impossible.) The task then is to "remove the confusion that is responsible for the misguided philosophical argument" (6). In other words, our pre-philosophical beliefs are to be preserved, and the linguistic muddle generating the philosophical challenge is identified and expunged, thereby dissolving the problem. This contrasts with T-philosophical efforts to devise sceptical views or error theories that deny that the putative phenomenon obtains (or that we are warranted in believing that it obtains), or to devise revisionist theories that abandon normally held views about the phenomenon or heroic theories that regard the phenomenon as genuine but intrinsically paradoxical (29–32).

Let's turn to what Horwich has to say about numbers (2012, 12–16). Talk of numbers is familiar and ubiquitous. We utter sentences such as "Seven is prime" and "Seven is greater than five." Here "seven" apparently serves to refer to a certain object, a certain number. But, because paradigmatic objects are ordinary physical objects, we find ourselves asking the same sort of questions about a number as we do about a physical object:

Where is it located?
What is it made of?
How do other things interact with it?
How can information about it reach us?

According to Horwich, our inability to answer these questions misleads us into thinking that numbers are "either hopelessly mysterious or else could not really be as we naively take them to be" (2012, 13). He agrees that there are numbers and that numbers are (as he puts it) objects "in the ordinary sense" (53; this sense is not further specified). But I think that this is enough to get the problem of our knowledge of numbers off the ground.

For any sort of object, if you think that objects of that sort exist, it seems reasonable for us to ask, and for you to tell us, how you know that there are such objects.[7] Answering the question serves a dual social purpose. By getting to know how you know some fact, we too can get to know that fact. And by telling us how you know that fact, we can check that you meet the standards we require for something to be knowledge (perhaps relative to a certain context). The problem is, as Horwich admits (2012, 12), that we are not able to say how we get information about numbers. That calls into question the assumption that we do have knowledge of them.

Horwich tries to counter this threat. He says that it is based on exaggerating the analogies between numbers and physical objects, such as planets, raising "the same questions about numbers that we normally ask about planets; and to be perplexed when we can't answer them" (2012, 15–16). But, as indicated, the questions do not arise because of any analogies that we might want to draw. They are general questions that we can ask about objects of any sort, not just physical objects. If you think that there is an economic recovery, or a god, or a way to checkmate in three moves, or a number seven—none of which is an ordinary physical object—there is a good question about how you know these things. Moreover, if we do have knowledge of numbers, then we would be well placed to answer the other questions on Horwich's list. If we have that knowledge, then we ought not to be perplexed about saying where the number seven is located or what it is made of or how other things interact with it. (Our answers might be that these questions have a false presupposition—that numbers are located and that they can cause events.) But, at any rate, the answers ought to be forthcoming, given our knowledge of numbers.

In fact, it is odd that Horwich thinks that these other questions cannot be answered. He thinks that our naïve view of numbers is that they are abstract objects (2012, 16). Yet it is widely agreed by philosophers that, as a matter of definition, abstract objects lack location, composition, and the potential for causal interaction. But these negative answers make the last question on the list—How can we get information about numbers?—all the more pressing and perplexing.

The weakness of Horwich's response to the challenge facing our knowledge of numbers can be brought out by seeing that his response can be deployed to close down debate about the existence of any sort of object, provided that it is unlike an ordinary physical object. Leibniz, Kant, and Hegel believed that there were such things as monads, noumena, and the

---

[7] A referee says that Horwich's reply would be that this is (within scare quotes) "reasonable" only within philosophy. But, first, I'm unclear what work the scare quotes are supposed to be doing. Second, the referee is insinuating that there is something somehow defective about a question that only a philosopher would ask. Such an insinuation needs supporting argument; none is offered. I can't see why the question "How do we know there are numbers?" would be defective, whereas Horwich's statement "There are numbers" is licit, when both utterances occur in a philosophical context.

world-spirit, respectively. You might be tempted to ask how they could know that there were such things. A Horwich-inspired response, however, would have it that you are confused in wanting to ask that question. You are unwittingly drawing analogies between ordinary physical objects and these philosophical exotica and you are asking a question that can reasonably be asked only about physical objects. Note as well that the more exotic the sorts of philosophical objects in question are, the more they are unlike ordinary physical objects. By Horwich's reckoning, this makes the analogies between them still weaker, thereby correspondingly diminishing sceptical doubts about them. To my mind, however, the weaker the analogies, the *stronger* sceptical doubts about how we can have knowledge of them. The stronger the analogies between numbers and ordinary physical objects, the more similar the account of our knowledge of numbers might be to the account of our knowledge of ordinary physical objects. The weaker the analogies, the less similar the accounts will be. But then we are beggared to give an account of our knowledge of numbers. Let me develop this line of thought by the following two points.

First, Horwich decries T-philosophy for conjuring problems from "irrational over-generalizations" (2012, 19). Yet Horwich's own diagnosis of the origin of the problem of our knowledge of numbers is itself the result of a dubious over-generalization: namely, that *any* philosophical problem about our knowledge of any sort of object is underpinned by misplaced analogies with our knowledge of physical objects.

In sum, not only does Horwich's response prove too much—banishing reasonable sceptical worries about knowledge of monads, the world-spirit, and noumena—it is irrelevant to the problem of our knowledge of numbers. Now, a referee failed to see why this is so, citing Hegel and Brandom's alleged insights into "the categories of object and property." Such a surprising invocation, however, cries out for substantive supporting argument. That aside, let me put my challenge as simply as I can: we have reasonable sceptical worries about knowledge of souls (one supposed kind of non-physical object); why not about numbers (another such kind) as well? Moreover, this worry becomes more pressing in the absence of any plausible account of how we could get knowledge of them. Since Horwich eschews devising any philosophical theories, his official position prevents him from filling this absence, and so the worry cannot be addressed, at any rate by this means.

My second point is that the problem of our knowledge of numbers can be established without drawing analogies with our knowledge of anything else (following Field 1991, introduction). For any sort of object, if we believe there are objects of that sort, it is reasonable to try to explain how we get information about such objects. We cannot get information about numbers in the ways in which we get information about concrete objects. It also seems that we cannot explain how we can get information about numbers. Setting up the problem in this way does not appeal to any analogy with our knowledge of physical objects; if anything, the comparison with our knowledge of physical objects reveals a disanalogy. However we know about numbers, it is not by the same way in which we know about physical objects.

Accordingly, the problem of our knowledge of numbers resists dissolution, and Horwich's more general contention that philosophical problems are pseudo-problems is undermined.

6. Conclusion

In response to Williamson, Horwich entertains the fallback position that some of his claims are empirical theoretical conjectures (2013, e24). He takes this to be consistent with a rejection of T-philosophy. To illustrate his idea, Horwich suggests that the claim that a word w's meaning is w's basic regularity of use is "an *a posteriori* constitution theory (on a par with 'water is H_2O')—an account whose acceptance is perfectly consistent with Wittgenstein's metaphilosophy" (e24).[8] This manoeuvre leaves me at a loss about what remains at issue between the Wittgensteinian and the T-philosopher; the manoeuvre seems less of a fallback than a collapse of the debate. What Horwich is proposing is an instance of philosophical theorising explicitly modelled on theorising in science. A theory of how word meanings are constituted by word use is a reductive theory, in the sense of a theory showing how some facts are less basic than others. That makes Horwich's theory a piece with *a posteriori* philosophical theories about, for example, how the mental reduces to the physical (Smart 1959) or how the moral reduces to the non-moral (Boyd 1988). A constitution theory denies that the target phenomena—say, word meanings—are too messy and vague to admit systematic investigation, and it provides a simple, exceptionless, and informative principle or set of such principles that govern those phenomena. Such a principle would also have explanatory potential because it stratifies reality into surface appearance (what word w means) and underlying determinants (facts about w's basic regularity of use). What more does the T-philosopher need?

Acknowledgments

My thanks to the organisers and participants of the 2021 conference *New Directions in Metaphilosophy* at the University of Kent. I'm also grateful to

---

[8] This is offered as a fallback position because Horwich's first line of defence is that he is offering a definition of the meaning of the expression "word meaning." But that defence has difficulties of its own. According to it, Horwich is offering an *a priori* analysis of the concept of meaning and thereby faces the various objections that he himself makes against the project of analysis—that there are no successful, informative analyses, that most concepts are vague, and that most concepts apply to a messy range of phenomena.

two referees for detailed comments. Thanks as well to Fraser MacBride for valuable discussion.

References

Armstrong, D. M. 1978. *Nominalism and Realism: Universals and Scientific Realism*, volume 1. Cambridge: Cambridge University Press.

Bennett, Karen. 2017. *Making Things Up*. Oxford: Oxford University Press.

Boyd, Richard. 1988. "How to Be a Moral Realist." In *Essays on Moral Realism*, edited by Geoffrey Sayre-McCord, 181–222. Ithaca, N.Y.: Cornell University Press.

Carnap, Rudolf. 1950. *Logical Foundations of Probability*. Chicago: University of Chicago Press.

Chalmers, David. 1996. *The Conscious Mind: In Search of a Fundamental Theory*. Oxford: Oxford University Press.

Chalmers, David. 2011. "Verbal Disputes." *Philosophical Review* 120: 515–66.

Clendinnen, F. John. 1998. "Note on Howard Sankey's 'Induction and Natural Kinds'." *Principia* 2: 125–34.

Craig, Edward. 1990. *Knowledge and the State of Nature*. Oxford: Clarendon Press.

Cruse, Pierre. 2007. "Van Fraassen on the Nature of Empiricism." *Metaphilosophy* 38: 489–508.

Dummett, Michael. 2010. *The Nature and Future of Philosophy*. New York: Columbia University Press.

Dupré, John. 1981. "Natural Kinds and Biological Taxa." *Philosophical Review* 90: 66–90.

Earman, John. 1993. "Underdetermination, Realism, and Reason." *Midwest Studies in Philosophy* 18: 19–38.

Field, Hartry. 1991. *Realism, Mathematics and Modality*. Second edition. Oxford: Blackwell.

Horwich, Paul. 1982. "How to Choose Between Empirically Equivalent Theories." *Journal of Philosophy* 79: 61–77.

Horwich, Paul. 2012. *Wittgenstein's Metaphilosophy*. Oxford: Oxford University Press.

Horwich, Paul. 2013. "Reply to Timothy Williamson's Review of *Wittgenstein's Metaphilosophy*." *European Journal of Philosophy* 21: e18–e26.

Horwich, Paul. 2020. "Sosa's Theory of Knowledge." *Synthese* 197: 5225–32.

Kanamori, Akihiro. 2008. "Cohen and Set Theory." *Bulletin of Symbolic Logic* 14: 351–78.

Kornblith, Hilary. 2002. *Knowledge and Its Place in Nature*. Oxford: Oxford University Press.

Krugman, Paul. 2011. "Does Economics Still Progress?" *New York Times* (September 27). https://krugman.blogs.nytimes.com/2011/09/27/does-economics-still-progress/

Ladyman, James. 2004. "Discussion: Empiricism Versus Metaphysics." *Philosophical Studies* 121: 133–45.

Lewis, David. 1973. *Counterfactuals*. Oxford: Blackwell.

Lewis, David. 1983. "New Work for a Theory of Universals." *Australasian Journal of Philosophy* 61: 343–77.

Linsky, Bernard, and Edward N. Zalta. 1995. "Naturalized Platonism vs. Platonised Naturalism." *Journal of Philosophy* 92: 525–55.

Lynch, Michael. 1998. *Truth in Context: An Essay on Pluralism and Objectivity*. Cambridge, Mass.: MIT Press.

Rosen, Gideon. 2010. "Metaphysical Dependence: Grounding and Reduction." In *Modality: Metaphysics, Logic, and Epistemology*, edited by Bob Hale and Aviv Hoffmann, 109–35. Oxford: Oxford University Press.

Schindler, Samuel. 2018. *Theoretical Virtues in Science: Uncovering Reality Through Theory*. Cambridge: Cambridge University Press.

Smart, J. J. C. 1959. "Sensations and Brain Processes." *Philosophical Review* 68: 141–56.

Stalnaker, Robert 2001. "Metaphysics Without Conceptual Analysis." *Philosophy and Phenomenological Research* 62: 631–36.

Swoyer, Chris. 1999. "How Ontology Might Be Possible: Explanation and Inference in Metaphysics." *Midwest Studies in Philosophy* 23: 100–131.

Tappenden, Jamie. 1995. "Extending Knowledge and 'Fruitful Concepts': Fregean Themes in the Philosophy of Mathematics." *Noûs* 29: 427–67.

Tappenden, Jamie. 2008a. "Mathematical Concepts and Definitions." In *The Philosophy of Mathematical Practice*, edited by Paolo Mancosu, 256–75. Oxford: Oxford University Press.

Tappenden, Jamie. 2008b. "Mathematical Concepts: Fruitfulness and Naturalness." In *The Philosophy of Mathematical Practice*, edited by Paolo Mancosu, 276–301. Oxford: Oxford University Press.

van Fraassen, Bas C. 1976. "On the Radical Incompleteness of the Manifest Image." In *PSA: Proceedings of the Biennial Meeting of the Philosophy of Science Association, 1976, Vol. 1976, Volume Two: Symposia and Invited Papers*, 335–43. Chicago: University of Chicago Press.

van Fraassen, Bas C. 1980. *The Scientific Image*. Oxford: Oxford University Press.

Williamson, Timothy. 2007. *The Philosophy of Philosophy*. Oxford: Blackwell.

Williamson, Timothy. 2013. Review of Paul Horwich, *Wittgenstein's Metaphilosophy*. *European Journal of Philosophy* 21: e7–e10.

Wittgenstein, Ludwig. 1958. *The Blue and Brown Books*. Oxford: Blackwell.

PART 2

HOW TO DO PHILOSOPHY

CHAPTER 4

ON THE CONTINUITY OF METAPHYSICS WITH SCIENCE: SOME SCEPTICISM AND SOME SUGGESTIONS

JACK RITCHIE

1. Three Kinds of Continuity

Metaphysics is normally understood as an attempt to say how things are (and perhaps must be). Science too, at least if we are realists, is an attempt to describe the world. How should we understand the connection between these two activities? Are they in competition?

Most contemporary philosophers think not. Science and metaphysics ought to and do, when done well, complement each other: metaphysical theorizing is in some sense continuous with scientific investigation. There are different ways of cashing out this idea of supposed continuity, but they can, I think, be usefully grouped into three broad (and overlapping) strategies.

On one popular conception of the relation between science and metaphysics, although metaphysicians are concerned with more general questions than those that arise in science—what are things, properties, laws, fundamental structure, and so on—the methods that are used to answer metaphysical questions are the same as those used by the natural sciences. The best theory is the one that fits all the data and displays various theoretical virtues, like simplicity and fecundity. A second strategy takes the metaphysical project as an attempt to synthesize the diverse theories and ideas of the natural sciences and perhaps also ordinary commonsense knowledge. One way to do so is to argue that there is a general metaphysical picture or worldview that is best supported by our scientific knowledge. It is the philosopher's job both to articulate this general theory and to show how (if they do) non-fundamental aspects of reality fit into this picture. Physicalism is a version of this way of doing metaphysics, and so too is ontic structural realism. Finally, in the foundations of physics community the

Examining Philosophy Itself. Edited by Yafeng Shan.
Chapters and book compilation © 2023 Metaphilosophy LLC and John Wiley & Sons Ltd.
Published 2023 by John Wiley & Sons Ltd.

project of interpreting our fundamental theories is often offered as the best way, perhaps the only way, to pursue metaphysics.

My aim here is largely negative. There are, I contend, fundamental problems with all three of these metaphysical projects—at least if the aim is to discover the truth. I end on a positive note. If we give up on the idea that truth is the goal of metaphysical inquiry, there are new and interesting ways to understand the value of metaphysics.

1.1. Methodological Continuity: The Abductive Method in Metaphysics

When it comes to first-order metaphysical matters metaphysicians rarely agree. Some are nominalists, some Platonists. Some possible-worlds sceptics, others realists. Some are Humeans about laws, others believe in natural necessity. Add your own favourites. What is remarkable, though, is that beneath this first-order disagreement there is widespread consensus regarding the appropriate methods of metaphysics. Ted Sider, John P. Hawthorne, and D. W. Zimmerman express the idea well: "[M]etaphysicians use standards for choosing theories that are like the standards used by scientists (simplicity, comprehensiveness, elegance, and so on)" (2008, 8).[1]

Some prefer to use different language. David Lewis talks about the serviceability of a hypothesis. David Armstrong describes what he is doing in terms of inference to the best explanation. Timothy Williamson uses the term "abduction." But once these ideas are spelled out, it quickly becomes clear that they are all variations on a single theme. A thesis is serviceable for Lewis if "[it] is fruitful; that gives us good reason to believe that it is true" (1986, 4). According to Armstrong, "the best explanation explains the most by means of the least" (1984, 73). Williamson characterises his abductive method this way: "Apart from its relation to the [evidence], the more [a metaphysical theory] has the intrinsic virtues of a good theory, the better (ceteris paribus). ... In brief, it should combine simplicity with strength" (2016, 266).

All these views owe a debt to Quine and his conception of both the nature of philosophy and the methodology of science. Famously Quine argued that philosophy and science are continuous.[2] In characterising how scientists come to accept a theory, for example like the molecular hypothesis, he provides an analysis on which the claims of Sider and others are clearly modelled: "The benefits credited to the molecular doctrine may be divided into five. One is simplicity. ... Another is familiarity of principle. ... A third is scope. ... A fourth is fecundity. ... The fifth goes without saying: such testable consequences of the theory as have been tested have turned out well" (1966, 234).

---

[1] See also Paul 2012 for a similar but more fully developed view.

[2] "Our acceptance of an ontology is, I think, similar in principle to our acceptance of a scientific theory" (Quine 1980, 16).

For the sake of simplicity and brevity, I will use Williamson's term and call this Quine-inspired way of proceeding the abductive method in metaphysics.

1.1.1. Justification of the method? In light of the near perfect unanimity regarding appropriate methods, one might expect a core part of the work of the methodologically self-conscious metaphysician would be to undertake a detailed investigation into the abductive methods used in science and how and when they can be adapted to metaphysical concerns. Surprisingly, that is not what we find.[3] Typically, if any defence of abductive methods is offered at all, a quick two-step argument is given. First, some examples of supposedly abductive inferences in the sciences are offered: evolutionary biology (Paul 2012, 12) and Big Bang cosmology (Williamson 2016, 266) are two favourites.[4] Then we are told: "If such theoretical desiderata [that make for a good abduction] are truth conducive in science, they are also truth conducive in metaphysics" (Paul 2012, 21).[5]

That no fuller defence of abduction is offered is particularly surprising because, as Williamson himself notes: "[I]t [is] far from clear what makes abduction such a good method. For instance, why should aesthetic criteria such as elegance contribute to the pursuit of truth?" (2016, 268).

I think it would be strange if a crucial part of scientific practice involved a method that had no obvious justification; and this ought to raise a concern among metaphysicians about whether they have correctly interpreted theory choice in science. As we will see below, they have not. When we turn to consider some real scientific examples, it quickly becomes obvious that abductive considerations of the sort described by Sider and others appear to play little or no role in deciding theoretical disputes in science.

1.1.2. Three case studies. This point, I think, has been made often in the philosophy of science literature (see, e.g., van Fraassen 2002, 12–13; Ladyman 2012; and Saatsi 2017), but it will be useful to rehearse a few examples that illustrate the claim. In particular, it is worth considering some of the favourite examples of supposedly scientific abductions mentioned above. Many of these involve existence claims, and so they provide a nice contrast with the arguments given in ontology for the existence, for example, of possible worlds or mereological fusions.

Consider first Quine's example of atoms and molecules. Penelope Maddy (1997, 137–41) has discussed this case in detail. As she shows,

---

[3] Quine is an exception. Quine and Ullian 1970 provides a detailed discussion of the role of theoretical virtues in science. Much of the discussion makes it sound as though the virtues play a pragmatic as opposed to epistemic role.

[4] Although she claims it is common, Paul in fact does not give any actual examples of abduction at work in evolutionary theory but does give a brief account of modelling in ecology. Williamson's paper mostly explores cases of abductive reasoning outside science.

[5] It is also this conditional claim that Brenner (2017) defends.

when we look at the state of the atomic hypothesis as it developed throughout the nineteenth century, it displayed all the theoretical virtues that Quine lists. Maxwell and Boltzmann used the notion of the atom or molecule to develop the kinetic theory which offered, among other things, general explanations of thermodynamic principles. The atomic hypothesis was used to explain ratios of combination in chemistry, and later more sophisticated chemical formulae and rules of interaction. The theory was simple, broad in scope, uniting both physical and chemical knowledge, and apparently highly explanatory. Nevertheless, there was widespread scepticism about the existence of atoms among both chemists and physicists. Wilhelm Ostwald (1904) expressed a view typical of many when he said: "[T]he atomic hypothesis has proved to be an exceedingly useful aid to instruction and investigation. ... One must not, however, be led astray by this agreement between picture and reality and combine the two."[6] What decisively moved the scientific community towards belief in atoms was Jean Perrin's experimental work on colloids in the early twentieth century. Perrin was able to demonstrate the random nature of Brownian motion, thereby ruling out competitors to the atomic hypothesis that took thermodynamic properties to be basic. Using theoretical ideas of Einstein and others, Perrin determined the absolute atomic masses for the atoms in his solutions, where before only mass ratios had been determined, and used his measurements to derive Avogadro's number in multiple and, importantly, theoretically independent ways, all of which were in broad agreement. It was this work, which used experimental data to rule out competitors and provided direct empirical grounding[7] for certain properties of the atom, like size and mass, that persuaded the scientific community of the truth of the atomic hypothesis.[8]

Consider now the Big Bang. The simple abductive model suggests a quick inference from the discovery of the microwave background to the truth of the existence of a big bang. But again, as John Norton's (manuscript, chap. 8) recent work demonstrates, the real history is more complicated. The mere existence of the microwave background radiation was not enough to convince the physics community of the Big Bang hypothesis. All cosmologies will predict some background radiation, since all posit charged matter. What was needed was evidence of something more specific: that the radiation had a thermal character with a black body spectrum and a temperature of 2.7 K.

After the initial discovery of some background radiation in 1965 by Penzias and Wilson, it took another twenty or so years of empirical and

---

[6] Quoted by both Ney (1972, 30) and Maddy (1997, 138).

[7] The term "empirical grounding" I take from van Fraassen (2009). He develops a very detailed and sophisticated account of the notion in his own discussion of Perrin.

[8] As can be seen in later editions of Ostwald's 1908 textbook: "I have satisfied myself that we have arrived a short time ago ... at experimental proof for the discrete or particulate nature of matter" (quoted in Nye 1972, 151).

theoretical work to establish that the background radiation had the character predicted by Big Bang cosmology and, equally important, that rival Steady State cosmologies could not provide a mechanism that could explain the character of the radiation.[9] Here again what is decisive is not an appeal to "theoretical virtues" but further empirical work.

The discovery of the Higgs boson offers a third example. The Higgs mechanism offers an attractive and simple explanation for how gauge bosons involved in the weak interaction (the W and Z bosons) can have mass (a fact confirmed by experimental work). The bosons interact with a new field, the Higgs field. But this nice explanation was not judged enough by the physics community to warrant belief in the Higgs field. Only in 2012, when the Higgs boson was discovered, and so other possible mechanisms for explaining the mass of the gauge bosons were ruled out, were physicists convinced. And so only then, and nearly fifty years after he first published his paper, was Peter Higgs (along with François Englert) awarded the Nobel Prize.

The contrast between science and metaphysics highlighted by these examples is so obvious that it is a little embarrassing to note: in science, but not in metaphysics, at some point, relative to background knowledge, empirical evidence is taken to play a decisive role. But we will look in vain for any similar experimental data or other evidence used to discriminate among metaphysical rivals.

1.2. A Response

One response that might be made is to accept the contrast illustrated but insist the difference highlighted is one of degree, not kind. Although the evidence in favour of a metaphysical hypothesis is never decisive in the way it can be in science, nevertheless explanatory considerations in both fields provide some good reasons for belief. One could argue, for example, that even before the discovery of the Higgs boson, the explanatory benefits of the theory made it reasonable to have a high degree of confidence in the Higgs mechanism. The same, or at least something similar, can be true in metaphysics. Metaphysical theories are supported to some, non-conclusive degree by abductive considerations.[10] Again, Sider provides a good example of this sort of thinking:

> Skeptics often ask too much of metaphysical arguments. A priori metaphysical arguments should not be faulted for not being decisive.

[9] Through multiple textbooks and reports, Norton, like Maddy, shows how scepticism gradually turned to belief.

[10] Another related idea, presented to me when I gave this piece as a talk, might be that abduction is a first step in metaphysical argument, winnowing the possible down to the plausible. If this is the correct way to understand the role abduction plays in metaphysics, then some story must be told of how we get from presumably multiple plausible options to the single best supported theory. I know of no such account in the literature on metaphysics.

For suppose the evidential support conferred by such arguments is fairly weak, though non-zero. Then the support for a typical metaphysical theory, T, will be weak. But the only support for T's rivals will also be from a priori metaphysical arguments. Thus T may well be better supported—albeit weakly—than its rivals. One would then be reasonable in giving more credence to T than to its rivals. Metaphysical inquiry can survive if we are willing to live with highly tentative conclusions. Let's not kid ourselves: metaphysics is highly speculative! It does not follow that it is entirely without rational grounds. (Sider 2001, xv)

The case made here is, on the face of it, quite odd. What metaphysicians can reasonably hope to offer their interlocutors are considerations that one view, although not well supported, is better supported than any rival. But taking Sider's own presentation of the state of metaphysical theorising as correct, surely the rational attitude to take to any metaphysical debate would be agnosticism.[11]

It is useful here to contrast what is at stake in metaphysical discussion with more practical matters. I might come to believe, or more probably act as though I believe, that it will rain, even if the weather forecast predicts showers with less than 50 percent confidence. Obviously, that is because there are clear practical matters at stake in getting things wrong here. I risk not just acquiring a false belief but getting wet too. But in metaphysics no such practical stakes are in play. All I risk is failing to adopt a true belief or mistakenly adopting a false one.[12] When nothing other than the truth or falsity of my beliefs is at stake, I have no obligation to take a view on any matter or act in any way at all, and surely one should not if even the advocates of metaphysical views think the evidence in favour of their claims is very weak. Given that and a reasonable pessimism that we will ever get the kind of decisive evidence we find in the empirical sciences, actual belief in any metaphysical theory does indeed seem to be without any rational ground on Sider's conception.[13] Since truth and thus rational belief are meant to be the goals of metaphysical inquiry, Sider's defence suggests no rational agent should pursue metaphysics, given there are no grounds for thinking it will ever meet its goals.

---

[11] Sider's account indeed seems oddly to embrace a standard criticism of abduction: the best theory may be the best of a bad lot. Interestingly, Sider interprets scientific realism in the same way (2020, 53).

[12] See van Fraassen 1989 and 2002 for a similar argument.

[13] There are more permissive views of rationality defended by van Fraassen (1989; 1999) and Chakravartty (2017) in which we could take a metaphysician like Sider to be individually rational in holding a metaphysical claim so long as certain minimal coherence conditions are met. This offers a different way to draw the contrast between metaphysics and science. Reasons offered in science are meant to persuade others; that they are public but metaphysical "evidence" really reflects the personal predilections of the metaphysician in question.

1.3. Simplicity in Science

Bad as this conclusion is, things are in reality much worse for the metaphysician. Once we pick into the details of science and see how what Williamson calls "aesthetic" virtues play a role in theory choice, it is clear where these virtues have an evidential role in science that this role could not carry over to metaphysical debates. Consider, for example, simplicity, a virtue that appears on the lists of all the philosophers mentioned above. Under what conditions, if ever, could we say that of two hypotheses the simpler is more likely to be true?

A great deal of detailed work has been done on this subject in recent philosophy of science (e.g., Sober 2016; Norton manuscript; Kelly 2007). One thing this work has uncovered is that the concept of simplicity is used in many ways, but below I concentrate on just one straightforward idea, what is sometimes called parsimony: we ought to prefer theories that postulate fewer entities or properties, all things considered.

Consider first a simple example. You are sitting in your office working on a paper, and suddenly all the lights in the building go out at the same time. One explanation is that all the bulbs in the building have coincidentally and simultaneously failed. A different explanation is that there has been a power cut. The first explains the event in terms of lots of independent causes; the second in terms of one common cause. Clearly the common cause explanation is better. Why?

Well, because the simultaneous failure of all the lights is highly probable given the power-cut theory, but the simultaneous failure of the bulbs is very unlikely on the multiple-cause theory. Simplicity or parsimony here is really a proxy for likelihood.

Similar forms of inference can be found in real science. For example, in evolutionary biology, we may sometimes reasonably infer that the existence of a common trait in two species, not shared by a third, is evidence the first two species have a closer common ancestor than either shares with the third. The reasoning here is broadly similar to the light-bulb case. It is more likely that a common trait would have a common cause (a shared ancestor with the trait) than two independent causes. In real evolutionary biology, making good on this kind of argument requires the justification of many other assumptions. For one, we must have some reason to think that the trait in question is not the result of convergent evolutionary processes; for another, some knowledge of how the trait is manifested in a common ancestor of all three species is needed. Further background knowledge can strengthen the inferences. If we have grounds to think a trait is maladaptive, and so less probable than an adaptive trait, this can be strong evidence of a more recent common ancestor. But here again, as in the simpler light-bulb case, what is doing the inferential work will be judgements about relative likelihoods.[14] In fact, what even these brief examples show is that parsimony considerations are only evidentially relevant given certain background facts are taken to hold. There is no sound general rule that the more parsimonious theory is more likely true.

Could the same sort of explanation be used in metaphysics? It is certainly possible to think of cases that seem to have some of the same structure as the light-bulb case. Consider the metaphysics of properties. Say there are three red snooker balls in front of me. One explanation of what they have in common is to say that all three balls instantiate the very same universal of redness; another would be to say that each ball is in part made up of a red trope and that these tropes are exactly similar. In the first case sameness of property is explained by appeal to one thing, in the second by three things. We might think parsimony favours the explanation in terms of a single universal by analogy with the light-bulb case.

The rationale for preferring the single cause of multiple-light-bulb failure is simply because:

P(all the lights go out simultaneously (observed association)/power cut (single cause))≫P(all the lights go out simultaneously (observed association)/each individual bulb fails (multiple cause)).[15]

Clearly, though, no such objectively justifiable inequality holds in the case of universals and tropes. As metaphysical theses, it is by the lights of each theory a necessary truth that each red thing instantiates the universal red or that each red thing has a part that is a red trope. The likelihoods, if we can talk meaningfully about them in this case, of all three balls being red for each metaphysical hypothesis would be 1.

In general, this will always be true. Common-cause explanations, where they hold, depend on making relative likelihood judgements, but since metaphysical hypothesis are typically meant to be necessary truths, no such similar judgement can be made.

In a purely formal way, a metaphysician might claim a similar inequality could be justified. If we are strictly subjective Bayesians, we ought to interpret the probabilities as credences, subjective degrees of belief. So, the thought, say, that realism about universals is simpler than trope theory could be understood as a claim about different metaphysicians' priors. While such a rationale might be probabilistically coherent, since there would be no objective basis to these different judgements about the likelihoods, it would have no persuasive force.[16] In the case of the light bulbs, we

[14] For more on the complexities of this kind of inference and its applications in evolutionary biology see Sober (2016, chap. 3, and 2008, chap. 4).

[15] The details of this sort of inference are laid out in Sober 2016, 102–17.

[16] This is a way to reconstruct Chakravartty's (2017) voluntarism in ontological matters. Different philosophers can rationally hold a variety of different views because of their different priors and differing judgements about likelihood. Again, the contrast with science is clear. There must be empirical evidence that justifies these probabilities or background judgements.

can get estimates of the relevant probabilities from frequencies of light-bulb failure. Something similar, although more complex, is true in the evolutionary case. But nothing, other than the prejudice of the individual metaphysician, could similarly ground the different credences imagined here.

In one narrow sense, Paul and metaphysicians advocating the abductive method are right. It is possible to find reasoning that involves simplicity judgements in some sciences, like evolutionary biology. But in a more fundamental way they are wrong. Simplicity judgements where they provide warrant are grounded in empirically supported background knowledge, like the relative likelihood judgements discussed above.[17] These forms of reasoning have no more than a formal analogue in metaphysics. It is false to claim that if simplicity judgements are truth conducive in biology or other sciences, they are truth conducive in metaphysics.

As we have seen in our discussion of Sider, even if we were to accept metaphysicians' self-understanding of their abductive method, it never provides grounds for belief. But we should not accept that conception. Where we see something like theoretical virtues in play in science, that reasoning cannot be employed in metaphysics.[18]

2. Continuity of Content, Part 1: The Worldview

Let us turn from strategies that seek to make metaphysics methodologically continuous with science to strategies that seek in some way to make science and metaphysics continuous in terms of their content. Consider first the idea that our best science supports a general worldview.

The most popular version of this idea is physicalism. Physicalists claim that everything is physical, or in some appropriate way dependent upon the physical. The work of the metaphysician concerns what Jackson (1998) calls placement problems: to show how things like minds, morals, or numbers can be accommodated in the physicalist picture. Different forms of physicalism diverge in how they treat the apparently non-physical. Some are reductionists, some eliminativists, some favour technical notions like supervenience as a way of articulating a non-reductive relation between

---

[17] There is a more straightforward connection between simplicity and probability given by the simple fact that $P(a\&b) \leq P(a)$. But this truism cannot be used to justify any interesting metaphysical claims. We can't argue that, say, mereological nihilism is more probable than a common-sense ontology that admits chairs because $P(atoms\&chairs) \leq P(atoms)$, since the mereological nihilist obviously holds a stronger view than just the thought that mereological atoms exist; she believes in an addition that chairs *don't* exist. Obviously, it is not true in general that: $P(a\&b) \leq P(a\& \sim b)$.

[18] The case I have made is brief. A metaphysician might claim there are other ways to understand the role simplicity plays in theory choice. That we should concede is possible. But the metaphysicians' case cannot be made by highlighting a mere possibility. We are owed an account of what this alternative view is. Without it, the claim that theoretical virtues like simplicity play a role in metaphysics is without merit.

the physical and the non-physical. Most physicalists probably favour a combination of all three, using different relations for different cases of the non-physical.

Another version of the worldview strategy is ontic structural realism (OSR), the view, roughly, "that there are no 'things' [at some fundamental level] and that structure is all there is" (Ladyman 2007).[19] Like physicalists, OSRists are concerned to say something about how the non-fundamental or non-physical fits into this picture. And like physicalists, they diverge in how they do this. James Ladyman and Don Ross (2007) try to accommodate the ontology of the non-fundamental sciences, a position they call Rainforest Realism. Steven French (2014), in contrast, defends an eliminativist position.

There are then two steps in the defence of such a worldview. First, the defence of the general picture itself. Second, the project of accommodating the non-fundamental. It is the first move where continuity with science is typically claimed, and so it is this step I focus on below: the notion that the general worldview is supported by our best science.[20]

2.1. Physicalism, the Completeness of Physics, and Hempel's Dilemma

Let's turn to physicalism first. The claim that the content of physicalism is continuous with science derives from the idea that a weaker but related thesis, the completeness of physics, is empirically well supported.[21] The completeness of physics thesis states that to account for physical phenomena we only ever need to appeal to physical properties, states, and laws. This contrasts with other domains. In psychology, for example, we will often have to advert to non-psychological states to explain psychological states. Your current pain, for example, might be explained by the physiological fact that you have stubbed your toe. Physics is different because the laws of physics, unlike the laws of other disciplines, are universal and complete. Physicalism proper is derived from the completeness of physics by noting that non-physical states have (apparently) physical effects; beliefs cause bodily movements, for example. Hence (ruling out the possibility

[19] It could be that OSR is a particular form of physicalism, but Ladyman and Ross (2007) present their view in contrast to at least more traditional forms of physicalism.

[20] Jackson (1998), for example, thinks conceptual analysis plays a crucial role in addressing placement problems. Ladyman and Ross's (2007) way of accommodating the non-physical seems more thoroughly naturalistic, appealing to information-theoretic ideas. Ladyman and Ross's official view is that really only the second step counts as metaphysics: see their Principle of Naturalistic Closure (2007, 40ff.). I take this to be a highly idiosyncratic definition, one clearly contradicted by other things Ladyman says: for example, "OSR is any form of structural realism based on an *ontological or metaphysical thesis* that inflates the ontological priority of structure and relations" (2007; italics added).

[21] See especially Papineau 1993, chap. 1. Papineau 2001 offers a slightly more sophisticated historical argument.

of systematic overdetermination), those non-physical states must either be identical to physical states or in some appropriate way be dependent on physical states or not real: the three possible answers corresponding to the reductive, non-reductive, and eliminative forms of physicalism mentioned above.

But what, we may ask, do physicalists mean by physics when they say it is complete? One answer, robustly naturalistic, would be to defer to science. Physical properties and objects are those described in (fundamental) physics. This answer leads to an obvious problem. Current physics is incomplete. There are many facts and phenomena unexplained by current science, from sonoluminescence to high-temperature superconductivity to better-known examples like quantum gravity, dark matter, and dark energy. It seems reasonable to expect that future physical theories will need to be revised to account for at least some of these phenomena. Any claim that everything is physical or dependent upon the physical, where physics is understood this way, will be false.

We could, then, try to define the physical by appeal to future physics. This will lead to vacuity. Since we have no idea what the content of this future physics will be, we can give no clear sense to physicalism defined this way.

2.1.1. Take the first horn. This problem, that physicalism is either false or lacks clear content, is often called Hempel's dilemma, and there is a vast literature that tries to respond to it.[22] One strategy offered by Andrew Melnyk is to take the first horn of the dilemma. According to Melnyk, we should define the physical in terms of "those theories which are the object of consensus among current physicists" (2003, 15). Although physicalism so defined is likely false, Melnyk claims it is better supported by the evidence than any alternative metaphysical view and so more probable than any of its rivals. This strategy is analogous to Sider's defence of the abductive method in metaphysics, and it clearly suffers from the same problem. Even if it is true that there is more support for physicalism so defined than for its rivals, this would not provide grounds for belief in physicalism if the evidence in its favour remains weak. But as with Sider, the situation is even worse than this. Those theories that are the object of consensus among physicists include quantum theory (QT) and general relativity (GR). QT and GR are clearly incompatible with each other as standardly presented, since among many other things space-time is curved in GR but flat in QT. Attempts to combine the theories by quantising the gravitational field by analogy with the other fields of quantum field theory leads to impossibilities, such as infinite

---

[22] See Ney 2008a for a good summary of the relevant literature. Some responses accept that physicalism is not a thesis. See for example Poland 1994, who thinks of physicalism as a research programme, and Ney 2008b, who claims it is a stance. I have sympathy for these views, but clearly they are no longer metaphysical claims.

probability values. The probability that any such combination of theories is true must then be zero, and so it cannot be the case that Melnyk-style physicalism is more probable than its rivals.[23]

2.1.2. Via negativa.

An alternative and more common strategy is the so-called *via negativa*.[24] Instead of defining the physics in physicalism by appeal to contemporary science, physics is defined negatively, as, for example, the not fundamentally mental. Advocates of this view claim that this gives clear content to physicalism in a way that allows metaphysicians to make sense of the traditional mind-body problem: physicalists think physics so defined is complete, dualists deny this.

The via negativa converts a sweeping worldview into a rather parochial position, one that forgoes telling us anything of interest outside the mind-body problem. But even so, it is not in fact clear whether this does solve the problem of providing clear content to physicalism, since it remains unclear exactly how to cash out the idea of the not fundamentally mental. Take, for example, a metaphysical theory of consciousness like Chalmers' (1996) pan-protopsychism. It seems a case can be made that since fundamental entities are only *proto*-conscious on Chalmers' view, this conception of how things are is compatible with physicalism defined in terms of the not fundamentally mental. But intuitively for many, that will seem wrong. Chalmers' panprotopsychism is meant to be an archetype of a non-physicalist view. One might fiddle with the definition to exclude the fundamentally *proto*-mental. If we do that, then what about theories of consciousness that envisage revisions and enrichments of fundamental physics like Roger Penrose's (1997) orchestrated objective reduction? Should we see the moves made here as involving a kind of *proto*-consciousness in the objective reduction of the wave function? Stipulations might be offered, but it is hard to see what principled answers could be given.

But there is a more fundamental difficulty with the via negativa: it undermines the idea that content of physicalism is supported by our best science. When we define the physical in terms of physical theory, there is a prima facie, if somewhat abstract, case to be made for its completeness by appeal to things such as physical laws, as we saw above. When we turn to the mishmash of things that are included in the not fundamentally mental, it is unclear what empirical or theoretical reason there is to believe in the completeness of that domain. There are obviously many examples of phenomena where appeal to mental causes seems necessary to explain

---

[23] There are of course many speculative theories of quantum gravity, such as string theory and loop quantum gravity, which try to overcome these problems. But none of these is the object of consensus among practicing physicists, and for good reason, since all face serious conceptual problems.

[24] See Spurrett 2017; Montero and Papineau 2005; Papineau and Spurrett 1999. Ney 2008a aptly calls this an *a priori* strategy.

non-mental phenomena; conscious mental states are surely one such group. Physicalists might assume that these states will be reduced to or explained by something not fundamentally mental, but if any such questions remain empirically open, as they do in the case of consciousness, there appear to be no empirical grounds to accept the claims of the physicalist. Physicalists pursuing the via negativa can arguably avoid the charge of vacuity or obvious falsity, but their view is then no longer continuous in any meaningful way with the sciences.[25]

2.2. Ontic Structural Realism

Physicalists struggle to provide clear content to physicalism because of the incomplete and open-ended nature of current science. Ontic structural realism was in part conceived to address similar issues in the philosophy of science and so might seem better placed to offer a coherent worldview genuinely supported by current science.

According to structuralists, although science, especially physics, is subject to revolutionary change, typically we will find that mathematical structures are retained, at least approximately, through revolutions. So, for example, although, in the shift from Fresnel's wave theory to Maxwell's electromagnetic theory of light, key metaphysical posits like the ether are jettisoned, the equations Fresnel employed to describe the relative intensities of reflected and refracted light traversing two media are retained. The structural realist says it is these mathematical structures that we should be realists about.[26]

A distinctively *ontic* form of structural realism is obtained by combining this kind of realism with some philosophy of physics. Particles as described in non-relativistic quantum theory have some very strange properties. What one might take naturally to be permutations of different bosons or fermions do not correspond to different physical states according to the theory. Advocates of OSR suggest the best way to make sense of this is to reject the idea that there are any individual particles with intrinsic properties.[27] Instead, our fundamental ontology should include only the structures described in our physics, and jettison commitment to fundamental things.[28]

2.2.1. What is structure? What, though, do OSRists mean when they talk about ontic *structure?* Some statements of the view make it seem utterly mysterious. "[I]f one were asked to present the ontology of the world

---

[25] See Ritchie 2008, chap. 5, for a more detailed account of this worry.

[26] See Worrall 1989 for the classic statement of this view.

[27] See Weyl 1931 (quoted in French 2019a) for a pithy statement of the problem and Ladyman 1998 for the structuralist solution.

[28] Some will say these things don't exist, others that they are metaphysically derivative.

according to ... [general relativity] one would present the apparatus of differential geometry and the field equations and then go on to explain the topology and other characteristic of the particular model ... of these equations. ... There is nothing more to be said" (Ladyman and Ross 2007, 159).

This way of expressing what structure is gives rise to the obvious problem of how one can meaningfully distinguish the represented *concrete* physical structure from the representing *abstract* mathematical structure, the field equations.[29] In more recent writings both Ladyman (2011) and French (2014, chap. 8) seem to agree that the right way to respond to this objection is to admit "that there is in the world some causal or nomological structure that is represented by logical and mathematical relationships in our theoretical thought" (Ladyman 2011, 421).[30] So it is these further nomological or modal facts that differentiate physical from mathematical structure.[31]

It remains somewhat unclear exactly what this claim amounts to; how exactly the modal part permeates the structure, where and how far. We might, for example, be able to understand what is meant by these additional modal commitments when it comes to laws of nature. OSRists take a non-Humean view of laws, and these additional non-Humean elements differentiate the laws from the mathematics used to represent them. But even if we were to accept this move, it would not be enough to make the required notion of structure sufficiently determinate. A set of structurally understood non-Humean laws would not by itself be enough to pick out the real physical world from all its nomological equivalents; for example, a world exactly like ours except where the initial distribution of matter to anti-matter was reversed. To distinguish these two possibilities, the OSRist would have to have a way of understanding how such modal notions could permeate structure beyond laws in a way compatible with their metaphysical denial or down-playing of individuals and intrinsic properties.[32]

---

[29] See van Fraassen 2006 for a very clear statement of this objection.

[30] Similar appeals to modal structure can be found in the earlier works: French and Ladyman 2003 and Ladyman and Ross 2007. But it has not always been so clear that the invocation of modal properties is the answer to the worries raised by van Fraassen. Ladyman and Ross (2007, 158) say elsewhere that they "refuse to answer" the question of what distinguishes mathematical from physical structure.

[31] Berenstain and Ladyman (2012) make the general and multi-component case for structuralists, including natural necessity, in their metaphysics. They do not say how to reconcile the two ideas.

[32] French struggles mightily with this in his 2014; see especially chapter 10, where he appeals to the idea of "existential witnesses" to bridge the gap from the general to the particular. Chakravartty (2017, chap. 5) argues this amounts to simply positing the idea of a concrete relation as part of one's fundamental ontology. In a later discussion (Chakravartty 2019 and French 2019b), the acceptance of one or another way of making sense of de re necessity seems to turn on theoretical virtues like parsimony. For reasons given above, such considerations cannot be compelling.

2.2.2. OSR and the return of Hempel's dilemma. Even if OSR and modal realism can be successfully combined into a coherent view, a familiar problem lurks round the corner. Despite structural realism's claim to offer an account of what gets preserved through scientific revolutions, OSRists encounter a version of Hempel's dilemma. The problem can be put like this: What *exactly* is the structure that we are supposed to believe in according to the structural realists? It can't simply be *all* the structural elements of our current theories. We know from the history of science that structure as well as ontology sometimes get discarded. The flat structure of space described in Newtonian mechanics is discarded and replaced with the curved structure of space-time in general relativity. It seems reasonable to expect that the same will happen with current physics: as we try to develop a theory of quantum gravity, the structure of the field equations of general relativity will likely be revised in unknown ways.

Structural realists seem to agree. As French and Ladyman put it: "The advocate of OSR is not claiming that the structure of our current theories will be preserved simpliciter" (2011, 31). How, then, are we to fix the content of OSR once we acknowledge this? French and Ladyman say: "The job of predicting what will be preserved and what abandoned by future science belongs to science itself" (2011, 32). So, it looks as though the real fundamental structures will only become apparent in some unknown future physics. OSR, then, seems impaled on the second horn of Hempel's dilemma.

In some places, it looks as though Ladyman and Ross are willing to grasp in a Melnyk-like way the first horn: "One consequence of naturalism that cannot be avoided is that if our current scientific image of the world changes much, as we suppose it will, then it will then turn out that the best current metaphysics is substantially wrong" (2007, 35).

As with similar admissions from Sider and Melnyk, this presumably rules out belief in our "best" metaphysical theory, and so with it the idea that it makes sense to think that truth is the goal of metaphysical inquiry.

Perhaps this is unfair. After all, the structural realist is still committed to the idea "that from a structuralist point of view it is possible to explicate the continuity in scientific theories" (French and Ladyman 2011, 31) and "hold[s] fallibilism about science to be compatible with optimism about epistemic progress in science. This argument carries directly over to scientifically motivated metaphysics" (Ladyman and Ross 2007, 35).

One way to make sense of this would be to think of the scientific realism part of OSR as in part an attitude—an attitude, as Ladyman and Ross have it, of optimism. The OSRists are committed to the idea that however things turn out in future science, there will be a story to tell of the approximate retention of the old science in terms of the new at the structural level. One might complain that if OSR is part attitude, then it is not the kind of thing apt to be true or false and so not a metaphysical position at all; but maybe the key idea is here just the thought that if the scientific realist can coherently claim current science is likely to be strictly false, and yet approximately true, then the OSRists can say the same of their metaphysical position.

Familiar worries must return. On the one hand, there is the question of whether we can make sense of this claim. Even setting aside the trouble we have had in trying to clarify the notion of structure generally, there are grounds to think we cannot. Kerry Mackenzie (2020) has recently argued that if we take the essence of OSR to be given by a slogan like "all fundamental properties are extrinsic," the approximate truth of OSR must mean either (1) that *approximately* all fundamental properties are extrinsic or (2) that all fundamental properties are *approximately* extrinsic. The latter is unintelligible. Properties are either extrinsic or not; and if not extrinsic, they are intrinsic. The former implies that at least some properties are not extrinsic. But opponents of OSR have taken the admission of just one intrinsic property to be sufficient to refute OSR conclusively.[33] So again we teeter between claims that are not truth evaluable and those that are clearly false.

On the other hand, even if we reject Mackenzie's argument, there seems no very good reason to accept that OSR is approximately true. Ladyman and Ross make it sound as though the approximate truth of OSR is supposed to piggyback on the approximate truth of our current science. But even (generously) granting our current theories are approximately true in the way favoured by structuralists, that would by itself demonstrate nothing about the approximate truth of the much more specific claims of OSR. After all, it seems easy enough to imagine situations in which although current science is at some structural level approximately continuous with the final true theory, that theory might make essential reference to individuals in a way that is inconsistent with the ontology of OSR. Some additional reason for thinking OSR might be approximately true that goes beyond the approximate truth of our current theories is therefore needed. It is difficult to see what that could be.[34]

3. Continuity of Content, Part 2: Interpretation

Confident pronouncements of a metaphysical project continuous with science are not hard to find among philosophers of physics. Here is a typically robust statement from Tim Maudlin: "Metaphysics is ontology. Ontology

[33] See Chakravartty (2012, 204), for example. Almost all metaphysical positions admit some extrinsic relations: spatial, temporal, and causal being the most common. So, it is unclear what the interesting point of contrast of OSR would be if the thesis is just that it is likely some fundamental properties are extrinsic.

[34] Another way to put this point is related to the problem of the underdetermination of interpretations discussed below. Even if we imagine some ideal physics that emerges in the infinite long run that physics will be likely be subject to multiple interpretations, some of which diverge from OSR. Ladyman and Ross (2007, 9) are aware of this problem but don't seem to offer any solution. See van Fraassen 2007 for more discussion.

is the most generic study of what exists. Evidence for what exists, at least in the physical world, is provided solely by empirical research. Hence the proper object of most metaphysics is the careful analysis of our best scientific theories (and especially of fundamental physical theories) with the goal of determining what they imply about the constitution of the physical world" (2007, 104).

The most common way this project has been pursued is through offering *interpretations* of our current physical theories. This project has been very successful—too successful, in fact.

Consider non-relativistic quantum mechanics. Quantum theory seems to call out for interpretation, since in the form taught to undergraduates the theory appears incomplete or worse yet inconsistent. Quantum mechanics seems to have two different dynamical principles. An undisturbed quantum system evolves in accordance with the Schrödinger equation, which is strictly deterministic. Once a measurement is made, however, a quantum system evolves indeterministically according to the Born rule. The theory is incomplete, since no information is given in the theory about what constitutes a measurement and so therefore why one principle would in any given interaction apply rather than the other. The theory could be considered inconsistent if we take both principles to be in play at the same time, since, as I have noted, one is deterministic and the other not, and so they imply different results when a measurement is made.

There are answers to these worries. Bohm theorists (Bohm 1952) make sense of quantum mechanics by adding to its ontology. Every particle has a well-defined position but no other non-contextual properties and is pushed about by a pilot wave. Conformity to the Born rule is ensured by cooking up the initial distribution of all the particles in the universe in just the right way.

Advocates of the so-called GRW theory (Ghirardi, Rimini, and Weber 1986) alter the underlying dynamics of quantum theory, adding non-linear elements to the Schrödinger equation that bring about spontaneous collapse of the wave function and so measurement results that are in agreement with the Born rule.

Many-worlds theorists take the Schrodinger dynamics to be complete. In this view every possible measurement result is realised in a multiverse. The probabilities of the Born rule can be recovered by adding some very plausible assumptions and some decision theory (Wallace 2012).

These are the three favoured textbook interpretations of quantum mechanics. In recent years new and interesting interpretations have been offered. Richard Healey (2017) provides what he calls a pragmatist interpretation, which treats certain parts of quantum theory as non-representational. Quantum Bayesianism (Fuchs 2002) is the even more radical idea that quantum states represent the epistemic state of an agent. Carlo Rovelli's (1996) Relational interpretation offers a kind of rehabilitation of the original Copenhagen interpretation, in which measurement results and so properties are always relative to some further system.

Most agree that at least the three now standard interpretations are all consistent and make the same predictions as conventional quantum mechanics.[35] But very obviously they describe very different worlds, in some cases with very different laws. The work done to develop these theories has been exemplary. Too good, in fact, for the metaphysician. For all this work shows that there is no good reason to favour any one interpretation over any other. The good naturalist ought to be agnostic towards the varied metaphysical postulates of these rival theories. So here again the project of devising a metaphysics that aims at truth and is continuous with science fails.

4. Re-thinking the Aims of Metaphysics

I have offered a brief but, I think, compelling case that there is no truth-seeking metaphysical project that can properly be said to be continuous with science. It is not difficult to see why. The methods of science are empirical, the methods of metaphysics are not. The claims of physics and other sciences are incomplete, likely to be revised in unknown ways and open to multiple interpretations. Metaphysicians want to go beyond the claims of science in either claiming some insight into the fundamental aspects of reality or offering a particular interpretation of our current science. Such claims, where they are intelligible, clearly must go beyond the empirically well-supported theories of our best science and so cannot, any more than their rivals, claim support from science.

One response might be to abandon the broad naturalism of all three approaches and hope to pursue metaphysics in some other purely rationalist way.[36] If this is the course you favour, I wish you good luck, but I'd like to hear what methods, if not abductive ones, will take metaphysicians to true conclusions about how the world is; and how insight about how the world works can be achieved independently of empirically successful science. A better response to the problems raised would be simply to re-think the aims of metaphysics. Each of the strategies I have considered can be reconstrued as an activity with some value if we move away from thinking the aim of metaphysics is to tell us how the world is.

---

[35] Wallace (2020) offers an interesting argument for the Many Worlds theory: only the MWT can be extended from non-relativistic quantum mechanics to other successful applications of quantum theory, like quantum field theory and solid state physics. I tend to agree with Callender (2020) that this tells us something about the differences in ambition of these rival interpretations rather than about their intrinsic value. But I also think many of the newer interpretations—pragmatist, relational, for example—can be extended in the same way as the MWT. Wallace denies this, but discussion of this point would require a separate essay.

[36] Peter van Inwagen (2007) takes this line in his response to van Fraassen 2002, where a similar criticism of the abductive method in metaphysics is offered. It is unclear precisely what his alternative method is.

4.1. *Interpretation as a Means of Exploring a Theory*

Consider first the work in the foundation of physics. What value are the multiple interpretations that those working in the philosophy physics have offered if underdetermination and incompleteness precludes us from believing any? One answer is inward looking. The different interpretations of, say, non-relativistic quantum mechanics tell us important things about the theory itself. It is, for example, natural for a student of quantum mechanics to think, given its irreducibly probabilistic nature, that the theory must be indeterministic. But both the Bohm theory and the Many Worlds theory provide us with a way to understand quantum mechanics in which this is not so. Equally, GRW shows us there is a consistent interpretation of quantum mechanics that is indeterministic. All three interpretations provide us with a way of thinking of quantum mechanics as a consistent theory, a possible way the world could be.

Learning the multiple ways a theory may be interpreted may also have practical, outward-looking benefits. New interpretations of a theory may suggest new ways the theory may be developed; and this is often how advocates of rival interpretations justify their preference for one over another. Carlo Rovelli, for example, finds his preferred interpretation, relational quantum mechanics, congenial as a framework for developing a theory of quantum gravity.

If the function of interpretation is to serve as an inspiration for future physical theory, then clearly, since we do not yet have that theory, and there may be many possible valuable avenues of inquiry, a multiplicity of interpretations is desirable. This clearly contrasts with a discipline that aims at truth. There can only be one true theory, and so what is ultimately desirable is to land on that unique truth. It should also affect the practice of interpreters of science. Once we have arrived at a consistent interpretation, our work is done. If another consistent interpretation comes along that in no way threatens or undermines the original work. They are equally valuable; no ink need be spilled to show that one is better than another in some non-empirical way.[37]

---

[37] This view of the value of interpretation obviously has affinities with van Fraassen 2007, 54–55, and perhaps also Ruetsche 2015. Ruetsche's emphasis is slightly different and more fine-grained. She is concerned to show that successful applications of a theory are best understood as involving several, incompatible interpretations. Interpretation is a good in allowing the successful elaboration of theory in many new settings. It might be that the work of Morganti and Takho (2016) fits here too. They emphasise interpretation and the idea that metaphysical theorising explores the realm of the possible. If all that means is finding consistent ways to interpret theories, we are I think in broad agreement and this is a valuable activity, for reasons set out above. If it is meant as an exploration of some special modal realm, understood in terms of essence, distinct from the actual world described by science, as it sometimes seems, I find it harder to understand.

4.2. *Metaphysics as Targetless Model Building*

Something similar can be said about certain projects in more mainstream analytic metaphysics. A useful way to think of some metaphysical theorizing is that it is analogous to a certain kind of modelling used in science and some philosophy of science. The most common sort of model deployed in the sciences involves offering a partial representation of a target phenomenon. Global climate models, for example, offer a representation of the large-scale processes that affect the climate and can, if well calibrated, offer good predictions of the future. Although some have suggested metaphysics resembles this activity (see Paul 2012 and Godfrey-Smith 2006), I think a better analogy is with so-called targetless models. Some models are not meant to represent, even partially, any real system. These models are models of a theory, and their value often lies in allowing us to explore aspects of a theory or other constraints.

For example, John Norton (2003) offers this simple model of a Newtonian system. Imagine a particle sitting at the apex of a radially symmetric dome. One solution to the relevant equations would be for the particle to remain at rest indefinitely. Norton shows, though, that it is also compatible with the laws of motion that the ball starts sliding down the dome at any time and in any direction. From this simple model, Norton argues, Newtonian mechanics allows for a kind of indeterminism.

What makes a targetless model like Norton's a good and interesting model is not that it tells us about how some worldly system behaves or even how some such system could behave. There are no domes or balls of the sort Norton describes. Very obviously Newtonian mechanics is strictly false. The real interest here is in learning something about indeterminism. A system can be governed by what we take to be strictly deterministic laws but nevertheless still in some sense be indeterministic. We have learnt something not about the world but about a theory—Newtonian mechanics—and a concept—determinism. Some kinds of metaphysical theorising can be thought of in analogous way. Consider debates about the causal exclusion problem from the 1990s. These begin with some general presuppositions: the completeness of physics; that mental events are not identical to physical events; that the mental supervenes on the physical; and so on. From these presuppositions we can generate a picture or, if you like, a model of the relation of mental to physical states that looks like this:

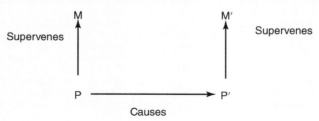

The challenge is to show, given these assumptions, how it can ever be that M-like events can cause anything.

As normally understood, this model is supposed to have a target. It is meant to represent relations between real mental and physical events. Our discussion of Hempel's dilemma, however, ought to lead us to reject the idea that we can make determinate sense of properties satisfying these constraints. Better, then, to think of this as not representing a real system, even in some approximate way. Its value, like Norton's dome, consists in allowing us to explore certain concepts. The model of mental causation allows us to explore the possible connections between various weakly theorized concepts, like causation and supervenience. So-called solutions to the problem are often simply suggestions about new ways to think about these very general relations.[38] For example, Stephen Yablo suggests we can make sense of M-like events in the model being causes if we think of the supervenience relation in terms of the determinate-determinable relation and apply what he calls a principle of proportionality.[39] It does not matter that there is no good reason to think anything we might call a mental property and anything we call a physical property really stand in such relations. The model is better thought of as teaching us about or at least allowing us to explore the relationship between the concepts of causation and supervenience.[40]

4.3. Metaphysics as Metaphor

Finally, some metaphysics, maybe physicalism and ontic structural realism are examples, is best thought of as a kind of picture making or, maybe better, metaphor mongering. As we have seen, there are ways of articulating physicalism or OSR that are either obviously false or not truth evaluable. But this is true of many metaphors too. "Everything is physical" might be strictly false in the same way as "All the world's a stage" or perhaps indeterminate in truth-value like, arguably, "Brevity is the soul of wit." But, of course, metaphors intimate much more than their literal meaning. Statements of physicalism or OSR could be the same; perhaps conveying

---

[38] I think the debates in the so-called special composition question could be versions of this.

[39] A deterministic cause is proportional to its effect if it includes no more than is necessary to bring about its effect.

[40] A referee helpfully suggested this might be similar to the toolbox idea elaborated in French and Mackenzie 2012 and 2016 and in French 2018. Maybe. It could be that this way of elaborating concepts is useful for the practice of interpretation understood in the way I favour. Then again, for this practice to be worthwhile it need not have any such use. Norton's model is illuminating about the concept of determinism. Yablo's arguably is about the connections between supervenience and causation. That illumination or understanding can by itself be enough. I of course disagree with French and Mackenzie that this work is a useful tool for a respectable kind of naturalised metaphysics. For the reasons given above, I think there is no such metaphysics.

attitudes. When philosophers say everything is physical, they are intimating their deference to science perhaps, or their suspicion of postulating new entities to explain consciousness. When advocates of OSR say it's structure all the way down, they mean to indicate to us maybe the strangeness of current science. And perhaps nothing even as determinate as this is conveyed, just a tantalizing indeterminate picture. Here, then, is a third successor project. Metaphysics so understood is not a theoretical enterprise but a kind of creative writing aimed at intimating various attitudes and other states in interesting prose.

5. Conclusion

There is no truth-seeking metaphysical project that can be said to be truly continuous with science. The methods of metaphysics cannot be assimilated to natural science, and the incomplete and open-ended nature of contemporary science means no general conclusions about the nature of reality can be drawn from it. But I recommend to metaphysicians not despair but a reconstrual of their aims. What is called metaphysics may be a useful way of exploring our scientific theories, a way of investigating how concepts like determinism or causation relate, or even a kind of creative prose. Though none of these projects aims to describe the fundamental structure of reality, all are worthwhile.

Acknowledgments

Many thanks to audiences in Zagreb and the University of Kent for helpful feedback on an ancestor of this piece and two referees for many useful suggestions and criticisms. Special thanks to Yafeng Shan for his patience and good advice.

References

Armstrong, D. M. 1984. *What Is a Law of Nature?* 1st ed. Cambridge: Cambridge University Press.
Berenstain, N., and J. Ladyman. 2012. "Ontic Structural Realism and Modality." In *Structural Realism: Structure, Object, and Causality*, edited by E. M. Landry and D. P. Rickles, 149–68. Dordrecht: Springer
Bohm, D. 1952. "A Suggested Interpretation of the Quantum Theory in Terms of Variables, I and II." *Physical Review* 85: 166–93.
Bokulich, A., and P. Bokulich, eds. 2011. *Scientific Structuralism*. Boston Studies in the Philosophy of Science, volume 281. Dordrecht: Springer.
Brenner, A. 2017. "Simplicity as a Criterion of Theory Choice in Metaphysics." *Philosophical Studies* 174, no. 11: 2687–2707.
Callender, C. 2020. "Can We Quarantine the Quantum Blight?" In French and Saatsi 2020, 57–77.

Chakravartty, A. 2012. "Ontological Priority: The Conceptual Basis of Non-Eliminative, Ontic Structural Realism." In *Structural Realism: Structure, Object, and Causality*, Western Ontario Series in Philosophy of Science, edited by E. M. Landry and D. P. Rickles, 187–206. Dordrecht: Springer

Chakravartty, A. 2017. *Scientific Ontology: Integrating Naturalized Metaphysics and Voluntarist Epistemology*. New York: Oxford University Press.

Chakravartty, A. 2019. "Physics, Metaphysics, Dispositions, and Symmetries—À la French." *Studies in History and Philosophy of Science: Part A* 74: 1–15.

Chalmers, D. J. 1996. *The Conscious Mind: In Search of a Fundamental Theory*. Oxford: Oxford University Press.

French, S. 2014. *The Structure of the World: Metaphysics and Representation*. Oxford: Oxford University Press.

French, S. 2018. "Toying with the Toolbox: How Metaphysics Can Still Make a Contribution." *Journal for General Philosophy of Science / Zeitschrift für Allgemeine Wissenschaftstheorie* 49, no. 2: 211–30.

French, S. 2019a. "Identity and Individuality in Quantum Theory." *Stanford Encyclopedia of Philosophy* (Winter 2019 Edition), edited by Edward N. Zalta. https://plato.stanford.edu/archives/win2019/entries/qt-idind/

French, S. 2019b. "Defending Eliminative Structuralism and a Whole Lot More (or Less)." *Studies in History and Philosophy of Science: Part A* 74: 22–29.

French, S., and J. Ladyman. 2003. "Remodelling Structural Realism: Quantum Physics and the Metaphysics of Structure." *Synthese* 136, no. 1: 31–56.

French, S., and J. Ladyman. 2011. "In Defence of Ontic Structural Realism." In Bokulich and Bokulich 2011, 25–42.

French, S., and K. McKenzie. 2012. "Thinking Outside the Toolbox." *European Journal of Analytic Philosophy* 8, no. 2: 42–45.

French, S., and K. McKenzie. 2016. "Rethinking Outside the Toolbox." In *The Metaphysics of Contemporary Physics*, Poznan Studies in Philosophy of Science and the Humanities, vol. 104, edited by Tomasz Bigaj and Christian Wüthrich, 25–54. Leiden: Brill.

French, S., and J. Saatsi. 2020. *Scientific Realism and the Quantum*. Oxford: Oxford University Press.

Fuchs, C. 2002. "Quantum Mechanics as Quantum Information (and Only a Little More)." http://arXiv.org/abs/quant-ph/0205039

Ghirardi, G., A. Rimini, and T. Weber. 1986. "Unified Dynamics for Microscopic and Macroscopic Systems." *Physical Review D* 34 (D): 470–91.

Godfrey-Smith, P. 2006. "Theories and Models in Metaphysics." *Harvard Review of Philosophy* 14, no. 1: 4–19.

Healey, R. 2017. *The Quantum Revolution in Philosophy*. Oxford: Oxford University Press.

Jackson, F. 1998. *From Metaphysics to Ethics: A Defence of Conceptual Analysis*. Oxford: Clarendon Press.

Kelly, K. 2007. "A New Solution to the Puzzle of Simplicity." *Philosophy of Science* 74, no. 5: 561–73.

Ladyman, J. 1998. "What Is Structural Realism?" *Studies in History and Philosophy of Science* 29: 409–24.

Ladyman, J. 2007 "Structural Realism." *Stanford Encyclopedia of Philosophy* (Winter 2020 Edition), edited by Edward N. Zalta. https://plato.stanford.edu/archives/win2020/entries/structural-realism/

Ladyman, J., 2011. "Scientific Representation: A Long Journey from Pragmatics to Pragmatics." *Metascience* 20, no. 3: 417–42.

Ladyman, J. 2012. "Science, Metaphysics and Method." *Philosophical Studies* 160, no. 1: 31–51.

Ladyman, J., and D. Ross, with D. Spurrett and J. G. Collier. 2007. *Every Thing Must Go: Metaphysics Naturalized*. Oxford: Oxford University Press.

Lewis, D. K. 1986. *On the Plurality of Worlds*. Oxford: Blackwell.

Maddy, P. 1997. *Naturalism in Mathematics*. Oxford: Oxford University Press.

Maudlin, T. 2007. *The Metaphysics Within Physics*. Oxford: Oxford University Press.

McKenzie, K. 2020. "A Curse on Both Houses: Naturalistic Versus A Priori Metaphysics and the Problem of Progress." *Res Philosophica* 97, no. 1: 1–29.

Melnyk, A. 2003. *A Physicalist Manifesto: Thoroughly Modern Materialism*. Cambridge: Cambridge University Press.

Montero, B., and D. Papineau. 2005. "A Defence of the Via Negativa Argument for Physicalism." *Analysis* 65, no. 3: 233–37.

Morganti, M., and T. E. Tahko. 2016. "Moderately Naturalistic Metaphysics." *Synthese* 194, no. 7: 2557–80.

Ney, A. 2008a. "Defining Physicalism." *Philosophy Compass* 3, no. 5: 1033–48.

Ney, A. 2008b. "Physicalism as an Attitude." *Philosophical Studies* 138, no. 1: 1–15.

Ney, M. J. 1972. *Molecular Reality*. London: Macdonald.

Norton, J. D. 2003. "Causation as Folk Science." *Philosophers' Imprint* 3, no. 4: 1–22.

Norton, J. D. Manuscript. *"The Material Theory of Induction."*

Otswald, W. 1904. *The Scientific Foundations of Analytic Chemistry*. 2nd ed. London: Macmillan.

Otswald, W. 1908. *The Scientific Foundations of Analytic Chemistry*. 3rd ed. London: Macmillan.

Papineau, D. 1993. *Philosophical Naturalism*. Cambridge, Mass.: Blackwell.

Papineau, D. 2001. "The Rise of Physicalism." In *Physicalism and Its Discontents*, edited by C. Gillett and B. Loewer, 3–36. Cambridge: Cambridge University Press.

Paul, L. 2012. "Metaphysics as Modeling: The Handmaiden's Tale." *Philosophical Studies* 160, no. 1: 1–29.

Penrose, Roger. 1997. *The Large, the Small and the Human Mind*. Cambridge: Cambridge University Press.

Poland, J. 1994. *Physicalism: The Philosophical Foundations*. Oxford: Oxford University Press.

Quine, W. V. O. 1966. "Posits and Reality." In *The Ways of Paradox and Other Essays*, 233–41. New York: Random House. First published in 1960.

Quine, W. V. O. 1980. *From a Logical Point of View*. 2nd rev. ed. Cambridge, Mass.: Harvard University Press.

Quine, W. V. O., and J. S. Ullian 1970. *The Web of Belief*. New York: Random House.

Ritchie, J. 2008. *Understanding Naturalism*. Stockwell: Acumen.

Rovelli, C. 1996. "Relational Quantum Mechanics." *International Journal of Theoretical Physics* 35: 1637. arXiv:quant-ph/9609002

Ruetsche, L. 2011 *Interpreting Quantum Theories: The Art of the Possible*. Oxford: Oxford University Press.

Ruetsche, L. 2015. "The Shaky Game +25, or: On Locavoracity." *Synthese* 192, no. 11: 3425–42.

Saatsi, J. 2017. "Explanation and Explanationism in Science and Metaphysics." In *Metaphysics and the Philosophy of Science: New Essays*, edited by M. Slater and Z. Yudell, 162–91. Oxford: Oxford University Press.

Sider, T. 2001. *Four-Dimensionalism: An Ontology of Persistence and Time*. Oxford: Clarendon Press.

Sider, T. 2013. "Against Parthood." *Oxford Studies in Metaphysics* 8: 237–93.

Sider, T. 2020. *The Tools of Metaphysics*. Oxford: Oxford University Press.

Sider, T., J. P. Hawthorne, and D. W. Zimmerman. 2008. *Contemporary Debates in Metaphysics*. Malden, Mass.: Blackwell.

Sober, E. 2008. *Evidence and Evolution: The Logic Behind the Science*. Cambridge: Cambridge University Press.

Sober, E. 2016. *Ockham's Razors: A User's Manual*. Cambridge: Cambridge University Press.

Spurrett, D. 2017. "Physicalism as an Empirical Hypothesis." *Synthese* 194, no. 9: 3347–60.

Spurrett, D., and D. Papineau. 1999. "A Note on the Completeness of Physics." *Analysis* 59, no. 261: 25–29.

van Fraasen, B. C. 1989. *Laws and Symmetry*. Oxford: Blackwell.

van Fraassen, B. C. 2002. *The Empirical Stance*. New Haven: Yale University Press.

van Fraassen, B. C. 2006. "Structure: Its Shadow and Substance." *British Journal for the Philosophy of Science* 57, no. 2: 275–307.

van Fraassen, B. C. 2007. "Structuralism(s) About Science: Some Common Problems." *Aristotelian Society Supplementary Volume* 81, no. 1: 45–61.

van Fraassen, B. C. 2009. "The Perils of Perrin, in the Hands of Philosophers." *Philosophical Studies* 143, no. 1: 5–24

van Inwagen, P. 2007. "Impotence and Collateral Damage: One Charge in Van Fraassen's Indictment of Analytical Metaphysics." *Philosophical Topics* 35, nos. 1–2: 67–82.

Wallace, D. 2012. *The Emergent Multiverse: Quantum Theory According to the Everett Interpretation*. Oxford: Oxford University Press.

Wallace, D. 2020. "On the Plurality of Quantum Theories: Quantum Theory as a Framework and Its Implications for the Measurement Problem." In French and Saatsi 2020, 78–102.

Weyl, H., 1931. *The Theory of Groups and Quantum Mechanics*. Translated by H. P. Robertson. 2nd ed. London: Methuen.

Williamson, T. 2016. "Abductive Philosophy." *Philosophical Forum* 47, nos. 3–4: 263–80.

Worrall, J. 1989. "Structural Realism: The Best of Both Worlds?" *Dialectica* 43, nos. 1–2: 99–124.

Yablo, S. 1992. "Mental Causation." *Philosophical Review* 101, no. 2: 245–80.

CHAPTER 5

IN DEFENSE OF ORDINARY LANGUAGE PHILOSOPHY

HERMAN CAPPELEN AND MATTHEW McKEEVER

The Ordinary Language Movement in twentieth-century philosophy is typically associated with the work of the later Wittgenstein, Ryle, Austin, and, to some extent, Strawson.[1] The movement was massively influential, but today it's unusual to find philosophers self-ascribing that label. In some circles, the label "ordinary language philosophy" is slightly derogatory—an indication that the work is somewhat outdated and methodologically flawed. In this essay, we want to counteract that attitude. Some of the core ideas behind the movement are and should be central to work done in all parts of philosophy. We try to articulate how and why ordinary concepts are central to much of philosophy (in a way that they are not to, say, physics). We develop our positive view by responding to some anti–ordinary language arguments found in David Chalmers's paper "Verbal Disputes" (2011). We then contrast our positive view of the role of language in philosophy with that found in Timothy Williamson's *Philosophy of Philosophy* (2007).

1. When Ordinary Language Does and Doesn't Matter

We'll start with some paradigms of inquiries where ordinary, non-theoretic notions play no significant role:

---

[1] The seminal texts in the tradition include Austin 1962, some of Ryle's papers (1971), and perhaps Strawson's work on "descriptive" metaphysics (1959). For an overview, see Parker-Ryan 2012. Relevant also is the so-called contemporary ordinary language philosophy (Hansen 2014, 2020). This includes work in experimental philosophy, but also mainstream subdisciplines of contemporary philosophy, including ones discussed below. One way to view the present essay is as exploring the foundations of contemporary ordinary language philosophy.

Examining Philosophy Itself. Edited by Yafeng Shan.
Chapters and book compilation © 2023 Metaphilosophy LLC and John Wiley & Sons Ltd.
Published 2023 by John Wiley & Sons Ltd.

Doesn't matter: Physicists study mass, and in so doing they don't care about the ordinary notion of "mass" or how ordinary speakers of English use the expression "mass." Biologists who study genes don't care about the ordinary notion of "gene." Economists who study inflation don't care much about the ordinary notion of "inflation." When doctors study cancer, the last thing they need to think about is the ordinary notion of "cancer." Mathematicians and logicians don't care about facts about how ordinary speakers use the word "infinite." In all these cases, there's an entrenched theoretical notion that's well defined within the respective disciplines.

With that in mind, why should philosophers care about the ordinary notions of knowledge, or freedom, or goodness? Why don't they just introduce new technical terms, in the way these scientific disciplines do, and leave behind the English words "knows," "free," and "good"?

In many parts of philosophy there is a deep deference to and focus on the ordinary concept, with an accompanying interest in the lexical item that expresses that concept. This essay is an effort to explain why and to defend that strategy. Before we get to the normative point—that deference to the ordinary is a good thing—first some data about the various ways deference to ordinary language permeates many parts of philosophy. Note the strength of the claim, which is important: we take deference to ordinary language to permeate *many* parts of philosophy, but not all. That would be much too strong.[2] The generic generalizations below, accordingly, are to be understood as generics, that is, as expressing a variable quantificational force that varies by domain (deference to ordinary language is ubiquitous in formal semantics but barely present in philosophy of biology, for example). With that in mind:

- *Epistemology:* Epistemologists are interested in knowledge and the conditions under which people can obtain knowledge. Here is one thing epistemologists typically *don't do:* they don't just start their papers with a technical definition of "knows" and then use that in their theorizing. They are concerned with what ordinary speakers talk about when they

---

[2] In addition, we don't maintain what we could roughly think of as the converse claim that if something is of philosophical interest, there is an ordinary language term for it. A pessimistic meta-induction should convince one of this: depression is of philosophical interest, but until somewhat recently there was no term picking out exactly that state (there were of course things like "melancholy," "ennui," and "spleen," but they aren't quite the same). Inevitably, our language is to some future language as nineteenth-century English is to our language with regard to "depression." And we *also* don't think that even if a term exists in ordinary language, and is of philosophical interest, it's worth studying its ordinary usage. "Substance" is an example—we shouldn't try to learn about, say, bare particulars by seeing what the folk say about substances. We thank a reviewer for making us get clear here (and for the "substance" example).

use "knows." They are also interested in what ordinary speakers think and say when they use such terms. This is why over the past thirty years many of the most central debates and theories in epistemology have, in large part, been inextricably intertwined with data about the lexical semantics of "knows." This is most obviously so for discussions between contextualists, invariantists, and relativists about knowledge.[3] These debates are also the background for the most important contemporary discussions of skepticism (e.g., DeRose 1996; Cohen 1988). We see the same in other domains of epistemology. Thus Jason Stanley and Timothy Williamson (2001) argue that knowing how is a species of knowing that, explicitly basing their view on the semantics of knowledge-how attributions. Ian Rumfitt (2003) demurs and uses as evidence the fact that languages such as French, ancient Greek, Latin, and Russian lexicalize knowledge how and knowledge that differently. Across huge swathes of epistemology, then, ordinary language is important.[4]

- *Moral philosophy:* Here is something moral philosophers typically *don't do:* they don't just start their papers and books with stipulative definitions of "good," "bad," and "ought" and then use them in their theorizing. Instead, they pay careful attention to what ordinary speakers think and say when they use those terms. A snapshot of some of that work: at the start of the twentieth century (at least per the potted history of analytic philosophy that suffices for our purposes), G. E. Moore (1903) set the tone for ethical theorizing with his defense of moral intuitionism, which placed heavy and somewhat spooky constraints on both the ontology and the epistemology of value. A couple of decades later, logical positivists and others reacted to that and proposed noncognitivist theories of value (notably Ayer [1936] and Stevenson [1944]), according to which there was no nonnatural reality out there for us to intuit. In cutting out the world from our theory of value, they were left with the explanatory burden of explaining our value-laden thought and talk, and emotivism, as its name suggested, proposed that such thought and talk expressed our feelings about parts of the natural world as opposed to expressing nonnatural properties or states of affairs. That in turn inaugurated a research program thriving to this day of making sense of how moral talk, syntactically and semantically seemingly on a par with fact-stating talk, can interact with it while having such a foreign purpose. In 1965,

---

[3] Respectively, discussion in DeRose 1996; Cohen 1998; Hawthorne 2003; MacFarlane 2014, chap. 8; and much else.

[4] We are not the first to draw attention to this in the context of ordinary language philosophy. See Hansen 2014 and 2020 and Ludlow 1999. Not all epistemologists are concerned with ordinary language. If one is working on epistemic logic, for example, one might be interested in proving soundness and completeness, and ordinary language won't be of any help. And in some cases the debate itself may turn on whether ordinary language is an adequate source of evidence, as when one assesses Moore-style anti- skeptical arguments.

Geach focused energy on his Frege-Geach problem, which presents the issue acutely. If "Eating meat is wrong" expresses disapproval, a noncognitive attitude (stylized in the literature as "Boo eating meat!"), then how do we explain the acceptability of "If eating meat is wrong, then we should subsidize R&D for lab-grown meat" in light of the fact that "if boo eating meat!, then we should subsidize R&D for lab-grown meat" is nonsense. For some important recent work, see Schroeder 2008; Charlow 2014; and Silk 2015, and references therein. While the (often quite technical) details don't matter to us, we should note that this literature is deeply immersed in the careful analysis of ordinary thought and talk. An inability to handle certain natural language embeddings involving ethical vocabulary is viewed—in this research program—as involving important consequences all across the foundations of metaethics.[5]

Attention to the ordinary notions have proved useful throughout philosophy. Here are a few more examples:

- *The nature of belief and thought:* Here is something philosophers of mind who are interested in the nature of belief *don't do:* they don't start their papers and books by introducing stipulative definitions -of "belief," "hope," and so on and then talk about whatever those stipulations pick out. They try to figure out what is expressed by the ordinary notions of "belief" and "hope." They are interested both in the phenomenon picked out by the ordinary notion and by the thoughts and beliefs speakers have when they use it. Much of this literature relies on linguistic data about belief reports. For example, data about what kinds of expressions can be substituted *salva veritate* within the scope of "believes that," the nature of opacity, and the kind of ambiguity manifested by "John believes someone in this room is a spy," which provides evidence of a difference between de re and de dicto beliefs. This has spawned much work in mind and language and philosophical logic for more than half a century.[6]
- *The nature of truth:* Here is something philosophers who are interested in the nature of truth typically *don't do:* they don't start their papers and books by stipulating a meaning of "true" and then theorize about what the stipulation picks out. Instead, such philosophers aim to describe what the ordinary truth predicate stands for (if anything) and what

---

[5] Again, there are many exceptions. For example, some utilitarians will not approach the topic through ordinary language but will instead use technical terms. Ordinary language doesn't and shouldn't constrain thinking about, say, the nonidentity problem.

[6] E.g., Quine 1956; Kaplan 1968; Salmon 1986; Hawthorne and Manley 2012; Keshet 2010; Chalmers 2006; and much, much else. Exceptions include philosophers who introduce a technical term like "mental representation" and use that as their core theoretical term, bypassing the need for ordinary language.

speakers think and believe when they use it. In doing so, a great deal of linguistic data have been helpful. Deflationary theories of truth (e.g., Horwich 1998, stemming from Ramsey 1927), for example, note the undeniable fact that the word "true" is used to generalize over utterances (when we say "Everything Kripke said was true") and, not being able to find any other facts about truth (such as correspondence), conclude that that fact exhausts the function of "true," and that accordingly utterances of the form "*P* is true" just say. Linguistic data, then, work in tandem with metaphysical exploration (or skepticism thereof) to produce minimalism; but minimalism without the linguistic data wouldn't be much of a theory at all. In the same vein, an important constraint on theorizing about the liar paradox is that we get an account of "contingent liar sentences" (made famous by Kripke 1975), perfectly natural sentences that lead to big logical complications. A logician proposing a theory of "trueish," a technical notion for which definitionally Liar paradoxes didn't arise, wouldn't get much attention.[7]

- *The theory of generics and genericity:* What are generics and genericity? Work in psychology shows that generic generalizations, those expressed by sentences like "Tigers are striped," are cognitively fundamental, a way of thinking about the world that arises before explicit quantification. In addition, other work shows that we tend to make cognitive mistakes with such thoughts. We need to understand the manifestation of genericity in language in order to fully understand these quirks—like our being much more likely to judge generics that attribute dangerous or striking properties true of a given kind even if few members of that kind possess the property, and thus to behave in a certain way.
- *Theory of causation:* Theorists of causation have paid close attention to how the verb "to cause" works. For example, its context sensitivity has been a subject of much discussion (see, e.g., Lewis 1973, 558; Schaffer 2012; and Swanson 2012 for a helpful overview). And particular theories about semantics have been thought to be relevant for our metaphysics of causation. An example discussed by Swanson shows this. George Lakoff (1965) influentially argues that sentences like the ones below have the same "deep structure":

- Floyd caused the glass to melt.
- Floyd melted the glass.

Although this view is contested, Eric Swanson points out: "The *truth of this hypothesis (or a hypothesis close to it) would be profoundly important to philosophical thought about causation.* Among other things it would

---

[7] Some salient exceptions to this generalization include those in the Tarskian tradition who think the natural language conception of "truth" is problematic and work more or less with a stipulative version.

open up a whole new range of causal locutions against which to test our metaphysical theories of causation" (2012, 772; our emphasis). The exact details aren't important—see Swanson 2012 and references therein if you're interested in the behavior of such idioms—it's that, again, natural language seems relevant to metaphysical theorizing.

- *Philosophy of time:* Peter Ludlow is quite explicit that "we can gain insight into the metaphysics of time by studying the semantics of natural language" (1999, xvi). Very roughly, he thinks that the famously differing cognitive and behavioral significance of sentences like the following, where now is time t, of someone uttering in a Starbucks far from the office "I have a meeting now" and "I have a meeting at t" is best explained by a theory of reality, in particular time, according to which nowness is a metaphysically important feature of the world, capable of guiding action, which is to say a non-B-theoretic theory of time. And, in fact, for reasons like this, Ludlow defends the A-theory. On such a way of approaching metaphysics, language is straightforwardly very strong evidence in favor of metaphysics, and while Ludlow's language-first approach to metaphysics is surely heterodox today, it shouldn't be discounted without consideration.

What these cases illustrate is that much important work in core parts of philosophy are what we'll call ordinary language guided (OL guided).

> *OL guidance:* An investigation is OL guided if it aims to investigate (and understand) those parts of the world that a particular ordinary language expression picks out and, in so doing, is in part guided by data about the relevant ordinary language terms.

Our sense is that the examples above are not isolated—they are typical of much good work in contemporary philosophy. OL guidance doesn't cover everything one might associate with "ordinary language" philosophy: there's little of the typical Wittgensteinian paraphernalia of "form of life," "grammatical rules," and so forth. Despite that, there's at least an ordinary language sense in which OL guidance is a form of ordinary language philosophy.

Having established that OL guidance describes many areas of contemporary philosophy, we can turn to a normative question: Is OL guidance a good thing or would it be better for these parts of philosophy to leave ordinary language behind and instead develop terminology that's more precise and crafted to particular theoretical tasks? We think OL guidance is not just good but essential, and we'll develop our argument for that in response to a Chalmers-style objection to OL-guided philosophy.

2. A Chalmers-inspired Objection to OL Guidance

David Chalmers's paper "Verbal Disputes" contains a powerful argument against OL guidance. Rather than going through the details of Chalmers's view of verbal disputes, the method of elimination, and the subscript gambit, we'll present our version of an anti-OL-guidance argument that can be extracted from that paper. The conclusion is that we *shouldn't* be OL guided and that the practice described above is misguided.

The argument starts with three core claims and then some elaborations.[8]

1. *Conceptual pluralism:* If an ordinary language expression, T, semantically expresses concept C, there will be indefinitely many other concepts, C1 ... Cn, that are in the vicinity of C.[9] Don't assume that C is causally, normatively, or explanatorily privileged. Explore the entire neighborhood.
2. *Property pluralism:* If an ordinary language term, T, denotes a property P, there will be indefinitely many neighborhood properties: P1 ... Pn, that are in the vicinity of P.[10] Don't assume that P is causally, normatively, or explanatorily privileged. Explore the entire neighborhood.
3. *Pluralism as default assumption:* Conceptual and property pluralism should be the default assumption in philosophy: to give priority to C or P is a fetishistic attachment to ordinary language.

As a corollary this yields what we can call *pluralistic philosophy:* Since what T happens to pick out isn't more philosophically interesting than all the other concepts and properties in the vicinity of T, the question "What is T?" shouldn't be philosophers' primary focus. Instead, we should explore the entire neighborhood of properties and concepts, and then see what causal, normative, and explanatory work each can do.

Applied to "knows," this means we shouldn't be particularly interested in what "knows" denotes. It might be JTB + (something), but finding that

---

[8] Based on this passage in Chalmers's "Verbal Disputes": "[T]here are *multiple interesting concepts* (corresponding to multiple interesting roles) in the vicinity of philosophical terms such as 'semantic,' 'justified,' 'free,' and *not much of substance depends on which one goes with the term.* The model also leads to a sort of *pluralism about the properties* that these concepts pick out. For example, it naturally leads to a sort of *pluralism about the properties* that these concepts pick out. For example, it naturally leads to semantic pluralism: there are many interesting sorts of quasi-semantic properties of expressions, playing different roles. It leads to epistemic pluralism: there are many different epistemic relations, playing different roles. It leads to gene pluralism: there are many different things that deserve to be called 'genes,' playing different roles. The same goes for confirmation pluralism, color pluralism, and so on" (2011, 539–40; our emphasis).

[9] We don't assume anything particular about concepts, except that they are associated with expressions (perhaps as denotations) and play some role in thought.

[10] As in footnote 9, we are agnostic about the nature of properties, apart from being committed by what we say to the claim that they are abundant.

"something" (whether it's some kind of safety condition or something else) isn't philosophically significant. Instead, we should articulate all the properties in this vicinity: P_1, P_2, ... , P_n (JTB, JTB + safety, JTB + X, reliabilism, and so on). Once we know the truths about each of these, including their explanatory roles, then we know all that's worth knowing. There can be a residual debate about which one of these the English word "knows" denotes, but an obsession with that question is, according to Chalmers, a form of fetish. This point generalizes: it applies to "freedom," "time," "art," "causation," "beauty," "democracy," and other core philosophical terms. In realizing this, philosophy can free itself from the shackles of ordinary language philosophy.

Why would it be fetishistic to take an interest in which property the English word "knows" (or "art" or "causation" or ...) picks out? Because, and here we're paraphrasing Chalmers, once we know the truth about all properties in the relevant vicinity (for example, about JTB, JTB + safety, reliabilism, and so on), the extra true belief (for example, which one of these "knows" happens to pick out) does not correspond to any significant increase in our understanding of the world.[11] Here are some quotations from Chalmers that give a sense of his view:

> In practice, sensible philosophers and scientists who are not concerned with metalinguistic matters are almost always willing to set aside these residual questions [about which of P_1, P_2, P_3 are in fact denoted by P] as insignificant. As always, these residual questions carry *with them a distinctive sort of pointlessness*. If we are interested in understanding, it is best to simply move on. (2006, 537–38; our emphasis)

And:

> [T]he significance of the residual question (once the other questions are settled) seems to reduce to the significance of the linguistic question of what [philosophical terms] refer to, and has *"no interest of its own."* (536; our emphasis)

And:

> If we are not concerned with language, then we should not be concerned with the missing sort of knowledge. (536)

---

[11] Other than the metalinguistic piece of information: that this is the property denoted by "knows." The argument isn't denying that it is a fact that that one property is denoted by that expression. It's not even saying that such information is worthless. What it *is* saying is that its epistemic value is much less than the value obtained by exploring all the different instances of T_n.

3. Defending OL-Guided Philosophy Against the Chalmers-Inspired Objection

The Chalmers-style objection fails for two big reasons, both of which reinforce the normative conclusion that a version of ordinary language philosophy is both a good and an essential philosophical methodology.

3.1. Care

Put abstractly, the objection to Chalmers is this: It's not a fetish to care about, for example, the ordinary notion of knowledge, because that's the notion speakers use when they talk and think. The term "knowledge" denotes what they care about. If you care about what people care about and if their caring (just like their talking and thinking) plays important explanatory roles, then T should be the center of attention.

We'll illustrate this using some of Timothy Williamson's claims in *Knowledge and Its Limits* (2000). The central thesis in Williamson's book is that knowledge is a sui generis mental state, not reducible to a combination of truth, belief, justification, something else, or any combination of thereof. This sui generis mental state plays important explanatory roles, Williamson argues. For example, it explains facts about assertion, evidence, and action, which is to say it explains a lot. No matter what you think about the details of this view, one thing is clear: it is knowledge and not knowledge$_1$ or knowledge$_2$ or knowledge$_n$ that has these properties. In other words, it is what "knowledge" denotes that plays these important explanatory roles.

Here is a helpful way to think about it. Knowledge is a core philosophical topic because it's the thing that matters to humans, it's what we talk and think about, and what motivates us. The same is not true about "knowledge$_1$" "knowledge$_2$," and so forth. It's because knowledge matters in these respects (and "knowledge$_1$" "knowledge$_2$," and so forth don't) that epistemology is about knowledge, and not "knowledge$_1$." This is why it is not a fetish—to use Chalmers's terminology—to care about the denotation of "knows." Imagine a Chalmers-style cluster of knows-properties: $K_1 \ldots K_n$. The K that "knows" picks out will be superspecial and worthy of very special attention because it plays such important explanatory and motivational roles in our lives. The Ks in $K_1 \ldots K_n$ are not on a par: the one denoted by "knows" has a distinctive philosophical halo.

This point generalizes and shows why it's a good thing for philosophers with certain aims to be OL guided:

CARE *(as reason for OL guidance):*

(i) If one aim of theorizing in a domain is to understand what ordinary speakers think and talk about using an ordinary language term, T, then we have to figure out what the denotation of "T" is (because the denotation of "T" is what they're talking about).

(ii) If one aim of theorizing in a domain is to understand what ordinary speakers say and think when they use "T," then we have to understand the meaning of "T" (because that meaning is what constitutes the content of their talk and thought).

Both of these aims then require OL guidance. We'll say of those who have such aims that they care.

CARE explains the different ways in which apparently identical topics are treated in the sciences and in philosophy. Physicists working on time don't care, because it doesn't make much difference to them what ordinary speakers are talking about or thinking about when they use the term "time." They're not in the business of explaining and understanding human thought and agency. That is a big part of the reason, plausibly, why in fact philosophers of time don't tend to concentrate too much on words like "time."[12] Many philosophers, however, care. That's why philosophers of time are OL guided, while physicists are not. The same goes for terms like "causation." If you care about the role of thought and you talk about causation among ordinary speakers, you'll be OL guided. Importantly, not all theorists of causation care: the aim of their research might be to understand the nature of scientific laws or explanations, and that can lead them to be interested in a phenomenon in the neighborhood of causation, say causation$_1$. But some do. We expand on this limited nature of OL guidance below.

CARE as a motivation for OL guidance also explains why technical terminology isn't OL guided. When Kripke introduced the term "rigid designator," he wasn't OL guided. In particular, he wasn't guided by the meaning that "rigid" has in English. None of Kripke's discussion of rigidity, and none of the subsequent discussion, focused on how the term "rigid" is used in English. One reason for that was a complete disconnect between the phenomenon Kripke was investigating and anything that speakers say or think using the term "rigid."[13]

According to the Chalmers-style argument, we shouldn't care about what, say, the word "freedom" picks out. We should just learn as much as possible about all the properties in the freedom vicinity. If we've done that but don't know what the word "freedom" picks out, we're not missing anything more than an insignificant metalinguistic fact: "[A]t worst [we're missing] one of those facts under a certain linguistic mode of presentation"

---

[12] At the same time, those philosophers who do attend to ordinary language talk in thinking about the metaphysics of time, such as Ludlow (1999, xiv–xvi), explicitly do so because they think metaphysics should mesh with facts about human language and behavior, like the supposed semantic and action-guiding difference mentioned above between temporal indexicals and names of times.

[13] That said, there are of course mild associative motivations for the choice of terminology. Kripke wouldn't have named rigidity "stinky designation" or "funny designation." That would just be confusing.

(Chalmers 2011, 536). In other words, all we're "missing" is information about which of the properties in the freedom vicinity the word "freedom" picks out. If we are not concerned with language, then "we should not be concerned with the missing sort of knowledge" (536). CARE shows that this is a fundamentally mistaken line of thought. Knowledge of the semantic value of a string of letters isn't *all* you're missing. You're also missing the content of our talk and thought: what we are saying and thinking when we use "freedom." You're missing what we agree and disagree over when we use the term. Finally, you're missing that which plays important roles in motivating and coordinating our actions. That points to a further "worldly" fact that's being missed: the phenomenon in the world we care about is the one that "freedom" picks out.

3.2. An Objection to CARE

We can here imagine someone, inspired perhaps by Chalmers's fetishism objection, remarking:

> The argument against Chalmers will be compelling only *if* we accept (what of course many philosophers have thought) that philosophy has the particular aim of understanding ourselves. If *that* is what we are doing then it seems clear why ordinary language should matter. It's less clear why it should if our interest isn't (as it were) so self-directed.

Here is the overall structure of our argument. Suppose someone cares about one or more of (i) to (iii):

(i) What humans say or think using natural language.
(ii) What motivates our actions.
(iii) The phenomena in the world that we care about (and that motivates our actions).

For someone with those interests, OL guidance is a good strategy. The data given at the beginning of the essay show that this lesson has been absorbed and that those interests are broadly shared. Two points are worth noting here. First, (i) to (iii) are not just about *ourselves* (our thought and talk), as the objection has it. It is also about the phenomena in the world that we think and talk about, and that motivate our actions. The subject of philosophy is, to a large extent, what we care about. We care about the big questions, about what knowledge and truth and justice are, and we care about these questions because these notions are cognitively and conatively central to our lives, and they are central, in turn, because they are *important*. So it's a methodology that goes via human concerns out into the world. Investigation into the relevant worldly phenomena is not a linguistic investigation. As Austin says, "[W]e are using a sharpened awareness of words to sharpen our perception of, though not as the final arbiter of, the phenomena" (1957, 182). And second, we have not, so far, *advocated* for having the interests in (i) to (iii). We're observing that philosophers across the discipline have these interests, that the interests are reflected in their methodology, and that they are good motivation for careful attention to various properties of ordinary language expressions.

This last point, however, is a bit too modest. While we have no interest, or competency, in being the interest police, it does strike us as implausible to claim that an interest in (i) to (iii) somehow isn't appropriate or isn't appropriately philosophical. If philosophy is anything, it is, at least, what good philosophers have been doing. The interests (i) to (iii) are a good description of much important philosophical work. None of that is to deny that those who don't share those interests are also doing philosophy or that they have deviant interests and should be converted.

3.3. Anchoring

So far, we've been letting the proponent of the Chalmers-style argument get away with talking about property vicinities, for example properties in the *vicinity* of freedom or knowledge. This notion of a vicinity, or grouping or neighborhood, of properties and concepts is at the core of the Chalmers-style argument. However, and this is closely related to CARE, we need a deep understanding of the ordinary language notion in order to create vicinities. We call this the ANCHORING role of ordinary language. "Vicinity" makes sense only relative to an anchoring point: there's no such thing as a vicinity *simpliciter* (just as there's no such thing as "nearby" *simpliciter*). So the first question to ask is: "Vicinity of what?" If again we use "knowledge" as an illustration, the answer seems obvious: we're talking about concepts and properties in the vicinity of *knowledge*. The point generalizes: we're interested in vicinities around *freedom*, *belief*, *causation*, and so on. In all these cases, the anchoring point is an ordinary language expression, and then we somehow define a similarity relation to it. That gives us the scope of the relevant vicinity. If that's how the vicinities are generated, then, again, an interest in what the ordinary language expression picks out is not a fetish. On the contrary, it's a precondition for engaging in the kind of pluralism that Chalmers advocates, as well as for those theorists, like the theorists of causation just considered, who don't need to care about the ordinary notion in their research.[14] The underlying principle can be summarized as ANCHORING.

ANCHORING: The meanings and denotations of ordinary language expression serve as anchoring points for conceptual vicinities: The

---

[14] Chalmers appeals to the idea of a functional or explanatory role. Note that these must be the explanatory roles of something. That something is the ordinary language notion.

conceptual vicinity of T is whatever is relevantly similar to T. In order to find what's relevantly similar to T, you first need to know a lot about T. The process of vicinity creation starts with an understanding of T. The relevant kind of understanding of T comes through OL guidance.

Here's an analogy to make this vivid. Suppose we try to define a cluster of cities: those that are similar to Paris. In order to do that, we can't just say: "Oh, it doesn't much matter what 'Paris' denotes—an obsession with that is just a fetish." On the contrary, the cluster creation can't get off the ground without detailed knowledge of what "Paris" denotes. You cannot assess relative similarity with Paris without relying on knowledge about the properties of Paris. Even if you agree with Chalmers that conceptual vicinities are important and that we should not privilege the concepts that happen to be picked out by the ordinary language terms, the anchoring point is crucial. If ANCHORING is correct, then identifying the conceptual vicinities relies on OL guidance.

Note that ANCHORING applies across the board. In particular, it applies to what some might call deferential terms. According to externalist orthodoxy, many ordinary language terms, such as "arthritis," "contract," and "brisket," have their extensions determined by a subset of the linguistic community, the experts. Call such terms expert-deference terms (E-D terms). An initial thought is that E-D terms don't require OL guidance, and that CARE and ANCHORING don't apply, because meanings are determined by these experts. The experts can do whatever they want with them, and they don't need to heed OL guidance. Maybe "time" is like that: it's an E-D term, so its meaning is determined by the experts, and the experts are the physicists. On this view, the physicists are using the ordinary language term, but they are in charge. They can do whatever they want with it and don't need any OL guidance. In Tyler Burge's original (1979) thought experiment, the central argumentative move involved just such a change: we're asked to imagine that the medical community decides to use "arthritis" as a term that denotes ailments that can occur in the thigh, thus overruling the ordinary language notion.

This line of thought is too simplistic, for three reasons. First, experts are not free to introduce meanings willy-nilly. If the medical experts were to decide tomorrow that "arthritis" denotes a certain kind of wart on the toes, then they would just have introduced an ambiguity. The wiggle room experts have is restricted by ANCHORING in the ordinary notion. Just how ANCHORING restricts is a difficult question, but we don't need a full account of how the restriction works in order to see that there are restrictions. Second, not all terms are E-D terms. Timothy Williamson and Miranda Fricker are experts in epistemology, but they don't determine what "knows" or "knowledge" means in the mouths of ordinary speakers.

The speech community doesn't defer to Williamson and Fricker on judgments about "knowledge" in the way they defer to doctors on "arthritis." Speakers of English don't defer to Allan Gibbard's judgments about what "good" or "ought" denotes. Gibbard defers to them. The same goes for most of the terms mentioned in the introductory part this essay. "Time," however, is a tricky case. That brings us to the third point: even when there is deference, it's something that's difficult to discern and assess the effects of. How do you discover whether "time" is different from "knows" with respect to E-D status? You pay careful attention to the behavior of speakers. That involves paying close attention to the way in which the ordinary notion is used; that is, you need OL guidance *even if just to reassure yourself that you don't need OL guidance.*[15]

4. Talking Stock: From CARE and ANCHORING to Ordinary Language Philosophy

We've made three claims:

(i) OL guidance as a matter of fact dominates large parts of philosophy.
(ii) OL guidance is a good and inevitable methodology because of CARE and ANCHORING.
(iii) OL-guided philosophy is a form of ordinary language philosophy.

Of these, we have done the least to defend (iii) but we don't want to get into a verbal dispute about how to use the term "ordinary language philosophy." There certainly are people who would want to use that expression to denote something that incorporates more elements from Ryle or Austin, and if so we'll just be concessive and let people use the term in many different ways. We think ours is one reasonable usage. Nevertheless—and without getting into detailed exegesis of Austin—it's worth noting that a thought at least close to CARE is expressed in the following seminal passage from "A Plea for Excuses":

[15] A reviewer suggested another reason we might want OL guidance: what they call "cognitive fluency." Speakers of a natural language will normally have acquired a capacity to recognize (in a wide range of cases) whether a widely used term of ordinary language (such as "know," "cause," "ought") applies or not. This is what competency with an ordinary language term typically consists in. The result of that familiarity is a kind of cognitive fluency: an ability to apply the term in new contexts and to assess its use by others, without excessive cognitive effort. This not only simplifies thinking, talking, and theorizing, it also contributes to our ability to understand what different instantiations of, say, a predicate have in common. This contrasts sharply with terms that are artificially cooked-up. To employ such terms can require an extensive learning period, there's bound to be initial cognitive resistance, and the training period will not be of the kind familiar for natural language terms. This isn't to deny that technical terms can be improvements on OL terminology, but there's an initial cognitive investment and an inevitable lack of fluency compared to what we have with terms from ordinary language.

In view of the prevalence of the slogan "ordinary language," and of such names as "linguistic" or "analytic" philosophy or "the analysis of language," one thing needs specially emphasising to counter misunderstandings. When we examine what we should say when, what words we should use in what situations, we are looking again not merely at words (or "meanings," whatever they may be) but also at the realities we use the words to talk about: *we are using a sharpened awareness of words to sharpen our perception of, though not as the final arbiter of, the phenomena.* (1957, 182, italics ours)

It seems that this is just what happens when we think about the behavior of "knows." Our sharpened awareness of how "knows" is context sensitive sheds light on knowledge, which is what we as thinkers and actors care about. The contemporary contextualist in epistemology, maybe, is just Austin with help from Kaplan; maybe ordinary language philosophy never died, it just changed form, and learned Montague grammar.

So far, we haven't said much about just what kind of information we get from paying attention to ordinary notions—of how exactly ordinary language guides us. How exactly does it enable us to see the phenomena more clearly? We don't have a full answer to that and we're not sure it's worth trying to get a fixed taxonomy of the kinds of insights that might be gained. One reason for this is highlighted by Austin in that same paper: "Certainly ordinary language has no claim to be the last word, if there is such a thing" (1957, 11). We certainly aren't aiming to defend a "linguistic idealist" or a constructivist view according to which we can read our theory of the world off our language. The guidance of language is variable, fallible, and unsystematic. It is *one* source of insight that combines with other assumptions, both substantive and methodological, and its guidance can always be overridden. For example, faced with the seeming context sensitivity of "knows" one can and should (and people do) wonder whether the data can be explained away, and whether the contextualist explains all we want.

Nevertheless, here are some schematic ways in which ordinary language guides us in combination with other substantive and methodological assumptions:

- The context sensitivity of "T" tells us something about the nature of Ts, but what it tells us will depend on your view of the semantics-pragmatics distinction, your view of speech reports, your view about intuitions about cases, and many other things.
- The (putative) opacity of belief reports will tell you something about the nature of beliefs, but just what it'll tell you will depend on your explanation of opacity and cognitive significance, your view of the logical form of belief sentences, and a more general theory of the distinction between

de re and de dicto beliefs, which might in turn depend on cutting-edge work in syntactic theory.

- Here is an example from the *Stanford Encyclopedia*'s entry on "love" (Helm 2008). It starts with an observation about ordinary conversations:

In ordinary conversations, we often say things like the following:

1. I love chocolate (or skiing).
2. I love doing philosophy (or being a father).
3. I love my dog (or cat).
4. I love my wife (or mother or child or friend).

What follows from this being said in ordinary conversations is an open question. Even if the observation of ordinary usage is correct (as it no doubt is in this case) you get no philosophical mileage without doing more philosophy. In this case the author goes on to make various assumptions about how "what is meant by 'love' differs from case to case." With that assumption in mind, the author focuses on the kind of personal love picked out in (4) as primary and says that "(3) may be understood as a kind of deficient mode of the sort of love we typically reserve for persons." The author's strategy here is fairly typical: to start with an observation about ordinary language, then to make a number of additional assumptions: for example, that there's an ambiguity of some sort ("what is meant by 'love' differs"). That's not something you can read off ordinary conversation. You get that only from starting with doing more theorizing. This illustrates how observations about ordinary usages combine with theoretical assumptions as the starting point for theorizing about the phenomenon picked out by the ordinary notion.

So the take-home message here is that ordinary usage alone doesn't give us much philosophical insight. It needs to interact with assumptions about a potentially extremely broad range of other issues and in particular assumptions about the nature of semantics and pragmatics, the metaphysics of meanings, the connections between semantic content and speech-act content, the nature of speech acts, and so on. That "and so on" is not a cop-out but a way of saying that we don't think there's an a priori limit to the kinds of considerations that can be relevant.

Not only is the payoff from OL guidance dependent on additional assumptions, often there will be no payoff at all. Suppose you want to learn about the denotation of "Georg Wilhelm Friedrich Hegel." It's a proper name, it can be used in certain syntactic positions in various sentences, it can't always be substituted by a coreferential term in a sentence *salva veritate*. All that will tell you nothing helpful whatsoever. Note that this is so even if you satisfy CARE. You want to know something about the object denoted by an ordinary language expression, that is, "Hegel." If you want to learn about Hegel, then you have to read thick books by and about Hegel. Studying the philosophical or linguistic literature on proper names won't help you.[16]

So one thing that we think any ordinary language philosophy needs to be sensitive to is that it (like everything else) isn't first philosophy, and one goes wrong if one thinks it is. And here we take ourselves to be heeding Austin's famous dictum that while ordinary language is never the "last word," it *is* the "first word"—it is the starting place for theorizing about many areas of philosophy.[17]

5. Contrast with Williamson's Instrumentalism About Ordinary Language

We want to end by comparing our view of ordinary language philosophy to the view outlined by Timothy Williamson in *The Philosophy of Philosophy* (2007). This is not only because he has interesting things to say but because his view of the recent history of analytic philosophy and the "linguistic turn" represents, we think, a widely held view among mainstream contemporary analytic philosophers. Logical positivism and ordinary language were language-oriented metaphilosophies that were decisively brushed aside when Kripke came along and showed us how to do metaphysics again. From that angle on our recent history, the reliance shown above in recent philosophy on language should seem methodologically unsound, something hard to square with analytic philosophy's current self-image according to which it's a discipline concerned with finding out truths about the world, not merely limning our conceptual or linguistic scheme. We hope to offer a way of bringing our self-image into line with philosophical reality, and Williamson is an ideal interlocutor for this.

In the first part of that book, Williamson argues against what he calls the "linguistic turn" in philosophy, but that doesn't mean, he points out, that language has *no* role to play in philosophical theorizing. He is keen to place front and center "the liveliest, exactest, and most creative achievements of the final third of [the twentieth] century" (2007, 19), namely, "the

---

[16] This is not to deny that CARE and ANCHORING play a role in the study of Hegel. In order to find out about Hegel's theories, you need to find out stuff about what the person denoted by "Hegel" wrote. You can't just ignore "Hegel" and introduce "Hegel$_1$," "Hegel$_2$," and so on for each potential interpretation and then say: "I don't care which one 'Hegel' denotes because that's just a fetish." Or you could try to, but historians of philosophy would probably shout at you for it.

[17] One of us is committed to the idea that an important philosophical project—conceptual engineering—involves assessing ordinary language (see, e.g., Cappelen 2018). Conceptual engineering, so understood, is a project that goes hand in hand with ordinary language philosophy: it has to start with an understanding of what we already have. It then assesses and finally suggests ameliorations.

revival of metaphysical theorizing, realist in spirit, often speculative, some-times commonsensical" (19), associated with people like Armstrong, Fine, and Kripke, a metaphysics that isn't "primarily concerned with thought or language at all" (18), but he realizes that even the most realist metaphysi-cian can't overlook language. Language, after all, is the means by which we theorize. To use Williamson's example, for an analytic metaphysician to disdain language in his theorizing would "resemble an astronomer who thinks he can safely ignore the physics of telescopes because his interest is in the extra-terrestrial universe" (46). Williamson goes on: "Analytic phi-losophy at its best uses logical rigor and semantic sophistication to achieve a sharpness of philosophical vision unobtainable by other means. To sacri-fice those gains would be to choose blurred vision. Fortunately, one can do more with good vision than look at eyes" (46).

Expanding on this thought in the afterword, Williamson writes:

> Explicit compositional semantic theories for reasonable fragments of particular natural languages also have the great methodological advantage of being comparatively easy to test in comparatively uncontentious ways, because they make specific predictions about the truth conditions (or assertability conditions) of infinitely many ordinary unphilosophical sentences. The attempt to provide a semantic theory that coheres with a given metaphysical claim can therefore constitute a searching test of the latter claim, even though semantics and metaphysics have different objects. (285)

From Williamson's discussion, we could extract the following view:

> (INSTRUMENTALISM): Language can serve as a *tool* to help us under-stand the objects of philosophical study by helping us to make clear the nature of the arguments we make for philosophical claims.

Williamson-style instrumentalism fails to capture the full significance of ordinary language. That failure undermines some (but not all) of Williamson's criticism of the linguistic turn in *The Philosophy of Philoso-phy*. At the beginning of this essay, we noted an indisputable asymmetry between, say, epistemology, on the one hand, and physics, on the other. Epistemologists, including Williamson (see, for example, the careful treatment of linguistic data in Williamson 2005), rely extensively on data about "knows," in a way that has no analogue in physics (the properties of the words "thing," "mass," and "energy" play zero role in physics, for example). Instrumentalists predict that there should be no asymmetry. What Williamson says about analytic philosophy could surely also be said about physics, where italicization indicates our changing of Williamson's text: "*Physics* at its best uses logical rigor and semantic sophistication to achieve a sharpness of philosophical vision unobtainable by other means"

(2007, 46). And: "A *physicist* who disdains language in his theorizing would resemble an astronomer who thinks he can safely ignore the physics of telescopes because his interest is in the extra-terrestrial universe" (46).

Nonetheless, Williamson is aiming to capture an asymmetry. He asks, "Why should considerations about thought and language play so much more central a role in philosophy than in other disciplines, when the question explicitly under debate is not itself even implicitly about thought or language?" (45). Here is another version of his instrumentalist answer:

> The paradigms of philosophical questions are those that seem best addressed by armchair considerations less formal than mathematical proofs. The validity of such informal arguments depends on the structure of the natural language sentences in which they are at least partly formulated, or on the structure of the underlying thoughts. That structure is often hard to discern. We cannot just follow our instincts in reasoning; they are too often wrong. ... In order to reason accurately in informal terms, we must focus on our reasoning as presented in thought or language, to doublecheck it, and the results are often controversial. Thus questions about the structure of thought and language become central to the debate, even when it is not primarily a debate about thought or language. (45)

Again, this fails to capture the asymmetry. The validity of any argument articulated using a natural language depends on "the structure of the natural language sentences" used to articulate the argument. This is just as true about political science as it is about biology, geology, or chemistry. It's wildly implausible that philosophers care more about the validity of their arguments than do contributors to those other disciplines. Even the most formal of disciplines care about the structure of the arguments they use. Typically those arguments are presented as a mixture of a formal language and a natural language, with the latter dominating. If you want some illustrations, take a look at some random samples, say, Hannes Alfven's book *Cosmological Electrodynamics* (1963), a foundational work in plasma physics, or a more recent paper about black holes, say, Laura Ferrarese and David Merritt's "A Fundamental Relation Between Supermassive Black Holes and Their Host Galaxies" (2000). Core elements of the arguments are articulated in natural language, and whatever need for clarity philosophers have, physicists have.

This is not intended to be a sophisticated point. Any intellectual endeavor needs logical rigor and semantic sophistication. To be sharp it needs the semantic tools we use to formulate our theories and assess our arguments. These are weak constraints on theorizing. Philosophy, as practiced in the examples with which we began, needs more. In philosophy, ordinary language use in some way provides something that a theory in a given domain needs to fit with. A theory in epistemology needs to fit with how ordinary people use "know" in a way that a theory of gravity doesn't have to fit with how we use "gravity." Philosophy takes more from ordinary language—Williamson-style instrumentalism can't explain why philosophy takes more—and instrumentalism fails as a way of capturing the distinct importance of language for philosophy.

Moreover, it's not as if moving to a formal language removes the need for carefulness of the kind Williamson describes: it's just as crucial for those using mathematical symbols as it is for those using English words. Instrumentalism fails to capture the supposed distinctness of appeals to language in philosophy as opposed to other disciplines.

Overgeneralization isn't the only problem with Williamson-style instrumentalism. Instrumentalism also fails to capture a distinctive way in which OL guidance plays a role in philosophy. To see this, let us return to Williamson's analogy of language as a telescope: "Some contemporary metaphysicians appear to believe that they can safely ignore formal semantics and the philosophy of language because their interest is in a largely extra-mental reality. They resemble an astronomer who thinks he can safely ignore the physics of telescopes because his interest is in the extra-terrestrial universe. In delicate matters, his attitude makes him all the more likely to project features of his telescope confusedly onto the stars beyond" (2007, 46). While this is a fascinating and helpful analogy in many ways, there's an important disanalogy between language and telescopes. Terms such as "knowledge," "freedom," and "ought" are topic determining in a way that a telescope is not. A telescope we're free to move around and point at whatever we feel like. "Knows," on the other hand, is fixed on knowledge and can't be moved. One corollary of our ANCHORING principle: core philosophical terms serve as anchors for philosophical investigations in a way that "thing" and "matter" don't anchor investigations in physics. Ordinary language is not just a tool or instrument for seeing the world better. It also determines what it is we look at, and—sometimes—it tells us things about what we look at.

Acknowledgments

Thanks to three anonymous *Metaphilosophy* reviewers for helpful comments.

References

Alfven, Hannes. 1963. *Cosmological Electrodynamics*. Oxford: Clarendon Press.
Austin, John. 1957. "A Plea for Excuses." *Proceedings of the Aristotelian Society* 57: 1–30.
Austin, John Langshaw. 1962. *How to Do Things with Words*. Oxford: Clarendon Press.

Ayer, A. J. 1936. *Language, Truth and Logic*. London: V. Gollancz.

Burge, Tyler. 1979. "Individualism and the Mental." *Midwest Studies in Philosophy* 4, no. 1: 73–122.

Cappelen, Herman. 2018. *Fixing Language: An Essay on Conceptual Engineering*. Oxford: Oxford University Press.

Chalmers, David J. 2006. "The Foundations of Two-Dimensional Semantics." In *Two-Dimensional Semantics: Foundations and Applications*, edited by Manuel Garcia-Carpintero and Josep Macia, 55–140. Oxford: Oxford University Press.

Chalmers, David. 2011. "Verbal Disputes." *Philosophical Review* 120, no. 4: 515–66.

Charlow, Nate. 2014. "The Problem with the Frege-Geach Problem." *Philosophical Studies* 167, no. 3: 635–65.

Cohen, Stewart. 1998. "Contextualist Solutions to Epistemological Problems: Scepticism, Gettier, and the Lottery." *Australasian Journal of Philosophy* 76, no. 2: 289–306.

DeRose, Keith. 1996. "Knowledge, Assertion and Lotteries." *Australasian Journal of Philosophy* 74, no. 4: 568–80.

Ferrarese, Laura, and David Merritt. 2000. "A Fundamental Relation Between Supermassive Black Holes and Their Host Galaxies." *Astrophysical Journal Letters* 539, no. 1, L9–L12

Geach, P. T. 1965. "Assertion." *Philosophical Review* 74, no. 4: 449–65.

Hansen, Nat. 2014. "Contemporary Ordinary Language Philosophy." *Philosophy Compass* 9, no. 8: 556–69.

Hansen, Nat. 2020. "'Nobody would really talk that way!': The Critical Project in Contemporary Ordinary Language Philosophy." *Synthese* 197, no. 6: 2433–64.

Hawthorne, John. 2003. *Knowledge and Lotteries*. Oxford: Oxford University Press.

Hawthorne, John, and David Manley. 2012. *The Reference Book*. Oxford: Oxford University Press.

Helm, Bennett W. 2008. "Love." In *Stanford Encyclopedia of Philosophy*, edited by Edward N. Zalta (Fall 2021 Edition).

Horwich, Paul. 1998. *Truth*. Oxford: Clarendon Press.

Kaplan, David. 1968. "Quantifying In." *Synthese* 19, nos. 1–2: 178–214.

Keshet, Ezra. 2010. "Split Intensionality: A New Scope Theory of De Re and De Dicto." *Linguistics and Philosophy* 33, no. 4: 251–83.

Kripke, Saul. 1975. "Outline of a Theory of Truth." *Journal of Philosophy* 72, no. 19: 690–716.

Lakoff, George. 1965. "On the Nature of Syntactic Irregularity." Ph.D. dissertation, Harvard University.

Lewis, David. 1973. "Causation." *Journal of Philosophy* 70, no. 17: 556–67.

Lewis, David K. 1996. "Elusive Knowledge." *Australasian Journal of Philosophy* 74, no. 4: 549–67.

Ludlow, Peter 1999. *Semantics, Tense, and Time: An Essay in the Metaphysics of Natural Language*. Cambridge, Mass.: MIT Press.

MacFarlane, John. 2014. *Assessment Sensitivity: Relative Truth and Its Applications*. Oxford: Oxford University Press.

Moore, G. E. 1903. *Principia Ethica*. New York: Dover.

Parker-Ryan, Sally. 2012. "Ordinary Language Philosophy." *Internet Encyclopedia of Philosophy*.

Quine, Willard van Orman. 1956. "Quantifiers and Propositional Attitudes." *Journal of Philosophy* 53, no. 5: 177–87.

Ramsey, F. P. 1927. "Facts and Propositions." *Aristotelian Society Supplementary Volume* 7, no. 1: 153–70.

Rumfitt, Ian. 2003. "Savoir Faire." *Journal of Philosophy* 100, no. 3: 158–66.

Ryle, Gilbert. 1971. *Collected Papers*. London: Hutchinson.

Salmon, Nathan. 1986. *Frege's Puzzle*. Atascadero, Calif.: Ridgeview.

Schaffer, Jonathan. 2012. "Causal Contextualisms." In *Contrastivism in Philosophy: New Perspectives*, edited by Martijn Blaauw, 35–63. London: Routledge.

Schroeder, Mark. 2008. *Being For: Evaluating the Semantic Program of Expressivism*. Oxford: Oxford University Press.

Silk, Alex. 2015. "How to Be an Ethical Expressivist." *Philosophy and Phenomenological Research* 91, no. 1: 47–81.

Stanley, Jason, and Timothy Willlamson. 2001. "Knowing How." *Journal of Philosophy* 98, no. 8: 411–44.

Stevenson, Charles. 1944. *Ethics and Language*. New Haven: Yale University Press.

Strawson, Peter. 1959. *Individuals: An Essay in Descriptive Metaphysics*. London: Routledge.

Swanson, Eric. 2012. "The Language of Causation." In *The Routledge Companion to the Philosophy of Language*, edited by Delia Graff Fara and Gillian Russell, 716–28. London: Routledge.

Williamson, Timothy, 2000. *Knowledge and Its Limits*. Oxford: Oxford University Press.

Williamson, Timothy. 2005. "Knowledge, Context, and the Agent's Point of View." In *Contextualism in Philosophy: Knowledge, Meaning, and Truth*, edited by Gerhard Preyer and Georg Peter, 91–114. Oxford: Oxford University Press.

Williamson, Timothy. 2007. *The Philosophy of Philosophy*. Oxford: Wiley-Blackwell.

Wittgenstein, Ludwig. 1953. *Philosophical Investigations*. Edited by G. E. M. Anscombe and R. Rhees and translated by G. E. M. Anscombe. Oxford: Wiley-Blackwell.

CHAPTER 6

TESTING AND DISCOVERY: RESPONDING TO CHALLENGES TO DIGITAL PHILOSOPHY OF SCIENCE

CHARLES H. PENCE

1. Introduction

While digital humanities is not a new discipline (precursors may be found as far back as Garfield 1955; de Solla Price 1965; or Busa 1980), its application has exploded in recent years, thanks in no small part to the advance of, on the one hand, digitization methods that have enabled us to access large corpora of text, images, social media posts, and other source material that have the potential to radically reshape our understanding of a number of traditional questions in the humanities; and, on the other hand, increasing access to computational power and advances in algorithms for the analysis of data that have enabled us to more easily draw relevant inferences for study in the humanities. This has been no less true in the case of philosophy. Numerous texts in the history of philosophy have now been digitized, in part through projects like Early English Books Online (EEBO) and Eighteenth Century Collections Online (ECCO). To this can be added the increasing volume of journal literature in contemporary philosophy that is now available digitally, as well as native-digital philosophical resources such as the *Stanford Encyclopedia of Philosophy*. These have been matched by an increasing accessibility of sophisticated methods of textual analysis, network analysis, visualization, bibliometrics, and more, all of which can help us to find empirically grounded responses to traditional philosophical questions.

The possibilities for the use of digital methods are all the more apparent for branches of philosophy—most emblematically, and my focus here, the philosophy of science, though also moral philosophy, philosophy of religion, experimental philosophy, and others—that engage with bodies of knowledge generated in other disciplines, as well as for the history of

Examining Philosophy Itself. Edited by Yafeng Shan.
Chapters and book compilation © 2023 Metaphilosophy LLC and John Wiley & Sons Ltd.
Published 2023 by John Wiley & Sons Ltd.

philosophy, where the relevant body of knowledge would be the prior products of philosophers themselves.[1] For philosophers of science, these methods could provide new ways of looking at the work done by scientific practitioners, whether through the lens of their journal articles (Ramsey and Pence 2016), laboratory notebooks, social media accounts (Rogers 2013), or results in the form of large collections of scientific data (Leonelli 2016).[2]

For this promise to pay off, however, we need to critically consider exactly when and how these tools can be best applied. As with every technological fix in any domain of human inquiry, when we are possessed of such tools we run the serious danger of either a hasty rejection of novel methods or an equally hasty inference that digital approaches will be a panacea for every question in the future of philosophy.

What exactly, then, are these tools supposed to be used for? In this essay, I consider two very common answers to this question—that the digital humanities should be used for the *testing of philosophical hypotheses,* and that they should be used for the *discovery of new hypotheses.* Each of these uses is obvious, and as I hope to demonstrate, both are essential for the full promise of digital philosophy to be realized. That said, there is a certain apparent tension between the two. As we will see, one cannot simultaneously use the same data to derive a hypothesis and test that same hypothesis—a fact that has led some to call for the wholesale rejection of discovery in favor of hypothesis testing.

Drawing on two case studies from elsewhere—in data-driven science and in history—I attempt to offer a new way to think about, and potentially resolve, this apparent tension between testing and discovery, by more precisely illuminating exactly what it is that's at stake in this controversy. While the case studies I discuss seem at first to be relatively disperse, and are drawn from different fields with different concerns, I argue that in fact they both derive from the same kind of underlying concern. That is, they are both, in the end, reminders that we must explore the relationship between our background preexisting philosophical positions and the kind of inferences

---

[1] I regret that I lack the space to extensively pursue the connections between this work and parts of philosophy beyond the philosophy of science. While my focus here is thus limited, I hope readers will be able to see how this might generalize to these other areas where digital work can provide a valuable "input" to philosophical reflection.

[2] I am using "philosophy of science" here to stand for a wide array of allied kinds of philosophical pursuits. The precise details of the ways in which digital methods will be useful will certainly depend on whether the effort is best understood as "contemporary philosophy of science (PoS)," "history of philosophy of science (HOPOS)," or "history and philosophy of science (HPS)." The data upon which we rely, for example, might be either the contemporary scientific process (PoS), the historical works of scientists (HPS), or the historical works of philosophers of science (HOPOS). I stick with "philosophy of science" for brevity's sake in the rest of this article, but I believe that the considerations that I raise here will be valid for any of these approaches to philosophical work. (My thanks to Laura Georgescu for encouraging me to bring out this point.)

that we might hope to draw in digital philosophy. In claiming a mantle of "empiricism" or (more problematically) "objectivity" for these digital results—a claim that, whether explicit or implied, is practically inescapable in some form or another—we must be very sure that we are aware of the ways in which those empirical conclusions might depend upon our extant conceptual structure.

In doing so, I argue, we will find means to take advantage of *both* hypothesis discovery and hypothesis testing, without abandoning either one wholesale. I conclude by raising a handful of questions as targets for future work, which, while largely unresolved, will, I claim, form a crucial companion to applications of digital philosophy in the years to come.

2. What Is Digital Philosophy?

While applications of digital philosophy are now becoming ubiquitous enough that many readers will be familiar with them already, it merits a brief pause here to describe the kinds of studies that I have in mind.[3] Perhaps the most common use of these tools thus far has been in what we might call "mapping" of the field of philosophy itself. What kinds of questions have philosophers been interested in, and when? How have these trends changed over time, and how has the reflection of them in our published works matched or differed from the accounts of our own field that we tell in the history of philosophy? To point to just one particularly striking example of such work, Christophe Malaterre, Jean-François Chartier, and Davide Pulizzotto (2019) have constructed a corpus of articles from the journal *Philosophy of Science* spanning seventy years, from 1934 to 2015 (Figure 1). Their work uses a process known as *topic modeling*, on which an unsupervised algorithm (that is, an algorithm that does not require its users to input significant amounts of domain knowledge in advance) breaks a corpus up into a collection of topics, roughly analogous to the subjects that each article might discuss (Blei 2012). Such a topic model shows us some classic features of the history of the philosophy of science that we might expect—for instance, the decreasing importance of logic and philosophy of language for philosophy of science (indicating their increasing independence as subdisciplines of philosophy) and the explosion of philosophy of biology beginning in the 1970s.

But these tools are useful not only for a retrospective understanding of philosophy—they also can help us test extant philosophical claims. To take one recent example, Moti Mizrahi (2020) has considered whether scientific publications tend to offer support for or counterexamples to some of the most common accounts of scientific progress. It should be

---

[3] Anyone not in need of such a refresher should feel free to move on to the next section.

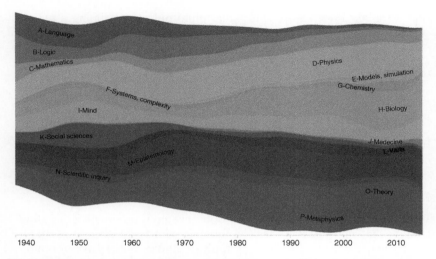

FIGURE 1. The evolution over time of large categories of topics in the journal *Philosophy of Science*, from 1934 to 2015. Figure in Malaterre, Chartier, and Pulizzotto 2019.

clear enough that a philosophical theory about the nature of "progress" in the sciences (for instance, that science progresses in terms of approach to the truth, or increased understanding, or accumulation of empirical knowledge) should have at least some kind of empirical upshot—if it is right, scientists should tend to describe the lasting consequences of their work in certain ways (say, using terms connected to knowledge, understanding, or truth) and should avoid describing those consequences in other ways. While Mizrahi's analyses are not definitive, they seem to offer evidence against truth-based views of scientific progress and for knowledge-based or understanding-based views.

Third and finally, we might see these tools as useful for the generation of new philosophical hypotheses. In my own prior work, I have evaluated what I call the "network of discourse" surrounding a debate over the nature of heredity in the history of biology at the turn of the twentieth century (Pence 2022). This discourse network can be understood as the picture we get when we consider authors to be "connected" each time one author mentions another in a particular context—here, a few decades from the correspondence pages of the journal *Nature*. As it turns out, such a network does not merely recapitulate the already-known networks of "allies" in this debate, or networks of training and mentorship, also already well understood (Kim 1994). On the contrary, what appears is a different network (Figure 2), in which authors who are heavily invested in debating one another actually

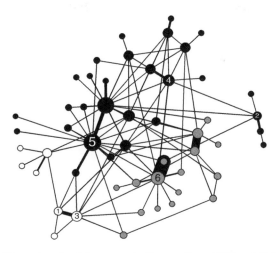

FIGURE 2.   The network of discourse in *Nature,* from 1900 to 1904. W. F. R. Weldon and William Bateson, the two central players in the debate at issue, are labeled 1 and 3, and we can see them relatively isolated from the rest of the discussion in the letters to the journal. Figure 4 in Pence 2022.

seem to *remove themselves* from the mainstream of scientific discourse, leading me to propose, at least tentatively (more case studies being certainly required) a sort of "professional debater" or "paradigm warrior" category of social actor in the development of scientific theories.

Again, it is not my purpose here to evaluate the merits of these particular examples. But I hope that this brief tour of some recent examples of digital philosophy of science can provide a window into the potential of these methods for philosophical investigation. In all these cases, the idea is to begin treating the outputs of the scientific or philosophical process as empirical data, aided in each case by our access to massive databases of those outputs and the kinds of analytical tools needed to understand them in compelling and useful ways.

3. Hypothesis Testing and Discovery

Even this short presentation, however, gives rise to a very important question that is in some sense an obvious one to pose to any new methodology: What is it that these methods are good for?

The answer to this question is less straightforward than it might seem, perhaps highlighted by the different aims of Mizrahi's and my own work as just discussed above. Clearly, these digital tools are extremely useful for the discovery of new and unexpected trends in the data, which might readily lead us to propose novel philosophical hypotheses in order to explain them. I tentatively offered an amendment to the standard account of the social structure of the historical controversy that I discussed, adding to it another class of scientific actor that could, at least potentially, be revealing in the analysis of a number of other vitriolic and public scientific controversies.

Indeed, the cultivation of what we might call "serendipitous discovery" is often an explicit target of scholars working in the digital humanities.[4] This focus derives from a related worry that one might have about the proliferation of digital technologies, hyperlinked references, and so forth: the process of searching for and finding academic information has radically changed. In the process, we have lost some of the randomness that at times led to important academic insight. Think, for instance, of looking for a book in the library, only to come away with several more nearby on the shelf, or of picking up a paper issue of a journal and reading more than the one sought-for article. With this in mind, dedicated efforts to design browsing or analysis systems that encourage such serendipity—think of an academic version of the "more items like this one" found at many online retailers—have been undertaken.

That said, any formulation of a new hypothesis *after* consulting a particularly large dataset comes with a serious problem. If one has a dataset of sufficient size, it's essentially guaranteed that it will be filled with what have become known as "spurious correlations." It has already been noted in a digital humanities context by Lev Manovich that any methodologies targeted at sampling of large datasets (in his case, of images) run the risk of remaining, nonetheless, nonrepresentative (Manovich 2012, 259).[5] And as Cristian S. Calude and Giuseppe Longo have formally demonstrated, "the more data, the more arbitrary, meaningless and useless (for future action) correlations will be found in them" (2017, 600), where here a meaningless correlation is defined as one that could be produced in a randomly generated dataset with no relation to real-world, empirical fact. The presence of such spurious correlations has as an obvious consequence that one cannot simply "read off" theoretical commitments from a dataset, no matter its size or how carefully it was constructed. But more subtly than this, it also entails that we have an obligation to engage in at least some degree of active prevention: how can we be sure that the promising and novel hypothesis our

[4] For instance, Deb Verhoeven, following Martin Weller, discusses the expansion of discovery as an explicit role for digital humanities work (Arthur and Bode 2014, 210); in the same volume, Sydney Shep underlines "search and discovery" as two of the key challenges "in big data sources that often deliver masses of unfiltered hits and whose subsequent systematic reorganization mirrors existing knowledge structures or assumptions" (Arthur and Bode 2014, 79).

[5] Strikingly, Manovich presents similar problems not only for the identification of trends within such a corpus of images but also for the visualization over time of such corpora.

analysis has shown us is not just the result of a fortuitous coincidence of bits?[6]

There are, to be sure, many ways in which one might respond to this challenge—but one of the most common propositions has been a fairly extreme one. Many have called for a wholesale turn to hypothesis-driven research in these kinds of big-data contexts.[7] That is, if we simply *abandon* the use of digital tools as serendipitous avenues for discovery and do not employ such large datasets until and unless we have formulated a prior hypothesis, then we can honestly claim that any results we produce serve as unbiased tests of that hypothesis.[8] Think here of the work of Mizrahi mentioned above, which took as its starting point the collection of existing philosophical theories concerning scientific progress and used textual analysis as a way to offer evidence for or against each one.

The foregoing has been too vague, however, and these problems deserve a further degree of exploration. What exactly is it that's taken to be actually (or potentially) the flaw in these cases of serendipitous discovery, such that the generalizations produced are invalid, and how is it that hypothesis-driven research might avoid them? To close this section, I want to lay out three ways in which we might imagine what "goes wrong" in problematic cases and then, in the next two sections, I consider connections with two other fields that might give us tools useful for elaborating and better understanding them.

First, we might be worried that we are interpreting our data through a preexisting theoretical frame or on the basis of an already-formulated hypothesis (or even just a hunch). In that case, we would run the serious risk of conflating *theory construction* with *theory testing*. After all, it is no surprise if the very data that we had in mind when we *derived* a given theory would go on to be compatible with that theory; we cannot then claim that those same data serve to test or confirm it. This is an old problem in the philosophy of science; there is a long debate concerning whether there is a difference between "predicted" evidence and merely "accommodated" evidence, with no real consensus concerning just exactly what the difference between the two consists in (Douglas 2009 contains a nice summary). However it is worked out in the details, it seems that the construction/testing

---

[6] It is also important to note that, in addition to the size of our datasets leading to problems of spurious correlation—the clearest and least escapable such problem, and hence the example that I detail here—we also need to keep in mind that no dataset can possibly be constructed in a "neutral" manner (boyd and Crawford 2012), and no analysis tool is "free" of assumptions about the data that it analyzes (for one striking recent example, see Buolamwini and Gebru 2018), leading to yet more sources of skepticism about the validity of such generalizations.

[7] The arguments that I present for this claim in this section come largely from the sciences, but they have been echoed in the digital humanities literature as well; see, for instance, Underwood 2017.

[8] This is not to say that interpreting the results of those analyses automatically becomes straightforward, but at least we cannot be accused of cherry-picking favorable evidence. I provide an example of an extreme view that entirely rejects discovery in the next section.

relationship here is at best extremely complex, and at worst could threaten to undermine any work that does not take this distinction seriously.

Second, we might fear that being in some sense *too flexible* in our methods of analysis could lead to biased conclusions. It is increasingly recognized that even absent cases of outright academic fraud, researchers of good faith still operate in an environment of extreme external pressure—to publish, obtain positions and grants, and so forth. These kinds of pressures can lead even scrupulous researchers to take advantage of the freedom present within standard scientific practices to make methodological "tweaks" to render their work more attractive (Smaldino and McElreath 2016). For instance, one might stop an analysis short as soon as one finds a result that looks "interesting," not evaluate a full range of parameters for a given algorithm because an early attempt met expectations, or make a series of methodological choices with the goal of rendering a hoped-for result "clearer" or "more perspicuous." Again, such tweaks don't (necessarily) constitute outright fraud—but they can nonetheless provide a path by which biases could enter into research practice via prima facie innocuous methodological decisions.

Third, and perhaps most nebulously, we might be worried that we're not approaching our source material with an apt set of concepts—that in engaging in digital analysis at all, we're failing to engage with that material on its own terms. This a relatively slippery idea, but we might imagine it in line with what Christia Mercer has called the Getting Things Right Constraint in the history of philosophy: the injunction that "historians of philosophy should not attribute claims or ideas to historical figures without concern for whether or not they are ones the figures would recognize as their own" (2019, 530). As Mercer notes, such a principle is essentially second nature in contemporary work on early modern philosophy (her case study). While this principle is perhaps not quite as ubiquitous in the philosophy of science, one can certainly find all of the undercurrents of, for instance, distrust in rational reconstruction and concern for the views of practitioners across contemporary philosophy of science, especially in such areas as the burgeoning philosophy of science in practice movement (Soler et al. 2014). We might thus find at least some apparent support for a modified version of the Getting Things Right Constraint—philosophers of science should not attribute claims or ideas to practicing scientists without concern for whether or not they are ones those scientists would recognize as their own.[9] If digital methodologies do really threaten this increasingly widely accepted principle, then this would constitute good reason to be skeptical of them.

---

[9] As Mercer herself underlines (2019, 300), because this principle is phrased in negative terms (a kind of philosophy *not* to do), there are numerous ways of practicing philosophy consistent with such a principle.

4. The "Preregistration Revolution"

How might we begin to approach these three interrelated problems surrounding hypothesis and discovery in digital philosophy of science? In this section and the next, I want to turn to two case studies, taken from disciplines outside philosophy, to draw out some ways in which philosophers might begin to engage constructively with these kinds of worries, moving past a view of testing and discovery as mutually exclusive.

To begin, let's consider an example from contemporary, data-driven empirical science: *pre-registration*. The concept of preregistration first began to take hold in the life and psychological sciences, both because of the massive amounts of data that these sciences began to generate in the 2000s (especially with the advent of inexpensive, fast DNA sequencing; for a humorous take on the situation, see Sagoff 2019) and because of the failure of several high-profile results to replicate when tested by multiple groups (Munafò et al. 2017). The basic idea is this: if scientists begin a research project by publicly stating the hypotheses to be tested, the ways in which those tests will be undertaken, and the empirical results that would indicate either confirmation or refutation of those hypotheses, then many of the worries surrounding the first two problems I mentioned in the last section (conflation of theory construction and testing, and flexibility in analysis) would be circumvented.

Preregistration has been approached by scientists in surprisingly philosophical terms, and at times with an almost religious fervor. Nosek and colleagues, for instance, begin a theoretical introduction to preregistration by introducing the distinction between prediction and accommodation (which they call postdiction). They continue: "To make confident inferences, it is important to know which is which. Preregistration *solves* this challenge by requiring researchers to state how they will analyze the data before they observe it, allowing them to confront a prediction with the possibility of being wrong" (2018, 2605, emphasis added). Notably, the advantages of preregistration will vary depending upon what exactly it is that we are preregistering. On the one hand, preregistration of the hypothesis we hope to test targets the first problem I mentioned above. As Alison Ledgerwood puts it, this sort of preregistration ensures that "we should only adjust our confidence in a theory in response to evidence that was not itself used to construct the theoretical prediction in question" (2018, E10516). Preregistration of a complete plan of experimental analysis, on the other hand, targets the second worry above, that the data have not unduly influenced our choice of algorithm or methodology of analysis; "flexibility in researcher decisions can inflate the risk of false positives" (Ledgerwood 2018, E10516).

While preregistration might seem more difficult to envisage in a digital-humanities context than a scientific one, the practice could certainly be adapted and utilized to good effect. Preregistering the scope of a corpus, for instance, would guard against the addition of further documents after initial analyses if expected results failed to materialize. Preregistering the plan for applying a given algorithm—think, for instance, of detailing the ways in which the parameters for a topic model would be tuned, the number of topics selected, their quality or coherence evaluated, and so on—could potentially alleviate worries that these choices rely too much on personal preference. Despite the fact that human interpretation of topic-model coherence, among many other examples, remains "the gold standard" (Röder, Both, and Hinneburg 2015, 400), it can be difficult to convince peer reviewers that such human-driven choices are well motivated. Making the limits and role of subjective evaluation particularly clear and declaring them in advance—rendering moot any objection that these choices could have been made with the intent of influencing study outcomes—could make this justificatory process easier.

That said, I do not want to argue here that preregistration is necessarily a silver bullet for these two problems in either scientific or philosophical practice. Perhaps the largest issue for the application of preregistration to the digital humanities concerns the very nature of *replication* itself. To the extent that preregistration in the natural sciences is often targeted at the resolution of failures of replication, this is simply not an issue that is relevant for research in the humanities. There is only one sequence of historical events in the sciences, and only one Kuhnian theory of scientific revolutions—we cannot perform an experiment to see if perhaps a different way of understanding the natural world (say, one with no Newton) could have yielded a different evaluation of Kuhn's approach to theory change. Further, we can see that preregistration has often been presented in precisely the way that I have already cautioned against above, namely, as rejecting entirely the use of digital tools for discovery, in favor of pure hypothesis testing.

I think two potential responses to these critiques are important to highlight here. First, as I noted above, acknowledging that there is no clear crisis of "replication" in the humanities is not to say that there are not *other* uses for preregistration that would be useful in philosophical contexts. Philosophers using digital methods are just as subject as our scientific colleagues to worries surrounding, as I discussed in the last section, for instance, the potential for our unforced choices in methodology to constitute a path for the introduction of bias. To return to the example I discussed just above, imagine that in preparing a topic model I am interested at least in part in the dynamics of a specific concept within my corpus. If the first model I generate has a reasonable coherence score and seems to be free of meaningless or duplicate topics, and my concept of interest is particularly well picked out by one specific topic, there will be a natural pressure to accept this model and move on. This wouldn't in any straightforward sense be a fraudulent practice—this kind of judgment call is found throughout this kind of work. But it is worth questioning whether the presence of my desired concept in the model in fact exerted an undue influence on my choice, one that could have been avoided had I preregistered a plan for the evaluation and selection of models.

Second, I think that a careful look at the motivation behind preregistration begins to distill an important way to frame any potential response to all three of the problems that I detailed in section 3. Preregistration draws our attention to the importance of the relationship between the data that we have derived and the generalizations and analyses that we might produce from them, bin at least two different ways. First, in what ways have the very data themselves influenced some generalization drawn from them? Can those data be said to be testing that generalization, or not? And second, have those data influenced the choice of analysis method or the parameters used to produce the generalization itself? As I reconstruct the state of play a bit later on, I believe this question of the influences or relationship that holds between the data and these other aspects of our philosophical work is precisely the one that we need to ask—it opens space for a variety of more complex and nuanced answers that can better allow us to explore the use of both serendipitous discovery and hypothesis testing.

5. The Whig Interpretation of History

In 1931, the British historian of politics and science Herbert Butterfield, otherwise primarily known for works on the history of Christianity in England, published a short volume entitled *The Whig Interpretation of History*. Butterfield was bothered by what he took to be a destructive characteristic shared by many political histories of the day, "the tendency in many historians to write on the side of Protestants and Whigs, to praise revolutions provided they have been successful, to emphasize certain principles of progress in the past and to produce a story which is the ratification if not the glorification of the present" (1931, v). Such histories—*whiggish* histories—take both the success and the moral rectitude of our present moment for granted. The job of the historian, Butterfield decries, becomes to write a history that can explain how it is that we are now so right, and how it was that so many historical actors could have been so wrong for so long. The problems with any such story are manifold, but perhaps the most succinct way to put the problem is the one laid out by the environmental historian William Cronon: "Thanks in part to Butterfield, we now recognize such narratives as teleological, and we rightly suspect them of doing violence to the past by understanding and judging it with reference to anachronistic values in the present, however dear those values may be to our own hearts" (2012, 5). History is a deeply contingent affair; any approach that identifies within it "goals," whether descriptive states of affairs or normative clusters of values, should be kept at arm's length.

Butterfield himself is a difficult figure to parse, and exactly how historians across the twentieth century responded to his work makes for a fairly complex story (Sewell 2003). But the way in which Butterfield's caution was taken up by one particular discipline—the history of science—is not a complex story. The perils of whiggism are perhaps the most serious in crafting the history of science, where the pressure of contemporary theory weighs heavily and a realist epistemology could lead one to think that we are, in fact, steadily approximating the truth in the long run (about which more later). In that sense, the rejection of whiggism has been widely and deeply adopted by the community of historians of science. As Michael Gordin puts it, "In some ways, a militant hostility to Whiggish narratives *defines* the history of science against other fields, and one can often spot historians of science at a talk when they query the potentially Whiggish approach of a speaker in, say, military or legal history" (2014, 417).

Such an adherence makes a great deal of sense—one could surely point to numerous examples of whiggish histories that entirely obscure the actual practice of historical scientists.[10] But as David Hull rightly notes, an opposition to whiggism is only a negative constraint on the practice of the history of science, and just what is supposed to replace it is far less clear. The choice simply to accumulate historical facts and interpret them as minimally as possible—a sort of maximally "anti-whiggish" interpretation—seems to be no better solution. In Hull's words, "an inductivist philosophy of history is no less a philosophy of history because it is inductivist and widely shared by other historians" (1979, 2). At the very least, such an interpretation *is still an interpretation* and thus owes us a justification every bit as much as any whiggish interpretation would.

This was not lost on Butterfield in his original critique. He wrote there that "[o]ur assumptions do not matter if we are conscious that they are assumptions, but the most fallacious thing in the world is to organize our historical knowledge upon an assumption without realizing what we are doing, and then to make inferences from that organization and claim that these are the voice of history. It is at this point that we tend to fall into what I have nicknamed the whig fallacy" (1931, 23–24). Again, it is not the presence of assumptions per se that is the problem—it is the relationship between those background assumptions and the generalizations that follow after them that counts. We need not search for "a dispassionate scientific understanding of the past" (Jardine 2003, 132) or attempt to deny the fact that "the histories we write typically end somewhere different from where they begin" (Cronon 2012, 5). Rather, we have no choice but to embrace and defend the interpretive choices that we make.

It is here, I claim, that we find a commonality between preregistration and the example of whiggish history. Again, our attention is drawn to the question of what kinds of background theories we should "let into" our narratives and how we should justify our having done so. In section 3,

---

[10] The first chapters of introductory science textbooks are particularly likely to be offensive in this regard.

I mentioned Mercer's introduction of the Getting Things Right Constraint in the history of early modern philosophy. The argument that she goes on to make, however, is not to indict people for failing to adhere to this constraint. On the contrary (rephrased for our case here), she argues that the second-order question of whether or not to be "whiggish" is far less interesting, as it happens, than the first-order question of which kinds of context or background should in fact inform a particular explanation of interest (Mercer 2019).

We could see a number of ways in which this concern about whiggishness might manifest itself in work in digital philosophy. Any time that textual analyses are extended across a long time span, we run the risk that, whether for technical reasons (such as the dramatically larger number of articles and books published in recent decades) or conceptual ones (the analysis of conceptual or disciplinary structures, say, that only make sense in a contemporary context), the categories that we use to analyze sometimes quite historically remote texts will apply only with some degree of infelicity to the texts analyzed. The same could be said for citation-network or other scientometric analyses across large temporal, subject-area, or geographic scales—systems of publication, collaboration, mentoring, and training are highly situated both in time and in space, and it requires careful attention to detail to avoid precisely the kind of unjust extrapolation that Butterfield has in mind.

Of course, a host of ways to respond to this charge have been deployed in the historical literature, and I want to close this section by picking up on a provocative idea from the biologist and historian of science Ernst Mayr. Mayr spent much ink in the 1980s and 1990s defending himself against (entirely deserved) charges of whiggishness in his historical works on the life sciences. To justify his work, however, he pointed to particular features of the relationship between the subject matter of the history of science and the generalizations drawn from that subject matter: "[The charge of whiggishness] was based on the erroneous assumption that a sequence of theory changes in science is of the same nature as a sequence of political changes. Actually the two kinds of changes are in many respects very different from each other. ... [I]n a succession of theories dealing with the same scientific problem each step benefits from the new insights acquired by the preceding step and builds on it" (1990, 302). Put differently, Mayr is appealing to the very nature of science itself—for all that he is here using a naive, "accumulation of facts" picture of the scientific process that is today rather discredited—in order to claim that a certain kind of relationship between his background knowledge (namely, his knowledge that the future history of science would turn out in a particular way) is indeed relevant and acceptable to draw upon in telling that historical tale (rather than being perniciously whiggish). I consider a potential philosophical analogue to this kind of move in the next section.

To sum up the last two sections, then, I have argued that we can interpret the apparent tension between hypothesis and discovery in digital methods in the philosophy of science instead as a set of demands for the explanation of relationships or influences between our philosophical presuppositions and data, on the one hand, and the generalizations that we draw from those data, on the other. With Butterfield, we can question which of the influences that our theoretical or philosophical background might have on those results are in fact legitimate. With Nosek and Ledgerwood, we can interrogate the relationship between the data themselves and the inferences drawn from them. And with Mayr, we can more speculatively imagine what characteristics of the material that we're aiming to describe might be relevant for our conclusions.

6. From Demands to Open Challenges

In this section, I want to draw on another piece of recent work in which several coauthors and I laid out an approach to understanding the place of digital analyses in a more general framework for doing empirical philosophy of science (Lean, Rivelli, and Pence 2022). While the full structure of that paper's argument will not be necessary to my purposes here, I want to borrow its central reconstruction of what exactly that process looks like—that is, as a three-step procedure beginning with the scientific literature, moving to generalizations about that literature, and finally using those generalizations to inform conclusions in empirical philosophy of science (Figure 3).[11] The essential idea is that Figure 3 represents the "core" of an empirical approach to the philosophy of science. One begins with a body of products of the scientific process—be it journal articles, datasets, laboratory notebooks, or other such traces. One then attempts to construct generalizations from that empirical corpus about how it is that science works, whether in that particular laboratory or, more often, in that field or in science as a whole. This generalizing step is often the key move in such research, as we attempt to demonstrate that the scientific process shows certain kinds of reliable features that we can use to make philosophical inferences. Finally, we have to figure out how to construct such philosophical claims based upon those generalizations—how exactly can they be shown to be relevant for philosophical concerns?

In laying out where these demands for further explication fit into that three-part structure, I believe we will find ways in which we can transform those demands into challenges for future work on digital philosophy of science—in short, set some positive goals for scholars invested, as I am, in advancing this field and its prospects.

---

[11] In phrasing these in terms of scientific literature, I am reflecting my own group's focus on textual analysis; I believe the same considerations clearly apply to other parts of digital philosophy.

FIGURE 3. An excerpted portion of the central figure from Lean, Rivelli, and Pence 2022, representing schematically how scientific literature might inform empirical philosophy of science.

Let's begin with the common thread picked out by both the examples of preregistration and whig history. In both cases, we found evidence that Figure 3 needs at least one more box and arrow. In addition to being informed directly by the scientific literature, the generalizations that we draw will, of course, also be informed by our extant philosophical commitments, adding another "input" to the middle node in Figure 3. No reading of any text can occur in a philosophical vacuum. But this also turns into the first open challenge for philosophers wishing to use these methods. How exactly should we evaluate the potential impacts of our prior philosophical commitments on these empirical analyses? What kinds of such biases might exist, and how could we detect their presence or absence? If we want to produce an analysis independent of one such presupposition, how would we do so?

In general, because the methods of digital philosophy are so new, there is very little work directed at answering these questions in a philosophical context. Digital humanists, who have produced a fair bit of sustained critical analysis of their own tools and methods (e.g., Rogers 2013; Arthur and Bode 2014; Estrada 2014; Berry and Fagerjord 2017; and the discussion of the role of stylometrics in the analysis of Henry James present in Hoover 2007), have of course not done so with the peculiar concerns of philosophers in mind.[12] There is thus a significant space here for further work. We should encourage the pursuit of systematic study of the relationship between philosophical commitments and the very analysis tools of digital philosophy themselves. For example, it seems likely that differing views about the very nature of the scientific process will lead to different conclusions about how we ought to interpret the empirical signals coming from our study of scientific texts (Lean, Rivelli, and Pence 2022). It is also worth considering whether this extends not only to our views of social or community epistemology but also to ontology and metaphysics. Will adopting a realist or an anti-realist ontology, for instance, alter the appropriate epistemic attitude toward the results of these empirical analyses? More remotely, could our commitments to theories of causation, for instance, have downstream impacts on how we think about the nature of

---

[12] Jeremy Trevelyan Burman (2018) has also considered similar questions from the perspective of digital methods in the history of psychology.

these scientific products and the digital inferences we draw from them? These kinds of questions deserve to be explored in greater detail.

Second, consider the challenge raised by Nosek and colleagues, inspired by preregistration. As philosophy isn't faced with a replication crisis, the fervor present in preregistration advocates in the sciences would likely be misplaced in a digital-philosophy context. But that said, one can still defend the use of preregistration in cases where there is a chance for our unforced methodological choices to have undue influence on the results of our analyses. More broadly, one might be inspired by these kinds of worries to focus in a more dedicated way on the development of *best practices* regimes for digital analyses in philosophy. In much the same way that scientific data analysis is often governed by informal norms surrounding which software packages to use, default settings that should be respected, and so forth, we should encourage the development of these same sorts of norms in philosophical practice. As anyone who has been to a scientific journal club (reading group) meeting can attest, the very first action of any scientist confronted with a new article is to turn to the methods section and make sure that these choices all pass muster. In the language of Figure 3, we could consider this a reinforced emphasis on the arrow connecting the scientific literature to those generalizations—the technical details of this process clearly are extremely important.

Some such work already takes place, of course, in digital humanities journals, or in the particular technical papers that describe methodological advances, and these papers are fairly routinely cited by philosophers doing digital work. But spaces for dedicated philosophical discussion of this kind remain somewhat rare, with these methodological and technical points often being pushed into appendices or online-only content rather than developed and discussed as integral parts of our analytic work. Here, perhaps most of all, we have a need for sociological or professional change in order to build spaces for this kind of work. Some of these issues surround publication and credit. Broader digital humanities journals often aren't welcoming venues for philosophers, who in this case would largely be reworking questions already tackled by scholars in literary studies, history, or library science years or decades ago. Another issue involves interdisciplinarity. We have a great opportunity here to learn from other colleagues in the digital humanities, though often this philosophical commitments requires building bridges with communities that have historically been relatively remote from philosophy.

Third, and finally, consider the Mayr-inspired point about the very nature of the philosophy of science itself. Does and should our subject matter itself constrain the kinds of questions that digital methods might ask, or the kinds of answers that we might expect those questions to receive? One might call this a question of the *internal structuring* present within the philosophy of science: are there certain kinds of relationships between our methodological choices, the empirical facts on the ground,

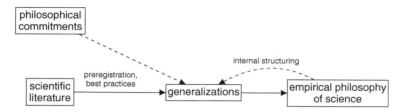

FIGURE 4. A modified version of Figure 3, adding in the kinds of concerns that might be raised by taking seriously the worries about practice in digital philosophy that I have raised here.

and our philosophical views, such that analyses taking some of these connections for granted are justified, while others are not? We might envision this as an arrow moving backwards from the third to the second box in Figure 3—that is, a connection between the nature of empirical philosophy of science itself and the generalizations that we might draw from the scientific literature (see the final resulting diagram in Figure 4).

An extreme example of this kind of structuring, for instance, might be found in radical skepticism about the external world.[13] Obviously, a view such as this will have far-reaching consequences for our other philosophical positions, as well as for what we might expect to find (or not) in the "empirical" record. A less extreme example might be Richard Boyd's argument for scientific realism. Quickly surfacing in arguments between Boyd and authors like Bas van Fraassen (1980), one of the points at issue between the scientific realist and the scientific anti-realist is the legitimacy of argument via inference to the best explanation. And yet, it is not only in science that such arguments occur—perhaps the most common way of interpreting the argument for scientific realism itself in philosophy of science is as a (philosophical, rather than scientific) inference to the best explanation. In that sense, our first-order views about ontology are directly tied to our second-order views about appropriate methodology. As Boyd himself puts it, "If what is at issue is the legitimacy of abductive inferences to theoretical explanations in general, then there is a kind of circularity in the appeal to a particular abduction of this sort in the defense of scientific realism. ... I suggest that our assessment of the import of the circularity in question should focus not on the legitimacy of the realist's abductive inference considered in isolation, but rather on the relative merits of the overall accounts of scientific knowledge which the empiricist and the realist defend" (1983, 80–81). That is, Boyd argues that the threat of circularity present here (using abduction to argue for the legitimacy of abduction) can be viewed as virtuous rather than vicious, if only we step back from the

---

[13] Thanks to Timothy Williamson for raising this example.

details of the fine-grained arguments for and against abduction itself and instead target the overall coherence of the systemic approaches that the realist and anti-realist offer us.

To be sure, there is no invocation here of digital methods in philosophy of science. But I think exactly this kind of relationship or "feedback" between different portions of our philosophical perspectives is what we should be on the lookout for, given a "whiggish" worry about the ways in which our philosophical positions might either support or undermine the use of some empirical tools. I have no clear predictions about where this kind of work might lead—but a clear demonstration of the *lack* of such internal structure would be no less valuable.

7. Conclusion: Future Steps

I began my argument here by pointing out an apparent tension in the reasons for which we might use digital methods in the philosophy of science. On the one hand, these methods can show us a host of unexpected and interesting features of the scientific process, features that might be exactly the kind of inspiration needed to develop new philosophical views. But on the other hand, and following on the concerns about spurious correlation and implicit assumptions present in the analysis of big data, it has been argued that the use of these two tools for discovery is dangerous and that we might instead be better off considering them as tools for the restricted *testing* of particular hypotheses, not their generation.

Such a tension puts us in an unenviable position, as taking either approach alone seems to deny us some of the real power of digital philosophy. The generation of novel hypotheses has already been important both in scientific contexts (e.g., Wilkinson and Huberman 2004; Altman et al. 2008) and in humanities contexts (e.g., see the discussion of the birth of "nouveaux observables" by means of digital analysis in Rastier 2010). We thus would be ill served by the outright rejection of either approach in favor of the other. A nuanced way to extract the advantages of both hypothesis testing and novel hypothesis generation is required.

This same tension has appeared in fields beyond philosophy—I thus turned to two such examples, one from contemporary data-driven science and one from the history of science. These other views of this same problem helped to shift our frame from one of testing versus discovery to a less binary view of the relationship between our data or background philosophical views, and the empirical results that we might draw from them. In the last section, I made this frame yet more precise, by splitting that question of relationships into three particular challenges for future digital philosophy of science.

To conclude, I want to consider how we might start to address these challenges. As I briefly noted in the last section, I believe that this largely turns on building institutional and professional spaces in which philosophers can discuss the kinds of questions that I have raised here. Three kinds of considerations are, I have argued, especially important. Philosophers need ways in which we can:

1. Work to illuminate the influences of our philosophical commitments on our empirical work;
2. discuss methodological questions and best practices in detail, perhaps with the aid of preregistration; and
3. explore whether the nature of philosophical questions themselves will alter that work.

As I mentioned, it's also unclear whether and when such work would be acceptable for publication in philosophy journals, and thus we may have community-level reforms to undertake as well, building opportunities for sharing and discussion among practitioners in this area.

In short, while digital methods in philosophy of science have much promise, I believe that this promise has to be tempered by careful and reflective thought about where, when, and how such methods will be most useful, as well as whether the kinds of uses that we envision for them will actually enable us to produce higher-quality philosophy. Much exciting work remains to be done.

References

Altman, Russ B., Casey M. Bergman, Judith Blake, Christian Blaschke, Aaron Cohen, Frank Gannon, Les Grivell, et al. 2008. "Open Access Text Mining for Biology—the Way Forward: Opinions from Leading Scientists." *Genome Biology* 9, suppl. 2: S7. doi:https://doi.org/10.1186/gb-2008-9-S2-S7.

Arthur, Paul Longley, and Katherine Bode, eds. 2014. *Advancing Digital Humanities: Research, Methods, Theories*. Basingstoke: Palgrave Macmillan.

Berry, David M., and Anders Fagerjord. 2017. *Digital Humanities: Knowledge and Critique in a Digital Age*. Cambridge: Polity.

Blei, David M. 2012. "Probabilistic Topic Models." *Communications of the ACM* 55, no. 4: 77. doi:https://doi.org/10.1145/2133806.2133826.

boyd, danah, and Kate Crawford. 2012. "Critical Questions for Big Data." *Information, Communication and Society* 15, no. 5: 662–79. doi:https://doi.org/10.1080/1369118X.2012.678878.

Boyd, Richard N. 1983. "On the Current Status of the Issue of Scientific Realism." *Erkenntnis* 19, nos. 1–3: 45–90. doi:https://doi.org/10.1007/BF00174775.

Buolamwini, Joy, and Timnit Gebru. 2018. "Gender Shades: Intersectional Accuracy Disparities in Commercial Gender Classification." *Proceedings of Machine Learning Research* 81: 1–15.

Burman, Jeremy Trevelyan. 2018. "Digital Methods Can Help You ... If You're Careful, Critical, and Not Historiographically Naïve." *History of Psychology* 21, no. 4: 297–301. doi:https://doi.org/10.1037/hop0000112.

Busa, R. 1980. "The Annals of Humanities Computing: The Index Thomisticus." *Computers and the Humanities* 14, no. 2: 83–90.

Butterfield, Herbert. 1931. *The Whig Interpretation of History*. London: Bell.

Calude, Cristian S., and Giuseppe Longo. 2017. "The Deluge of Spurious Correlations in Big Data." *Foundations of Science* 22, no. 3: 595–612. doi:https://doi.org/10.1007/s10699-016-9489-4.

Cronon, William. 2012. "Two Cheers for the Whig Interpretation of History." *Perspectives on History* 50, no. 6: 5.

de Solla Price, D. J. 1965. "Networks of Scientific Papers." *Science* 149, no. 3683: 510–15. doi:https://doi.org/10.1126/science.149.3683.510.

Douglas, Heather E. 2009. "Reintroducing Prediction to Explanation." *Philosophy of Science* 76, no. 4: 444–63. doi:https://doi.org/10.1086/648111.

Estrada, Daniel. 2014. "In Defense of the Digital Humanities as a Science." *Academia.edu*.

Garfield, Eugene. 1955. "Citation Indexes for Science: A New Dimension in Documentation Through Association of Ideas." *Science* 122, no. 3159: 108–11. doi:https://doi.org/10.1126/science.122.3159.108.

Gordin, Michael D. 2014. "The Tory Interpretation of History [Review of Hasok Chang, *Is Water H₂O?: Evidence, Realism and Pluralism*]." *Historical Studies in the Natural Sciences* 44, no. 4: 413–23. doi:https://doi.org/10.1525/hsns.2014.44.4.413.

Hoover, David L. 2007. "Corpus Stylistics, Stylometry, and the Styles of Henry James." *Style* 41, no. 2: 174–203.

Hull, David L. 1979. "In Defense of Presentism." *History and Theory* 18, no. 1: 1–15.

Jardine, Nick. 2003. "Whigs and Stories: Herbert Butterfield and the Historiography of Science." *History of Science* 41, no. 2: 125–40. doi:https://doi.org/10.1177/007327530304100201.

Kim, Kyung-Man. 1994. *Explaining Scientific Consensus: The Case of Mendelian Genetics*. New York: Guilford Press.

Lean, Oliver M., Luca Rivelli, and Charles H. Pence. Forthcoming. "Digital Literature Analysis for Empirical Philosophy of Science." *British Journal for the Philosophy of Science*. doi:https://doi.org/10.1086/715049.

Ledgerwood, Alison. 2018. "The Preregistration Revolution Needs to Distinguish Between Predictions and Analyses." *Proceedings of the National Academy of Sciences* 115, no. 45: E10516–17. doi:https://doi.org/10.1073/pnas.1812592115.

Leonelli, Sabina. 2016. *Data-Centric Biology: A Philosophical Study*. Chicago: University of Chicago Press.

Malaterre, Christophe, Jean-François Chartier, and Davide Pulizzotto. 2019. "What Is This Thing Called Philosophy of Science? A Computational Topic-Modeling Perspective, 1934." *HOPOS* 9, no. 2: 215–49. doi:https://doi.org/10.1086/704372.

Manovich, Lev. 2012. "How to Compare One Million Images?" In *Understanding Digital Humanities*, edited by David M. Berry, 249–78. London: Palgrave Macmillan. doi:https://doi.org/10.1057/9780230371934_14.

Mayr, Ernst. 1990. "When Is Historiography Whiggish?" *Journal of the History of Ideas* 51, no. 2: 301–9.

Mercer, Christia. 2019. "The Contextualist Revolution in Early Modern Philosophy." *Journal of the History of Philosophy* 57, no. 3: 529–48. doi:https://doi.org/10.1353/hph.2019.0057.

Mizrahi, Moti. 2020. "Hypothesis Testing in Scientific Practice: An Empirical Study." *International Studies in the Philosophy of Science* 33, no. 1: 1–21. doi:https://doi.org/10.1080/02698595.2020.1788348.

Munafò, Marcus R., Brian A. Nosek, Dorothy V. M. Bishop, Katherine S. Button, Christopher D. Chambers, Nathalie Percie du Sert, Uri Simonsohn, Eric-Jan Wagenmakers, Jennifer J. Ware, and John P. A. Ioannidis. 2017. "A Manifesto for Reproducible Science." *Nature Human Behaviour* 1: 0021. doi:https://doi.org/10.1038/S41562-016-0021.

Nosek, Brian A., Charles B. Ebersole, Alexander C. DeHaven, and David T. Mellor. 2018. "The Preregistration Revolution." *Proceedings of the National Academy of Sciences* 115, no. 11: 2600–2606. doi:https://doi.org/10.1073/pnas.1708274114.

Pence, Charles H. 2022. "How Not to Fight About Theory: The Debate Between Biometry and Mendelism in *Nature,* 1890–1915." In *The Dynamics of Science: Computational Frontiers in History and Philosophy of Science*, edited by Grant Ramsey and Andreas De Block. pp. 147–163. Pittsburgh: University of Pittsburgh Press.

Ramsey, Grant, and Charles H. Pence. 2016. "evoText: A New Tool for Analyzing the Biological Sciences." *Studies in History and Philosophy of Biological and Biomedical Sciences* 57: 83–87. doi:https://doi.org/10.1016/j.shpsc.2016.04.003.

Rastier, François. 2010. "Sémiotique et linguistique de corpus." *Signata: Annales des sémiotiques / Annals of Semiotics* no. 1 (December): 13–38. doi:https://doi.org/10.4000/signata.278.

Röder, Michael, Andreas Both, and Alexander Hinneburg. 2015. "Exploring the Space of Topic Coherence Measures." In *Proceedings of the Eighth ACM International Conference on Web Search and Data Mining*, 399–408. Shanghai: ACM. doi:https://doi.org/10.1145/2684822.2685324.

Rogers, Richard. 2013. *Digital Methods*. Cambridge, Mass.: MIT Press.

Sagoff, Mark. 2019. "Can Hypothesis-Driven Research Survive the Sequence-Data Deluge?" *Microbial Biotechnology* 12, no. 3: 414–20. doi:https://doi.org/10.1111/1751-7915.13377.

Sewell, Keith C. 2003. "The 'Herbert Butterfield Problem' and Its Resolution." *Journal of the History of Ideas* 64, no. 4: 599–618. doi:https://doi.org/10.1353/jhi.2004.0010.

Smaldino, Paul E., and Richard McElreath. 2016. "The Natural Selection of Bad Science." *Royal Society Open Science* 3, no. 9: 160384. doi:https://doi.org/10.1098/rsos.160384.

Soler, Léna, Sjoerd Zwart, Michael Lynch, and Vincent Israel-Jost, eds. 2014. *Science After the Practice Turn in the Philosophy, History, and Social Studies of Science*. New York: Routledge.

Underwood, Ted. 2017. "A Genealogy of Distant Reading." *Digital Humanities Quarterly* 011, no. 2.

van Fraassen, Bas C. 1980. *The Scientific Image*. Oxford: Clarendon Press.

Wilkinson, Dennis M., and Bernardo A. Huberman. 2004. "A Method for Finding Communities of Related Genes." *Proceedings of the National Academy of Sciences* 101, suppl. 1: 5241–48. doi:https://doi.org/10.1073/pnas.0307740100.

CHAPTER 7

ATTENTIONAL PROGRESS BY CONCEPTUAL ENGINEERING

EVE KITSIK

1. Introduction

Conceptual engineering—evaluating and improving concepts—is currently a hot topic. Many conferences, papers, and books are devoted to it. Proposals have been made to engineer the concepts of knowledge (Fassio and McKenna 2015; Nado 2021), truth (Scharp 2013), gender and race (Haslanger 2000), sexual orientation (Dembroff 2016), and misogyny (Manne 2018), to name just a few. Is all that attention to conceptual engineering justified? Some have doubts (e.g., Deutsch 2020a, 2020b; and 2021).[1] One line of thought underlying such doubts is that introducing new terms and reassigning old ones just enables more convenient ways of thinking and talking, but the important part is what we think and what we say: philosophy is about the world, not about concepts. Conceptual engineering, one might say, perhaps has its place in the preparatory phase of philosophical work, where we get our tools cleaned up and ready to go, but not in philosophizing itself, where we put the tools to use.[2]

My target is not specifically that line of thought but more generally someone who does not understand why conceptual engineering is getting so

---

[1] Deutsch singles out "pragmatic re-engineering," that is, merely changing speaker-meanings, as unworthy of attention: "[C]onceptual engineering, conceived as pragmatic re-engineering, deserves no more attention or hype, and the amount it has received thus far strikes me as fairly absurdly overblown" (2021, 11). Elsewhere, Deutsch extends this assessment to changing semantic meanings: "Changing semantic meanings is also utterly ineffective as a method of philosophy, one useless for solving philosophical problems" (2020b, 13).

[2] One might go even further, as Deutsch (2020a) appears to, and insist that there is no need for cleaning up: the ordinary concepts perform just fine at allowing us to refer to the relevant things in the world. But another conceptual conservative, Austin, suggests that some cleaning might be required: "[W]ords are our tools, and, as a minimum, we should use clean tools" (1956, 7).

Examining Philosophy Itself. Edited by Yafeng Shan.
Chapters and book compilation © 2023 Metaphilosophy LLC and John Wiley & Sons Ltd.
Published 2023 by John Wiley & Sons Ltd.

much attention as a philosophical method and suspects that the attention is largely undeserved. This essay offers one way of understanding the significance of conceptual engineering for philosophy, granting that it might not be the only way. Also, I am concerned only with how we can make philosophical progress by evaluating and improving the concepts that *philosophers* use, not with engineering the concepts used by nonphilosophers, such as natural or social scientists or society at large.

My proposal is especially fitting for the target I described: someone who suspects that conceptual engineering is getting too much attention. Such a target accepts the assumption that it is important to distribute philosophical attention well—for example, conceptual engineering should not get more than its fair share. That assumption about the importance of distributing attention well is crucial for my defense of conceptual engineering. I argue that by engineering the concepts that philosophers use, we can configure the prevailing patterns of attention in philosophy for the better. Furthermore, conceptual engineering thereby contributes to philosophical progress, either by focusing philosophers' attention on more important questions or by facilitating epistemic progress with the traditional questions, construed in a coarse-grained way.

The essay is structured as follows. In section 2, I clarify what I mean by "attention" and "configuring patterns of attention." I then discuss the different ways in which we can engineer concepts to configure the attention patterns in philosophy for the better: by engineering agenda-setting terms, such as "philosophy" and "metaphysics" (section 3); by constructing concepts to guide attention to neglected matters (section 4); by reassigning central terms, such as "belief" and "knowledge" (section 5); and by eliminating "red herring" concepts from philosophical discourse (section 6). In section 7, I explain how such attention configuring can contribute to philosophical progress. In section 8, I offer some concluding remarks.

2. Configuring Attention for the Better

An account of attention that works well enough for my purposes, without being crucial for them, is that attending to something is selecting it for action, including merely mental action (Allport 1987; Neumann 1987; Wu 2014). The things that we attend to, in this sense, are the parts of the world or our experience that we are attuned to and oriented toward, that we select for contemplating, praising, condemning, drawing conclusions from, grabbing, operating, running away from, and so on. In yet other words, the things that we attend to are salient for us. (These things may be merely in the mind or are phenomena in the external world—I leave this open.)

In order to talk about configuring patterns of attention for the better, we need to think of such patterns as good or bad, better or worse, right or wrong. As Watzl (2022) points out, in a paper delineating the ethics of attention as a field of inquiry, this field is largely unexplored, compared to, say, the ethics of belief.[3] But we do make normative judgments about attention. For example, we argue about whose statue should be in the central square, who should be taught as part of the canon, and whether conceptual engineering should get so much attention.

My preferred account of attention, as selection for action, suggests a way of outlining an ethics of attention. If attention is selection of action, then we can evaluate both the selected object and the action that it is selected for. We thus ask: Are the right things selected for the right actions? Or, to put it another way: Are we attuned to the right things in the right ways? Are the right things salient to us in the right respect, in the right circumstances?[4] Even when we merely complain that someone or something gets too much or too little attention, we usually have in mind a certain kind of attention, certain actions that the object is selected for (or not). For example, when we say that more attention should be given to women in professional meetings, we have in mind attention that involves taking seriously their ideas and not, for example, ridiculing or sexualizing attention.

This essay is concerned with improving *patterns* of attention, not single instances of (im)proper selection for action. For example, when we complain about a driver's negligent slip of attention that resulted in an accident, this criticism concerns an instance of improper attention. The driver momentarily failed to select the surrounding traffic for observing and reacting. But we can also complain about *patterns* of attention, for example, a driver's pattern of failing to pay proper attention to the traffic. Further, we can distinguish between individual and collective patterns of attention. For example, we can complain that an individual is unduly concerned with other people's looks or that they think too much or too little about diet and health; and we can make similar complaints about the collective patterns of attention in contemporary Western societies.

Problematic collective patterns of attention, as Gardiner (2022) points out, are not always reducible to individuals' problematic patterns of attention. Using Gardiner's example, suppose that female-pattern heart disease is under-researched, compared to male-pattern heart disease. This is not a problem with the individual researchers' patterns of attention: there is nothing wrong with an individual focusing exclusively on male-pattern heart disease, to study it in depth. The problem only emerges at the collective level, due to the lack of researchers focusing on female-pattern heart disease.

---

[3] This is changing, however: there are several research projects under way on the ethics (norms, ideals, and so forth) of attention.

[4] Although Watzl (2022) does not frame attention in terms of selection for action, he makes a similar distinction between "manner-based" and "content-based" norms of attention. And Gardiner (2022) similarly writes about being attuned to the right things in the right ways.

Now, I am concerned with philosophers' collective patterns of attention: how we can configure these patterns for the better by engineering the concepts that philosophers use. I am thus concerned with shaping what phenomena, issues, or whole research areas philosophers tend to select for philosophical action, for thinking about and discussing, for raising questions about, and for forming hypotheses in response to existing questions. When we complain that philosophers are thinking and talking too much about, say, conceptual engineering, knowledge, and grounding, or that they are not thinking and talking enough about, say, wars and education, then we are complaining about the collective patterns of attention in philosophy. The point of such complaints is not that no philosopher should focus exclusively on knowledge, or that all philosophers should do at least a bit of work on wars. The problem, if there is one, emerges at the collective level.

How can we configure such collective patterns of attention? Two sorts of factors can be shaped: the "internal" and the "external" setup. Watzl, who also mentions engineering attention, focuses on external factors: "Our world is attentionally engineered. ... Channels for attention are carved into the fabric of our homes, the news we watch, the social media we consume, and into the urban landscapes around us" (2017, 1). If problematic channels of attention are carved into our environment, then we can shape the environment to shape the patterns of attention for the better. Gardiner (2022) similarly focuses on the ways in which we can modify the environment to bring about the desired change in patterns of attention. For example, in order to draw other scientists' attention to female-pattern heart disease, individuals could raise questions about it at conferences or feature it on syllabi, and institutions could offer funding opportunities and prizes or host conferences on the topic. This is all about changing the environment in which the target subjects (those who are to attend to the neglected issue of female-pattern heart disease) find themselves in.

I suggest that conceptual engineering can also be a way of shaping patterns of attention—shaping them from the "inside" rather than by shaping the environment. To make vivid the distinction between the internal and the external aspects of the attentional configuration, consider the following example. Conference rooms are set up so that the chairs are facing the speaker, who is well visible and audible: the external setup facilitates selecting the speaker for listening. But perhaps some audience members are uninterested in the topic or have prejudices related to the speaker's age or gender. Then their internal setup does not favor attending to the speaker. Statues on central squares, funding and publication opportunities for certain topics, and prime-time or front-page news are parts of an external setup that facilitates attending to certain things rather than others. And concepts, which I now turn to, are parts of the internal setup. Our minds as well as our environment shape what we attend to; and we can shape our minds as well as our environment to configure attention for the better.

A qualification is immediately called for: the distinction between engineering the environment and engineering minds (including the concepts in the minds) is a rough one. We will not go drilling into brains, after all. Presumably, conceptual engineering will also involve interfering with the environment (for example, with how the people that one encounters tend to use words). But I do put concepts in individual minds: they are not floating in the external world. That might make one think that semantic internalism is presupposed here. But it is not: we need not identify the relevant "concepts" (those that conceptual engineers evaluate and improve) with semantic meanings, as, for example, Cappelen (2018) does. We can instead take the relevant concepts to be the meanings that speakers associate with their words, that is, speaker meanings (Pinder 2021). Or we can construe the concepts as bodies of information associated with a label and retrieved by default in categorizing and other judgment making (Machery 2017; Isaac 2020). Such bodies of information can include prototypes, exemplars, and theorylike structures. Both the bodies of information that we automatically draw on and the definitions that we consciously endorse play a role in the internal setup of attention patterns.

3. Engineering Agenda-Setting Concepts

How can we shift philosophers' patterns of attention by engineering such internal concepts? At a very general level, we can engineer what I call "agenda-setting concepts," such as the concepts of philosophy, metaphysics, and epistemology. These concepts set the agenda in the sense that they delineate what philosophers should do, as philosophers, either generally or in a subdomain; and these concepts also shape the priorities within the agenda, insofar as they involve some division between the core and the margins.

Such agenda-setting concepts influence what philosophers pay attention to: what they select for action, what is salient to them as a potential object of philosophical (or metaphysical, epistemological, and the like) inquiry. This can work in various ways. Philosophers can—perhaps unconsciously—self-regulate their activity, aligning their topics with what they think of as properly or centrally philosophical. But a philosopher's agenda-setting concepts can also influence the attention-configuring environment that other philosophers find themselves in. For example, a journal editor's agenda-setting concepts can contribute to the journal publishing mostly on "core" topics; and other philosophers will then face the papers published in that journal as a part of their external setup, in which these topics are salient, making this audience more likely to work on these topics themselves.

Concerns have been raised that such agenda-setting concepts can be exclusionary or marginalizing. Dotson, for example, critiques the gate-keeping culture of philosophy that requires diverse approaches to legitimize themselves as "philosophical" with reference to dominant standards and expectations. She suggests that even Priest's seemingly permissive view of philosophy, as "intellectual inquiry in which *anything* is open to critical challenge and scrutiny" (Priest 2006, 202), can become constrictive, within such a culture (Dotson 2012, 26). Regardless of what one thinks of Priest's definition, a narrow concept of philosophy, when widely accepted, can surely make it harder for nonconforming philosophers to disseminate their work and have it taken seriously, or even to embark on such work in the first place.[5] In addition to exclusionary views of philosophy, a problematic core/periphery distinction has been criticized. For example, Kitcher (2011) argues that our "image" of philosophy, which presents abstract and theoretical philosophy as the "core," gets things wrong: applied philosophy that engages with the challenges of the time should rather have that central status.[6] Brake is also not content with the current core/periphery division, but instead of turning it around would rather dissolve any evaluative division of this sort: "[N]o topics should be off the table *a priori* as unphilosophical or marginal; the evaluative distinction between margin and center in philosophy should be abandoned altogether" (2017, 35).

Similar concerns have been raised about "metaphysics" and "epistemology." Barnes (2014) argues that some accounts of what metaphysics is exclude feminist metaphysics of gender by putting too much emphasis on fundamentality, whereas gender is a nonfundamental phenomenon. The worry seems to be that the metaphysics of gender might not get the attention it deserves when it is denied a place within an established and central field of philosophy, such as metaphysics.[7] Further, Rooney complains about the marginalization of feminist epistemology, the "assumption that feminist epistemology is not epistemology 'proper'" (2011, 3). Here as well this assumption apparently has to do with how we implicitly represent the core and the margins of epistemology.

Since some of these criticisms of agenda-setting concepts are about how this or that philosopher has defined, say, "philosophy" or "metaphysics," it is worth emphasizing that the agenda-setting concepts of interest are usually not consciously endorsed and enforced definitions. To illustrate this,

---

[5] Solomon has also raised the worry about the exclusionary concept of philosophy: "Our critical scrutiny today should be turned on the word 'philosophy' itself, along with its history, to realize that what was once a liberating concept has today become a constricted, oppressive, and ethnocentric one" (2001, 101).

[6] It should be noted that applied philosophy has become much more mainstream and well respected over the past decade.

[7] An alternative reading is that feminist metaphysics just *is* metaphysics (and a particularly valuable part of it), and hence the criticized definitions of metaphysics get the extension wrong. But this reading misses an important aspect of the worry: failure to classify feminist metaphysics as metaphysics is somehow bad for feminist metaphysics, in a way that goes beyond wrongful misclassification. It should also be mentioned that Sider (2017) and Schaffer (2017) have responded to the criticism, defending their respective accounts.

consider Jenkins's recollection of how a fellow student, at a social event in the beginning of their graduate studies, commented on her field of research, the metaphysics of gender: "That's not philosophy." Jenkins reflects: "[I]t seemed to me that his reaction arose in part from genuine bemusement: my project really was not recognisable to him as a philosophical enterprise" (2014, 262). The fellow student did not appeal to a definition of philosophy that Jenkins's project failed to satisfy. Perhaps he had in mind a prototypi-cal philosopher or philosophical project, or a collection of exemplars, some more central than others, and metaphysics of gender did not seem to fit in. Whatever exactly went on in that young man's head, this is plausibly how agenda-setting concepts often work: not by people endorsing and enforcing explicit definitions but by people drawing on implicit bodies of information.

Just as racism does not originate from racial slurs, philosophical trends and tendencies do not originate from the agenda-setting concepts. But racial slurs do play a role in perpetuating racism, and the fight against racism cannot ignore that. Similarly, agenda-setting concepts play a role in perpetuating the trends and tendencies in philosophy. Accordingly, these concepts are potential points of intervention when the trends and tendencies are problematic or suboptimal.

So, one way of configuring the patterns of attention in philosophy is by evaluating and improving our agenda-setting concepts. It is not obvious how to go about changing these concepts, or how to even establish what they are currently like and in what regards they need improving. But with such questions, the fast-developing field of conceptual engineering can, one hopes, help.

4. Constructing Concepts

There are also more microlevel ways of configuring philosophical atten-tion by engineering concepts. One of these is by introducing new terms that do not yet have important uses in philosophy, in order to draw attention to something worthy of attention. Chalmers offers examples of fruitful conceptual innovations in philosophy, including supervenience, grounding, Carnap's intension, Frege's sense, Grice's implicature, Kripke's rigid designator, Gendler's alief, and Fricker's epistemic injustice and its varieties (2020, 4–6). We can also construct new lower-level agenda-setting concepts, to guide attention to less determinate sets of issues and phe-nomena; examples include the concepts of political epistemology, social epistemology, and social ontology.

The idea is not that without the introduced terms we would be unable to speak or think about the relevant phenomena. After all, when a term is introduced, one must define it or otherwise indicate what it means or how it is to be used, in the context. So, in principle, we could use those definitions or indications every time. On such grounds, Deutsch holds that stipulative introduction is generally a matter of "syntactic convenience" and unremarkable as a philosophical method: "Stipulative introduction won't reveal whether we have free will, all women are subordinated, or knowledge is justified true belief. In fact, it seems that most of its value derives from syntactic convenience: via stipulative introduction, we can replace longer descriptions ('desk chair with five legs') with a shorter, single term ('brollop')" (2020a, 3945).

Of course, we sometimes just introduce technical terms to avoid writing out an extended description every time. This makes life easier for the writer and the readers, without reconfiguring the patterns of attention in the discipline. But the above examples are more significant: new phenomena or issues have been successfully put on philosophers' shared agenda.

Just announcing a name for something, however, does not put it on shared agendas. The ingenious part in such attentional reconfiguration is identifying neglected significant phenomena and convincing others of their significance. One might think that perhaps the ingenious part is not conceptual engineering. If, however, we think of conceptual engineering as improving the attentional configuration of philosophy, then identifying significant neglected phenomena and convincing others of their significance is surely a part of that job. Choosing a good label, such as "supervenience" or "grounding," is also a part of the job. But it would be question-begging for someone arguing against the significance of conceptual engineering to insist that only the relatively insignificant labeling phase counts as "conceptual engineering" and that the ingenious part of identifying the significant phenomena and convincing others of the significance does not.

5. Reassigning Central Terms

Perhaps more controversially and interestingly, we can also configure attention for the better by engineering terms that already have important uses in philosophy and elsewhere. The reengineering of agenda-setting concepts, discussed above, is a variety of this; but here I am concerned with "smaller" concepts denoting specific phenomena, rather than research areas.

An example is Schwitzgebel's case for a pragmatic concept of belief. He draws a distinction between the intellectualist concept, according to which belief consists in intellectually endorsing a proposition, and his preferred pragmatic concept, which additionally requires a wide range of relevant behavioral and phenomenal dispositions. Schwitzgebel's main example is the following (2021, 354–55). Daniel (a fictional character introduced by Schwitzgebel) intellectually endorses the view that low-wage workers deserve as much respect as well-paid people. Yet, it strikes Daniel as rude when a poorly dressed customer interrupts a well-dressed man's conversation with a shop employee; and he has a passing feeling that something is wrong when he sees a migrant laborer in a nice plane seat with extra leg room, while a rich-looking fellow is cramped in a middle seat.

And so on: Daniel's phenomenal reactions and behavior do not always fit what he consciously, intellectually endorses. He has the "intellectualist" belief but does not have the "pragmatic" belief. Schwitzgebel argues that the demanding pragmatic concept, which requires the full range of relevant dispositions, "directs our attention to what we ought to care about most in thinking about belief: our overall ways of acting in and reacting to the world" (351).

If we just wanted to talk about both kinds of "belief" conveniently and clearly, we could introduce terms like "intellectualist belief" and "pragmatic belief." But Schwitzgebel is against such equal treatment. He argues that pragmatic belief should get the attention that comes with the term "belief": "Central terms should track matters of central importance. In general, attaching central terms to phenomena of secondary importance risks misdirecting disciplinary attention, risks signaling to outsiders and new participants that the secondary phenomenon is more important than it is, and risks failing to make important patterns as salient as they should be" (2021, 359).

What makes pragmatic belief more attention worthy than mere intellectualist belief? Schwitzgebel emphasizes that it is important to get the full range of dispositions right and to align how we behave and react with what we intellectually endorse. Given that philosophers so often discuss how to get our "beliefs" right, what we should "believe" and why, it makes sense that "belief" should stand for the most important thing in the vicinity that we should get right. Schwitzgebel does allow philosophers to also discuss purely intellectualist beliefs, and how to get these right, but since this is a less important matter, it should not get the amplification that comes with the entrenched term "belief." Instead, he recommends using the term "judgment" for mere intellectual endorsement (2021, 359).

Although the argument from attention-worthiness is usually not put forth so explicitly, we can find more instances in the literature on conceptual engineering. For example, Clark and Chalmers (1998) proposed that the term "belief" should cover externally stored and easily accessible information as well as the beliefs stored in the head. Similarly to Schwitzgebel (although without using the word "attention"), Chalmers has justified using the term "belief" for the broader category with the centrality of the term: "[I]n practice the word 'belief' plays a central role in both social and scientific explanation. So attaching the word 'belief' to e-belief helps to create a mindset where e-belief can actually play those roles" (2020, 8). In passing, Chalmers has made a similar suggestion about "meaning": "In philosophy, 'meaning' functions as something of an honorific (it attracts people to its study), so if one thinks that meaning$_1$ is more important that meaning$_2$, one might hold that 'meaning' ought to be used for meaning$_1$" (2011, 542).

Further, Haslanger's proposal about gender terms and Manne's proposal about "misogyny" can be understood along these lines. Haslanger writes about her counterintuitive definitions: "[N]either ordinary usage nor empirical investigation is overriding, for there is a stipulative element to the project: *this* is the phenomenon we need to be thinking about" (2000, 34). In other words, the categories that she points to should receive philosophers' attention. Manne defines "misogyny," in contrast to the word's usual association with an individual's hatred for women, as "primarily a property of social systems or environments as a whole" (2018, 33). Although this is not explicit in Haslanger or Manne, both can be seen as insisting on using the old words because the familiarity and centrality of these words facilitates attending to the phenomena in the vicinity that are most in need of attention, given our relevant interests and purposes.

These examples suggest a general strategy: instead of engaging in lengthy debates related to ordinary terms and appealing to (what at least seem to be) linguistic intuitions, we could redirect at least some of these efforts toward identifying the most attention-worthy phenomena in the vicinity.[8] This is not to say that all interest in ordinary concepts (and the methods of conceptual analysis that serve such interest) is out of place. But there may well be matters more worthy of philosophers' attention, and it is no wonder that impatience is growing with the "navel-gazing," to use Eklund's term (2017, 192). To some extent, parochialism is counteracted by cross-cultural and cross-linguistic studies of, for example, epistemic concepts (Mizumoto, Stich, and McCready 2018; Mizumoto, Ganery, and Goddard 2020). But this still offers only a limited playground. Why not think about possible concepts in the vicinity of the English concepts, regardless of whether they prevail in any actual culture? Might reassigning the ordinary terms to such alternative concepts, within philosophy, help us attend to more attention-worthy phenomena?[9] These considerations are especially pressing for the *central* terms of philosophy, such as "belief," given their attention-attracting power.

But there are also pitfalls in generalizing this strategy, and these should be kept in mind. Consider "knowledge." Our agenda-setting concept of philosophy establishes epistemology as a core subfield, and the agenda-setting concept of epistemology in turn establishes knowledge as the top item on its agenda. Epistemology is often thought to revolve around knowledge: what knowledge is, how we get it, how we transmit it, whether we have it at all, and so on. Suppose, however, that there is a more valuable state

---

[8] Thinking about conceptual reengineering like this escapes the Strawsonian "change of subject" challenge (Strawson 1963): the *aim* of conceptual reengineering, on this view, is to redirect philosophers' attention to the most worthwhile subject for philosophers in the vicinity of the ordinary term. For a similar response to the change of subject challenge, see Knoll (2020), who argues that it is fine for conceptual engineers to change the topic, since changing topics for the better can in fact be seen as the aim of conceptual engineering.

[9] Grundmann writes, in this spirit, that even if there is no cultural variance in epistemic terms, the worry remains "that these terms might not refer to what is epistemically most relevant and valuable" (2020, 230).

in the vicinity that is more worthy of philosophers' attention. This is not wild speculation, since "knowledge," as standardly understood in philosophy, includes some pretty mundane states, such as the state that we are in when we know how many coins the man who will get the job has in his pocket. Let us call the more valuable state "the amazing state." Maybe it is knowledge about objectively important matters, or systematic knowledge, or both; maybe it is not any kind of knowledge but something else entirely. Currently, "knowledge" is thought to be what epistemology is centrally about. To give this place to the amazing state, should we then agree, among philosophers, to call the amazing state "knowledge"?

Even if this could work in principle, problems are likely to arise in practice. First, let us look at some issues of implementation. Even supposing that philosophers are willing to go along with this attention-configuring program, the current associations with the term "knowledge" might stand in the way, especially since philosophers will need to go on using the term in the old way outside philosophy. Philosophers might also need another term to talk about (good old mundane) knowledge, insofar as it deserves *some* attention, although not all the attention it is currently getting. Having both phenomena in the picture—what we used to call "knowledge" and now call something else, and what we now call "knowledge"—will make things even more confusing. Further, these psychological obstacles for motivated participants notwithstanding, it seems naive to expect that most philosophers would even try to go along with the program; widespread incompliance seems like a more realistic outcome.

Second, in addition to the implementation problems within philosophy, the move would create communication barriers with outsiders who use the term in the old way, reinforcing the impression of philosophy as something esoteric and not especially sensible. All things considered, it might be best to keep using "knowledge" in the old way, or reasonably close to the old way. Perhaps this means that we should restrict philosophical reassignments to the most attention-worthy candidates in the *immediate* vicinity, possibly the strands already present in ordinary usage. To some extent, such attention configuration has already happened with "knowledge." Philosophers usually assume that knowledge is factive: if you know that p, then p is true. But "know" is sometimes used non-factively in ordinary discourse, for example: "Everyone knew that stress caused ulcers, before two Australian doctors in the early 80s proved that ulcers are actually caused by bacterial infection" (Hazlett 2010, 501). Philosophers are mostly not bothered by this, aware that they can neglect aspects of ordinary usage, to focus on something worth focusing on.

Reassigning "knowledge" to the amazing state would likely go too far, then. But other conceptual engineering strategies can help with the attention configuration in such cases. For example, instead of engineering "knowledge," we could engineer the agenda-setting concept of epistemology, so that it would establish the amazing state as the top item on its agenda. We could also give the amazing state a better name—assuming that there isn't a perfectly fitting one, such as "understanding" or "wisdom," already available in ordinary language. (This is a simplified picture: there are probably many "amazing states," and perhaps also terrible states, that are good candidates for some of the attention that knowledge is currently getting. So, there is more work to do here than just describing and naming a single state and establishing it as the central one in epistemology.)

6. Eliminating Red Herrings

Eliminating concepts can also be seen as a way of configuring attention. Consider Chalmers's (2011) "method of elimination": asking the participants of potentially verbal disputes to restate their disagreement without certain terms. Resolving or clarifying disputes by this method directs the disputants' attention to worthier matters. For example, when we ban the word "alone" from a dispute over whether Lee Harvey Oswald acted alone, the dispute can be easily restated and clarified as one about whether somebody helped Oswald; but when we ban "planet" from a dispute over "Pluto is a planet," it is hard to find the remaining disagreement; hence the dispute is likely verbal: that is, only about the meaning of "planet" (Chalmers 2011, 527). The verbalness diagnosis suggests that we should end the dispute and concentrate our efforts on something else entirely.

Conceptual engineering is usually not thought to be about changing the ways people use terms in very local contexts, such as a single dispute between certain participants. Accordingly, we might not want to think of the term-banning interventions described above as instances of conceptual engineering. But consider instead proposals for philosophers to stop using certain terms (say, "epistemic" and "intuition") altogether, because this would make it clearer what, if anything, they disagree about, and would usefully redirect attention either to the crux of the disagreements or to different worthwhile issues (if there is no genuine disagreement pertaining to the original disputes). For example, Hazlett suggests that the term "epistemic" should receive this treatment: "Take any contemporary philosophical essay and consider each use of 'epistemic.' I submit that each is either superfluous—in which case to be stricken—or replaceable with alternative jargon—in which case to be so replaced" (2016, 547). (See also Cohen 2016 for related criticism of the term "epistemic.")

Perhaps some concepts in philosophy, then, are red herrings: they lead only to pointless verbal disputes, distracting philosophers from addressing the (underlying or more distant) attention-worthy questions. Eliminating the red herring concepts from philosophical discourse would then be a way of configuring philosophers' attention patterns for the better.

7. Attentional Improvement as Progress

We have seen how some varieties of conceptual engineering (reengineering the agenda-setting concepts and the central concepts of philosophy, constructing and eliminating concepts) can contribute to configuring philosophical attention for the better. These methods, in other words, help philosophers to attend to attention-worthy issues, to select the right objects for philosophical action. Now, how is this progress? We can think of this in two ways. First, focusing philosophers' attention on more important questions contributes to truth, knowledge, and understanding *about more important matters*—a distinct dimension of progress. Second, one might also say that attention configuration by conceptual engineering contributes to epistemic progress with the broad umbrella questions that philosophers have been tackling all along. Let us look at these options in turn.

The recent discussion on philosophical progress revolves around whether philosophy has made and can be expected to make significant progress, especially in comparison with the "hard" sciences.[10] A common view in that discussion is that philosophical progress is primarily a matter of gaining truth, knowledge, and/or understanding regarding philosophical questions (their answers or subject matters).[11] Sometimes, the issue is further constrained to progress with the "big" questions, such as the mind-body relationship or our knowledge of the external world (Chalmers 2015, 5). If gaining truth, knowledge, and/or understanding about (the answers to or the subject matters of) philosophical questions is indeed a dimension of philosophical progress, then another dimension seems to concern the importance and relevance of those questions. That other dimension is not always sufficiently recognized in the discussion on philosophical progress.[12] But it needs recognition: epistemic progress on insignificant questions is not worth much; and the more attention worthy the subject matter, the more valuable the truth, knowledge, and understanding.

[10] E.g., Chalmers 2015, Cappelen 2017, Stoljar 2017, Blackford and Broderick 2017, Hermann et al. 2020, Ross 2021, Dellsén, Lawler, and Norton 2021.

[11] For example, Stoljar (2017, 21) and Gutting (2009) focus on knowledge as the aim. Chalmers frames his benchmark for progress in terms of truth (collective convergence to the truth about the big questions); but he also suggests that pervasive disagreement is worrying because it shows that philosophers are not gaining knowledge, either individually or collectively (2015, 14–16). For discussions of understanding as the aim, see Hacker 2009, Graham 2017, Bengson, Cuneo, and Shafer-Landau 2019, Dellsén, Lawler, and Norton 2021, and Hannon and Nguyen manuscript.

[12] But Brake, for example, suggests that we should also recognize something like attentional progress: "We should reject the weight that is given to a narrow set of historically defined questions in measuring philosophical progress and consider philosophy's extension and application in different areas as a form of progress" (2017, 35). Similarly, Ross writes: "Wondering about a new and important question is a distinct form of progress in its own right" (2021, 750).

While truth, knowledge, or understanding regarding insignificant matters is not worth much, attentional progress alone is also not worth much.
For example, suppose that philosophers' attention shifted from the norms
of intellectualist belief to a more worthwhile topic, the norms of pragmatic
belief; and that they were hopelessly inept at investigating the former issue
and are just as inept at investigating the latter. It is doubtful that significant
progress has then been made merely in virtue of philosophers attending to
the more attention-worthy matter. Maybe philosophers would gain in terms
of the cognitive virtue of proper attunement. But it makes sense to think
of philosophers as serving the wider research community or the society at
large: delivering truths, knowledge, or understanding to others, rather than
acquiring epistemic or other goods for themselves. And from that perspective, mere attentional progress is rather like the progress made by someone
who never keeps their promises but consistently makes ever better, more
worthwhile promises—merely setting and frustrating greater expectations.
The value of attentional progress by conceptual engineering is thus conditional on philosophers' capability of securing other forms of progress,
that is, gaining truth, knowledge, or understanding. I do not discuss here
whether that condition is satisfied (but I see no reason to be particularly
skeptical).[13]

Instead, I briefly discuss another way in which we can think of attentional progress by conceptual engineering: not by shifting philosophers'
collective focus to more important questions, but by helping them to
address the same old questions. To explain: there is a sense in which
focusing on the norms of pragmatic belief, instead of the norms of
intellectualist belief, for example, changes the topic of discussion. But
there is also a broader topic that persists through the shift: How should we
govern our mental lives, what norms apply to representing and responding
to the world? Or even: How should we live? We can think of the conceptual
shifts, concept introductions, and concept eliminations as making salient
phenomena that are especially relevant for addressing such broad umbrella
questions, and thereby contributing to gaining truth, knowledge, and
understanding on important matters that have always given philosophers
sleepless nights. I leave it open whether we should cast attentional progress
by conceptual engineering in the first or the second way, and whether
and how these approaches could be combined; either approach suffices
to make good on the claim that conceptual engineering can contribute
to philosophical progress by configuring patterns of attention for the
better.

---

[13] For a response to skepticism related to pervasive disagreement in philosophy, see Cappelen 2017.

8. Concluding Remarks

I have argued that conceptual engineering deserves attention as a method that can contribute to philosophical progress, either by shifting philosophers' attention to more important questions or by making phenomena that are especially relevant for addressing the old umbrella questions of philosophy properly salient. If we care about what gets attention in philosophy, then we should care about conceptual engineering as a method that facilitates progress on that front. More specifically, we can make attentional progress by critically evaluating and improving our agenda-setting concepts, by constructing concepts that draw attention to attention-worthy phenomena, by reassigning central terms to the most attention-worthy phenomena in the vicinity, and by eliminating red herring concepts in order to redirect attention to more worthwhile discussions.

Further, acknowledging that conceptual engineering has this important role in philosophy—shaping philosophers' internal attentional configuration for the better—in no way threatens the view that philosophy is ultimately about the world and not about concepts. Conceptual engineering, on the contrary, facilitates engaging with the attention-worthy parts of the world.

Acknowledgments

I wish to thank the audiences of the online conference "New Directions in Metaphilosophy" at the University of Kent and the CONCEPT group's brown bag meeting at the University of Cologne, as well as Thomas Grundmann, Mark Pinder, and the referees for *Metaphilosophy* for very helpful comments and discussion.

References

Allport, Alan. 1987. "Selection for Action: Some Behavioural and Neurophysiological Considerations of Attention and Action." In *Perspectives on Perception and Action*, edited by Herbert Heuer and Andries F. Sanders, 395–419. Hillsdale, N.J.: Lawrence Erlbaum.

Austin, J. L. 1956. "A Plea for Excuses." *Proceedings of the Aristotelian Society*, new series, 57: 1–30.

Barnes, Elizabeth. 2014. "Going Beyond the Fundamental: Feminism in Contemporary Metaphysics." *Proceedings of the Aristotelian Society* 114, no. 3: 335–51.

Bengson, John, Terence Cuneo, and Russ Shafer-Landau. 2019. "Method in the Service of Progress." *Analytic Philosophy* 60, no. 3: 179–205.

Blackford, Russell, and Damien Broderick (eds.). 2017. *Philosophy's Future: The Problem of Philosophical Progress*. Hoboken, N.J.: Wiley Blackwell.

Brake, Elizabeth. 2017. "Making Philosophical Progress: The Big Questions, Applied Philosophy, and the Profession." *Social Philosophy and Policy* 34, no. 2: 23–45.

Cappelen, Herman. 2017. "Disagreement in Philosophy: An Optimistic Perspective." In *The Cambridge Companion to Philosophical Methodology*, edited by Giuseppina D'Oro and Søren Overgaard, 56–74. Cambridge: Cambridge University Press.

Cappelen, Herman. 2018. *Fixing Language: An Essay on Conceptual Engineering*. Oxford: Oxford University Press.

Chalmers, David. 2011. "Verbal Disputes." *Philosophical Review* 120, no. 4: 515–66.

Chalmers, David. 2015. "Why Isn't There More Progress in Philosophy?" *Philosophy* 90: 3–31.

Chalmers, David. 2020. "What Is Conceptual Engineering and What Should It Be?" *Inquiry*. https://doi.org/10.1080/0020174X.2020.1817141

Clark, Andy, and David Chalmers. 1998. "The Extended Mind." *Analysis* 58, no. 1: 7–19.

Cohen, Stewart. 2016. "Theorizing About the Epistemic." *Inquiry* 59, nos. 7–8: 839–57.

Dellsén, Finnur, Insa Lawler, and James Norton. 2021. "Thinking About Progress: From Science to Philosophy." *Noûs*, https://doi.org/10.1111/nous.12383

Dembroff, Robin A. 2016. "What Is Sexual Orientation?" *Philosophers' Imprint* 16, no 3: 1–27.

Deutsch, Max. 2020a. "Speaker's Reference, Stipulation, and a Dilemma for Conceptual Engineers." *Philosophical Studies* 177: 3935–57.

Deutsch, Max. 2020b. "Trivializing Conceptual Engineering." *Inquiry*. https://doi.org/10.1080/0020174X.2020.1853343

Deutsch, Max. 2021. "Still the Same Dilemma for Conceptual Engineers: Reply to Koch." *Philosophical Studies* 178, no. 11: 3659–70.

Dotson, Kristie. 2012. "How Is This Paper Philosophy?" *Comparative Philosophy* 3, no. 1: 3–29.

Eklund, Matti. 2017. *Choosing Normative Concepts*. Oxford: Oxford University Press.

Fassio, Davide, and Robin McKenna. 2015. "Revisionary Epistemology." *Inquiry* 58, nos. 7–8: 755–79.

Gardiner, Georgi. 2022. "Attunement: On the Cognitive Virtues of Attention." In *Social Virtue Epistemology*, edited by Mark Alfano, Colin Klein, and Jeroen de Ridder. New York: Routledge.

Graham, Gordon. 2017. "Philosophy, Knowledge, and Understanding." In *Making Sense of the World: New Essays on the Philosophy of Understanding*, edited by Stephen R. Grimm, 99–116. New York: Oxford University Press.

Grundmann, Thomas. 2020. "Conceptual Construction in Epistemology: Why the Content of Our Folk Terms Has Only Limited Significance." In

Ethno-Epistemology: New Directions for Global Epistemology, edited by Masaharu Mizumoto, Jonardon Ganery, and Cliff Goddard, 227–47. New York: Routledge.

Gutting, Gary. 2009. *What Philosophers Know: Case Studies in Recent Analytic Philosophy*. Cambridge: Cambridge University Press.

Hacker, P. M. S. 2009. "Philosophy: A Contribution, Not to Human Knowledge, but to Human Understanding." *Royal Institute of Philosophy Supplements* 65: 129–53.

Hannon, Michael, and James Nguyen. Manuscript. "Understanding Philosophy." https://philpapers.org/rec/HANUP (retrieved September 5, 2021).

Haslanger, Sally. 2000. "Gender and Race: (What) Are They? (What) Do We Want Them to Be?" *Noûs* 34, no. 1: 31–55.

Hazlett, Allan. 2010. "The Myth of Factive Verbs." *Philosophy and Phenomenological Research* 80, no. 3: 497–522.

Hazlett, Allan. 2016. "What Does 'Epistemic' Mean?" *Episteme* 13, no. 4: 539–47.

Hermann, Julia, Jeroen Hopster, Wouter Kalf, and Michael Klenk (eds.). 2020. *Philosophy in the Age of Science? Inquiries into Philosophical Progress, Method, and Societal Relevance*. London: Rowman and Littlefield International.

Isaac, Manuel Gustavo. 2020. "How to Conceptually Engineer Conceptual Engineering?" *Inquiry.* https://doi.org/10.1080/0020174X.2020.1719881

Jenkins, Katharine. 2014. "'That's not philosophy': Feminism, Academia and the Double Bind." *Journal of Gender Studies* 23, no. 3: 262–74.

Kitcher, Philip. 2011. "Philosophy Inside Out." *Metaphilosophy* 42, no. 3: 248–60.

Knoll, Viktoria. 2020. "Verbal Disputes and Topic Continuity." *Inquiry.* https://doi.org/10.1080/0020174X.2020.1850340

Machery, Edouard. 2017. *Philosophy Within Its Proper Bounds*. Oxford: Oxford University Press.

Manne, Kate. 2018. *Down Girl: The Logic of Misogyny*. New York: Oxford University Press.

Mizumoto, Masaharu, Jonardon Ganery, and Cliff Goddard (eds.). 2020. *Ethno-Epistemology: New Directions for Global Epistemology*. New York: Routledge.

Mizumoto, Masaharu, Stephen Stich, and Eric McCready (eds.). 2018. *Epistemology for the Rest of the World*. New York: Oxford University Press.

Nado, Jennifer. 2021. "Re-engineering Knowledge: A Case Study in Pluralist Conceptual Engineering." *Inquiry.* https://doi.org/10.1080/0020174X.2021.1903987

Neumann, Odmar. 1987. "Beyond Capacity: A Functional View of Attention." In *Perspectives on Perception and Action*, edited by Herbert Heuer and Andries F. Sanders, 361–94. Hillsdale, N.J.: Lawrence Erlbaum.

Pinder, Mark. 2021. "Conceptual Engineering, Metasemantic Externalism and Speaker-Meaning." *Mind* 130, no. 517: 141–63.

Priest, Graham. 2006. "What Is Philosophy?" *Philosophy* 81: 189–207.

Rooney, Phyllis. 2011. "The Marginalization of Feminist Epistemology and What That Reveals About Epistemology 'Proper'." In *Feminist Epistemology and Philosophy of Science: Power in Knowledge*, edited by Heidi E. Grasswick, 3–24. Dordrecht: Springer.

Ross, Lewis D. 2021. "How Intellectual Communities Progress." *Episteme* 18, no. 4: 738–56.

Schaffer, Jonathan. 2017. "Social Construction as Grounding; or: Fundamentality for Feminists, a Reply to Barnes and Mikkola." *Philosophical Studies* 174: 2449–65.

Scharp, Kevin. 2013. *Replacing Truth*. Oxford: Oxford University Press.

Schwitzgebel, Eric. 2021. "The Pragmatic Metaphysics of Belief." In *The Fragmented Mind*, edited by Cristina Borgoni, Dirk Kindermann, and Andrea Onofri, 350–75. Oxford: Oxford University Press.

Sider, Theodore. 2017. "Substantivity in Feminist Metaphysics." *Philosophical Studies* 174: 2467–78.

Solomon, Robert C. 2001. "'What Is Philosophy?' The Status of World Philosophy in the Profession." *Philosophy East and West* 51, no. 1: 100–104.

Stoljar, Daniel. 2017. *Philosophical Progress: In Defence of a Reasonable Optimism*. Oxford: Oxford University Press.

Strawson, P. F. 1963. "Carnap's Views on Conceptual Systems Versus Natural Languages in Analytic Philosophy." In *The Philosophy of Rudolph Carnap*, edited by Paul Arthur Schilpp, 503–18. Chicago: Open Court.

Watzl, Sebastian. 2022. "The Ethics of Attention: An Argument and a Framework." In *Salience: A Philosophical Inquiry*, edited by Sophie Archer. New York: Routledge.

Watzl, Sebastian. 2017. *Structuring Mind: The Nature of Attention and How It Shapes Consciousness*. Oxford: Oxford University Press.

Wu, Wayne. 2014. *Attention*. New York: Routledge.

CHAPTER 8

THE PHILOSOPHY OF LOGICAL PRACTICE

BEN MARTIN

1. Introduction

Contemporary philosophy of science and philosophy of mathematics are typified by their detailed analysis of the various facets of scientific and mathematical methodology, whether these be the norms of model building within a field of science (Braillard and Malaterre 2015), the notion of rigor that mathematicians adhere to when evaluating proofs (Hamami 2019), or the criteria scientists use when evaluating the utility of theoretical concepts (Brigandt 2010). In all of these cases, there is an acceptance that the philosophy of a research field should primarily be based upon the actual practices of experts within the field, rather than some idealised accounts of them.

The general rationale for this *practice-based approach* is clear, if often left explicitly unsaid (Soler et al. 2014). The sciences and mathematics, like any field of inquiry, are social enterprises, albeit rational social enterprises, whose aims, values, and techniques are the result of the collective actions and decisions of its practitioners.[1] Thus, any attempts to infer a picture of what scientific methodology *should look like* based upon our preconceptions of scientific rationality, or to determine what mathematical evidence *must be* given certain metaphysical assumptions about the nature of mathematical objects, are likely to distort the realities of the research areas and provide us with an impoverished view of the fields. Ultimately, such idealised accounts will be but castles in the air, no more insightful than an

---

[1] Note that this is not equivalent to proposing that a field's object of study, or the putative facts it discovers, are social constructions. There is no clear reason to think that the practice-based approach commits one to *social constructivism* about the domain (Soler et al. 2014). This is just as true for logic. While this point is important, addressing it will have to wait for another occasion.

Examining Philosophy Itself. Edited by Yafeng Shan.
Chapters and book compilation © 2023 Metaphilosophy LLC and John Wiley & Sons Ltd.
Published 2023 by John Wiley & Sons Ltd.

account of carpentry that fails to appreciate the intricacies of being a master carpenter. In comparison, if we build our accounts of these fields upon the ways in which they are actually practised by the experts within them, we can produce more detailed and accurate reflections of these incredible human enterprises.

Yet, while one of the prominent features of contemporary philosophies of science and mathematics has been the successful implementation of this "practice-based turn," the practice-based approach has yet to be systemically embraced within the philosophy of logic, with only a handful of papers explicitly using the approach to elucidate features of logic's methodology.[2] The nuanced accounts of model building within the climate sciences (Steele and Werndl 2013), and the values that underpin economic evaluations within public health (Cenci and Hussain 2019), are in stark contrast to the lack of a detailed appreciation of the various methods, aims, and values that constitute logic as a research area. It is still all too common for us to exclusively concentrate on what logical research *should look like* given our philosophical preconceptions about logic and its subject matter, rather than facing up to the reality of research in the field. This has led not only to an impoverished picture of some portions of logic's methodology but to a total neglect of others.

My goal here is to show that this predominant neglect of logical practice has been a mistake, by outlining the rationale and potential benefits for embracing a new practice-based approach to the philosophy of logic, by way of analogy with the benefits of the approach within the philosophies of science and mathematics. It is not my aim to argue that philosophy of logic as it is currently practised should be wholly replaced; the field as it stands has provided us with fruitful debates in some areas, such as whether we have good reason to endorse multiple logics simultaneously (Cook 2010) and what role logic plays (if any) in reasoning (Steinberger 2020). Instead, my proposal is for a new field of research, the *philosophy of logical practice* (hereafter, PLP), to sit alongside traditional philosophy of logic, which is better able to answer certain established questions about logic than traditional approaches and also has the benefit of opening up new fruitful areas of research.

My case for PLP proceeds as follows. Section 2 briefly outlines the general rationale for practice-based approaches, using established examples from the philosophies of science and mathematics. Section 3 then introduces PLP, detailing its motivation and aims. Sections 4 and 5 highlight the case for PLP, demonstrating how the positive considerations counting

---

[2] To note some examples of these papers: Dutilh Novaes 2012 uses the approach to identify the theoretical values that underpin our use of formal languages, Martin 2021b and 2021c use the approach to elucidate types of logical evidence and features of disagreements within logic, respectively, and Payette and Wyatt 2018 uses it to provide an account of explanations in logic (see Martin 2021a for competing analysis of logical explanations).

in favour of the approach in the philosophy of science and the philosophy of mathematics apply equally to the philosophy of logic. Section 4 outlines how PLP's methodology differs from that of traditional approaches to the philosophy of logic, and then shows how the former's methods are better suited to answering at least one prominent existent question in the philosophy of logic. In contrast, section 5 details how PLP adjusts the philosophy of logic's scope of inquiry, leading to new fruitful areas of research that have been neglected by traditional philosophy of logic.

2. The Practice-Based Approach

Practice-based approaches to the philosophy of a research field are jointly characterised by (i) their dissatisfaction with more traditional philosophical approaches to the field and (ii) their positive proposal for how to fix these shortcomings (Mancosu 2008; Soler et al. 2014). Prominent uses of the approach can be found in contemporary philosophy of science and philosophy of mathematics, with each containing research programmes built around the approach, in the form of the *philosophy of scientific practice* (PSP) and the *philosophy of mathematical practice* (PMP), respectively.

Both PSP and PMP are motivated by the perceived inadequacy of traditional philosophical approaches to the fields, on the basis of these traditional approaches producing accounts of the sciences and mathematics that are (i) *too idealised*, in virtue of being based upon *a priori* reflections of what we *want* science and mathematics to look like given our preconceptions of the fields, rather than reflecting the realities of research in these fields; (ii) *over-simplistic*, in failing to reflect the plurality of the fields' aims and methodologies; (iii) *too present centred*, by falling foul of a tendency to produce whig histories, presuming that the fields' histories are a story of smooth and unstoppable progress up to the present state of affairs; and (iv) *too end-product focused*, by concentrating on the properties of final theories or proofs and thereby neglecting the important processes that led to the discovery of these results, including communal processes (Carter 2019; Mancosu 2008).

An early, and particularly prominent, example of these concerns within the philosophy of science is Kuhn's (1962) criticism of Popper's (1959) falsificationism. Popper's account of the scientific method was denounced both for idealising scientific methodology, by presenting a naïve picture of scientific progress as a continual chain of ever more informative theories that perpetually become falsified, and for being too present centred, by presuming the aims and norms for evaluation of past scientific theories were the same as those of contemporary science. Further, Kuhn (1962) highlighted how past accounts of scientific methodology had been deficient by neglecting important features of scientists' research activities, such as the designing and testing of experimental equipment and its use in measuring constants. The failure of past theories of scientific methodology to recognise the various roles of experimentation within the sciences beyond the direct testing of hypotheses was further emphasised by Hacking (1983) and other New Experimentalists. Thus, according to both Kuhn and Hacking, past accounts of scientific methodology were deficient in virtue of paying too little attention to the rich variety of activities constituting part of the actual scientific method.

Similar concerns have been raised by advocates of PMP, with traditional approaches to the philosophy of mathematics being criticised for possessing too idealised a picture of mathematics and conceiving of mathematical knowledge wholly in the form of theorems evidenced by formal proofs (Corfield 2003). Contrary to this traditional view, it's been argued that mathematical understanding progresses in many ways, including through the abundant use of informal proofs, whose positive epistemic features cannot be reduced to those of formal proofs (Larvor 2012; Tanswell 2015). Further, in virtue of being too concerned with philosophically foundational issues, such as the metaphysics of mathematical objects and the epistemological puzzles resulting from these metaphysical pictures, traditional philosophy of mathematics has produced an over-simplistic picture of the mathematical enterprise, neglecting important features of contemporary mathematics, including the appraisal of definitions (Tappenden 2008) and the use of diagrams (Giardino 2017).

Conjoined with this negative component of the approach is the positive story of how the philosophy of these fields should then proceed in order to rectify the failures. The proposed solution requires both a re-evaluation of our *aims* when providing a philosophical account of a field and a modification in the *methods* we ought to use in order to appropriately meet these aims.

First, rather than attempting to build an account of the sciences and mathematics that conforms to our philosophical assumptions about the norms of rationality, possible sources of evidence, and viable metaphysical theories, we should instead aim to produce accounts that (i) reflect the reality of research in these fields; (ii) recognise the plurality of aims and methodologies found across them; (iii) situate results in the field within their proper historical context; (iv) recognise the development of, and changes in, the methodological norms within the fields; and (v) give equal attention to the processes of discovery as the properties of the final products (Corfield 2003; Soler et al. 2014).

Secondly, meeting these aims will require embracing new methods. To ensure that their proposals reflect actual research in the fields, philosophers will need to spend less time deliberating over how science and mathematics *could* operate given established epistemological theories and certain metaphysical assumptions about the fields, and more time looking in detail at how scientists and mathematicians actually reach their results. Much of this work will take the form of case studies, whether these be in-depth studies of the activities of an individual researcher (or research group) or wider studies of the norms within a particular sub-field (van Bendegem 2014). Historiographic studies are also commonly used, however, to trace the development of a particular prominent concept or track evolution of the methodological norms within a field (Krantz 2011), and studies from cognitive science are sometimes embraced to inform an account of how theories are evidenced or selected for (Giaquinto 2007).[3]

Through embracing these new aims and methods, both PSP and PMP have shown themselves to have two significant benefits over traditional approaches to the fields (Soler et al. 2014). First, the approach is able to provide more insightful answers to established and prominent questions about scientific and mathematical methodology than traditional philosophical approaches. Clear examples of this benefit are found within the already noted debate over what constitutes a proof within mathematics, where we now have a much more detailed appreciation of the standards of proof and why different forms of proof are valued (De Toffoli 2021; Hamami 2019), and in the long-standing debate over the nature of explanations in the sciences (Braillard and Malaterre 2015). In the latter case, before the development of the practice-based approach it had been assumed that there must be some essential characteristic shared by all instances of explanation, and thus a unified account of the phenomenon could be provided (see, e.g., Hempel 1965). Typically, these essentialist accounts struggled, in virtue of having to cope with numerous counterexamples and declaring a significant number of scientific explanations illegitimate (Woody 2015). In comparison, ever since philosophers of science dropped the essentialist assumption and began building accounts of scientific explanation from the bottom up, starting with instances of explanation from various sub-fields, research in the area has flourished, with detailed theories of the wide variety of forms of explanations found across the life (Brigandt 2013), medicinal (Qiu 1989), and physical sciences (Fisher 2003).

Secondly, the approach has opened up new important research questions about the fields that were previously neglected using traditional philosophical methods. This has been achieved through a combination of the approach's methodology facilitating a more detailed consideration of the activities of practitioners and further using these activities as a means to motivate new philosophical research questions, rather than simply imposing established philosophical questions upon the fields of inquiry. For instance, the approach has led to the investigation and a growing understanding of (i) the various sources of evidence that mathematicians rely upon, such as visualisation (Giaquinto 2007) and computer-aided

---

[3] For a more detailed discussion of the various methods of inquiry used within PMP see Hamami and Morris 2020.

proofs (Avigad 2008); (ii) what constitutes scientific understanding (de Regt 2017); (iii) the characteristics that mathematicians look for when devising and choosing formal notations (De Toffoli 2017); (iv) the role of (interdisciplinary) collaboration within the sciences (Andersen 2016); and (v) the theoretical virtues mathematicians prize within a piece of mathematics (Rota 1997).

Later, in sections 4 and 5, I argue that these same considerations that count in favour of PSP and PMP apply equally to PLP. Before that, however, we need to look at the motivations behind a practice-based approach to the philosophy of logic, and how this approach differs from traditional approaches to the field.

3. PLP Versus the Traditional Approach

3.1. The Motivation for PLP

In general terms, PLP aims to provide us with a new approach to the philosophy of logic, one more capable of reflecting the reality of research within the field of logic.[4] Like PSP and PMP before it, PLP is motivated by perceived deficiencies in the way that the philosophy of logic is traditionally practised. In particular, we can pinpoint *five* (interconnected) concerns with the traditional approach.

(i) It produces accounts of logic that *are far too idealised*. Philosophers will often build an account of logic based upon what they *expect* its subject matter, sources of evidence, and methodology to be, given certain philosophical presumptions about logic's properties, standards of rationality, and possible sources of evidence. What results is a picture of logic completely at odds with that practised by logicians.[5]

(ii) The traditional approach is *too focused on traditional philosophical concerns*. Significant time is spent on established philosophical questions that are divorced from the realities of logical research. One prominent example is the preoccupation with the *metaphysics* of logic, whether this takes the form of providing an ontology of logic (Sider 2011) or assessing the existence of logical facts and their nature (McSweeney 2018). While

---

[4] PLP should not be mistaken for the study of everyday reasoning; it is not an ethnography of reasoners. Rather, PLP is concerned with the theoretical field of logic and the activities of its practitioners. Of course, it may turn out that everyday reasoning is a topic of interest for logicians themselves, and this is an interesting question for the philosophy of logic. This doesn't mean, however, that the subject matter of PLP itself is this everyday reasoning. The distinction here is analogous to that between linguistics and the philosophy of linguistics. While linguistics is (among other things) the study of the linguistic practices of speakers, the *philosophy of* linguistics is concerned with the aims and methodology of linguistics as a field. What should count as the *field of logic* is another question, which I consider below. Many thanks to an anonymous referee for pushing me on this point.

[5] I consider an example of this concern from the epistemology of logic in section 4.

these debates are of potential philosophical interest, there is little to no attempt in them to relate the proposals to the actual means through which logics are developed or chosen by practitioners. Another example is the attempt to provide detailed accounts of traditional philosophical properties that logic putatively possesses, such as the necessity of its truths (McFetridge 1990) and the topic neutrality of its laws (Sher 1991). Again, while potentially of philosophical interest, rarely (if ever) do these accounts attempt to show that the formal systems regularly developed, analysed, and applied for various purposes in the field actually possess these putative properties, or how we would expect research in the field to be conducted in light of these properties.

(iii) The conclusions drawn in the traditional approach are often *too synchronically homogeneous*. In virtue of being preoccupied with traditional philosophical concerns, or too focused on certain uses of logic deemed "philosophically important," a significant portion of the projects that logicians are engaged in, and the uses these logics are put to, are neglected. While dynamic logics are commonly used to model the semantics of complex linguistic phenomena (Keshet 2018) and Church's type theory is now being used to model ethical reasoning in AI (Benzmüller, Parent, and van der Torre 2020), when it comes to discussing the aims and methods of logic, such applications are either ignored completely or dismissed as not being the canonical, philosophically significant application of logic.[6] What results is a far poorer view of the field, with prominent applications of logic and substantial practices in the field being neglected.

(iv) The proposals of the traditional approach are often *a historical* (leading to implicit *diachronic homogeneity*). In virtue of the propensity within contemporary philosophy of logic to build idealised accounts of logic based upon certain presumptions about rationality, knowledge, and logic's properties, what tends to result is an essentialist account of logic's aims and methods, which gives the impression that logic as a field is diachronically homogeneous. Just like the empirical sciences and mathematics, however, logic is a social enterprise with continually changing priorities and techniques. Given the availability of excellent resources on the history of logic (Haaparanta 2009), such presumed diachronic homogeneity is perhaps surprising. As we'll see in section 5, however, it is prominent in the literature.

(v) The traditional approach is *too end product focused*. Contemporary philosophy of logic concentrates primarily on the properties of *logics*, rather than on the processes that led to the formulation and evidencing of these logics, whether those of individual researchers or of the community. This is troublesome not only because it can lead us to neglect the many important techniques and methods that logicians use to develop, evidence, and apply their systems but also because it can result in hasty conclusions

---

[6] I revisit this topic in section 5.

about the field. For instance, following Haack (1978), there has been a tradition of understanding (dis)agreement within logic in terms of ways in which logics as theories can (dis)agree (Stei 2020). Given that various such competing logics are still advocated in the literature, some (Resnik 1999) have concluded that the persistent disagreement between candidate theories in the field is evidence that logic is more akin to ethics than to the sciences. This, however, neglects the significant ways in which *logicians* as participants in the debates agree, such as on how logics should be evaluated (relative to a purpose), the relative strengths and weaknesses of the various competing theories, and what would constitute sufficient evidence for the resolution of the debate (Martin 2021c) What results is a picture of theory evaluation and debate more similar to the sciences than to ethics (Martin and Hjortland 2021).[7]

PLP's positive proposal is to address these shortcomings of traditional philosophy of logic through a combination of re-orientating our theoretical aims back towards the practices of the field of logic and suitably diverging from the traditional approach in terms of its methodology and scope of inquiry.

3.2. The Aims of PLP

In order to ensure we avoid producing idealised accounts of logic, putting too much focus on traditional philosophical concerns, and thereby neglecting important features of the field's actual aims and methods, PLP explicitly orientates its goals towards the concrete activities of the field, giving primacy to these activities over traditional philosophical concerns. In particular, PLP aims to:

(i) Provide the most detailed and accurate account of the aims, epistemology, and methods of logic possible, including recognising the diversity of these features of the field.

(ii) Explore the philosophical repercussions of the full diversity of logicians' activities, beyond what has traditionally been considered to be of philosophical importance.

---

[7] Concerns over the lack of consensus and progress within logic also tend to be somewhat myopic, due to the ahistorical nature of contemporary philosophy of logic. Throughout the development of logic, there have been significant periods of consensus as well as recognition of progress (Haaparanta 2009). Very few contemporary logicians, for instance, deny that classical first-order logic is theoretically preferable to Aristotelian syllogistic logic as an account of mathematical reasoning, even if they admit it has its own weaknesses. This recognition should also go some way to addressing the concern that, whereas PSP and PMP are effective because both the empirical sciences and mathematics are successful fields of inquiry, exhibiting progress and stable consensus on many matters, the same is not true of logic, and thus the case for PLP's effectiveness is weaker. I hope to discuss this in greater depth elsewhere.

(iii) Provide analysis of how the activities of logicians impact traditional philosophical topics, such as the nature of knowledge, rather than, inversely, how established answers to philosophical questions impact our view of logic (as has been standard in the philosophy of logic).[8]

Motivating each of these aims is the working assumption that a philosophy *of logic* should be concerned with logic as it exists as a living, breathing discipline, and that our philosophical theories about logic should be built upon these practices, not in spite of them. According to PLP, it is not the purpose of the philosophy of logic to use logic as an instructive case study to evidence one's choice philosophical theory or to show how logical knowledge would be possible in light of one's favoured epistemology. Conducting one's philosophy of logic in this manner would, unjustifiably, suggest that logic as a field of research is somehow subservient to our wider philosophical theories and aims. Yet, just as with the empirical sciences and mathematics, logic is an important and diverse field of research that ought to be examined and analysed in its own right, and on its own field-specific terms. In other words, the practices of logicians have primacy, and it is these practices that should lead our philosophical analysis of logic.

Re-orientating the philosophy of logic's goals in this fashion requires changes both to its methodology and to its scope of inquiry in relation to traditional approaches. These changes, however, bring benefits analogous to those found with PSP and PMP. In the next section, I outline how PLP's methodology differs from traditional approaches, and the benefit this methodology brings in addressing established questions in the philosophy of logic. Then, in section 5, I show how alterations to philosophy of logic's scope of inquiry lead to PLP opening up new fruitful areas of research, neglected by traditional approaches.

---

[8] Here and elsewhere I've spoken of the *field of logic* and allowing practices within the field to dictate our accounts of logic's aims, methodology, and epistemology. Yet, one might plausibly be concerned that in order to identify and analyse these practices, one must have a prior conception of what constitutes the field of logic (and who is a member of it), which itself may be unduly influenced by one's philosophical views (unfortunately for PLP, given its motivations). Indeed, field specification is a problem for *all* practice-based approaches, given that they do not wish to excessively restrict the field's scope of inquiry due to preconceptions. Further, there is no straightforward answer. The delineation of research fields is a live research question within informetrics (Muñoz-Écija, Vargas-Quesada, and Rodriguez 2019), and the various measures we currently have at our disposal are not guaranteed to deliver the same results. They do, however, indicate that by beginning with certain paradigm cases of a logician and works within the field, we can then use citation, conference attendance, and publication venue data as reliable (if defeasible) evidence for membership in the field. While I provide some indication of how we foresee PLP expanding the philosophy of logic's scope of inquiry in section 5, I hope to discuss in more detail the available means to delineate the field and the repercussions for PLP elsewhere.

4. Benefit 1: Progress on Established Questions

4.1. The Methodology of PLP

PLP diverges from the methodology of traditional philosophy of logic in two noteworthy respects. First, it has a distinct *methodological starting point*. As with its predecessors in the philosophy of science and the philosophy of mathematics, PLP takes a bottom-up approach, beginning with case studies of instances of practice within the field. From these initial case studies, tentative conclusions are drawn and hypotheses proposed, to then be tested against further case studies. The aim is to steadily build up a detailed theory of particular elements of the field through a process of testing proposals against an ever-increasing number of case studies.[9]

In comparison, philosophy of logic traditionally has used a top-down approach, beginning with certain philosophical presumptions about the subject (Martin 2021b). These could take the form of assumptions about logic itself, such as its privileged status in virtue of its laws being formal, wholly general, and necessarily true, or wider philosophical assumptions, such as established accounts of what constitutes knowledge or rational standards of inquiry. From these postulates, philosophers of logic then attempt to *infer* viable theories about logic's aims, epistemology, or methods, with the adequacy of any proposal ultimately tested against the background of these presumptions, on the basis of the theory's ability to respect them. We'll consider a detailed example of this top-down approach from the epistemology of logic shortly.

Secondly, the approaches differ in the *evidential priority* they accord logicians' practices and philosophical background assumptions when the two clash. PLP treats the practices of experts within the field as the most reliable evidence we have to understand the field's aims, epistemology, and methods. This means that, in most cases, if these practices conflict with philosophical presumptions, whether about logic itself or about established epistemological or metaphysical theories, then it is the latter that should go in this context.[10]

In comparison, it's common within traditional philosophy of logic to dismiss cases of logical practice as irrational or unviable if they clash with certain philosophical conclusions. Take, for example, the proposal that logical laws are *constitutive of rational thought* (Leech 2015). One consequence

---

[9] Much as with PSP and PMP, it's likely that other interdisciplinary methods, such as results from cognitive science, will be useful to PLP when investigating certain questions, including the theoretical and aesthetic virtues logicians prize within systems. Discussion of the possibilities these further methods offer PLP is beyond the scope of the current essay, but I hope to explore this topic elsewhere.

[10] Why do I say *in most cases*? We must be open to the possibility that individual members of the community can make methodological mistakes and thus not reflect the general methodological norms of the field. This potential concern can be addressed through considering a range of case studies (Martin 2021b).

of this view is that if one fails to adhere to the (correct) logical laws, then one isn't reasoning rationally, which has consequences for the possibility of rational disagreement in logic. After all, if by definition a logician who does not adhere to the correct logical laws (whatever these are) cannot be reasoning rationally, their possibility of engaging in a *rational* disagreement with peers over the correct logic is precluded. This consequence, however, runs contrary to what we find in the literature. We find advocates of competing logics debating with one another not only over the comparative strengths and weaknesses of their candidates but also over the validity of important logical laws, such as *modus ponens* (Martin and Hjortland 2021). While for advocates of a practice-based approach this clash with logical practice spells a devastating blow to *constitutivism*, the constitutivists themselves seem content to admit that those who challenge the logical laws putatively constitutive of rational thought cannot be providing rational considerations (Martin 2021c), *even if* these challenges are taken seriously by their peers.

One of the significant benefits of PLP's bottom-up method, in comparison to traditional top-down approaches, is that it offers the opportunity of greater progress on established questions within the philosophy of logic. As a means of demonstrating this benefit of the practice-based approach, we'll now briefly consider how the approach has contributed to the contemporary debate from the epistemology of logic over how we come to know claims about deductive validity, providing progress where the traditional approach to the philosophy of logic has faltered.

4.2. *An Example from the Epistemology of Logic*

While there is wide disagreement within the philosophy of logic over what exactly constitutes deductive validity, whether it is facts about our natural languages, structural features of the world, or mathematical reasoning, there is a general consensus that one of the important philosophical applications that logical systems are put to is to adequately capture this deductive validity.[11] Given this, one important question for contemporary philosophy of logic is then how (philosophical) logicians come to evidence their candidate logics of validity. In other words, how do we come to know claims about deductive validity (Priest 2016; Williamson 2017)?

Philosophical tradition has it that logical evidence about validity must be both non-inferential and *a priori* (Martin 2021b). *Non-inferential*, for otherwise one would need to presume the validity of at least *some* rules of inference to establish the reliability of the inferences that partially constitute one's justification for the logical rules (Haack 1976). *A priori* because, first, no observable states of affairs directly demonstrate that a rule of inference is

---

[11] See Martin and Hjortland 2022 for the background to these debates over the metaphysics and epistemology of validity.

valid and, secondly, the possibility of *inferring evidence* for particular logical laws from empirical evidence is precluded by the non-inferentiality of logical evidence (Martin 2021b). Consequently, if these two starting assumptions are correct, we must have *unmediated a priori* access to the truth of logical laws about validity. This would distinguish logic's epistemology from both the empirical sciences and mathematics, with the former relying significantly upon *a posteriori* evidence and the latter involving inferences being made to establish results (Martin and Hjortland 2021).

Beginning with this pair of commitments, discussions of the epistemology of validity have traditionally embraced a top-down approach, by attempting to infer how knowledge of validity could be possible while respecting these traditional assumptions. Two accounts, in particular, have dominated the philosophical landscape: *logical rationalism* and *logical semanticism* (Martin 2021b). Both positions agree that the justification for logical laws of validity must be non-inferential and *a priori*, but they disagree on the source of this apriority. While according to rationalists evidence of validity lies in intuitions facilitated by a quasi-perceptual intellectual faculty, with which one simply *sees* that a particular logical law is true or inference valid (Bealer 1998; BonJour 1998), semanticists deny the need to posit a novel cognitive faculty to accommodate logical knowledge. Instead, we gain evidence for logical laws directly through linguistic proficiency. In virtue of understanding the meaning of the constituent terms of a logical law or inference, we automatically become justified in assenting to its truth or validity (Ayer 1936). In other words, logical laws are epistemically analytic (Boghossian 1996).

Importantly, neither rationalists nor semanticists are motivated in their accounts by the types of evidence logicians actually appeal to when justifying logics of validity. Instead, with the starting assumptions of logic's epistemic foundationalism and apriority, it's presumed that either rationalism or semanticism must be correct if we are to avoid the unfortunate sceptical conclusion that we don't possess knowledge of validity (Boghossian 2000). Further, the answer to the question of which of these two candidates we should then favour is made not on the basis of which candidate provides us with a more realistic answer to logical knowledge but rather, first, on the basis of which is more able to avoid undesirable sceptical conclusions and, secondly, on the basis of the compatibility of these accounts with further philosophical commitments their advocates embrace. For example, logical semanticists such as the logical positivists have traditionally been motivated to accept logic's analyticity on the basis of their scepticism about the existence of a special cognitive faculty providing direct rational insight into the truth of logical claims and, further, their desire to accommodate the putative necessary truth of logical laws without relying on a dubious notion of metaphysical necessity (Carnap 1963, 46). In other words, semanticists are commonly motivated by both metaphysical and epistemological naturalism (Warren 2020, chap. 1). By embracing analyticity, the semanticist can aim to account for the necessary truth of logic's laws in terms of linguistic conventions, rather than in terms of ways the world must be. In comparison, rationalists desire to uphold the objectivity of logic, which they believe the semanticist throws away by demoting logic to the status of conventions (BonJour 1998), and attempt to achieve this by rejecting naturalism and admitting both abstract non-spatiotemporal facts and a special faculty, *rational intuition*, to access them (Katz 1998).

What has resulted is a long-standing debate between rationalists and semanticists, in which the goal has been to undermine the viability of the competitor while staving off sceptical conclusions. On the semanticist side, this has consisted of appeals to naturalism (Warren 2020, chap. 1) and to the opacity of rational intuition as a faculty (Boghossian 2000, 231) in order to undermine rationalism, as well as of attempts to show that the permissibility of rule circularity can allow the semanticist to avoid sceptical conclusions (Boghossian 2000). In comparison, rationalists have attempted to undermine semanticism by appealing to classical Quinean concerns over the viability of analyticity and the dangers of committing ourselves to conventionalism (BonJour 1998, chap. 2).

Neither position, however, has been able to make significant progress and succeed, even by its own lights. While we still lack any case for the reliability of rational intuitions as a source of knowledge (De Cruz 2014), past advocates of the semanticist approach now question the viability of the rule circularity justification for logical knowledge (Boghossian 2014). When it comes to top-down approaches to logic's epistemology, therefore, we have reached something of an impasse. What is even more concerning, however, is that both positions problematize the actual debates logicians have over the validity of rules of inference and the forms of evidence these logicians appeal to. As has been shown through case studies, logicians appeal to a vast array of forms of evidence when arguing for their theories of validity, including the ability of their logics to: (i) solve pressing theoretical puzzles, such as the logico-semantic paradoxes; (ii) facilitate important mathematical results; and (iii) explain why mathematicians are warranted in making certain inferential moves within informal proofs (Martin 2021b; Martin and Hjortland 2021). That it's reasonable for logicians to appeal to these forms of evidence, as far as both rationalism and semanticism are concerned, is a mystery. In fact, both are committed to saying that the debates logicians are engaged in are epistemically inappropriate, in virtue of not being based on the forms of evidence sanctioned by their respective accounts (Martin 2021b). Thus, the top-down approach has produced not only an impasse but also accounts that problematize actual logical debates.

In comparison, through recent attempts to build an account of the epistemology of validity from the bottom up, beginning with the reasons logicians actually give to support their theories of validity, the practice-based approach has shown itself to have three advantages over the top-down approach. First, in virtue of taking the forms of evidence that logicians actually appeal to as a given and building an account of logic's epistemology up from these practices, the resulting theory should not problematize actual logical debates. Secondly, there's good reason to think that the approach will not lead to an impasse. The practice-based approach provides clear criteria for the success of an account of the epistemology of validity, in terms of the ability of the proposal to make sense of the forms of evidence logicians actually appeal to and the types of debates they engage in. Of course, having this clear set of criteria does not preclude that for a period of time we may have several candidate proposals that are equally viable. It does mean, however, that we can expect a particular proposal to gain greater traction over time than its competitors, in virtue of its expectations regarding logicians' practice being met to a greater degree as more cases are considered.

A third advantage of the practice-based approach is that while it is relatively young in comparison to top-down approaches, attempts to produce an account of the epistemology of validity using the practice-based approach have already delivered more detailed accounts than top-down approaches have so far managed. For instance, Martin and Hjortland 2021 shows how we can make sense of many of the forms of evidence logicians appeal to within a *predictivist* model of logical justification. According to this model, logical theories of validity are evidenced by their ability to (i) produce successful predictions about which inferences mathematicians will deem acceptable within informal proofs; (ii) explain why these particular inferences are acceptable in virtue of their form; and (iii) establish their compatibility with other well-established commitments, such as mathematical results, through the logico-semantic paradoxes. While ultimately the predictivist model may well be found to be flawed in some regard (as the practice-based approach would expect), the detailed account of logic's epistemology that the approach has already been able to produce (albeit tentatively) evidences its fruitfulness.

Combined, these considerations give us good reason to think that, over time, the bottom-up practice-based approach will be able to provide us with a more detailed and nuanced account of the epistemology of validity than top-down approaches. This is just one prominent example of the benefit PLP provides over traditional approaches, in offering progress to established debates within the philosophy of logic. The benefits with PLP do not stop here, however. In the next section, I highlight how PLP also opens up new fruitful areas of inquiry in virtue of expanding the philosophy of logic's scope of inquiry.

5. Benefit 2: New Fruitful Areas

As I noted in section 3, traditional philosophy of logic typically concentrates on established philosophical questions and how they relate to logic, be it the rationality of logic, the metaphysics of logic, or the epistemology of logic. Further, attention is paid almost exclusively to logics as objects, whether discussing how logics can provide normative guidance to reasoning or in what sense different logics can disagree with one another. In addition, when focus is placed on the aims and methodology of logic, consideration is restricted to those particular aims of logic that philosophers are interested in and how logics might be selected for in accordance with these purposes, thereby neglecting multiple other applications of logic. In this section, I outline three aspects in which PLP widens philosophy of logic's scope of inquiry, and highlight three corresponding new and fruitful research questions PLP raises in virtue of doing so.

5.1. Pure Logic

First, PLP recognises that logic as a field is concerned with both developing formal systems and studying these systems for their own sake (sometimes called *pure* or *mathematical* logic), and further applying these formal systems to various phenomena for different purposes (often known as *applied* logic). While contemporary philosophy of logic is well aware of this distinction (Priest 2006), little to no attention is ever paid to pure logic, in terms of its aims, content, and methods. This is a mistake, not only because pure logic constitutes a significant portion of the field of logic as a whole but also because by considering its activities we should gain a better understanding of how innovations within pure logic lead to breakthroughs in applied logic (just as technical innovations tend to lead to breakthroughs in the sciences) and a better understanding of the relationship between methodological norms within pure logic and (other) fields of mathematics. Answering both of these questions are important for philosophers of logic, given the recent interest in the extent to which logic is methodologically distinct both from mathematics (Sagi 2021) and from the empirical sciences (Martin and Hjortland 2021).

Let's focus momentarily on one notable research question that arises from widening philosophy of logic's scope to include consideration of pure logic: Which properties of formal systems are logicians interested in establishing, and why?

Just a cursory look at recent work in the field highlights the multitude of results that logicians are interested in establishing. First, logicians are concerned to establish that a given system has certain desirable properties. This can take the form of establishing a widely regarded beneficial property of logic, such as their decidability (Payne 2015; Wintein and Muskens 2016), but it also often takes the form of solving a non-generic open problem for a particular logic (Badia 2018; Uckelman, Alama, and Knoks 2014). For instance, Slaney and Walker (2014) set about establishing that the pure implication fragment of Anderson and Belnap's (1975) logic T has infinitely many pairwise non-equivalent formulae in one propositional variable; a particular instance of the problem set by Meyer (1970) for all substructural logics. Such cases raise interesting questions for the philosopher of logic. While a logic's decidability has clear practical implications when it comes to applying the logic in multiple contexts, the matter is less clear for some of these logic-specific open problems. Is there any shared characteristic behind the open problems logicians choose to address instead of those they deem less important? Further, are these open problems motivated by community-wide desiderata for a formal system, or are they research programme specific?

The import of this latter question is further raised by logicians' interest in demonstrating the limitations of a given system. These undesirable characteristics can have clear connections to widely shared desiderata of a system, as is the case with Kosterec's (2020) demonstration that the definition of substitution in Transparent Intensional Logic leads to a contradiction in the system, and Randall Holmes's (2019) proof that monadic third-order logic cannot provide a general representation of functions, but they need not have these connections. For instance, Yang (2013) demonstrates that the (putatively) relevant logic R fails to satisfy Anderson and Belnap's (1975) own relevance principle. Yet, of course, adherence to a relevance principle is a not a desideratum shared by the whole logic community. It is, therefore, an interesting question not only which characteristics are considered (un)desired within a formal system, and the relation of these desiderata to potential applications of logics, but also whether these desiderata are shared community wide or are peculiar to particular research programmes in the field.[12] The benefit of PLP is that it provides us not only with a means to generate these interesting research questions but with the clear and concrete means to go about addressing them as well.

5.2. Non-Philosophical Applications

A second way in which PLP widens philosophy of logic's scope of inquiry is that, rather than restricting it to those applications of logics that are deemed philosophically interesting (for whatever reason), PLP considers the full array of applications of logic, whether the use of fuzzy logics to model national incomes (Ferrer-Comalat, Corominas-Coll, and Linares-Mustarós 2020) or the use of possible-world semantics to model belief revision (Grove 1988). Considering the full diversity of these

---

[12] Let me raise here two further questions worthy of future study. First, I've mentioned that logicians are keen to establish a given system's decidability. This is understandable, but they are often interested in providing *multiple* sound and complete derivation systems for the logic (cf. Kamide 2018), without any clear rationale. What is the motivation here? Second, logicians are often interested in developing the resources to study a range of logics simultaneously, even if most of the (comparative) properties of these logics are already known (cf. Kamide 2021). Does this suggest that the development of new powerful tools is considered a good in and of itself, potentially for promising future use?

applications of logic is important, for it is only under these conditions that we can appropriately judge the fruitfulness of logic as a field, the full extent and diversity of its methodological norms, and whether similar standards of evaluation persist across all of logic's applications. Further, again, these questions are clearly important to philosophers, as the extent to which logic as a field possesses certain methodological features that align it with the sciences is a prominent debate in the literature (Martin and Hjortland 2021; Williamson 2017).

In addition, considering the array of logic's applications should help us address and evaluate certain prominent presumptions within the philosophy of logic, such as the long-standing assumption that there is some *primary* or *canonical* purpose to logic. While this assumption goes back at least as far as the terminist tradition in the twelfth century (Lu-Adler 2018, chap. 2), when nominalists and realists argued over whether logic's purpose was to capture the relationship between the *meaning* of terms or rather the *nature of objects* that terms denote, it still has its advocates now (Priest 2006). This is a little surprising, given that with the development of mathematical logic came the recognition that logical systems can be applied to distinct phenomena with myriad purposes. Kripke frames, for instance, are used to model multiple agents' mental attitudes within multi-agent systems in artificial intelligence (Wooldridge 2009), and linear logic has been fruitfully applied to model meaning composition in formal semantics (Dalrymple 2001). Yet, even given the acknowledgment of this fact, we find contemporary philosophers proposing that logical systems have a *canonical application*, whether this be the "analysis of reasoning" (Priest 2006, 196) or the "codification of logical consequence in natural language" (Cook 2010, 495).

Unfortunately, no detailed defences accompany these proposals. In the background seems to be a presumed *essentialism* about the aims of logic, based upon the perceived purposes of logic according to founding figures of the field, such as Aristotle and Tarski (Cook 2010, 495). Yet, even if historically accurate, any such appeal to historical precedent is bound to fall foul of the *embryonic fallacy*: the presumption that an activity has the same aims and purposes as when it was initially developed. Astronomy, for example, was originally developed with the purpose of facilitating astrological predictions (Campion 2008), yet that is far from the field's purpose now. Just as the techniques at disposal within a field change over time, so can its primary aims.

A strength of the practice-based approach is that, by explicitly recognising logic as a living breathing social activity constituted by the decisions and actions of its practitioners, it frees us of the need to assume that there is some primary or canonical aim that *defines* logic. The aims and purposes of logic are those given to it by its practitioners, and each deserves to be fully explored. By becoming over-preoccupied with one possible purpose of logic, it is likely that our view of logic's methods and epistemology will also be too narrow. After all, we should expect that practitioners will use methods and sources and evidence suitable for achieving their theoretical aims (Woody 2015). Consequently, the practice-based approach not only facilitates our exploring the full range of purposes to which logicians put their theories but in doing so also opens up the possibility that logic's methodology is not homogeneous—a research question that itself the practice-based approach is well suited to investigate.

5.3. Theory Development

A third widening aspect of PLP is that, in virtue of being an exemplar of the practice-based approach, PLP is primarily interested not in logics as objects of study but rather in logic as a field of research, including the many activities and norms that constitute the field. This includes the development of formal systems, the development of techniques in order to prove some desired results, and the communal processes that lead to the ultimate acceptance or rejection of a logic as (un)interesting or (un)successful for some given purpose.[13]

An excellent example of one of these processes that is worthy of study is the development and assessment of *concepts*. It is well recognised within the philosophy of science that scientists are engaged not only in theory choice but in concept development and choice as well, evaluating the relative fruitfulness of theoretical concepts (Brigandt 2010). Recent work has also been carried out on the criteria mathematicians use in assessing concepts (Tappenden 2008). In comparison, due to the neglect of a practice-based approach, we have lacked the resources to consider instances of concept development within logic, and identify the means through which logical concepts are evaluated and chosen. Yet, it's quite clear that, just as in the empirical sciences and mathematics, concepts are developed in order to solve theoretical problems in the field. For instance, Henkin's (1949) introduction of the concept MAXIMALLY CONSISTENT SET, in order to construct his completeness proof for first-order logic, and Kripke's (1963) development of the novel concepts RELATIONAL FRAME and ACCESSIBILITY RELATION, forming part of his relational semantics, provided a much-needed semantics for modal and intuitionistic logics. The question of how these concepts are developed, and their success assessed, is of interest not only to those working in the philosophy of language on the topic of conceptual engineering (Cappelen 2018) but again for the live

---

[13] The question of which practices or activities of a field, precisely, we should concentrate on when using a practice-based approach is a difficult question not only for PLP but also for PSP and PMP. Some within PMP (van Kerkhove and van Bendegem [2004]) have attempted to provide frameworks within which to think about the relevant mathematical practices worthy of study. While it may in future be viable (and fruitful) to provide such a framework for understanding the scope of logical *practices*, I trust such a framework isn't necessary either to defend PLP or to engage in its activities.

question of the extent to which logic's methodology mirrors that of the empirical sciences.

6. Conclusion

Unlike the philosophy of science and the philosophy of mathematics, the philosophy of logic has yet to recognise the importance of building its understanding of the field upon the actual practice of its researchers. My goal here has been to provide some initial motivation for embracing a practice-based approach within the philosophy of logic, showing that those considerations that justified a practice-based turn within the philosophies of science and mathematics apply equally to the philosophy of logic. While it should be recognised that more needs to be done in terms of vindicating PLP's promise through further successful applications of its method, these considerations should provide philosophers of logic with sufficient reason to take the approach seriously and explore its fruitfulness.

Acknowledgments

I am grateful to participants in the 2021 *New Directions in Metaphilosophy* conference at the University of Kent and to colleagues at the University of Bergen for their comments on a draft of this essay. I would also like to thank two anonymous referees for their detailed comments on a previous version of the essay.

References

Andersen, Hanne. 2016. "Collaboration, Interdisciplinarity, and the Epistemology of Contemporary Science." *Studies in History and Philosophy of Science A* 56: 1–10.

Anderson, Alan R., and Nuel D. Belnap. 1975. *Entailment: The Logic of Relevance and Necessity*, Volume 1. Princeton: Princeton University Press.

Avigad, Jeremy. 2008. "Computers in Mathematical Inquiry." In *The Philosophy of Mathematical Practice*, edited by Paolo Mancosu, 302–16. Oxford: Oxford University Press.

Ayer, Alfred J. 1936. *Language, Truth and Logic*. New York: Dover.

Badia, George. 2018. "On Sahlqvist Formulas in Relevant Logic." *Journal of Philosophical Logic* 47: 673–91.

Bealer, George. 1998. "Intuition and the Autonomy of Philosophy." In *Rethinking Intuition: The Psychology of Intuition and Its Role in Philosophical Inquiry*, edited by Michael DePaul and William Ramsey, 201–40. Lanham, Md.: Rowman and Littlefield.

Benzmüller, Christoph, Xavier Parent, and Leendert van der Torre. 2020. "Designing Normative Theories for Ethical and Legal Reasoning:

LoɢɪKEy Framework, Methodology, and Tool Support." *Artificial Intelligence* 287: 103348 (online).

Boghossian, Paul A. 1996. "Analyticity Reconsidered." *Noûs* 30: 360–91.

Boghossian, Paul A. 2000. "Knowledge of Logic." In *New Essays on the A Priori*, edited by Paul A. Boghossian and Christopher Peacocke, 229–54. Oxford: Clarendon Press.

Boghossian, Paul A. 2014. "What Is Inference?" *Philosophical Studies* 169: 1–18.

BonJour, Laurence 1998. *In Defense of Pure Reason*. Cambridge: Cambridge University Press.

Braillard, Pierre-Alan, and Christophe Malaterre. 2015. "Explanation in Biology: An Introduction." In *Explanation in Biology*, edited by Pierre-Alan Braillard and Christophe Malaterre, 1–28. Dordrecht: Springer.

Brigandt, Ingo. 2010. "The Epistemic Goal of a Concept: Accounting for the Rationality of Semantic Change and Variation." *Synthese* 177: 19–40.

Brigandt, Ingo. 2013. "Explanation in Biology: Reduction, Pluralism, and Explanatory Aims." *Science and Education* 22: 69–91.

Campion, Nicholas. 2008. *The Dawn of Astrology: A Cultural History of Western Astrology*. London: Hambledon Continuum.

Cappelen, Herman. 2018. *Fixing Language: An Essay on Conceptual Engineering*. Oxford: Oxford University Press.

Carnap, Rudolf. 1963. *The Philosophy of Rudolf Carnap*. Cambridge: Cambridge University Press.

Carter, Jessica. 2019. "Philosophy of Mathematical Practice: Motivations, Themes and Prospects." *Philosophia Mathematica* 27: 1–32.

Cenci, Alessandra, and M. Azhar Hussain. 2019. "Epistemic and Non-Epistemic Values in Economic Evaluations of Public Health." *Journal of Economic Methodology* 27: 66–88.

Cook, Roy T. 2010. "Let a Thousand Flowers Bloom: A Tour of Logical Pluralism." *Philosophy Compass* 5: 492–504.

Corfield, David. 2003. *Towards a Philosophy of Real Mathematics*. Cambridge: Cambridge University Press.

Dalrymple, Mary. 2001. *Lexical Functional Grammar*. Syntax and Semantics Series, vol. 34. New York: Academic Press.

De Cruz, Helen. 2015. "Where Philosophical Intuitions Come From." *Australasian Journal of Philosophy* 93: 233–49.

De Regt, Henk W. 2017. *Understanding Scientific Understanding*. Oxford: Oxford University Press.

De Toffoli, Silvia. 2017. "'Chasing' the Diagram—The Use of Visualizations in Algebraic Reasoning." *Review of Symbolic Logic* 10: 158–86.

De Toffoli, Silvia. 2021. "Reconciling Rigor and Intuition." *Erkenntnis* 86: 1783–1802.

Dutilh Novaes, Catarina. 2012. "Towards A Practice-Based Philosophy of Logic: Formal Languages as a Case Study." *Philosophia Scientiæ* 16: 71–102.

Ferrer-Comalat, Joan C., Dolors Corominas-Coll, and Salvador Linares-Mustarós. 2020. "Fuzzy Logic in Economic Models." *Journal of Intelligent and Fuzzy Systems* 38: 5333–42.

Fisher, Grant. 2003. "Explaining Explanation in Chemistry." *Annals of the New York Academy of Sciences* 988: 16–21.

Giaquinto, Marcus. 2007. *Visual Thinking in Mathematics: An Epistemological Study*. Oxford: Oxford University Press.

Giardino, Valeria 2017. "Diagrammatic Reasoning in Mathematics." In *Springer Handbook of Model-Based Science*, edited by Lorenzo Magnani and Tommaso Bertolotti, 499–522. Dordrecht: Springer.

Grove, Adam. 1988. "Two Modellings for Theory Change." *Journal of Philosophical Logic* 17: 157–70.

Haack, Susan. 1976. "The Justification of Deduction." *Mind* 85: 112–19.

Haack, Susan. 1978. *Philosophy of Logics*. Cambridge: Cambridge University Press.

Haaparanta, Leila, ed. 2009. *The Development of Modern Logic*. Oxford: Oxford University Press.

Hacking, Ian. 1983. *Representing and Intervening*. Cambridge: Cambridge University Press.

Hamami, Yacin. 2019. "Mathematical Rigor and Proof." *Review of Symbolic Logic*. Online first: doi:https://doi.org/10.1017/S1755020319000443

Hamami, Yacin, and Rebecca L. Morris. 2020. "Philosophy of Mathematical Practice: A Primer for Mathematics Educators." *ZDM Mathematics Education* 52: 1113–26.

Hempel, Carl G. 1965. "Aspects of Scientific Explanation." In *Aspects of Scientific Explanation and Other Essays in the Philosophy of Science*, 331–496. New York: Free Press.

Henkin, Leon. 1949. "The Completeness of the First-Order Functional Calculus." *Journal of Symbolic Logic* 14: 159–66.

Kamide, Norihiro. 2018. "Proof Theory of Paraconsistent Quantum Logic." *Journal of Philosophical Logic* 47: 301–24.

Kamide, Norihiro. 2021. "Lattice Logic, Bilattice Logic and Paraconsistent Quantum Logic: A Unified Framework Based on Monosequent Systems." *Journal of Philosophical Logic* 50: 781–811.

Katz, Jerrold J. 1998. *Realistic Rationalism*. Cambridge, Mass.: MIT Press.

Keshet, Ezra. 2018. "Dynamic Update Anaphora Logic: A Simple Analysis of Complex Anaphora." *Journal of Semantics* 35: 263–303.

Kosterec, Miloš. 2020. "Substitution Contradiction, Its Resolution and the Church-Rosser Theorem in TIL." *Journal of Philosophical Logic* 49: 121–33.

Krantz, Steven G. 2011. *The Proof Is in the Pudding: The Changing Nature of Mathematical Proof*. Dordrecht: Springer.

Kripke, Saul. 1963. "Semantic Analysis of Modal Logic I: Normal Modal Propositional Calculi." *Zeitschrift für mathematische Logik und Grundlagen der Mathematik* 9: 67–96.

Kuhn, Thomas. 1962. *The Structure of Scientific Revolutions*. Chicago: University of Chicago Press.

Larvor, Brendan. 2012. "How to Think About Informal Proofs." *Synthese* 187: 715–30.

Leech, Jessica. 2015. "Logic and the Laws of Thought." *Philosophers' Imprint* 15, no. 12: 1–27.

Lu-Adler, Huaping. 2018. *Kant and the Science of Logic: A Historical and Philosophical Reconstruction*. Oxford: Oxford University Press.

Mancosu, Paolo. 2008. "Introduction." In *The Philosophy of Mathematical Practice*, edited by Paolo Mancosu, 1–21. Oxford: Oxford University Press.

Martin, Ben. 2021a. "Anti-Exceptionalism About Logic and the Burden of Explanation." *Canadian Journal of Philosophy.*

Martin, Ben. 2021b. "Identifying Logic Evidence." *Synthese* 198: 9069–95.

Martin, Ben. 2021c. "Searching for Deep Disagreement in Logic: The Case of Dialetheism." *Topoi* 40: 1127–38.

Martin, Ben, and Ole T. Hjortland. 2021. "Logical Predictivism." *Journal of Philosophical Logic* 50: 285–318.

Martin, Ben, and Ole T. Hjortland. 2022. "Anti-Exceptionalism About Logic as Tradition Rejection." *Synthese.*

McFetridge, Ian G. 1990. "Logical Necessity: Some Issues." In *Logical Necessity and Other Essays*, edited by John Haldane and Roger Scruton, 135–54. London: Aristotelian Society Monograph Series.

McSweeney, Michaela M. 2019. "Logical Realism and the Metaphysics of Logic." *Philosophy Compass* 14:e12563 (online).

Meyer, Robert K. 1970. "R_I—The Bounds of Finitude. *Zeitschrift für mathematische Logik und Grundlagen der Mathematik* 16: 385–87.

Muñoz-Écija, Teresa, Benjamin Vargas-Quesada, and Zaida Chinchilla Rodríguez. 2019. "Coping with Methods for Delineating Emerging Fields: Nanoscience and Nanotechnology as a Case Study." *Journal of Informetrics* 13: 100976 (online).

Payette, Gillman, and Nicole Wyatt. 2018. "How Do Logics Explain?" *Australasian Journal of Philosophy* 96: 157–67.

Payne, Jonathan. 2015. "Natural Deduction for Modal Logic with a Back Tracking Operator." *Journal of Philosophical Logic* 44: 237–58.

Popper, Karl. 1959. *The Logic of Scientific Discovery*. London: Hutchinson.

Priest, Graham. 2006. *Doubt Truth to Be a Liar*. Oxford: Clarendon Press.

Priest, Graham. 2016. "Logical Disputes and the A Priori." *Logique et Analyse* 59: 347–66.

Qiu, Ren-Zong. 1989. "Models of Explanation and Explanation in Medicine." *International Studies in the Philosophy of Science* 3: 199–212.

Randall Holmes, Melvin. 2019. "Representation of Functions and Total Antisymmetric Relations in Monadic Third Order Logic." *Journal of Philosophical Logic* 48: 263–78.

Resnik, Michael D. 1999. "Against Logical Realism." *History and Philosophy of Logic* 20: 181–94.

Rota, Gian-Carlo. 1997. "The Phenomenology of Mathematical Beauty." *Synthese* 111: 171–82.

Sagi, Gil. 2021. "Logic as a Methodological Discipline. *Synthese*. Online first: doi:https://doi.org/10.1007/s11229-021-03223-3

Sher, Gila. 1991. *The Bounds of Logic*. Cambridge, Mass.: MIT Press.

Sider, Ted. 2011. *Writing the Book of the World*. Oxford: Clarendon Press.

Slaney, John, and Edward Walker, 2014. "The One-Variable Fragment of T→." *Journal of Philosophical Logic* 43: 867–78.

Soler, Léna, Sjoerd Zwart, Michael Lynch, and Vincent Israel-Jost. 2014. "Introduction." In *Science After the Practice Turn in the Philosophy, History, and Social Studies of Science*, edited by Léna Soler, Sjoerd Zwart, Michael Lynch, and Vincent Israel-Jost, 1–43. London: Routledge.

Steele, Katie, and Charlotte Werndl. 2013. "Climate Models, Calibration, and Confirmation." *British Journal for the Philosophy of Science* 64: 609–35.

Stei, Erik. 2020. "Disagreement About Logic from a Pluralist Perspective." *Philosophical Studies* 177: 3329–50.

Steinberger, Florian. 2020. "The Normative Status of Logic." *Stanford Encyclopedia of Philosophy* (Winter Edition), edited by Edward N. Zalta. https://plato.stanford.edu/archives/win2020/entries/logic-normative/

Tanswell, Fenner. 2015. "A Problem with the Dependence of Informal Proofs on Formal Proofs." *Philosophica Mathematica* 23: 295–310.

Tappenden, Jamie. 2008. "Mathematical Concepts: Fruitfulness and Naturalness." In *The Philosophy of Mathematical Practice*, edited by Paolo Mancosu, 276–301. Oxford: Oxford University Press.

Uckleman, Sara L., Jesse Alama, and Aleks Knoks. 2014. "A Curious Dialogical Logic and Its Composition Problem." *Journal of Philosophical Logic* 43: 1065–1100.

van Bendegem, Jean Paul. 2014. "The Impact of the Philosophy of Mathematical Practice on the Philosophy of Mathematics." In *Science After the Practice Turn in the Philosophy, History, and Social Studies of Science*, edited by Léna Soler, Sjoerd Zwart, Michael Lynch, and Vincent Israel-Jost, 215–26. London: Routledge.

van Kerkhove, Bart, and Jean Paul van Bendegem. 2004. "The Unreasonable Richness of Mathematics." *Journal of Cognition and Culture* 4: 525–49.

Warren, Jared. 2020. *Shadows of Syntax*. Oxford: Oxford University Press.

Williamson, Timothy. 2017. "Semantic Paradoxes and Abductive Method-
    ology." In *The Relevance of the Liar*, edited by B. Armour-Garb,
    325–46. Oxford: Oxford University Press.
Wintein, Stefan, and Reinhard Muskens. 2016. "A Gentzen Calculus for
    Nothing but the Truth." *Journal of Philosophical Logic* 45: 451–65.
Woody, Andrea I. 2015. "Re-orienting Discussions of Scientific Explana-
    tion: A Functional Perspective." *Studies in History and Philosophy of
    Science* 52: 79–87.
Wooldridge, Michael. 2009. *An Introduction to MultiAgent Systems*. 2nd
    ed. London: John Wiley and Sons.
Yang, Eunsuk. 2013. "R and Relevance Principle Revisited." *Journal of
    Philosophical Logic* 42: 767–82.

CHAPTER 9

ONE PHILOSOPHER'S MODUS PONENS IS ANOTHER'S MODUS TOLLENS: PANTOMEMES AND NISOWIR

JON WILLIAMSON

1. Introduction

Recall the two rules of inference, modus ponens (MP) and modus tollens (MT):

MP	MT
$\theta \rightarrow \phi$	$\theta \rightarrow \phi$
θ	$\neg\phi$
ϕ	$\neg\theta$

That one philosopher's modus ponens is another's modus ponens (henceforth, MP/MT) is the phenomenon that when one philosopher uses modus ponens to argue for some conclusion ϕ by appeal to $\theta \rightarrow \phi$ and θ, another might reasonably respond by simply denying ϕ and using modus tollens to undermine θ.[1]

Here is an example of Putnam's, which opens by discussing Quine's argument for ontological relativity:

> [E]ven *within* my language, or rather, within my metalanguage, I can define truth and reference in such a way that

---

[1] Here θ and/or ϕ may be logically complex propositions. Throughout the essay I follow standard practice in using "modus ponens" and "modus tollens" to refer either to rules of inference or to particular arguments that can be construed as appealing to applications of those rules of inference. Which usage is intended will be clear from the context.

Examining Philosophy Itself. Edited by Yafeng Shan.
Chapters and book compilation © 2023 Metaphilosophy LLC and John Wiley & Sons Ltd.
Published 2023 by John Wiley & Sons Ltd.

"Rabbit" refers to rabbits in my object language

comes out true, or in such a way that

"Rabbit" refers to mereological complements of rabbits in my object language

comes out true, without altering the set of true sentences of my object language in any way, and without altering the truth conditions for observation sentences as wholes; and in such a case, Quine tells us, there is no fact of the matter as to which reference/truth definition is correct. ...

In *Reason, Truth, and History* I used an argument similar to Quine's, but drew an opposite conclusion (thus illustrating the well known maxim that one philosopher's *modus ponens* is another philosopher's *modus tollens*). I argued there that metaphysical realism leaves us with no intelligible way to refute ontological relativity, and concluded that metaphysical realism is wrong. And I still see ontological relativity as a refutation of any philosophical position that leads to it. (Putnam 1994, 280)

Putnam takes the modus tollens route in response to Quine's modus ponens:

MP (Quine)	MT (Putnam)
$MR \rightarrow OR$	$MR \rightarrow OR$
MR	$\neg OR$
OR	$\neg MR$

Here MR stands for metaphysical realism and OR for ontological relativity.

It is characteristic of the MP/MT phenomenon that both parties agree with respect to the first, conditional premiss. The disagreement arises with respect to the second premiss and the conclusion. Note that nothing hangs on which party advocates the modus ponens and which advocates the modus tollens. By taking the contrapositive of the first premiss, Putnam's argument can be viewed as an instance of MP, and Quine's an instance of MT:

MP (Putnam)	MT (Quine)
$\neg OR \rightarrow \neg MR$	$\neg OR \rightarrow \neg MR$
$\neg OR$	MR
$\neg MR$	OR

Thus there is nothing in the logical form of these inferences to arbitrate between them. MP/MT does not admit a logical resolution.

MP/MT extrapolates beyond philosophy. For example, one can caricature some of the debate in the run-up to the 2020 U.S. presidential election as follows, where *TB* stands for "Trump is to be believed" and *AG* for "America is great again":

MP (pro-Trump)	MT (anti-Trump)
$TB \rightarrow AG$	$TB \rightarrow AG$
TB	$\neg AG$
AG	$\neg TB$

MP/MT is not, however, universally generalisable: it is not always reasonable to respond to an argument by modus ponens simply by denying the conclusion. Many arguments in mathematics, for example, can be cast as instances of modus ponens and are not so easy to resist when $\theta \rightarrow \phi$ and θ are supported by valid mathematical proofs. For example, suppose *PI* says of a particular structure *I* that *I* is a prime ideal in Boolean algebra *A*, and *MI* says that *I* is a maximal ideal in Boolean algebra *A*. The following modus ponens would not be easy to resist, where a proof is provided for both premisses:

MP (ideals)	MT (not viable)
$PI \rightarrow MI$	$PI \rightarrow MI$
PI	$\neg MI$
MI	$\neg PI$

The concern arises, then, that MP/MT poses a particular problem for philosophy. The aim of this essay is to clarify why MP/MT poses a problem for philosophy and to develop some strategies for resolving the problem in certain circumstances. In section 2, I argue that MP/MT poses a problem for the public practice of philosophy, because it makes it difficult for someone with no prior opinion about a conclusion of a philosophical argument to reach a reasoned opinion. I also distinguish this problem from standard epistemological scepticism. In section 3, I observe that arguments for the second premise of the MP or MT need to bottom out in some suitable form of public justification. Hence, I argue, appeals to philosophical intuition, evidence, truth, proof, and further philosophical argument fail to solve the MP/MT problem. In section 4, I discuss two examples from the area of formal epistemology: Cox's (1946) argument for probabilism and the argument of Hawthorne et al. (2017) for the Principle of Indifference. These arguments illustrate the limitations of mathematical proof in addressing MP/MT. I then develop two broad strategies that can help in some cases: an appeal to normal informal standards of what is reasonable (section 5), and argument by interpretation (section 6). I conclude in section 7 that these strategies require a shift in philosophical methodology towards a more prominent role for empirical justification and explication.

2. Why MP/MT Poses a Problem

MP/MT poses a problem because it raises the worry that very many philosophical arguments are what I call "pantomemes": arguments (often enthymemes) that are reasonable to resist simply by denying the conclusion. Schematically:

Oh yes it is!   Oh no it isn't!

$$\cdots$$

$$\frac{\cdots}{\phi} \qquad\qquad \frac{\neg\,\phi}{\cdots}$$

The concern is that very many philosophical arguments are instances of modus ponens, and, thanks to MP/MT, they are thereby pantomemes.

If very many philosophical arguments are pantomemes, then philosophy is in trouble. Suppose a third party who has no prior opinion about θ or ϕ wants to find out whether ϕ. Philosophers would point her to relevant arguments for and against ϕ. If, however, for each ϕ-argument there is a reasonable $\neg\phi$-argument, and vice versa, then philosophical arguments fail to provide grounds for preferring one of ϕ and $\neg\phi$ over the other. It thus seems practically impossible for our interested third party to come to a reasoned opinion about ϕ. Philosophy would at best be an amusing diversion—like a pantomime—not a reliable means of reaching reasoned opinions.

This worry applies to very many philosophical arguments, for the following reasons. First, as I explain below, philosophical arguments can be cast as (possibly enthymematic) inferences by modus ponens. Second, philosophical arguments are of a kind that can easily be challenged by MP/MT. Consider this second point. A philosophical argument is of interest to the extent that its conclusion is substantive and controversial. A controversial conclusion can be denied, however, and this opens the door to MP/MT.[2] The only way to resist MP/MT would be to provide a

---

[2] Indeed, it is sometimes claimed in jest that for each consistent philosophical position, and for many an inconsistent position, there exists some philosopher who advocates it. Insofar as there is more than a grain of truth to that maxim, one philosopher's modus ponens really is another's modus tollens.

justification of the premises of the modus ponens, of a sort that does not also apply to the premises of the modus tollens. In the case of mathematics, justification takes the form of proof from generally accepted axioms and definitions. But this avenue is not usually available to philosophical arguments. Even in the area of formal philosophy, philosophical premises are usually not all purely mathematical, and so not amenable to rigorous proof, as I illustrate in section 4. Moreover, it is hard to find generally accepted starting points in philosophy from which to begin proofs.

That philosophical arguments can be cast as arguments by modus ponens can be seen as follows. If an argument is intended to be deductive—that is, if the negation of the conclusion ϕ is taken to be incompatible with the conjunction θ of the premises—and the argument is not already in the form of an argument by modus ponens, then the conditional $\theta \rightarrow \phi$ can be taken to be an additional implicit premiss, subsuming it into the form of MP as set out above. If, on the other hand, the philosophical argument is intended to be inductive, that is, to render the conclusion plausible, then it can be cast as an instance of some inductive version of modus ponens and is susceptible to MP/MT, as I shall now show. For simplicity of exposition, we shall focus here on the case in which θ and ϕ are distinct atomic propositions and there is no further background information.

Any probabilistic logic validates the following inductive versions of MP and MT:

MP	MT
$\theta \rightarrow \phi$	$\theta \rightarrow \phi$
$\theta^{0.9}$	$\neg\phi^{0.9}$
$\phi^{[0.9,1]}$	$\neg\theta^{[0.9,1]}$

Here the modus ponens is to be read: if $\theta \rightarrow \phi$, and θ has probability 0.9, then ϕ has probability at least 0.9. Similarly for the modus tollens.[3]

For example, objective Bayesian inductive logic performs inferences using the probability function, from all those that satisfy constraints imposed by the premises, that has maximum entropy (Williamson 2017).

---

[3] Here the first premiss—the conditional—is taken to be certain, although this assumption can be relaxed, as we shall see below. There is nothing special about the value 0.9 here. To see this, consider for example the modus ponens. If the second premiss were θ^x, which attaches probability $x \in [0, 1]$ to θ, then one could calculate the probability of the conclusion as follows. The first premiss forces probability 0 on the state $\theta \wedge \neg\phi$. Probability x must thus be given to the remaining θ-state, $\theta \wedge \phi$. The remaining probability, $1 - x$, must then be divided between the two remaining states, $\neg\theta \wedge \phi$ and $\neg\theta \wedge \neg\phi$. Thus the probability of ϕ, which is the sum of the probabilities of $\theta \wedge \phi$ and $\neg\theta \wedge \phi$, must be between x and 1.

Objective Bayesian inductive logic validates the following versions of MP and MT:[4]

MP	MT
$\theta \to \phi$	$\theta \to \phi$
$\theta^{0.9}$	$\neg\phi^{0.9}$
$\overline{\phi^{0.95}}$	$\overline{\neg\theta^{0.95}}$

The above versions of MP and MT cover the case in which the conclusion is less than certain because the second premiss is less than certain. Alternatively, the conditional first premiss may be less than certain. In any probabilistic logic,

MP	MT
$\theta \to \phi^{0.9}$	$\theta \to \phi^{0.9}$
θ	$\neg\phi$
$\overline{\phi^{0.9}}$	$\overline{\neg\theta^{0.9}}$

In each case, the first premiss attaches probability 0.9 to the conditional $\theta \to \phi$.[5] Note that in the context of inductive logic, it is often more natural to consider conditional probability, rather than the probability of a material conditional. But the MP/MT problem also arises when conditional probabilities are used:

MP	MT
$\phi \mid \theta^{0.9}$	$\phi \mid \theta^{0.9}$
θ	$\neg\phi$
$\overline{\phi^{0.9}}$	$\overline{\neg\theta}$

Here the modus ponens is to be read: if the probability of ϕ conditional on θ is 0.9 and θ is true, then ϕ has probability at least 0.9.[6] Note that the

---

[4] In the case of the modus ponens, for instance, this is because the maximum entropy probability function gives the states $\neg\theta \wedge \phi$ and $\neg\theta \wedge \neg\phi$ the same probability, 0.05.

[5] Consider the MP, for example. The first premiss forces probability 0.1 on $\theta\wedge\neg\phi$, and the second premiss then ensures that $\theta \wedge \phi$ receives all the remaining probability, 0.9. ϕ is consistent only with the latter state, and so must receive probability 0.9.

[6] The conditional probability imposes a constraint on unconditional probabilities, namely, $P(\phi \wedge \theta) = 0.9\, P(\theta)$. We do not make the further assumption here that the conditional probability is *defined* by unconditional probabilities via the formula $P(\phi \mid \theta) =_{df} P(\phi \wedge \theta)/ P(\theta)$. Such a definition would not be compatible with the modus tollens, which gives θ zero probability. To see this, note that for the MT, $P(\phi) = 0$, so $0 = P(\phi \wedge \theta) = 0.9\, P(\theta)$, and hence $P(\theta) = 0$.

modus tollens yields a stronger conclusion than the modus ponens in this case. The two kinds of uncertainty can be combined, as follows.

MP	MT
$\phi \mid \theta^{0.9}$	$\phi \mid \theta^{0.9}$
$\theta^{0.9}$	$\neg\phi^{0.9}$
$\phi^{[0.81,1]}$	$\neg\theta^{[0.89,1]}$

Again, the modus tollens yields a stronger conclusion than the modus ponens.

In sum, philosophical arguments can straightforwardly be cast as arguments by modus ponens, and MP/MT applies to both deductive and inductive arguments by modus ponens.

*

It is worth observing that MP/MT is different to the standard problem of epistemological scepticism: it does not challenge the possibility of knowledge of the external world. The MP and MT parties may both think they know the conclusions of their arguments by virtue of their argumentation, and one of them may indeed be right. The problem is for an interested third party who has no prior opinion about θ or ϕ—how is she to be convinced one way or the other?

MP/MT is arguably a more serious problem than standard scepticism, for three key reasons. First, MP/MT is of practical as well as theoretical concern. There are few, if any, thoroughgoing philosophical sceptics who disavow all knowledge of the external world, yet there are many instances of arguments by modus tollens being used as serious responses to arguments by modus ponens, and vice versa. Second, MP/MT applies not only to claims about the external world but also to conclusions that are beyond the scope of standard scepticism: conclusions about the internal world, metaphysics, ethics, and so on. Third, scepticism is itself susceptible to MP/MT. Let K stand for "I know that," B for "I am a brain in a vat," and H for "This is a human hand in front of me." Consider:

MP (scepticism)	MT ("common sense")
$\neg K\neg B \rightarrow \neg KH$	$\neg K\neg B \rightarrow \neg KH$
$\neg K\neg B$	KH
$\neg KH$	$K\neg B$

Here the modus ponens represents the sceptical inference, while the modus tollens captures the "common-sense" response to scepticism. (This response is often attributed to Moore [1925], although Baldwin [1990, chap. 9, sec. 4] argues against this interpretation of Moore.)

Scepticism has been described as a scandal for philosophy (Kant 1781, B xxxix). Now a scandal can be a good thing because it can spark interest and engagement. MP/MT, on the other hand, is perhaps the bane of philosophy: it seems to undermine the whole public enterprise of philosophy.

3. Intuition and Public Justification

The common-sense response to scepticism is normally regarded as rather weak. The claim that when one apparently holds out one's hand one knows it is a human hand does, however, have the merit of agreeing with intuition. The question thus arises whether an appeal to intuition can mitigate the MP/MT problem. There are, after all, many advocates of appeals to intuitions in philosophy, including Bealer (1998, 2000), Williamson (2004), and Cath (2012), for example. If the second premiss of the modus ponens were more intuitive than that of the modus tollens, or vice versa, intuition would appear to favour one of the arguments over the other.

The difficulty here is that philosophical intuitions are notoriously subjective, and simply denying such an intuition is usually a reasonable response. Consider, for example, Ramsey's response to Keynes's intuition that there are logical probability relations between propositions:

> But let us now return to a more fundamental criticism of Mr. Keynes' views, which is the obvious one that there really do not seem to be any such things as the probability relations he describes. He supposes that, at any rate in certain cases, they can be perceived; but speaking for myself I feel confident that this is not true. I do not perceive them, and if I am to be persuaded that they exist it must be by argument; moreover I shrewdly suspect that others do not perceive them either, because they are able to come to so very little agreement as to which of them relates any two given propositions. ... If ... we take the simplest possible pairs of propositions such as "This is red" and "That is blue" or "This is red" and "That is red," whose logical relations should surely be easiest to see, no one, I think, pretends to be sure what is the probability relation which connects them. (Ramsey 1926, 161–62)

More generally, it is usually reasonable to respond to a philosophical argument by modus ponens that is grounded in intuition by putting forward a modus tollens that appeals to conflicting intuitions:

MP	MT
$\theta \rightarrow \phi$	$\theta \rightarrow \phi$
Intuitively: θ	Intuitively: $\neg\phi$
ϕ	$\neg\theta$

In fact, the proponent of the modus tollens does not even need to take $\neg\phi$ to be intuitive—she may have other reasons for doubting ϕ.[7] Since the first premiss, $\theta \rightarrow \phi$, is not under contention, this doubt about the conclusion ϕ of the modus ponens must extend to the second premiss, θ, however benign it may seem. (As we saw above, this is true of inductive as well as deductive arguments.) Hence, the MT proponent can reason as follows: I have grounds for denying ϕ, so, even though θ does seem benign, it must be a wolf in sheep's clothing, that is, a strong premiss formulated in such a way as to seem innocuous; therefore it should not trouble me that θ seems intuitive. We see, then, that the modus tollens can be a reasonable response to the modus ponens even where θ seems intuitive to the MT proponent and $\neg\phi$ does not. It is enough that the MT proponent has some other grounds for denying ϕ.

This consideration motivates a more general concern about the appeal to intuition. The worry is that it makes much philosophical argumentation look like artifice: that is, as trying to devise arguments by modus ponens in such a way that θ appears benign, even though from a logical point of view it is as strong as ϕ and should be as contentious as ϕ.[8]

*

We need to look further to find some means to resolve the MP/MT problem. It should by now be clear that to favour MP over MT we would need a form of public justification that applies to θ but not to $\neg\phi$. On the other hand, to favour MT over MP this kind of justification would need to apply to $\neg\phi$ and not to θ. Thus what we seek is an appropriate form of public justification. This would need to be public in the sense that it is available to all participants in the debate and objective enough to determinately favour one side over the other.

We saw that mathematical proof from a generally accepted starting point plays the required role in mathematics, but this form of public justification is seldom directly applicable to philosophical arguments, because it is rarely the case that all the premisses of a philosophical argument are purely mathematical, and because it is hard to find generally accepted starting points in philosophy. One might suggest that philosophical argument provides the required form of public justification, by analogy with mathematical proof. The problem of starting points remains, however. Unless there is a generally accepted starting point, we have regress: a philosophical argument for the second premiss θ will itself be susceptible to MP/MT.

[7] Presumably ϕ itself is not intuitively true—otherwise there would be no need for the MP proponent to argue for ϕ from a premiss that is supported by intuition. Thus, these other reasons are unlikely to conflict with intuitions about ϕ.

[8] We see an example of this in the next section, in relation to Cox's theorem. Cox originally presented his key premisses in a benign way, but when his argument was made rigorous, it became clear that the required premisses were no more benign than the conclusion.

I noted that an appeal to intuition is unsuccessful because intuition is personal and subjective, and it is reasonable to doubt a premiss that yields a contentious conclusion, even if the premiss is intuitive. Instead, one might suggest an appeal to evidence rather than intuition: the idea is that if θ is evidence and $\theta \rightarrow \phi$ is uncontentious, then ϕ can be established. Like intuition, however, evidence is personal, and though θ may be evidence for the MP proponent, it will not be evidence for the MT proponent, who argues that $\neg\theta$. This is the case under all the usual accounts of evidence—for example, evidence as knowledge (Williamson 2000), what is truly believed (Mitova 2017), what is rationally granted (Williamson 2015), or what is possessed as information (Rowbottom 2014). For example, if evidence is knowledge and θ is evidence for the MP proponent, then θ is believed by the MP proponent; however, it is not believed by the MT proponent, who argues against θ, so it is not evidence for the MT proponent. Hence, that the MP proponent takes θ as evidence will not trouble the MT proponent. Likewise, even if $\neg\phi$ is evidence for the MT proponent, it will not be evidence for the MP proponent, so the modus ponens is a reasonable response to the modus tollens.

Thus far I have suggested that intuition, mathematical proof, philosophical argument, and evidence each fail to provide the sort of public justification that could resolve the MP/MT problem. It is worth noting that an appeal to truth also fails to solve the MP/MT problem. Admittedly, if the two premisses of the modus ponens are true, then the conclusion of the modus tollens must be false, and vice versa. So there is a sense in which truth does adjudicate between the two arguments.[9] That at most one of these two arguments can be sound does not, however, imply that both cannot be reasonable. The problem remains that each argument offers a reasonable response to the other, where the truth of the second premiss of each argument is open to dispute. Moore (1939, 149), for example, suggests that it is enough to know H (that is, that this is a hand in front of me) for his response to scepticism to go through. This, however, is precisely what is at issue: the sceptic disavows this knowledge. Hence, the truth of KH cannot publicly arbitrate between the sceptical modus ponens and the "common-sense" modus tollens discussed above.

In response to these concerns, one might take issue with the claim that we need any kind of public justification at all. Perhaps philosophy is a personal journey and not in fact concerned with public persuasion. Perhaps the task of each philosopher is to add to the stock of arguments in the literature and to believe those propositions that best cohere with, best explain, or best unify, these arguments, her evidence, and her intuitions. It is compatible with this holistic enterprise that no philosophical argument is persuasive

---

[9] Under those views of evidence that take evidence to be factive, evidence adjudicates between the two arguments in a similar way. Under such views, if θ is evidence for the MP proponent and $\theta \rightarrow \phi$, then ϕ is true, so $\neg\phi$, being false, is not evidence for either party.

simpliciter, only relative to the entire literature and a particular philosopher's evidence and intuitions.

If this personalist response is correct, philosophy is necessarily elitist: only those who have mastered everything are in a position to form a view about anything. The personalist might bite the bullet here and accept that reasonable opinions are hard to come by in philosophy. But a further worry remains. The personalist response is also necessarily subjective: for any view, it may be reasonable to take the opposite view, provided one has sufficiently different intuitions and evidence. Thus, the personalist response merely concedes the point—it does not solve the MP/MT problem. Philosophical arguments remain pantomemes under this view. The fact is that philosophical arguments are usually presented as persuasive in their own right, and MP/MT threatens to undermine the conception of philosophy as a public practice that incrementally establishes claims by means of persuasive arguments.

4. Examples

Let us now consider two examples from the area of formal epistemology. These examples will help to illustrate the limitations of the use of mathematical proof in philosophical arguments. Sections 5 and 6 go on to use these examples to develop some more viable responses to the MP/MT problem.

The first example is known as Cox's theorem. This argument was originally put forward by Cox (1946). It takes the form of an argument by modus ponens, with first premiss $CS \rightarrow CP$ where CP is the claim that conditional credences are isomorphic to conditional probabilities and CS is a conjunction of "common-sense" conditions. Cox claims that these common-sense conditions hold, and he concludes that conditional credences are isomorphic to conditional probabilities. Cox's argument is one of an array of arguments for probabilism, that is, the view that rational degrees of belief are probabilities.

Now, Cox's original argument was invalid (Halpern 1999). In order to provide a rigorous argument, one needs to strengthen the common-sense conditions. Paris (1994, 24) provided a rigorous version, which can be stated as follows, where SL is the set of sentences of a propositional language L:

Theorem 1 (Cox/Paris). Suppose that a conditional belief function $\text{Bel}(\theta|\psi)$: $SL \times SL \rightarrow [0,1]$ is defined for each consistent ψ and each θ, that $\phi \wedge \psi$ is consistent, and

1. if θ is logically equivalent to θ' and ψ is logically equivalent to ψ', then $\text{Bel}(\theta|\psi) = \text{Bel}(\theta'|\psi')$,
2. if ψ logically implies θ, then $\text{Bel}(\theta|\psi) = 1$ and $\text{Bel}(\neg\,\theta|\psi) = 0$,

3. there is some continuous function $F: [0,1] \times [0,1] \rightarrow [0,1]$ which is strictly increasing in both coordinates on $(0,1] \times (0,1]$ such that $\mathrm{Bel}(\theta \wedge \phi | \psi) = F(\mathrm{Bel}(\theta | \phi \wedge \psi), \mathrm{Bel}(\phi | \psi))$,

4. there is some decreasing function $S: [0,1] \rightarrow [0,1]$ such that $\mathrm{Bel}(\neg\theta | \psi) = S(\mathrm{Bel}(\theta | \psi))$,

5. for any $a, b, c \in [0,1]$ and $\varepsilon > 0$ there are $\theta_1, \theta_2, \theta_3, \theta_4 \in SL$ such that $\theta_1 \wedge \theta_2 \wedge \theta_3$ is consistent and $\mathrm{Bel}(\theta_4 | \theta_1 \wedge \theta_2 \wedge \theta_3), \mathrm{Bel}(\theta_3 | \theta_1 \wedge \theta_2), \mathrm{Bel}(\theta_2 | \theta_1)$ are within ε of a, b, c, respectively.

Then there is a continuous, strictly increasing, surjective function $g: [0,1] \rightarrow [0,1]$ such that $g\mathrm{Bel}(\cdot | \tau)$ is a probability function on L, for any tautology τ.

While a mathematical proof does indeed provide a public justification for this theorem, the theorem itself constitutes only the first premiss, $CS \rightarrow CP$, of the modus ponens. There is ample room for someone who denies the conclusion to deny one or more of the conditions 1 to 5, or one of the other presuppositions of the theorem. For example, Shafer (2004) takes issue with conditions 3 and 4, and also the condition that there is a real-valued belief function. Colyvan (2004, 2008), on the other hand, denies the presupposition that this all takes place in classical logic. Conditions 1 and 2 would be challenged by anyone who thinks it too much to require that the agent in question be logically omniscient. Condition 5, which requires that the agent's credences assume denumerably many different values, is also contestable. Hence, despite the existence of a mathematical proof, the second premiss of the modus ponens lacks a suitable public justification, opening the door to MP/MT:

MP (Cox)	MT (anti-Cox)
$CS \rightarrow CP$	$CS \rightarrow CP$
CS	$\neg CP$
CP	$\neg CS$

*

Let us turn to a second example from the area of formal epistemology. Hawthorne et al. (2017) argued that the Principal Principle implies the Principle of Indifference, which we can write as $PP \rightarrow PoI$. Here PoI is a version of the Principle of Indifference that says one should believe a contingent atomic proposition to degree $1/2$, in the absence of any evidence that bears on the truth of that proposition. David Lewis's Principal Principle says that one should calibrate a degree of belief to a chance, given that chance and other admissible information. The Principal Principle needs to be accompanied by auxiliary conditions that specify facts about admissibility. Here is the key result:

> *Theorem 2 (Hawthorne and colleagues).* Suppose F is a contingent atomic proposition, $0 < x < 1$, and:

> *Principal Principle.* $P(A|XE) = x$, where X says that the chance A is x and E is admissible.

> *Condition 1.* If E is admissible and XE contains no information that renders F relevant to A, then EF is admissible.
> *Condition 2.* If E is admissible and XE contains no information relevant to F, then $E(A \leftrightarrow F)$ is admissible.
> Then $P(F|XE) = 1/2$ whenever E is admissible and XE contains no information pertaining to F or its relevance to A.

This result forms the conditional $PP \rightarrow Pol$, where Pol is the claim that $P(F|XE) = 1/2$ whenever E is admissible and XE contains no information pertaining to F or its relevance to A, and where PP encompasses the Principal Principle, conditions 1 and 2, and other presuppositions, including probabilism. (Note that this argument is directed at advocates of standard Bayesianism, in which probabilism is taken for granted.)

Again, there are two ways one can argue here. One can maintain with Hawthorne et al. (2017) that PP is well motivated and conclude Pol (the modus ponens), or one can endorse the modus tollens and argue that Pol being false tells against PP. Pettigrew (2020), Titelbaum and Hart (2020), and other detractors might be interpreted as taking this latter route, finding fault with conditions 1 and 2 in particular.

MP (Hawthorne et al.)	MT (anti–Hawthorne et al.)
$PP \rightarrow Pol$	$PP \rightarrow Pol$
PP	$\neg Pol$
Pol	$\neg PP$

In the next section I develop a strategy for telling between these two arguments, and we shall see that it provides just the sort of public justification that promises to resolve the MP/MT problem in certain cases.

*

These two examples typify the use of proof in formal philosophy. It is typical that mathematical proof provides a public justification for the first, conditional premiss of an argument. (In some cases—for example, Cox's theorem—the initial proof is invalid. As in Cox's case, the result can sometimes be reformulated, however, and made valid by strengthening the second premiss.) At this stage the first premiss becomes uncontentious, but the MP/MT problem then arises. This is because the substantive second premiss usually cannot be wholly justified by mathematical proof. Thus mathematical proof tends to be of limited use in resisting the MP/MT problem in philosophy.

5. Normal Informal Standards of What Is Reasonable

In this section and the next I put forward some positive proposals for tackling the MP/MT problem. In 5.1, I introduce normal informal standards of what is reasonable, or "nisowir" for short. We see in 5.2 that an appeal to nisowir can help to resolve the MP/MT problem. In 5.3, I note that this resolution is intended to be burden shifting and discuss concerns relating to circularity. In section 6 we turn to another strategy for addressing MP/MT, namely, argument by interpretation.

5.1. Explicating Nisowir

Let us consider the example of the Principal Principle and the Principle of Indifference in more detail. When defending the argument of Hawthorne et al. (2017) against critics, Landes, Wallmann, and Williamson (2021) argue that one can motivate the second premiss *PP* by appealing to normal informal standards of what is reasonable.

As Landes, Wallmann, and Williamson (2021) explain, David Lewis motivated his Principal Principle by means of a questionnaire, which begins as follows:

> First question. A certain coin is scheduled to be tossed at noon today. You are sure that this chosen coin is fair: it has a 50% chance of falling heads and a 50% chance of falling tails. You have no other relevant information. Consider the proposition that the coin tossed at noon today falls heads. To what degree would you now believe that proposition? Answer. 50%, of course. (Lewis 1980, 84).

The questionnaire provides helpful motivation because "we have some very firm and definite opinions concerning reasonable credence about chance. These opinions seem to me to afford the best grip we have on the concept of chance" (Lewis 1980, 84).

Landes, Wallmann, and Williamson (2021, § 2.1) provide a similar questionnaire:

Imagine you are a goat farmer, interested in the colour of the next goat to be born to your herd. Your evidence determines that the chance of that goat—Ashley, say—being brown (A) is 0.7. Consider three alternative scenarios, and ask yourself in each case what degree of belief in A would be reasonable:

(a)   You have no further evidence.
      Answer. Degree 0.7 stands out as uniquely reasonable.

(b)   You do have further evidence, namely some contingent atomic proposition F (e.g., the proposition that Finley, another goat, escapes).
      Answer. Still 0.7. Without any evidence that relates F to A, you have no grounds for any other choice. The chance of A gives robust grounds for believing A to degree 0.7.

(c)   You have instead evidence just that $A \leftrightarrow F$, for some contingent atomic proposition F (e.g., F says that Francis is brown and you learn that Ashley and Francis are identical twins, so $A \leftrightarrow F$).
      Answer. Still 0.7. With no other evidence bearing on F, learning that A and F have the same truth value doesn't tell you anything about A.

Landes, Wallmann, and Williamson (2021) argue that such questionnaires serve to identify normal informal standards of what is reasonable. These are norms of reasonableness that are conformed to widely enough to be considered normal or standard requirements. For example: the claim that one is rationally required to believe to the same degree that a fair coin will land heads and that it will land tails; the claim that one is rationally permitted to bet on either outcome at even odds.

There is a difference between these informal nisowir and formal conditions that can be used to explicate them. Lewis's Principal Principle, introduced in section 4 above, can be considered a formal explication of the nisowir that are elicited by his questionnaire. The auxiliary admissibility conditions 1 and 2, also introduced in section 4, explicate the nisowir elicited by scenarios (*b*) and (*c*) in the questionnaire of Landes, Wallmann, and Williamson (2021) quoted above.

Something needs to be said here about what it is to explicate nisowir. This is because the term "explication" was introduced by Carnap to apply only to concepts, not to nisowir: "The task of *explication* consists in transforming a given more or less inexact concept into an exact one or, rather, in replacing the first by the second" (Carnap 1950, 3). For example, the concept *temperature* explicates the comparative concept *warmer* (Carnap 1950, 12).[10]

We can understand an explication of nisowir to be analogous to Carnap's notion of explication of a concept. The task of explication of nisowir consists in replacing the more or less inexact nisowir by an exact standard of what is reasonable. Note that such an explication often needs to subsume a whole class of similar nisowir. The Principal Principle, for example, replaces many inexact nisowir concerning reasonable degree of belief that can be elicited from Lewis's questionnaire and others. Thus an explication of nisowir often needs to generalise, but not overgeneralise, a class of related nisowir. An explication of nisowir also needs to satisfy some other desiderata. Carnap provides four requirements for an explication of a concept, and these apply equally to an explication of nisowir: similarity to the explicandum, exactness, fruitfulness, and simplicity (Carnap 1950, sec. 3).

An explication of nisowir may invoke Carnapian explications of concepts. For example, *PP* explicates nisowir, and this explication presupposes that the concept of rational degree of belief is explicated by mathematical probability. (This move is appropriate here because the argument seeks to point out a consequence of the Bayesian framework. This move would not be appropriate in the context of Cox's theorem, which can be thought of as an argument in favour of a probabilistic explication of the concept of rational degree of belief.)

The possibility arises that certain nisowir might be explicated in different, mutually incompatible ways. Moreover, the current evidence may underdetermine which of these possible explications best balances the five desiderata introduced above—that is, the requirements that explications should appropriately generalise the nisowir, be similar to the nisowir, and be exact, fruitful, and simple.

It may be, however, that one of these explications stands out as best in some particular context. For example, in the context of the standard Bayesian framework, the Principal Principle arguably stands out as being

---

[10] While Carnap gave the process of explication its name, he was not the first to discuss this process. For example, Matthew Young argues as follows:

> [P]leasure and pain, heat and cold, probability and improbability, virtue and vice, which are estimated by degrees, are not measurable. ... Now to make quantities which consist of degrees, and therefore are not measurable, the subject of mathematical comparison, an arbitrary measure is assigned, by referring them to some measurable quantity to which they are related. Thus, in the graduation of the thermometer, an arbitrary measure is established for heat and cold, for the degrees of heat are referred to the expansion of the fluid contained in the thermometer, which is measurable, and to which heat is related. In the same manner, probability has no measure in itself; but an arbitrary measure is assigned to it, by referring it to the ratio of the number of chances by which the event may happen or fail; and thus it becomes the subject of mathematical calculation, in the same manner as the degrees of heat. (1800, 80–81)

the most natural way to explicate the nisowir elicited by Lewis's question-naire. Such an explication may not stand out as best in other contexts. For example, the Principal Principle would not be appropriate in the con-text of the framework of Dempster-Shafer belief functions, which does not presuppose that rational degree of belief can be explicated by conditional probability.

Suppose that some explication of nisowir stands out as best, by a long way, given the standard presuppositions of the context. We shall call such an explication a *canonical* explication of nisowir in that context.

5.2. How Nisowir Can Resolve MP/MT

An appeal to a canonical explication of nisowir can help with the MP/MT problem. If *PP* can be justified as a canonical explication of nisowir, and no such justification can be provided for ¬*PoI*, then this would favour the modus ponens over the modus tollens in the *PP→PoI* argument introduced in section 4.

Such a line of reasoning might be motivated more fully as follows:

1. Those informal standards of what is reasonable that have become entrenched as nisowir have become so because they have been par-ticularly conducive to our survival or to our achieving other goals.
2. Therefore, it is indeed reasonable to conform to such a norm. That is, a nisowir is justified, in the absence of any evidence against its rea-sonableness.
3. The role of an exact normative theory such as Bayesianism is to explicate and unify many nisowir, and to resolve any inconsistencies between nisowir, in order to provide guidance in complex situations where the nisowir do not suffice on their own.
4. In the context of standard Bayesianism, *PP* is a canonical explication of nisowir.
5. Therefore, in the context of standard Bayesianism, *PP* is justified in virtue of the nisowir that *PP* explicates being justified.
6. That *PP* implies *PoI* is justified by a mathematical proof.
7. Therefore, *PoI* is justified by a valid argument (by modus ponens) from justified premisses, in the context of standard Bayesianism.

This line of reasoning, if successful, shifts the burden of proof onto the proponent of the modus tollens. The MT proponent cannot simply respond with an analogous line of reasoning, because ¬*PoI* is not a canonical explication of nisowir. ¬*PoI* says that one is not rationally required to be indifferent between an atomic proposition and its negation, in the absence of any evidence relevant to that proposition. While some do indeed endorse this claim, many take the opposite view. Thus this claim is hardly a normal informal standard of what is reasonable. The fact is that the Principle of Indifference is very contentious—much more so than the Principal Principle.

This line of reasoning can be generalised to mitigate the MP/MT problem in a broad range of scenarios. Most directly, if the second premiss θ of an MP is any formal statement about what is reasonable or rational, then we can ask if it is a canonical explication of nisowir, in the relevant context. If it is, we can appeal to an analogous line of reasoning. As we have seen, one can argue that while PP is a canonical explication of nisowir, $\neg PoI$ is not. In the case of Cox's argument, neither the conjunction of the conditions of Cox's theorem nor the negation of its conclusion can plausibly be construed as a canonical explication of nisowir. Thus while this line of reasoning shifts the burden of proof to Bayesians who reject PoI, it favours neither Cox's MP nor the anti-Cox MT. This suggests that, ceteris paribus, Cox's MP fails to provide a persuasive argument for probabilism, and its detractors' MT fails to provide a persuasive argument against Cox's common-sense conditions.

The above line of reasoning can also be generalised to the situation in which θ is not a formal statement but is instead an informal statement about what is reasonable. In that case, we can ask whether θ is a nisowir, rather than a canonical explication of nisowir. If so, we can invoke a version of the above line of reasoning, but omitting steps 3 to 5.

A further generalisation is possible: if θ is any other proposition, one can ask whether normal informal standards of what is reasonable favour believing θ, when one is pressed on the matter. This consideration helps neither side of the Putnam-Quine disagreement, because both metaphysical realism and the negation of ontological relativity go beyond the diktats of normal standards of what is reasonable. A similar point can be made about the pro-Trump/anti-Trump instance of MP/MT. This consideration, however, is arguably applicable to the common-sense response to scepticism. Consider the common-sense modus tollens first. When I apparently hold out my hand in front of me, it would infringe normal informal standards of what is reasonable if I were to deny (or even, when pressed, withhold judgement on) the claim that I know that this is a human hand in front of me. Thus nisowir favour believing the second premiss of the common-sense MT. On the other hand, nisowir do not apparently favour believing the second premiss of the sceptical modus ponens, namely, that I don't know that I'm not a brain in a vat. Questionnaires could be used to support these two claims about nisowir. Such questionnaires would then provide a public justification of the two claims that would shift the burden of proof to the sceptic.

To summarise: if (i) the second premiss of a philosophical modus ponens is a nisowir or a canonical explication of nisowir, or nisowir favour believing the second premiss when pressed, and (ii) the second premiss of the corresponding modus tollens does not satisfy this condition, then there are grounds for siding with the modus ponens, against the modus tollens.[11] Any public justification of (i) and (ii)—for example, a Lewis-style questionnaire—can, when taken together with a public justification for the first premiss, provide the means to persuade an interested third party of the conclusion of the modus ponens. On the other hand, if nisowir underpin the second premiss of the modus tollens but not the second premiss of the modus ponens, then suitable public justifications of analogues of (i) and (ii) will shift the burden of proof to the MP proponent.

5.3. Discussion

It is important to emphasise that the appeal to nisowir is intended to be burden shifting rather than decisive. When applied to the common-sense response to scepticism, for example, it does not amount to a refutation of scepticism. But a shift in the burden of proof is enough to ward off the challenge posed by MP/MT because it is enough to favour one side over the other. If the MP is justified by nisowir but the MT is not, then it is not reasonable to respond to the MP by advocating the MT, in the absence of some suitable public justification of the MT that does not also apply to the MP. The philosophical argument in question is thus not a pantomeme.

It is also worth observing that the above motivation in terms of claims 1 to 7 appeals to certain empirical assertions. Claim 1, for example, is an empirical assertion; indeed, the origin of norms is an important question in sociology (Horne and Mollborn 2020).[12] In addition, the question of whether a purported nisowir is indeed a nisowir is an empirical question. The questionnaires of Lewis (1980) and Landes, Wallmann, and Williamson (2021) are intended to help us recognise nisowir. Where it is uncertain whether a purported nisowir is really a nisowir, a more structured survey may be required to settle the question; the methods of experimental philosophy can be of assistance in this regard. No attempt will be made at a sustained defence of these empirical claims here. Rather, the thesis of this section is that if certain empirical claims are true, then the MP/MT problem can be mitigated.

---

[11] It is crucial not to overlook condition (ii) here. For example, in order to maintain that the $PP \rightarrow PoI$ modus ponens is in a better position than the modus tollens, one needs not only to motivate the second premiss of the MP by appeal to nisowir but also to make a case that the second premiss of the MT cannot be so motivated.

[12] Claim 1 does not require that each individual nisowir confers evolutionary advantage; it is sufficient that the human capacity to generate such norms leads to evolutionary advantage (Clark 1990), or indeed some other sort of advantage, so that, in general, nisowir are likely to lead to advantage. Moreover, it is enough that individual nisowir are usually only of heuristic value, reliable in a typical range of circumstances, but not all. Such a nisowir can be relied upon unless the circumstance is known to be exceptional.

One might be concerned that claim 1 merely provides pragmatic motivation for claim 2, when what is needed is an epistemic justification. The step from 1 to 2 can, however, be made on epistemic grounds: one can argue that nisowir have become entrenched precisely because they lead to beliefs that are likely to be true; hence, it is reasonable to conform to them.

In addition, the motivation of section 5.2 is intended to be explanatory, rather than persuasive. It is intended to explain how an appeal to nisowir can resolve the MP/MT problem, rather than persuade a detractor that it solves the problem. This more limited ambition is appropriate because such a line of reasoning is itself a philosophical argument and thus prone to the MP/MT problem. To see this, note that the argument might be summarised as concluding that the MP/MT problem can be solved in certain situations (*MS*) on the grounds that nisowir have normative force (*NN*). This can be viewed as an argument by modus ponens, and opens the door to a response by modus tollens:

MP (pro-solution)	MT (anti-solution)
$NN \rightarrow MS$	$NN \rightarrow MS$
NN	$\neg MS$
MS	$\neg NN$

The pro-solution modus ponens is self-explanatory because, if sound, it explains why one should believe the contentious second premiss, and hence why one should believe the conclusion. This is because normal informal standards of what is reasonable favour believing *NN*, that is, that nisowir have normative force, when pressed to take some attitude towards *NN*. To see this, note for instance that if it is a nisowir that one ought to equivocate between a fair coin landing heads or tails, then normal standards favour believing—when pressed—that one ought to so equivocate. Hence, if we grant that the MP is sound and thus that *NN* is true, one can see why one would be justified in believing *NN*. This helps to explain why one would be justified in believing the conclusion, *MS*.

Of course, there is a circularity to this line of reasoning: the explanation of *NN* presumes its truth. Hence the ambition of the reasoning of section 5.2 is limited to explanation rather than persuasion. That a particular explanation only succeeds in explaining if it is true is not in itself a problem—many of our best explanations have this characteristic.[13]

In this section, then, we have seen that an appeal to nisowir, and canonical explications of nisowir, can provide a burden-shifting resolution to the

---

[13] One might think that this circularity precludes any grounds for favouring the pro-solution MP over the anti-solution MT. That conclusion, however, would be too quick. The pro-solution modus ponens, I have argued, is at least self-explanatory. On the other hand, the anti-solution modus tollens is not even self-explanatory: the truth of $\neg MS$ would not explain why one would be justified in believing $\neg MS$. To the extent that being self-explanatory is a virtue of an argument, this virtue favours the pro-solution MP over the anti-solution MT. Hence, that the MP is explanatory counts somewhat in its favour, despite the inherent circularity. Note that this reasoning is stable under the logical transformation discussed in section 1, where, by taking the contrapositive of the first premiss, one can construe the pro-solution argument as a modus tollens and the anti-solution response as a modus ponens.

MP/MT problem. We have also seen how this strategy can be applied to resolve the debate around $PP \to POI$ in favour of the modus ponens and the debate about scepticism in favour of the modus tollens, should suitable public justifications be provided. (The focus here has been on developing a general strategy to address MP/MT, rather than on providing detailed public justifications to support claims about particular arguments.) I have also developed a line of reasoning that—if its empirical claims are correct—can explain why the nisowir strategy is successful. In the next section I put forward another potential response to the MP/MT problem that can be used in combination with an appeal to nisowir.

6. Argument by Interpretation

Recall our two examples in formal epistemology, introduced in section 4. We have seen that the MP/MT problem can be mitigated in the case of the argument of Hawthorne et al. (2017) if we appeal to canonical explications of nisowir. This strategy, however, does not help Cox's argument. The question thus arises as to how best to motivate probabilism, given that Cox's argument falls to MP/MT. This question is important here because the argument of Hawthorne et al. (2017) presupposes probabilism.

Accuracy arguments for probabilism provide an alternative to Cox's argument (Joyce 1998; Predd et al. 2009; Pettigrew 2016). These arguments, however, are also susceptible to MP/MT, as we shall now see. Accuracy arguments for probabilism can usually be summarised as follows: rational degrees of belief minimise inaccuracy (MI), and an accuracy measure satisfies certain technical conditions including strict propriety (SP), so rational degrees of belief are probabilities (BP).

Strict propriety says that an accuracy function a should be such that each belief function Bel uniquely maximises its own expected accuracy,

$$\sum_{\omega \in \Omega} Bel(\omega)\, a(Bel, \omega),$$

where Ω is the set of possible worlds. The problem is that SP is very far from being a nisowir or an explication of nisowir. This opens the door to MP/MT:

MP (pro-accuracy)	MT (anti-accuracy)
$(MI \wedge SP) \to BP$	$(MI \wedge SP) \to BP$
$MI \wedge SP$	$\neg BP$
BP	$\neg(MI \wedge SP)$

Attempts to provide philosophical arguments for SP are prone to the same problem: they are not themselves grounded in nisowir (see, e.g., Campbell-Moore and Levinstein 2021). Thus, accuracy arguments apparently fail to provide a viable alternative to Cox's argument.

Perhaps the classic argument for probabilism is the Dutch book argument. This can be formulated as follows: degrees of belief are betting quotients (BQ), and rational betting quotients avoid sure loss (AL), so rational degrees of belief are probabilities (BP) (see, e.g., Paris 1994, chap. 3; Gillies 2000, chap. 4). A betting quotient is a value at which one would be prepared to bet for or against a given proposition: x is a betting quotient for proposition θ if one would consider xS a fair price to pay to receive S in return if θ turns out to be true, for an unknown stake S that may be positive or negative. The question is whether MP/MT poses a problem for the Dutch book argument:

MP (Dutch book)	MT (anti-Dutch book)
$(BQ \wedge AL) \rightarrow BP$	$(BQ \wedge AL) \rightarrow BP$
$BQ \wedge AL$	$\neg BP$
BP	$\neg(BQ \wedge AL)$

While normal standards of what is reasonable might favour believing that rational betting quotients avoid sure loss (AL), the same cannot be said for the claim that degrees of belief are betting quotients, BQ. BQ is an interpretation or explication of one's degree of belief in θ as the betting rate that one would consider fair, whether betting for or against θ. Hence the Dutch book MP can be viewed as an "argument by interpretation" (Williamson 2010, chap. 3, sec. 1): a key premiss proposition, BQ, provides an exact interpretation of degree of belief, and the viability of the argument hinges on this interpretation.

As Ramsey notes, "[T]he degree of a belief … has no precise meaning unless we specify more exactly how it is to be measured" (1926, 167). And, "The old-established way of measuring a person's belief is to propose a bet, and see what are the lowest odds which he will accept" (172). The latter quote suggests that the betting-quotient interpretation of degree of belief might be a canonical explication of the concept of degree of belief—that is, an explication that stands out as best, by a long shot, given the standard presuppositions of the context.

If so, this provides a further means to address the MP/MT problem: an appeal to canonical explications of concepts, in addition to nisowir and canonical explications of nisowir. The reasoning in favour of the Dutch book MP would thus be as follows: the first premiss is justified by a mathematical proof; the first conjunct BQ of the second premiss is justified in virtue of being a canonical explication of a concept; the second conjunct AL is justified by nisowir. If successful, this shifts the burden of proof to the proponent of the anti–Dutch book MT. Such a proponent must either provide grounds to reject the mathematical proof, the canonical explication of the concept of degree of belief, or the nisowir behind the claim that betting quotients that incur sure loss are irrational.

If the MT proponent were to reject the interpretation of degree of belief to which the MP appeals, the worry would arise that the MP proponent and the MT proponent are simply talking past each other. Thus the burden is on the MT proponent to provide grounds for denying that betting quotients offer a canonical explication of the concept of degree of belief. The natural way to do this would be to provide an alternative explication of the concept and argue that the betting-quotient explication does not stand out as superior to this alternative explication.

For example, the MT proponent might admit that the betting-quotient interpretation is exact, fruitful, and simple but point out that we do not, in practice, bet at the same rate for or against a proposition (see, e.g., Walley 1991, 3), raising this as a concern for the claim that the betting-quotient explication is sufficiently similar to the explicandum. The MT proponent might argue that this alternative dual-rate explication is better than the single-rate betting-quotient explication of degree of belief.

The advocate of the betting-quotient explication can, however, resist this conclusion by observing that when one allows different buy and sell rates, the Dutch book argument yields imprecise probability instead of standard precise probability, and that this leads to certain disadvantages. Imprecise probability is certainly less simple (see, e.g., Augustin et al. 2014; Troffaes and de Cooman 2014) and arguably less fruitful than precise probability, because it is a strictly weaker framework. Moreover, even if different rates for buying and selling bets are more realistic, that does not on its own imply that this alternative betting set-up is any closer to the explicandum than the single-rate betting-quotient approach. Indeed, while both precise and imprecise probabilists would take single-rate betting quotients to be an obvious indicator of strength of belief, it is much more doubtful that what is measured by two different rates for buying and selling is strength of belief, as opposed to, say, risk aversion.

In sum, then, the proponent of the Dutch book argument for probabilism can justify the claim that degrees of belief are betting quotients by invoking it as a canonical explication of the concept of degree of belief. The Dutch book argument can be thought of as an argument by interpretation, and this argumentative strategy provides a further weapon in the arsenal against MP/MT.

7. Conclusion

That one philosopher's modus ponens is another's modus tollens poses a serious challenge to philosophical practice. In order to decide between the modus ponens and the modus tollens one needs public justifications that can favour one argument over the other. Otherwise, philosophical arguments are mere pantomemes.

Mathematical proof is one kind of public justification, but it is generally not applicable to all the premises of a philosophical argument, even in areas such as formal epistemology. There are other kinds of public justification, however: evidence of normal informal standards of what is reasonable (nisowir), canonical explications of nisowir, and canonical explications of concepts can also be used to justify philosophical premises. The Dutch book argument for probabilism is interesting because it involves all three of these tools.[14]

This toolkit requires a shift in philosophical methodology. It is an empirical question whether a claim about what is reasonable is a nisowir. Answering such a question may require an appeal to questionnaires, such as the one provided by David Lewis, or the more systematic surveys of experimental philosophy. In addition, determining whether an explication is canonical requires careful weighing of desiderata. As Carnap noted, "The question whether the solution is right or wrong makes no good sense because there is no clear-cut answer. The question should rather be whether the proposed solution is satisfactory" (1950, 4).

To give a recent example, some might argue that Pearl's mathematisation of causality in terms of conditional probabilistic independence qualifies as a canonical explication of causality (Pearl 1988, 2000). It is exact, fruitful, and simple. Is it sufficiently similar to the explicandum? On the one hand, some have argued that it admits counterexamples (see, e.g., McKim and Turner 1997; Williamson 2005), and we might also question whether it can successfully accommodate the rich epistemology of causality, which arguably seeks evidence of mechanisms in addition to evidence of correlation (Russo and Williamson 2007). On the other hand, explication is a transformative process: it is the replacement of something informal by something exact, and this process can tolerate some significant discrepancies between explicandum and explicatum. When probability was axiomatized, for example, the informal concept, which was not universally taken to be additive (Bernoulli 1713), was replaced by an additive concept (Kolmogorov 1933). This kind of additive mathematisation of probability quickly became entrenched in mathematics and statistics as the canonical explication of the informal concept. The question thus arises whether the informal concept of causality might eventually be replaced by Pearl's mathematisation despite the infelicity of the explication. Time will tell; in this case we are apparently not yet in a position to make a judgement. In general, it can be very difficult to evaluate explications without some benefit of hindsight.

---

[14] There is no claim here that these tools are exhaustive, that is, that they provide the only means of addressing the MP/MT problem. MP/MT poses a challenge that must be met, however. If there are other tools, it is important to identify them and explain how they work.

A philosophical methodology that has a central place for nisowir and explication thus requires considerations rather alien to the usual a priori conceptual analysis and metaphysical theorising that currently characterise analytic philosophy. But some such transformation is required to avoid the impasse of MP/MT.

Acknowledgements

I am very grateful to Graeme Forbes, Mark Pinder, Jack Ritchie, Michael Wilde, and the anonymous referees for many helpful comments. This research was supported by funding from the Leverhulme Trust (grant RPG-2019-059) and the Deutsche Forschungsgemeinschaft (DFG, grant LA 4093/3-1).

References

Augustin, T., F. P. A. Coolen, G. de Cooman, and M. C. M. Troffaes. 2014. *Introduction to Imprecise Probabilities*. Wiley Series in Probability and Statistics. Chichester: Wiley.

Baldwin, T. 1990. *G. E. Moore: The Arguments of the Philosophers*. London: Routledge.

Bealer, G. 1998. "Intuition and the Autonomy of Philosophy. In *Rethinking Intuition: The Psychology of Intuition and Its Role in Philosophical Inquiry*, edited by M. DePaul and W. Ramsey, 113–27. Lanham, Md.: Rowman and Littlefield.

Bealer, G. 2000. "A Theory of the A Priori." *Pacific Philosophical Quarterly* 81, no. 1: 1–30.

Bernoulli, J. [1713] 2006. *Ars Conjectandi*. Translated by Edith Dudley Sylla. Baltimore: Johns Hopkins University Press.

Campbell-Moore, C., and B. A. Levinstein. 2021. "Strict Propriety Is Weak." *Analysis* 81, no. 1: 8–13.

Carnap, R. [1950] 1962. *Logical Foundations of Probability*. 2nd ed. London: Routledge and Kegan Paul.

Cath, Y. 2012. "Evidence and Intuition." *Episteme* 9, no. 4: 311–28.

Clark, A. 1990. "Connectionism, Competence, and Explanation." In *The Philosophy of Artificial Intelligence*, edited by M. A. Boden, 281–308. Oxford: Oxford University Press.

Colyvan, M. 2004. "The Philosophical Significance of Cox's Theorem." *International Journal of Approximate Reasoning* 37: 71–85.

Colyvan, M. 2008. "Is Probability the Only Coherent Approach to Uncertainty?" *Risk Analysis* 28, no. 3: 645–52.

Cox, R. T. 1946. "Probability, Frequency and Reasonable Expectation." *American Journal of Physics* 14, no. 1: 1–3.

Gillies, D. 2000. *Philosophical Theories of Probability*. London: Routledge.

Halpern, J. Y. 1999. "Cox's Theorem Revisited." *Journal of Artificial Intelligence Research* 11: 429–35.

Hawthorne, J., J. Landes, C. Wallmann, and J. Williamson. 2017. "The Principal Principle Implies the Principle of Indifference." *British Journal for the Philosophy of Science* 68: 123–31.

Horne, C., and S. Mollborn. 2020. "Norms: An Integrated Framework." *Annual Review of Sociology* 46, no. 1: 467–87.

Joyce, J. M. 1998. "A Nonpragmatic Vindication of Probabilism." *Philosophy of Science* 65, no. 4: 575–603.

Kant, I. [1781; 2nd ed. 1787] 1929. *Critique of Pure Reason*. Translated by Norman Kemp Smith. London: Macmillan.

Kolmogorov, A. N. [1933] 1950. *The Foundations of the Theory of Probability*. New York: Chelsea.

Landes, J., C. Wallmann, and J. Williamson. 2021. "The Principal Principle, Admissibility, and Normal Informal Standards of What Is Reasonable." *European Journal of Philosophy of Science* 11, no. 2: 36.

Lewis, D. K. [1980] 1986. "A Subjectivist's Guide to Objective Chance." In *Philosophical Papers*, 2: 83–132. With postscripts. Oxford: Oxford University Press.

McKim, V. R., and S. Turner. 1997. *Causality in Crisis? Statistical Methods and the Search for Causal Knowledge in the Social Sciences*. Notre Dame: University of Notre Dame Press.

Mitova, V. 2017. *Believable Evidence*. Cambridge: Cambridge University Press.

Moore, G. [1925] 2013. "A Defence of Common Sense." In *Philosophical Papers*, 32–59. London: Routledge.

Moore, G. [1939] 2013. "Proof of an External World. In *Philosophical Papers*, 127–150. London: Routledge.

Paris, J. B. 1994. *The Uncertain Reasoner's Companion*. Cambridge: Cambridge University Press.

Pearl, J. 1988. *Probabilistic Reasoning in Intelligent Systems: Networks of Plausible Inference*. San Mateo, Calif.: Morgan Kaufmann.

Pearl, J. 2000. *Causality: Models, Reasoning, and Inference*. Cambridge: Cambridge University Press.

Pettigrew, R. 2016. *Accuracy and the Laws of Credence*. Oxford: Oxford University Press.

Pettigrew, R. 2020. "The Principal Principle Does Not Imply the Principle of Indifference." *British Journal for the Philosophy of Science* 71, no. 2: 605–19.

Predd, J. B., R. Seiringer, E. H. Lieb, D. N. Osherson, H. V. Poor, and S. R. Kulkarni. 2009. "Probabilistic Coherence and Proper Scoring Rules." *IEEE Transactions on Information Theory* 55, no. 10: 4786–92.

Putnam, H. 1994. *Words and Life*. Edited by James Conant. Cambridge, Mass.: Harvard University Press.

Ramsey, F. P. [1926] 1931. "Truth and Probability." In *The Foundations of Mathematics and Other Logical Essays*, edited by R. Braithwaite, 156–98. London: Routledge.

Rowbottom, D. P. 2014. "Information Versus Knowledge in Confirmation Theory." *Logique et analyse* 57, no. 226: 137–49.

Russo, F., and J. Williamson. 2007. "Interpreting Causality in the Health Sciences." *International Studies in the Philosophy of Science* 21, no. 2: 157–70.

Shafer, G. 2004. "Comments on 'Constructing a Logic of Plausible Inference: A Guide to Cox's Theorem,' by Kevin S. Van Horn." *International Journal of Approximate Reasoning* 35: 97–105.

Titelbaum, M. G., and C. Hart. 2020. "The Principal Principle Does Not Imply the Principle of Indifference, Because Conditioning on Biconditionals Is Counterintuitive." *British Journal for the Philosophy of Science* 71, no. 2: 621–32.

Troffaes, M. C. M., and G. de Cooman. 2014. *Lower Previsions*. Wiley Series in Probability and Statistics. Chichester: Wiley.

Walley, P. 1991. *Statistical Reasoning with Imprecise Probabilities*. London: Chapman and Hall.

Williamson, J. 2005. *Bayesian Nets and Causality: Philosophical and Computational Foundations*. Oxford: Oxford University Press.

Williamson, J. 2010. *In Defence of Objective Bayesianism*. Oxford: Oxford University Press.

Williamson, J. 2015. "Deliberation, Judgement and the Nature of Evidence." *Economics and Philosophy* 31, no. 1: 27–65.

Williamson, J. 2017. *Lectures on Inductive Logic*. Oxford: Oxford University Press.

Williamson, T. 2000. *Knowledge and Its limits*. Oxford: Oxford University Press.

Williamson, T. 2004. "Philosophical 'Intuitions' and Scepticism About Judgement." *Dialectica* 54, no. 1: 109–53.

Young, M. 1800. "On the Force of Testimony in Establishing Facts Contrary to Analogy." *Transactions of the Royal Irish Academy* 7: 79–118.

CHAPTER 10

LINKING PERSPECTIVES: A ROLE FOR POETRY IN PHILOSOPHICAL INQUIRY

KAREN SIMECEK

1. Introduction

Philosophical interest in poetry has been dominated by the question of whether poetry can aid philosophical thought and promote philosophical inquiry.[1] This focus reflects a tradition of philosophers like Pope, Lucretius, Xenophanes, Parmenides, Empedocles, and Rumi presenting their philosophical work in verse. In addition, poets like William Wordsworth, T. S. Eliot, and Wallace Stevens have been celebrated as poet-philosophers, with some commentators arguing that their work should be seen as the product of philosophy through poetry. Beginning with Plato's banishing of the poets from his ideal Republic, however, arguments against poetry having a role to play in philosophical inquiry have tended to focus on poetry's (negative) relationship to truth (or, as John Koethe [2009] puts it, poetry's indifference to truth) and its inability to offer argument in support of any thesis it might advance. Although we may accept works of poetry as having philosophical themes, this does not amount to doing philosophy through poetry. One such argument hinges on the non-paraphrasbility of poetry and form-content unity.[2] The thought goes, if poetry is to play a role in philosophy, then it needs to be paraphrasable (that is, its content must be separable from its form). The assumption is that paraphrase is a mark of understanding and indicates that some proposition has a fixed meaning and that only a proposition with a fixed meaning can be evaluated in terms of truth or falsity. Poetry resists paraphrase: to change the words is to change the poem (what the poem does and what or how it means, which is often

---

[1] See Leighton 2015; Elliott 1967; Koethe 2009; de Gaynesford 2017; and Barfield 2011.

[2] For more on form-content unity in poetry, see Lamarque 2009b.

Examining Philosophy Itself. Edited by Yafeng Shan.
Chapters and book compilation © 2023 Metaphilosophy LLC and John Wiley & Sons Ltd.
Published 2023 by John Wiley & Sons Ltd.

plural or ambiguous). Therefore, poetry cannot play any role in (analytic) philosophical inquiry.[3] Peter Lamarque argues: "[I]f paraphrase is impossible in poetry, it is obligatory in philosophy. There could not be a serious philosophical thesis that could only be expressed in one way or indeed an argument that demanded unique phrasing. This makes philosophical content in poetry problematic, for the way that a poem supports its philosophical themes both determines what those themes are and is part of its allegedly unparaphrasable content" (2009a, 46).[4]

Building on the idea of form-content unity in poetry, Lamarque argues that although both poetry and philosophy involve abstract thought, thinking of poetry as akin to philosophy is a category error, for they have distinct aims and use of language. He argues that "[p]hilosophical conclusions do not arise out of personal response to particularity" (2009a, 49), yet poetry is concerned with particularity, and the reader ought to attend to the fine-grainedness of expression, that is, to the aesthetic experience of the particular words of the poem. He goes on to add: "To read poetry (of any kind) *as poetry* is to adopt a certain attitude of mind, a receptiveness, among other things, to fine-grained expression, the salience of perspective, and the play of images. Reading philosophy as philosophy encourages different expectations and invites different kinds of appraisal" (2009a, 51–52). For Lamarque, this marks a significant distinction: the reader of philosophical prose is called to evaluate it for its truth, whereas in reading poetry, the reader is only called to judge aesthetically.

John Gibson offers a related worry concerning the possibility of philosophy through poetry by arguing that to treat poetry as philosophy would require poetry to be analysed in terms of its meaning (in order to identify philosophical propositions), which is to misunderstand the nature of poetry. Gibson points out that much poetry resists attempts to grasp singular meaning; instead it engages the reader in reflection on thought and feeling. He argues that it is a mistake to treat "the language of the poem as one would treat any chain of descriptive sentences whose business it is to describe some real or imaginary state of affairs" (2018, 9). He goes on to add that although poetry and philosophy might share concerns of worldliness, that is, "a kind of common cultural property that belongs to neither the poet nor the philosopher, as a shared sense of worries, wonders, anxieties, and puzzles" (15), what each brings to these aspects of human life is simply "another way of working through the same cultural material" (16) with differing results. Sharing a common focus does not mean we ought to

---

[3] This is similar to the debate regarding the possibility of philosophy through film: "If it is contended that the exclusively cinematic insight cannot be paraphrased, reasonable doubt arises with regard to its very existence. If it is granted, on the other hand, that the cinematic contribution can and must be paraphrased, this contention is incompatible with arguments for a significantly independent, innovative, and purely 'filmic' philosophical achievement" (Livingston 1991, 12).

[4] See also Abbott 2019 for a similar point.

put poetry in the service of philosophy, or vice versa. We ought instead to see them as distinctly valuable in what they offer us in terms of understanding human life.

In response to such scepticism about the role of poetry in philosophical inquiry, my project here is to take a new approach by arguing that such arguments against using poetry in philosophical inquiry subscribe to a narrow conception of philosophy. Furthermore, in response to Gibson's worry, there's an important distinction to be made between treating poetry as philosophical (that is, demanding that poetry does what philosophy does or aims to do) and what we gain from reading poetry as valuable to the philosopher (for instance, helping the philosopher cultivate an intellectual virtue necessary for philosophical inquiry). On my view, poetry is not directly philosophical but can play an important role in developing the philosopher's awareness of how perspective shapes beliefs and thought processes. In making the case, I argue first for the need to understand philosophy as a collective and collaborative endeavour. In addition, philosophical methodology is not reducible to a conception of philosophy as aimed at conclusive proof. Although it may well be the case that we ought not to expect poetry to contribute a logical, reasoned argument to philosophy, this only rules out a very limited contribution poetry might make. Second, I argue that the notion of perspective is relevant to understanding philosophy as a collective endeavour. In the final part of the essay, I show how poetry cultivates an intellectual virtue essential to some forms of philosophical inquiry, namely, those relating to questions of value and human experience. In making the case, I appeal to the importance of perspective in philosophical inquiry and demonstrate how engagement with poetry not only helps the philosopher better appreciate the role perspective plays but also cultivates the ability to forge connections between perspectives, which is important in uncovering and evaluating shared perspectives as well as in evaluating one's own philosophical perspective.

2. Philosophy as Collective Versus Individualistic

Arguments suggesting that poetry cannot play a substantive role in philosophical inquiry appear to be motivated by a narrow view of what philosophy is and what its aims are. For example, Lamarque writes: "The relation between a poem and its themes is not the same as the relation of a philosophical work and its conclusions. We might be misled by talking of 'support' in both cases. A philosophical work supports its conclusions, and a poem supports its themes but they do so in different ways. ... In philosophy a conclusion is derived through principles of reasoning. Logic not rhetoric dictates whether the conclusion has adequate support" (2009a, 45).

Lamarque argues that in the case of philosophy there is an expectation that it will offer proof, whereas in poetry "[t]here is no call to test an argument or demand more proof" (2009a, 48). Here philosophy is viewed as something that aims at conclusive proof through use of logic and rational argument. On such a view, philosophical inquiry is reduced to an individualistic endeavour to develop arguments with sufficient support such that they are invulnerable to knockdown arguments (that is, arguments that do not have defeaters). It's clear that although some philosophical inquiry may well have the aim of conclusive proof, examples will be significantly limited (perhaps to fields of logic and metaphysics). Much philosophical thought that we value highly does not aim for conclusive proof at all (and it is not clear that it can be evaluated in terms of truth). For instance, appeal to intuitions, thought experiments, and case studies in philosophical investigations is widespread. In such cases, the aim is more modest: the philosophers are simply aiming for their theory to be "agreeable" to others, that is, to be judged as offering a systematic, strong, plausible case for a given view (in other words, the theory meets a set of theoretical virtues rather than being evaluated according to truth or falsity). Take, for example, Alvin Goldman's (1976) fake barns. Goldman proposes a thought experiment comparing two scenarios. In the first, the subject is surrounded by real barns and upon seeing a barn *knows* that it is a real barn. In the second, the subject who ordinarily encounters real barns is now surrounded mostly by fake barns and upon seeing a real barn that is indistinguishable from the fake barns has the belief but does not *know* that it is a real barn, because he would have believed it to be a real barn even if it were one of the fake ones.

Kristoffer Ahlstrom-Vij provides the following analysis of what Goldman is aiming to achieve:

> Philosophy sometimes resembles curve-fitting in the sciences. Goldman's aim is to investigate how "this change in our assessment [from the first to the second scenario is] to be explained." ... According to Goldman, the way to account for this pattern is by saying that we know that *p* only if the actual state of affairs in which *p* is true is discriminable by us from a relevant possible state of affairs in which *p* is false. Goldman is not thereby providing an argument for his data-points. Fitting data-points to a curve is not to justify one's data, and accounting for intuitions through philosophical theorising is no different on this score. If anything, it's the other way around: *ceteris paribus*, theories are justified in so far as they fit our intuitions. (2013, 822).

In other cases, the aim is to offer a way of viewing a particular problem such that connections to other philosophical beliefs are made salient. Take for instance philosophical attempts to show that certain features of human life are morally significant, such as James O. Young's 2008 *Cultural Appropriation and the Arts*, Miranda Fricker's 2007 *Epistemic Injustice*, and Annette Baier's 1986 "Trust and Antitrust"; all three works are highly cited and have inspired much discussion amongst the philosophical community.

In both kinds of cases, the philosopher is offering something up to prompt thought and reflection in the philosophical community. The best way to understand what the philosopher is doing is to see philosophy as something that is collaborative and depends on the exchange of thought within the philosophical community and its related communities.

In his *Philosophical Explanations,* Robert Nozick argues for a collaborative conception of the aim of philosophy as an alternative to foundationalism, or for philosophy as aimed at conclusive proof. He argues that we ought to collectively seek linkages between theories as a way of generating insights or knowledge that are more secure than what any one individual may come up with. We look for what general principles are supported by different theories or theoretical structures. On Nozick's collaborative model, we ought to let linkages emerge and embrace potential incompatibility and tension between different views. Rather than being in a position of having to defend p against possible counterarguments, Nozick recommends that we look to understand how p is possible in light of, or as well as, possible defeaters. He writes: "To see how p can be true (given these apparent excluders) is to see how things fit together. This philosophical understanding, finding harmony in apparent tension and incompatibility, is, I think, intrinsically valuable" (1981, 10). The task of the philosopher therefore lies in explaining how it is the case that p seems possible whilst at the same time understanding how arguments for *not-p* also seem to hold. According to Nozick, by re-orientating inquiry towards bridging gaps between arguments through explanation of their differences, we can make progress and identify general principles that are not vulnerable to knockdown arguments.

An alternative to philosophy as a truth-seeking enterprise is especially needed when considering philosophical investigations into questions of value in which a naturalistic understanding cannot be established and where discussion centres on appeal (via intuitions) to a shared understanding of what we value. David Lewis comments on the need to see philosophy as a collective enterprise in which we seek to collectively bring our intuitions (and the theories that emerge from them) into equilibrium. He writes: "Our common task is to find out what equilibria there are that can withstand examination, but it remains for each of us to come to rest at one or another of them" (1983, x). The context of Lewis's comment is similar to Nozick's; they both note that so-called knockdown arguments rarely have any purchase on those who subscribe to the target view. Building on Lewis's view, Helen Beebee argues that the individual aim is to develop philosophical views that are brought into equilibrium and inform our point of engagement with the community. She writes: "The fact that we bring to the table different sets of substantive assumptions and different methodological principles—the kinds of differences that generate intractable disagreements—is no threat to our ability to contribute to the aim of philosophy. On the contrary: such differences are precisely what generate the plurality of equilibria that it is our collective aim to uncover" (2018, 16). The collective project cannot progress without bringing together individual standpoints or perspectives (that represent a set of assumptions and methodological principles).

Beebee's rejection of philosophy as a truth-seeking enterprise arises from consideration of two key worries. First, Beebee argues that we have no agreed method for evaluating our intuitions, the theories we construct from them, and the theoretical virtues we appeal to in constructing theories: "[W]e have no grounds for trusting our intuitions. ... And we have no grounds for thinking that the theoretical virtues are truth-conducive; indeed, even if we grant that they are, we have no agreed methodological standard for trading them off against one another, and hence, where such trade-offs are what divide us, we have no more reason to believe our own theory than we do a theory whose (alleged) justification comes from making the trade differently" (2018, 8). A further challenge emerges from recognising the centrality of disagreement to the practice of philosophy; for every serious philosophical view, there is significant opposition to it that is not due to any epistemic failing. Beebee asks how we can "be justified in believing our philosophical views, when we know that equally capable, well-informed philosophers disagree with us" (9).

Furthermore, as Nozick argues, individual thinkers are more likely to accept what they already believe to be true. Belief and commitment to belief cannot be *imposed* from the outside on a particular thinker, for an individual thinker always has the option of rejecting the argument, however compelling (one might be prepared to simply suspend judgment or accept the charge of irrationality rather than modify belief). That's not to say that one doesn't modify belief on being presented with reasons but rather to say that this is not due to the supposed force of an argument. In order to adopt a new belief, that belief must have internal justificatory force for the individual; in other words, the reasons are evaluated by the individual in terms of fittingness with other beliefs held, that is, in terms of whether they can be brought into equilibrium.

On the kind of alternative pictures offered by Nozick, Lewis, and Beebee, the value of engaging with other thinkers and other possible theories is to aid philosophical criticism of our own philosophical views; in other words, to determine what can "withstand examination," which in turn demands that we each develop a philosophical perspective: "[I]n the case of philosophy the aim of the discovery of equilibria demands that we take on board a set of core assumptions and methodological prescriptions in order to develop and scrutinize an equilibrium position of our own that can withstand examination" (Beebee 2018, 22). Argument construction still has a role to play for individuals in their development of theories, but one's engagement with other people's arguments and theories is aimed at developing understanding of one's own philosophical view. Comparison to other perspectives highlights both what is shared with others and where there is conflict, with the latter indicating that more reflection is required for the individual (either to resolve the conflict by modifying one's own beliefs or to understand how and why someone might hold the conflicting position). The value of individually producing such theories through collaborative reflection lies in the understanding it yields collectively. As Nozick writes: "Embedding the world in the network of alternative philosophical theories and visions, seeing how each of these different philosophical possibilities gets a grip on the world, does produce understanding. The major philosophical theories of continuing interest are readings of possible worlds accessible from here, that is, possible readings of the actual world. We understand the world by seeing it in its matrix of possibilities, in its possibility neighborhood" (1981, 21).

Taking such an approach doesn't have to mean giving up on truth as an ideal, but it expands the aims of philosophy to include understanding as a value alongside truth in that both enable progress in thought. Both the practice of uncovering equilibria and forging connections will provide understanding even if they fall short of offering truth. As Nozick argues, "[E]xplanation locates something in actuality, showing its actual connections with other actual things, while *understanding* locates it in a network of possibility, showing the connections it would have to other nonactual things or processes. (Explanation increases understanding too, since the actual connections it exhibits are also possible)" (1981, 12). Understanding offers insight through showing how things connect and interconnect, and what might be shared or shareable with others in the philosophical community. Whether or not this maps on to what is true, it still reveals something important about human experience, how we make sense of the world and the cognitive resources we use in doing so.

3. From Individual to Shared Perspectives

In light of the discussion in the previous section, I now want to argue that one's perspective shapes one's approach to philosophical inquiry (both methodological commitments and beliefs). The aim here is not to deny the value of philosophical argument and attempts at proof but to demonstrate the challenges to philosophical inquiry as a collective and collaborative practice rather than as merely an isolated, individual project. If we embrace philosophy as a collective endeavour, it becomes clear that we need to learn not only to appreciate our own philosophical perspectives but also how one's own perspectives are related to others and how we might go about forging shared perspectives. As Beebee suggests, our task is twofold: we not only ought to seek coherence or, as she puts it, bring equilibrium within our own view (to generate one's own philosophical perspective), we also need to seek connection with others to generate equilibria that can withstand examination, in other words, open up our theories to other thinkers to connect with and evaluate in a way that meets philosophy's aim as a collective and collaborative endeavour.

Nozick also hints at perspectivism in philosophical practice: "[K]nowing the world involves seeing the different ways it can be viewed" (1981, 21). Understanding different ways in which the world is viewed is not just a matter of perceptual or experiential point of view but the way one prioritises and processes information. According to Elisabeth Camp, "[A] perspective is an open-ended disposition to notice, explain, and respond to situations in the world—an ability to 'go on the same way' in assimilating and responding to whatever information and experiences one encounters" (2017, 78). In other words, a perspective is an idiosyncratic network (or map—see Camp 2007) of concepts (and their associations), beliefs, and commitments (further beliefs entailed by explicitly held beliefs) that configures value (how we prioritise sets of beliefs, and so on, as more firmly held—this could be due to the usefulness of a belief, experience as evidential, or as related to a conception of morality, and so forth). Such a network governs one's judgment (how we apply such beliefs) that shapes the way one responds, interprets (processes information), and acts in the world. It is through an understanding of one's thinking as perspectivally informed that one can see that one is never able to isolate a philosophical question to consider it from a neutral point of view (a view from nowhere); one will always orientate oneself towards or against it, for one's own beliefs and commitments are at stake. How we articulate the question, what we consider relevant to the question, and how we approach trying to answer it are all shaped by one's first-person perspective.

On the "proof" model, one takes one's argument as having direct relevance for others, for instance, by assuming shared intuitions and appreciation of connecting reasoning, that is, assuming that any rational thinker will accept the premises as true and accept all moves to establishing the conclusion. Such a view assumes one is able to reason independently of one's first-person perspective, yet any new beliefs resulting from proof must be brought into the fold of one's existent set of beliefs and commitments. One's perspective is not neutral but configures a sense of value and import that one will find difficult to see otherwise. It is not a flat structure but hierarchical, with certain beliefs, commitments, values, and so on held more centrally or firmly than others. Furthermore, there are beliefs and commitments that are more firmly entrenched than others, depending on how they are configured within the network, thereby making the task of epistemological criticism harder. It is not enough to evaluate individual beliefs without awareness of how they figure in one's way of thinking.

Perspectives can be improved and refined: there can be a sense of progress at the individual level by the way a perspective develops in response to apparent conflict, incompatibility, and tension and through accommodating a greater number of beliefs that cohere in relation to a greater diversity of questions. To achieve this, what is needed is a mode of inquiry that seeks out what is shareable with others, and only after one has achieved a sense of a shareable human perspective or set of shared perspectives (that is, first-person plural perspectives) is one in a position to evaluate one's own thinking (as it creates tension or incompatibility with one's first-person singular perspective). As suggested by Thomas Nagel's (1986) notion of "the objective self," individuals have the capacity to abstract and generalise from their own idiosyncratic point of view to consider what is shareable with others at the interpersonal level. Whereas Nagel's analysis involves positing an objective self as distinct from the individual, subjective self, I am merely suggesting that one can reflect on one's own perspective in terms of the different layers from which it is constructed—as more or less general and more or less shared with others. A. W. Moore makes a similar point, arguing that when considering certain things of human significance, we must have a sense of the human perspective. Without such a sense of the human perspective we would fail to appropriately understand that situation, person, or action because it is tied to human life. Moore writes: "In order to identify with other people, we must learn to rise above our own points of involvement; but not above every point of involvement; not above a *human* point of involvement" (1997, 25). What philosophy can offer us to enhance our thinking is a method for modifying our perspectives by "letting linkages" emerge and creating shared perspectives that reflect the commonality or overlap between individual perspectives that aims to capture a "human perspective." The ideal here may well be to reach a human perspective, as Moore puts it, but it is much more likely that such a perspective is not in fact singular but plural, as Beebee's conception of the aims of philosophy suggests, and requires individuals to bring their own individual perspectives together, with the individual and the shared perspectives forming a feedback loop.

4. Linking Perspectives Through Poetry

I want now to consider how lyric poetry, understood as essentially per-spectival, can help the philosopher appreciate what it is to engage with other perspectives and develop the skills for identifying and developing connections between perspectives. In the case of a poem, we are engaging with something that relies on shared language and invokes shared concepts; therefore, the reader is encouraged to move beyond their idiosyncratic per-spective to a more sharable perspective, a human perspective. What the poem does is give us an awareness of the different perspectives one can adopt by setting up an encounter with other perspectives presented as part of a complex whole, rather than demand we understand it as a unified whole. If we have any hope of reaching human/shared perspectives or, to use Lewis and Beebee's terms, "equilibria that can withstand examination," the philosopher must first practice linking perspectives in order to reach what might be shared and shareable with others.

Alison Denham observes that "[a] poem can enable us to understand its subject from a particular subjective, experiential point of view by eliciting affective, perceptual and cognitive responses appropriate to that perspective" (2015, 189). Peter Lamarque comments that "poetic subjects themselves are perspectival. They are the expression of a poetic speaker and it is not merely contingent how the subject is expressed or presented; indeed what the subject is is partially determined by how it is expressed" (2009a, 49). Hannah Kim and John Gibson also argue that poetry is fundamentally perspectival: "[T]he I of lyric poetry is often nothing more than a center of perceptual, cognitive, and affective *attention*: the subject of *an* experience. It is a self effectively reduced to a perspective" (2021, 108). If a poem can, to some extent, provide an experience of another perspective, then it provides an opportunity to seek linkages between perspectives and identify insights from a human/shared perspective. In "Beyond Narrative" (Simecek 2015), I argue that lyric poetry is inherently perspectival and that in reading a poem what we are trying to do is appreciate how the poem is treating some subject, that is, we regard the poem as expressing interconnected thoughts, images, feelings towards some subject; the poem in some sense tries to help us to make the connections that the poem is suggesting. In other words, a poem is offering a way of perceiving or thinking about some object of joint attention (that is, its subject) that the reader is invited to share.

The easiest way to motivate the view that poetry is perspectival is to use an illustrative example. Let's take Wallace Stevens's "Thirteen Ways of Looking at a Blackbird" (Stevens 1954).

> V
> I do not know which to prefer,
> The beauty of inflections
> Or the beauty of innuendoes,
> The blackbird whistling
> Or just after.

The perspective of the work is gestured at with the use of repetition of words and sounds ("er"; "Or"; "beauty"; "The"; "s") that presents the words as a unit (in this case a stanza, but the repetition of words and sounds also occurs across the whole work).[5] As a reader, I am encouraged to follow the feeling of connectedness with cognition: how can I make sense of this as a unit of meaning? The connection between "the beauty of inflections" and "the beauty of innuendoes" through the connecting word "or" and the repetition of "the beauty of" leads to awareness of a supposed relationship here that the poem enacts by offering "inflections" as an alternative to "innuendoes." There's also the mirroring of the two disjunctive sentences. This

---

[5] Ribeiro (2007) takes repetition to be central to what makes *poetry* poetry.

gets me so far in my understanding of the working of the poem. The poem merely shows me *that* the sentences are connected, not *how* they ought to be connected. The latter is left to me to attempt to resolve.

In each canto of the poem, the blackbird represents the anchor point of the perspective, or way of looking. It is the concrete imagery ("the blackbird whistling") that draws on one's (imagined) visual perception and acts as the object of joint attention (shared between me and the poem). What surrounds the blackbird image in each canto connects the visual image with ways of connecting to possible associations, mirrors, linkages. For instance:

IV
A man and a woman
Are one.
A man and a woman and a blackbird
Are one.

Although the blackbird is merely named at this point in the poem, the previous cantos have contributed to the imagery that the word "blackbird" carries forward ("Among twenty snowy mountains, / The only moving thing /Was the eye of the blackbird" and "The blackbird whirled in the autumn winds" invoking images of an actual blackbird that the reader brings to the poem). Again, the unfolding of the stanza is affectively connected, and on a linguistic level the extension of "A man and a woman" to "A man and a woman and a blackbird" seems straightforward. But to appreciate why the blackbird ought to be placed in such a relationship with "a man and a woman," work needs to be done by the reader. The reader cannot, however, simply draw on her own understanding of blackbirds to provide a resolution but must consider how the blackbird is situated in the work. To make sense of this, the reader must forge connections between her own perspective and that of the poem.

The perspective on offer in a poem represents other ways of thinking and other ways of valuing that are manifested in the focus and prioritising of certain thoughts, images, and feelings captured by the structure of the poem, as seen above with the example of "Thirteen Ways of Looking at a Blackbird." The act of trying to understand the poem involves abstracting away from my idiosyncratic perspective to an appreciation of my perspective as a human subject. Reaching such abstraction allows me to appreciate more that is shareable with others on the basis of a way of thinking that is available to me by extrapolating the shareable from the individualistic. Not everything will be resolvable in the poem, in virtue of the work's perspective being equally idiosyncratic. A sense of resolution is found, however, in the feeling of finding common ground. Reading poetry engages one in a particular kind of thinking activity, trying to negotiate the perspective of the poem from one's own first-personal perspective in play with all its baggage of linkages between concepts and beliefs, associations, and sense of import. Where individual tensions and incompatibilities emerge is also of value, showing the limits of one's perspective, including one's grasp of a human (shareable) perspective. What one can't grasp is just as important as what one can in terms of what that reveals about the self.

To illustrate how one's attempts to engage with and appreciate a work of poetry can cultivate the intellectual virtue of linking perspectives or generating equilibria, let's consider Robert Gray's "The Drift of Things" (Gray 2006) alongside Lucretius's *De rerum natura (The Nature of Things)*, book 1 (Lucretius 2008). One reason for selecting these examples is that both deal with the same philosophical themes; in fact, Gray's poem is a response to Lucretius's work. By looking at them side by side, we can see how each offers a different way of understanding, perceiving, and knowing the external world yet also come to appreciate linkages between them. It may strike the reader that the examples of Gray and Lucretius show poetry's contribution as too limited, for it is a small body of poetic works that are concerned so directly with philosophical themes. To re-cap, however, what philosophical inquiry as a collaborative endeavour must do is seek explanations that matter at both the individual and the collective level. The philosophical value of such poetry is not in its treatment of philosophical themes but in showing what it means to engage with another's perspectival thoughts, feelings, and experience and what it is to understand another's perspective through commonality, that is, by appreciating what is shared or shareable between one's own perspective and the other's.

The poems have distinct identifiable orientations: Lucretius focuses on the world with a sense of objectivity, whereas Gray focuses on the subjective encounter with things. Both focus on our sensation of things, both as sensations external to the human mind and as sensations that arise from one's own thoughts and feelings, but the prioritisation of these is different in each. For Lucretius, sensations of thoughts and feelings are secondary to sensations of the external world. For Gray, the focus is on the way things figure in our lives with feeling and value. What I hope to illustrate here is that Gray's poem is the product of such a collaborative mode of inquiry and that as readers we must seek the linkages not only between Gray's world view and Lucretius's but also our own, which includes our pre-theoretical perspective on things as they figure in our own lives. I then illustrate how aiming at explanation can enable linkages to emerge between these two very different (philosophical) perspectives. Unfortunately, there isn't space to provide a detailed study of each work in full. Instead, I have selected key passages that appear to focus on the same kind of thing, offering fertile ground for letting linkages emerge.

Here's an extract from Lucretius (lines 132–47):

—To start with, the first rule
is that nothing can come from nothing, not even by will of the gods.
Mortal men are afraid as they look about them and see
the many things that happen on earth and up in the sky,
and they cannot tell why or how and therefore think that gods
must bring them about by fiat. But if our axiom holds
and nothing can come of nothing, then we are obliged to look further
to learn what we want to know—how each thing was created
and how, without the gods, all things have come to be.
Consider the contrary case—that being could come from non-being
and that anything could arise from anything or from nothing,
without even a seed. Men could emerge from sea-foam,
scaly creatures could come swarming up from the earth,
and birds could burst forth from the sky. In meadowlands or deserts
cattle and wild beasts could simply appear at random,
and trees could bear any fruit haphazardly, for all
would be able to bring forth all, interchangeably.[6]

It is here that Lucretius presents his atomism, and in his making a case for this, rationality is contrasted with fantasy; he treats them as oppositional. The first half of the extract is void of imagery. Instead, it contains the language of fact ("that," "things," "being"), cognition ("know," "think"), and logic ("why," "how"). Yet the evidence for the axiom "nothing can come from nothing" is an appeal to *imagined impossibilities*, such as men emerging from sea-foam and animals popping into view. In contrast, Gray presents a series of *imagined possibilities* (lines 14–16):

A jetty in reeds, and clouds on water;
the bus that rides the dust like a surfboard;
a lizard trailed out of a mailbox drum,
inert, all the long-shadowed afternoon;
the planks on mud, from where chickens' pollard
is thrown; a skirmishing of cherry trees
in bloom, with sabres of wind; the looped vines
of sea-foam; or trees in an avenue
toward exalted snow—these are each itself
and no other thing. It's plurality
we experience, it is differences
not the smear of Oneness

The perspective on offer in Gray's poem prioritises the vividness of experience of certain things from a human perspective. The descriptions are not

---

[6] There are a number of well-respected translations of Lucretius's work, largely for philosophers. I have, however, chosen a translation (by D. R. Slavitt [Lucretius 2008]) that best respects *De rerum natura* as primarily a poetic work.

attempting to be flat descriptions or matters of fact about perception but
capture the character that the human eye perceives things as having ("a
skirmishing of cherry trees," "sabres of wind," "exalted snow") and therefore how they figure in human life as experienced. This is an extension of
Lucretius's treatment of imagery in which things are named without a sense
of the human. On Lucretius's poem, George Santayana comments: "We
seem to be reading not the poetry of a poet about things, but the poetry
of things themselves. That things have their poetry, not because of what we
make them symbols of, but because of their own movement and life, is what
Lucretius proves once for all to mankind" (1910, 34). The human, however,
is still required to recognise the poetry of things.

> Imagine a mighty wind that comes up to beat on the ocean
> to overwhelm huge ships and scatter the clouds in the sky,
> sweeping along the plains with hurricane force that trees
> bow down to or rise up to join as their branches fly,
> and the blasts are so strong that even the mountains shudder.
> You can feel its fury and hear its savage, threatening howling.
> You cannot see this wind that roils the sea and sweeps
> the earth and harries the cloud across the sky's expanses
> this way and that, but you do not question that it is there. (lines 249–59).

Both Lucretius and Gray are concerned with what cannot be literally
perceived by the senses. For Lucretius that means the microscopic; for Gray
that means meaning, interpretation, and value. The two perspectives are
not strictly incompatible; instead we can see them as merely focusing on
different aspects. Lucretius is concerned with how it is that things can exist;
Gray is concerned with how we experience the existence of things. Bringing
the two together yields the following insight: there's a way of understanding
the external world as separate yet inseparable from the human perspective.

The poet's perspective does not seek to deny the perspective of the
philosopher. Gray's poem uses some of the language of Lucretius but
re-orientates certain ideas to point to what is in Lucretius's work but not
taken as significant, that is, the poetic imagery. Ultimately, what emerges
from reflection on the two poems together is the general idea that no
matter how we point to things in the world, we can never experience them
as distinct from ourselves. It is only through reflection on our sensations
of thoughts and feelings about them that we have some hope of catching
a glimpse of their existence. And where we find this is in the unknown,
unknowable, and unexplainable. In other words, this is Gray's attempt
to understand the idea of oneness in Lucretius's philosophy. Things
aren't literally one whole, although they may have shared origins, yet our
experience of them through sensation is of unity (lines 36–43):

> And these things flow into one another
> as quietly as smoke, unhesitant,

unhampered. Glittering smoke of the world.
The differences in them do not exclude
their unity; the unity doesn't
detract from difference. Still, there can't be
one stuff, or "energy,"
beneath all this
that has remained itself, and that is "pure."

Here we have another modification of Lucretius's thought. Although it may be true that everything has some shared origin, that sameness is not left unaltered as things have changed.

When we are in queues for the banks of Lethe
we'll recall, attentive as candle flames,
not only faces, but things we have known,
and with intensity that is surprised—
the stance of grass at the foot of palings
one storm-lit afternoon; the night, an ocean
among its ice-floes; whatever flung us
into the furthest transcendence we've found. (lines 178–85)

Gray seems to be arguing that all we have is metaphor: through every attempt to access the nature of things, all we catch is a glimmer. Lucretius attempted to go beyond metaphor to speak directly of the nature of substance, the material world; but as Gray's poem shows, what we care about as human subjects is the wonder of the world in which we live, which in the words of Lucretius "could not have come from nothing." Although written only about Lucretius, Santayana's words sum up nicely how these two perspectives come together: "Nothing comes out of nothing, nothing falls back into nothing, if we consider substance; but everything comes from nothing and falls back into nothing if we consider things—the objects of love and of experience" (1910, 45), that is, how things figure in our lives as individual human subjects who experience the world in particular ways, with all its meaning and significance for us.

Both Lucretius and Gray are concerned with the observable and the imaginable, but how we observe and what we imagine is not neutral. To study the nature of things requires the subjective, human perspective; we feel and respond to the world. Although both Lucretius and Gray seek connection, what connects them is something provided by the human intellect. Ultimately, a perspective. For Lucretius, this perspective must be ordered and logical; for Gray, chaotic and wonderous. A seeming incompatibility emerges between these two perspectives, yet that does not preclude finding some common ground between them that reflects aspects of the human perspective and general experience. The beauty of Gray's poem is the ineffable. The perspective of the poem is just out of reach, cannot be fully articulated, and this is also true of the subject matter. The poem re-creates the experience of trying to get beyond visual perception to things themselves, but all we have is visual perception as a means to do this. The poem is an allegory of our first-personal and perspectival way of engaging with the world—we can feel the edges of our perspective but cannot know what it is like to live outside it. What I *can* do within my own first-personal perspective, however, is consider what is particular to me and what is potentially shared and shareable with others as fellow human beings.

The rejection of the thesis that poetry can play a role in philosophical inquiry is based on a limited understanding of the practice of philosophy. Not only might philosophy aim at truth or conclusive proof, there are still philosophical questions for which truth is out of reach, such as questions of value and understanding human experience where we cannot provide a naturalistic account and instead need to rely on appeal to intuitions. In such cases, what is needed is for the individual philosopher to uncover points of agreement and commonality between individual philosophical perspectives as a way of meeting the philosophical aim of understanding. Reading poetry offers a valuable experience of trying to appreciate another's perspective from one's own that can trigger awareness of a process of seeking linkages that has value for philosophical inquiry. Consequently, by engaging with poetry, one can better appreciate what it is to engage in philosophical inquiry as a collective endeavour. What is important is the practice of engaging with other perspectives and trying to find connections as a way of seeking shared perspectives that emerge through the exchange of thought with others.

Through this discussion of Lucretius's *De rerum natura* and Robert Gray's "The Drift of Things," I have demonstrated how general insights can emerge from seeking linkages between perspectives by appreciating the common ground between them, that is, by trying to understand the nature of things from a shared, shareable, human perspective. Aiming to adopt a human perspective does not require that one get outside one's own perspective (that is, adopt an objective point of view that's distinct from one's own perspective). Instead, the task in uncovering general principles related to the human perspective requires that I attempt to understand other perspectives to identify what *might* be common or shareable. Such a process serves an important role in engaging in epistemological criticism of one's own views and philosophical perspectives. By forging connections between perspectives, we open up our own perspective to examination via what connects them with and disconnects them from other perspectives. Furthermore, my defence of poetry's role in philosophical inquiry is consistent with Gibson's understanding of meaning in poetry. An advantage of my view is that poetry can play a role for philosophy in virtue of poetry's resistance to fixed meaning and paraphrase. It is precisely what makes understanding poems difficult that cultivates the intellectual virtue of linking perspectives that is valuable to philosophy conceived of as a collective endeavour.

Acknowledgments

I would like to thank Eileen John, Rafe McGregor, Paul Standish, and Emma Williams for helpful discussion of these ideas. Special thanks to Yafeng Shan for his immensely useful comments and suggestions on an earlier draft.

References

Abbott, M. 2019. "Philosophy and Lyric Poetry." In *The Palgrave Handbook of Philosophy and Literature*, edited by Barry Stocker and Michael Mack, 221–39. London: Palgrave Macmillan.

Ahlstrom-Vij, K. 2013. Review of *Philosophy Without Intuitions* by Herman Cappelen. *Philosophical Quarterly* 63, no. 253: 821–23.

Baier, A. 1986. "Trust and Antitrust." *Ethics* 96, no. 2: 231–60.

Barfield, R. 2011. *The Ancient Quarrel Between Philosophy and Poetry*. Cambridge: Cambridge University Press.

Beebee, H. 2018. "Philosophical Scepticism and the Aims of Philosophy." *Proceedings of the Aristotelian Society* 118, no. 1: 1–24.

Camp, E. 2007. "Thinking with Maps." *Philosophical Perspectives* 21, no. 1: 145–82.

Camp, E. 2017. "Perspectives in Imaginative Engagement with Fiction." *Philosophical Perspectives* 31, no. 1: 73–102.

Denham, A. 2015. "Ethical Estrangement: Pictures, Poetry and Epistemic Value." In *The Philosophy of Poetry*, edited by J. Gibson, 183–204. Oxford: Oxford University Press.

de Gaynesford, M. 2017. *The Rift in the Lute: Attuning Poetry and Philosophy*. Oxford: Oxford University Press.

Elliott, R. K. 1967. "Poetry and Truth." *Analysis* 27, no. 3: 77–85.

Fricker, M. 2007. *Epistemic Injustice: Power and the Ethics of Knowing*. Oxford: Oxford University Press.

Gray, R. 2006. "The Drift of Things." In *Nameless Earth*. Manchester: Carcanet.

Gibson, J. 2018. "What Makes a Poem Philosophical?" In *Wittgenstein and Modernism*, edited by K. Zumhagen-Yekplé and M. LeMahieu, 130–52. Chicago: University of Chicago Press.

Goldman, A. I. 1976. "Discrimination and Perceptual Knowledge." *Journal of Philosophy* 73 (November): 771–91.

Kim, H., and J. Gibson. 2021. "Lyric Self-Expression." In *Art, Representation, and Make-Believe: Essays on the Philosophy of Kendall L. Walton*, edited by Sonia Sedivy, 94–111. New York: Routledge.

Koethe, J. 2009. "Poetry and Truth." *Midwest Studies in Philosophy* 33, no. 1: 53–60.

Lamarque, P. 2009a. "Poetry and Abstract Thought." *Midwest Studies in Philosophy* 33: 37–52.

Lamarque, P. 2009b. "The Elusiveness of Poetic Meaning." *Ratio* 22, no. 4: 398–420.

Leighton, A. 2015. "Poetry's Knowing." In *The Philosophy of Poetry*, edited by J. Gibson, 162–82. Oxford: Oxford University Press.

Lewis, D. 1983. *Philosophical Papers, Volume I.* New York: Oxford University Press.

Livingston, P. 1991. "Theses on Cinema as Philosophy." *Journal of Aesthetics and Art Criticism* 64, no. 1: 11–18.

Lucretius. 2008. *De rerum natura (The Nature of Things): A Poetic Translation.* Translated by D. R. Slavitt. Berkeley: University of California Press.

Moore, A. W. 1997. *Points of View.* Oxford: Clarendon Press.

Nagel, T. 1986. *The View from Nowhere.* Oxford: Oxford University Press.

Nozick, R. 1981. *Philosophical Explanations.* Cambridge, Mass.: Harvard University Press.

Ribeiro, A. C. 2007. "Intending to Repeat: A Definition of Poetry." *Journal of Aesthetics and Art Criticism* 65, no. 2: 189–201.

Santayana, G. 1910. *Three Philosophical Poets: Lucretius, Dante, and Goethe.* New York: Cooper Square.

Simecek, K. 2015. "Beyond Narrative: Poetry, Emotion and the Perspectival View." *British Journal of Aesthetics* 55, no. 4: 497–513.

Stevens, W. 1954. "Thirteen Ways of Looking at a Blackbird." In *The Collected Poems of Wallace Stevens.* London: Faber and Faber.

Young, J. 2008. *Cultural Appropriation and the Arts.* Oxford: Wiley-Blackwell.

PART 3

DOING PHILOSOPHY

CHAPTER 11

GROUNDING INTERVENTIONISM: CONCEPTUAL AND EPISTEMOLOGICAL CHALLENGES

AMANDA BRYANT

1. Introduction

Philosophers have recently drawn substantive connections between grounding and causation, by drawing attention to their shared formal, metaphysical, and epistemic features.[1] Grounding is standardly taken to be an asymmetric metaphysical dependence relation that either *is* explanatory or *backs* explanation, wherein some derivative fact or entity obtains or exists in virtue of some more fundamental fact or entity.[2] Grounds are also standardly (though not universally) taken to metaphysically necessitate that which they ground.[3] Typical examples include: Socrates grounds Singleton Socrates, the fact that P and the fact that Q together ground the fact that P∧Q, the fact that P grounds the fact that P∨Q, God's love grounds the pious (or vice versa), natural features ground moral features, truthmakers ground truths, and fundamental physical facts ground biological facts.

Grounding is normally thought to differ from causation in some key respects. For instance, grounding can relate abstract relata, is synchronic, and relates more fundamental relata to less fundamental ones. By contrast, causation only relates concrete physical events, is diachronic, and typically relates equally fundamental relata (inter-level causation being an

---

[1] See Schaffer 2016 and Alastair Wilson 2018a, 2018b, and 2021. For critical responses, see Bernstein 2016 and Koslicki 2016. See also Wang 2020 for discussion.

[2] For introductions to grounding, see Audi 2012; Fine 2012; Raven 2015; Rosen 2010; and Schaffer 2009. On the connection between grounding and explanation, see Dasgupta 2017; Glazier 2020; Maurin 2019; and Thompson 2016.

[3] See deRosset 2010; Rosen 2010; and Trogdon 2013. For dissenting views, see Leuenberger 2014 and Skiles 2015.

Examining Philosophy Itself. Edited by Yafeng Shan.
Chapters and book compilation © 2023 Metaphilosophy LLC and John Wiley & Sons Ltd.
Published 2023 by John Wiley & Sons Ltd.

unusual and contested sort of case). Nevertheless, philosophers have also emphasized a number of features in common. Grounding and causation are both standardly thought to be irreflexive, asymmetric, transitive metaphysical dependence relations of a productive nature, intimately bound up with explanation, and aptly captured by counterfactual conditionals.

Those who emphasize the parallels between causation and grounding have attempted to extend the conceptual and formal resources of interventionism to grounding. For instance, Alastair Wilson claims: "The deep structural similarity between grounding and causation suggests that the asymmetry of grounding is reflected in an asymmetry of consequences of interventions. If we intervene to change the ground fact, the grounded fact changes. If we intervene to change the grounded fact, the ground fact is unchanged" (2021, 1123). According to this line of thought, interventionist conditionals capture important features of grounding. Similarly, Schaffer uses interventionist language to describe a test for grounding claims: "[T]here is a straightforward and informative ... working test of token grounding to be had, in terms of counterfactual covariation: wiggle the ground, and the grounded wiggles" (2016, 74). So there is some initial inclination in the literature to enfold grounding under the interventionist rubric. Call the resulting view (precisified below) *grounding interventionism*.

Causal interventionists face foundational challenges to the articulation and defense of their view, which have been well explored in metaphysics and philosophy of science.[4] They include, most prominently, the challenge of cashing out the central notion of an intervention in a way that is not viciously circular. Nevertheless, causal interventionism remains an attractive theoretical alternative in certain respects, partly due to the capacity of counterfactual conditionals to capture and explain a heterogeneous array of cases (Paul 2009), as well as the elegance and power of the formal machinery that accompanies it (Pearl 2000). It is natural to hope that accounting for grounding in interventionist terms might prove similarly fruitful.

Before getting too optimistic about the prospects for grounding interventionism, however, a number of substantive questions must be addressed. First, what does it mean to "wiggle the ground," as it were, and to see if the grounded wiggles? That is, what are grounding interventions, and what do they involve? Second, what are the epistemic credentials of grounding interventionism? That is, is wiggling the ground and seeing what happens a good way to find out about grounding? Can would-be grounding interventionists offer a satisfactory epistemological story about how we can come to know or form justified beliefs about grounding? The aim of this essay is to address both sorts of question.

---

[4] See such works as Hitchcock and Woodward 2003; Meek and Glymour 1994; Pearl 2000; Spirtes, Glymour, and Scheines 2000; Woodward 1997; 2000; and 2003; and Woodward and Hitchcock 2003.

We may begin to address them by looking to antecedent articulations and refinements of the substance of causal interventionism. In particular, to help clarify what it might mean to wiggle the ground, we may consider how causal interventionists have characterized wigglings. They standardly characterize the class of causal interventions as not limited to actual manipulations or practically possible ones, since causation is often independent of what we actually do and of what is practically possible for us to do. For example, Woodward points out that past events and large-scale cosmological events are uncontroversially causal, notwithstanding the impossibility of our manipulating them (2003, 10). So the relevant class of interventions must include counterfactual interventions. Evaluating the relevant counterfactuals sometimes requires us to countenance *far out* (that is, modally remote) scenarios.[5] It will be instructive to attend to this feature of causal interventions, because—as we will see—grounding interventionism likewise requires us to countenance far out counterfactual scenarios.

Since counterfactuals are so central to causal interventionism, the epistemology of counterfactuals is a natural place to begin considering how the causal interventionist's epistemological story might go. All sorts of philosophical and psychological work has been done on the epistemology of counterfactuals.[6] I will consider three (mutually compatible) suggestions about what enables and constrains counterfactual reasoning. First, I consider Williamson's (2007b) epistemology of counterfactuals, which assigns a prominent role to the imagination. On that view, imagination is the key cognitive capacity that allows us to perform the needed counterfactual evaluations, and wiggling a causal or grounding relatum is an *imaginative* act. Second, I consider structural equation models, which formally represent causal and grounding dependencies and potentially illuminate relations among concepts and claims of interest. Finally, I consider the potential for background theory to constrain counterfactual evaluation. Evaluating the epistemic credentials of grounding interventionism will then require determining whether the epistemic resources at issue—imagination, structural equation models, or theoretical constraints—can adequately constrain our assessments of grounding counterfactuals.

I argue below that when imagination is taken to be the primary basis for evaluating interventionist counterfactuals, interventionist

[5] For convenience, I occasionally invoke the metaphor of modal distance, but I don't wish to hang much on it, since it suggests a kind of linear progression of difference from actuality (merely logical possibilities always differing most from reality as compared to merely metaphysical possibilities, as compared to merely physical possibilities) that breaks down under scrutiny, with carefully chosen examples. I thank Anand Vaidya for drawing this to my attention.

[6] See, for instance, Byrne 2007; Hoerl, McCormack, and Beck 2011; Ichikawa 2011; Kroedel 2012 and 2017; Mandel, Hilton, and Catellani 2005; Schulz 2017; and Williamson 2007a and 2007b.

frameworks—whether causal or grounding—require us to stretch our imaginative resources beyond their adequacy conditions. In cases where experience doesn't constrain imaginative simulations, imagination calls on antecedent intuitions that lack adequate epistemic footing. If that's true, then causal interventionism and grounding interventionism alike invoke an epistemically deficient form of modal rationalism. Moreover, I point out that structural equation models can at best complement an independent epistemology of interventionist counterfactuals, because they require prior knowledge of the structural equations they encode. Lastly, I argue that holding fixed certain background theories can constrain our evaluation of some interventionist counterfactuals but that counternomics and countermetaphysicals again force us toward an unacceptably rationalist modal epistemology.

Let me be clear in advance about the strength of my thesis. I do not argue that grounding interventionism renders knowledge of grounding unachievable. I argue, rather, that the epistemic credentials of grounding interventionism are limited—cognizance of which should temper erstwhile high hopes that the interventionist framework can imbue theories of ground with increased objectivity, greater scientific respectability, or improved capacity for discovery. There are a spectrum of cases running from straightforward and unproblematic cases to intractable ones. My central claim is that none of the candidate epistemological stories gets us very far past the easy end of the spectrum. Moreover, since grounding theorists don't typically confine themselves to the easy end, the available epistemological options don't go very far toward vindicating metaphysical practice.

Section 2 describes Woodward's causal interventionism and considers some possible formulations of grounding analogs. Section 3 details the causal interventionist's notion of an intervention before using it to guide the articulation of an analogous ground-theoretic notion. Section 4 concerns the epistemology of interventionist counterfactuals. It addresses three (potentially complementary) approaches to counterfactual evaluation, respectively involving imagination, structural equation models, and theoretical constraint. At the same time, it evaluates the capacity of each approach to generate knowledge or justified belief concerning causation and grounding. Section 5 concludes the essay.

2. Interventionisms

Theories of causation have many different aims—they can concern causation itself, causal patterns, causal explanation, causal discovery and prediction, causal concepts and language (or their use in certain contexts), causal learning and reasoning, effective strategies, and so forth. For the purposes of this essay, I conceive of causal interventionism as a primarily ontological project, that is, as the project of non-reductively accounting for causation and identifying causal relationships. I take Woodward's (2003) account as an exemplar. On Woodward's account, relationships between two variables are causal when (roughly) intervening on one variable results in a change to the other (2003, 45). Assuming from here on that X and Y are not identical:

> *Causal interventionism:* X causes Y iff there is a possible intervention on X that changes the value of Y.

Woodward qualifies the view in a number of fine-grained ways, which I omit in the interests of maintaining a simple and general sense of the view. As I have already noted, since there are salient senses in which interventions need not be possible, the view is also amenable to counterfactual formulation:

> *Causal interventionism (counterfactual):* X causes Y iff there is a possible intervention on X that, were it carried out, would change the value of Y.

A natural place to start when formulating grounding interventionism would be by constructing an exactly parallel view. Such a view would say, roughly, that two variables represent a grounding relation when intervening on one variable results in a change to the other. Formulated counterfactually, we get the following view. Assuming from here on that α and β are not identical:

> *Grounding interventionism (counterfactual):* α grounds β iff there is a possible intervention on α that, were it carried out, would change the value of β.

Note that I have changed the variables from the causal formulation to reflect potential differences in kind between causal relata and grounding relata. Without any explicit restriction to the ranges of the variables, causal interventionism and grounding interventionism appear to make precisely the same condition sufficient for causation and for grounding. In fact, they appear to collapse counterfactual dependence with causation and grounding, respectively, in a way that would be immediately implausible to anyone who thinks counterfactual dependence tracks multiple kinds of metaphysical dependence. At any rate, grounding and causation are standardly thought to have incompatible features. In particular, as I mentioned at the outset, grounding is normally thought to be synchronic and causation diachronic; but a relation cannot be both at once, since one relatum is either temporally copresent with another or not.[7] If that's right,

---

[7] I borrow this characterization of the synchronic/diachronic distinction from Jessica M. Wilson (n.d), who convincingly argues that the distinction is not between temporal instantaneity and extension but rather temporal copresence and noncopresence. It is also worth noting that Alastair Wilson argues that the apparent distinction between causation and grounding in terms of their respective diachronicity and synchronicity "does not run deep" (2018b, 729).

then without further qualification, causal interventionism and grounding interventionism are incompatible, because they entail that any case of causation is a case of grounding, and vice versa. This presents a problem for anyone wishing to endorse a package deal of both interventionisms.

The ranges of the variables, however, typically *are* restricted by the aptness conditions of the relevant interventionist models. For instance, Schaffer specifies aptness conditions for causal models and for grounding models, according to which the variables range over events and entities, respectively (2016, 67 and 74). Would-be grounding interventionists who take the relata of grounding relations to be facts would have to formulate that condition differently. If causation and grounding are indeed mutually exclusive, their challenge would be to do so in a way that precludes a single dependency from fitting both the causal model and the grounding model. This would presumably require holding fixed a philosophical background theory according to which facts and events are categorially distinct.[8]

An alternative to relying on aptness conditions alone to adequately restrict the application of each interventionist view would be to weaken the views by removing their sufficiency conditions. In the case of grounding interventionism, the resulting view would be as follows:

Grounding interventionism (weak): α grounds β only if there is a possible intervention on α that, were it carried out, would change the value of β.

Since we are not in the business of providing a reductive account, this appears to be a reasonable amendment to the view. Even this weakened formulation, however, apparently admits of counterexample. For instance, suppose that P grounds P∨Q. It is possible to wiggle P without the truth of the disjunction wiggling.[9] Where both P and Q are true, P and Q *each* fully ground the disjunction. This is a case of *grounding overdetermination* (Koslicki 2015) that is analogous to cases of symmetric causal overdetermination, in which some effect has more than one operative and individually sufficient cause. As such, it is a case of grounding that does not satisfy the necessary condition posited by *grounding interventionism (weak)*.[10]

Suppose we stipulate that grounding interventions must wiggle *all* putative grounds. That would mean we could not capture as much grounding

---

[8] I thank an anonymous referee for encouraging me to consider aptness conditions such as these more explicitly.

[9] Thanks to Claudio Calosi for raising this counterexample.

[10] If the affinities between grounding and causation do indeed run deep, then it isn't surprising that the cases that make trouble for causal interventionism—including symmetric overdetermination and preemption—make trouble for grounding interventionism, too. Grounding interventionists such as Schaffer and Alastair Wilson acknowledge such problems and hold only that the interventionist framework works for a range of suitably unproblematic cases.

structure as we would like, since we would not have the means to say that in cases of symmetric grounding overdetermination each ground is individually sufficient for grounding. Another response would be to argue that cases of symmetric grounding overdetermination can be bracketed, by suggesting that they are an artifact of a sui generis kind of *logical* grounding (Correia 2014), which requires an independent account. Yet symmetric grounding overdetermination may not be so easily bracketed. Alastair Wilson describes it as "commonplace" and gives an example that does not seem merely logical: the potion's being poisonous is grounded in its containing 1 gram of arsenic and also in its containing 1 gram of strychnine (2018b, 743). A further response to grounding overdetermination would be to weaken grounding interventionism still further, so that it posits neither necessary nor sufficient conditions for grounding but instead says that *some* counterfactual conditionals track *some* grounding relations. Without general principles stating when and why the counterfactual analysis applies, however, such a view would not be particularly illuminating.

A more promising response might be to selectively negate the influence of any symmetrically overdetermining relata. Woodward suggests that, in cases of symmetric overdetermination, causal interventionists can get the right result for a particular cause X by, roughly, "freezing" the influence of other direct causes and finding that an intervention on X will change the value of Y (2003, 83).[11] This maneuver exploits the thought that the causal dependence of Y on X "fails to express itself in counterfactual dependence only because [the other symmetrically overdetermining cause] happens to be present as well" (83); if we remove the influence of other symmetrically overdetermining causes, we find the appropriate counterfactual dependence. A parallel approach to grounding overdetermination might motivate a revision to *grounding interventionism (weak)*, such that, roughly, the relevant intervention on α would change the value of β, supposing we have negated the influence of any symmetrically overdetermining grounds.

Even with such a qualification, the initial formulations of grounding interventionism might still be thought to be confused. I have designed them to capture Schaffer's and Alastair Wilson's idea that grounding interventions target *grounds*. Arguably, however, cases of *grounding preemption* show that this approach sometimes gets the direction of necessity and dependence wrong. I discuss grounding preemption in greater detail in section 4.2. The gist of the problem is that grounded facts or entities can have multiple full grounds that perform their grounding role only when the others don't. For instance, supposing a thing's redness grounds its being colored, we can wiggle the ground (by making the thing blue) without changing the grounded (the thing will still be colored). According to this line of thought, it is misguided to intervene on the grounds,

---

[11] For the formal details required to prevent this approach from being too permissive, see Woodward 2003, 82–84.

because the grounded doesn't counterfactually depend on the ground. The counterfactual dependence between ground and grounded runs in the opposite direction, so that if the grounded were to change (such that the thing were no longer colored), the ground would thereby change as well (the thing would no longer be red). In such cases, the interventionist must wiggle the *grounded* and see whether the *ground* wiggles.[12] To capture these sorts of cases, grounding interventionists might revise their view in the following way, which would make it structurally disanalogous with causal interventionism:

> *Grounding interventionism (disjunctive):* α grounds β only if there is a possible intervention on α or β that, were it carried out, would change the value of the other variable.

Arguably, this revised approach does not capture the motivation for the initial view, which was that grounds are like causes. It's *causes* we intervene on, since the arrow of determination flows from cause to effect, and that's the objective asymmetry we want to capture. According to this argument, the same goes, mutatis mutandis, for grounds. So grounding interventionists may insist that the view has to be formulated in terms of possible interventions on grounds, while instead proposing special ways of bracketing or precluding preemption cases.[13]

Overdetermination and preemption aside, one might still think grounding interventionism is inherently confused. In particular, it may be argued that some cases of grounding appear to involve bidirectional metaphysical necessitation—and that there is a fundamental lack of fit between such cases and the interventionist paradigm. For instance, wiggling Socrates automatically wiggles Singleton Socrates, *and vice versa*. Wiggling Singleton (whatever that might mean!) automatically wiggles Socrates. This suggests that some alleged grounding relata have a coarse-grained modal relationship that interventionist counterfactuals simply don't capture: the relata necessarily coexist, so there is no asymmetric counterfactual dependence between them, and accordingly you cannot intervene on one relatum independently of the other. We might suspect that this is a bug of the example at issue—but the Singleton example is generally taken to be paradigmatic of grounding.

The grounding formalism can allay some of these concerns. For instance, Schaffer explains: "[T]he idea that one can 'surgically intervene' requires a kind of modularity condition on grounding, which corresponds to a free

---

[12] I thank Fabrice Correia for bringing this to my attention.

[13] For instance, on Alastair Wilson's view (2018a and 2018b), the problem of preemption doesn't arise, because interventions cut off alternate grounding routes by definition. The right kind of intervention on a red object makes it *colorless* rather than blue—yet, were such an intervention accomplished, the object would (*per impossibile*) nevertheless remain red. I thank Al for raising these points in correspondence.

recombination assumption for the more fundamental," in which "one can adjust one of the more fundamental parameters while leaving the others as is" (2016, 71). We can represent Socrates and Singleton Socrates using distinct variables and encode their alleged asymmetric dependence into the equations we use to model them (73). This means that the formalism in which we enfold grounding "must tolerate" countermetaphysical and counterlogical scenarios (71), for which one needs a non-vacuous semantics.[14] So we can force asymmetry into the grounding models. Whether this truly resolves the concern that some paradigm cases of grounding intuitively fail to exhibit asymmetric dependence is open to debate.

We have considered some initial formulations of grounding interventionism involving counterfactual interventions being necessary and sufficient for grounding, being sufficient only, targeting grounds only, and targeting either grounds or grounded facts/entities. I do not privilege any of the formulations that I have canvassed. My aim has been just to consider some of the available options. In the process, I hope to have illuminated some initial choice points, challenges, and potential bones of contention. I leave finer-grained articulations and defenses of the view to its would-be proponents.

3. Interventions

Having sketched some basic formulations of grounding interventionism, I can now proceed to ask what, precisely, a grounding intervention could be. I start by considering how causal interventionists have precisified their notion of an intervention. Again, I take Woodward's (2003) view as the model. On that view, *intervention* is a token-level causal notion (2003, 98). Moreover, interventions need not be human manipulations; on the contrary, they bear no essential connection to human agency. Instead, an intervention on X with respect to Y changes the value of X in such a way that if any change occurs to Y, "it occurs only in virtue of the change in the value of X and not through some other causal route" (94). In other words, the intervention changes the value of X, such that any resulting change to Y *goes through* X, as opposed to resulting from some cause that merely correlates with the intervention. Woodward also stipulates that the change to X must be a result of the intervention alone (96). In essence, an intervention *alone* changes the value of X, which *directly* changes the value of Y.

It is well known that this conception of intervention invokes causation, for it is not clear what "directly changing" the values of variables could be if not causal. Accordingly, the notion of an intervention does not provide independent purchase on causation, and it makes causal interventionism

---

[14] On the semantics of countermetaphysicals, see Wilson 2018a.

circular. Woodward stresses, however, that his intention is not to provide a reductive account; instead, he intends to nontrivially elucidate causal concepts, claims, and the relations among them (2009, 253–54). Moreover, he argues that the circularity in question is non-vicious (2009, 254–55).

In cashing out the notion of an intervention, Woodward also characterizes interventions in terms of ideal experiments. Interventions are what we would do ideally—that is, if all practical impediments were removed—to test for causal relations (2003, 46). The appeal to ideal conditions is needed because interventions need not be practically possible. In fact, Woodward claims, they need not even be *physically* possible: "[C]ommitment to a manipulability theory leads unavoidably to the use of counterfactuals concerning what would happen under conditions that may involve violations of physical law" (2003, 132; emphasis removed). For instance, we know that the gravitational attraction of the moon causes the behavior of the tides. According to Woodward, while it may be physically impossible to change the position of the moon alone or to perform similar interventions, we can still assess what would happen in such counterfactual scenarios and be confident in the resultant causal and explanatory claims. The counterfactuals that capture causal relations will inevitably include such counternomics.

If the modal scope of the "possible" in "possible intervention" is not limited to practical possibility or physical possibility, where does that leave us? Woodward claims: "[A]n intervention on X with respect to Y will be 'possible' as long as it is logically or conceptually possible for a process meeting the conditions for an intervention on X with respect to Y to occur" (2003, 132). This means that the relevant modal space is remarkably broad. The only counterfactuals that cannot provide a test of the truth of causal claims are "those for which we cannot coherently describe what it would be like for the relevant intervention to occur at all or for which there is no conceivable basis for assessing claims about what would happen under such interventions" (2003, 132). This means that causal interventionism requires us to assess counterfactuals inhabiting some of the farthest reaches of modal space. For that reason, causal interventionism requires a powerful modal epistemology.

With a clearer sense of the notion of a causal intervention in hand, we can now consider what a grounding intervention might be. If causal and grounding interventions are analogous, then in the case of grounding, the relevant counterfactuals track token grounding relations. Let us say, closely following Woodward's characterization of causal interventions, that a grounding intervention on one variable with respect to another changes the value of the one in such a way that if any change occurs to the other, it occurs in virtue of that first change.

Note that, just as causal interventionists invoke causation in their conception of an intervention, grounding interventionists similarly invoke grounding. This is suggested by the presence of the "in virtue of" locution in the characterization I just gave, which grounding theorists take to signal grounding (Fine 2012). Hence, just as causal interventionism does not give independent purchase on causation, grounding interventionism does not give independent purchase on grounding. It is open to grounding interventionists to respond, as Woodward does, by emphasizing the non-reductive nature of their view and by suggesting that its value is in its nontrivial elucidation of networks of concepts and claims pertaining to grounding.

Having just noted the presence of the "in virtue of" locution in the characterization of a grounding intervention, we are well positioned to see that grounding interventionism offers a unique response to a much-discussed puzzle in the metaphysics of grounding: the question of what, if anything, grounds the grounding facts. Understood as an ontological thesis, grounding interventionism suggests that each token grounding fact obtains in virtue of a corresponding possible intervention. That is to say, possible interventions ground the grounding facts. Here the grounding interventionist faces the additional question of what grounds *those* second-order grounding facts, and so on. This issue has been addressed in different ways. Following Bennett (2011), interventionists might say that possible interventions ground the first-order, second-order, third-order grounding facts—and so on to infinity, resulting in a well-founded and nonvicious infinite regress. Alternatively, they might characterize the second-order (and higher) grounding facts as *autonomous* in Dasgupta's sense, that is, "not apt for being grounded," such that "the question of what grounds them does not legitimately arise in the first place" (2014b, 563; see also 2016). I leave it to defenders of the view to determine how best to further address the puzzle.

The most pressing question now is what changing the value of the relevant variables amounts to. Let's start with the causal case. On one natural interpretation, to change the value of X is just what it sounds like: to plug a particular value (0 or 1, let's say) in for X in the relevant causal model. This is, in effect, to add a condition or supposition to the model. But this cannot be what Woodward has in mind, because that would make all of the interventions at issue physically and, indeed, practically possible—even easy! After all, I can set the values of the variables as I like. So the interventions at issue are interventions not on our models but on the world. Changing the variable X must mean changing worldly circumstances in a manner at odds with the laws of physics. So let us say that, in the causal case, changing the value of X amounts to making some event occur or not occur.

As for grounding, what changing the value of α ultimately amounts to will depend on what sorts of things can be grounds. This is a matter of disagreement. Schaffer (2009) takes grounding relata to be objects; others take them to be facts (Audi 2012; Dasgupta 2014a; Fine 2012). If the relata are objects, then changing the value of α could mean bringing some object into or out of existence; in the case of facts, it could mean making some fact obtain or not obtain.

To make matters more concrete, let me appeal to some familiar examples. Take the following grounding claims:

Disjunction: The truth of P grounds the truth of P∨Q.
Singleton: The existence of Socrates grounds the existence of Singleton Socrates.
Euthyphro: God's desiring that P grounds its being good that P. (Wilson 2018b, 731–32)

In these examples, wiggling the ground requires, respectively, making P false, removing Socrates from history, and making God desire differently. Just as we asked about whether and in what sense causal interventions are possible, we can ask the same of these grounding interventions. Assume for convenience the standard nested model of possibility space, in which physical possibility is nested within a space of metaphysical possibility, itself nested within a space of logical possibility. Regarding the disjunction case, the possibility of the intervention is indeterminate, since whether and in what sense it is possible to make P false depends on what P says. In the case of Socrates, it is physically impossible (I assume) for us, temporally situated as we are, to remove him from history. Accordingly, the intervention in virtue of which the grounding relation holds inhabits the merely metaphysical space of possibility, outside the space of physical possibility.

As for God desiring differently, the details depend on the theology held fixed, but I take it no theist thinks anyone can *make* God do anything, given God's supposed omnipotence. It is an interesting question what sort of modality is at issue. For a human to force a change to God wouldn't break any physical laws, since (*pace* Spinoza) God is supposedly not part of the natural world they describe. One might think the intervention is metaphysically impossible or, for conceptual reasons, logically impossible.[15] Perhaps, in an ideal experiment, the human intervener would be omnipotent, too. In that case, we would get a variation of the paradox of omnipotence, which we might also interpret as a symptom of logical impossibility. Where grounding interventionism requires us to countenance counterlogicals, it takes us right off the standard map of modal space. These familiar examples suggest that grounding interventionism may require us to countenance counterpossible, countermetaphysical, and counterlogical interventions.

In fact, if one thinks that grounds are sometimes physically, metaphysically, or logically necessary—as grounding theorists surely do—then

[15] This example of an apparent physical possibility that is, at the same time, metaphysically impossible complicates matters by showing that we must refine either the standard characterization of physical possibility (in terms of consistency with physical law) or the standard nested picture of modal space.

examples like this will proliferate, since wiggling such grounds requires doing the impossible, in the respective senses. For instance, take the following claims:

1. The fact that nothing can travel faster than light grounds the fact that events occurring in different light cones are causally isolated.
2. The fact that water is H_2O grounds the fact that *this* sample of H_2O is a sample of water.
3. The law of noncontradiction grounds the fact that the statement "Whales are mammals" is either true or false but not both.

These are plausible candidates for grounding claims, because they involve a kind of non-causal explanation of particular facts by appeal to more general principles. Now, suppose we wiggle the grounds. Doing so would involve (1) making it possible for things to travel faster than light, (2) altering the essence of water, and (3) rendering false the law of non-contradiction. Arguably, the envisaged interventions are counternomic, countermetaphysical, and counterlogical interventions, respectively.[16] If such examples are any indication, grounding interventionism requires us to countenance interventions that are possible only at the farthest reaches of modal space.

Let's take stock. Grounding interventions can be understood in a manner closely parallel to causal interventions, that is, as changes to the value of variables representing grounding relata. Given that some of those interventions are impossible, "changing the value of variables" has to be understood in worldly terms. Depending on one's conception of the grounding relata, this might mean adding something to or deleting something from the roster of existents or making some fact obtain or fail to obtain. Just as causal interventionism requires that we assess counterfactuals whose antecedents are possible only in remote regions of modal space, grounding interventionism makes a similar demand. So both views ask us to make judgments about modally remote counterfactual scenarios. The next question I wish to address is: How might we do that?

4. Knowledge of Interventionist Counterfactuals

Since causal interventionism is the comparatively well-explored progenitor of grounding interventionism, it will be instructive to examine its epistemological credentials alongside those of grounding interventionism.

[16] In Woodwardian spirit, one might claim we have no clear conception of what these interventions would involve, that the relevant counterfactuals thus lack a clear meaning or truth-value, and that the interventionist framework has been overextended. In response, grounding interventionists must show that we *do* have a clear conception of the required interventions or else endorse a more permissive account of the meaningfulness of counterfactuals.

So how does the causal interventionist think we achieve our epistemic aims—whether knowledge, justified belief, understanding, confirmation, learning, or discovery—with regard to causation?

In the most epistemically ideal cases, we simply do the manipulations. That is the best way of finding out about causal dependencies. Where deriving a causal claim requires making a judgment about some practically possible intervention, sometimes it suffices to run inductions on prior experience of type-identical or suitably similar causal relations (cf. Roca-Royes 2017). Going beyond practical possibility, Woodward suggests that, as the sorts of creatures who can interact with and manipulate aspects of the world, we develop practices of causal inference and explanation, which we can extend from cases where manipulation is possible to cases where it's not (2003, 11). For physically possible interventions, our knowledge of the physical laws can guide our judgments. These sorts of piecemeal methods will only get us so far, however, especially relative to the vast space of logically possible interventions to which the causal interventionist indexes causality.

Is there anything more general that we can say in the elucidation of an epistemology that can underwrite interventionist frameworks? Given the centrality of counterfactuals to interventionist frameworks, such an epistemology would be, largely, an epistemology of counterfactuals. So it will be illuminating to consider which sorts of epistemic resources might figure into the assessment of counterfactuals generally and interventionist counterfactuals in particular. I consider three such resources below: (1) imagination, (2) structural equation models, and (3) theoretical constraints.

4.1. Imagination

I begin with Williamson's (2007b) epistemology of counterfactuals, to which there have been numerous critical responses.[17] My aim here is not to address the independent feasibility of the account but to see how conjoining it with causal and grounding interventionisms affects their epistemic credentials. Williamson suggests that the story of counterfactual knowledge is developmental and evolutionarily unmysterious. As individuals accrue experience over time, their experience conditions them into "patterns of expectation which are called on in [their] assessment of ordinary counterfactual conditionals" (2007b, 167). Importantly, counterfactual thinking often invokes the imagination, "radically informed and disciplined" by an empirical background of beliefs and an accompanying folk physics (143). Against that background, imaginative simulation allows us to discern, for instance, that "If the bush had not been there, the rock would have ended in the lake" (142).

---

[17] See Casullo 2012; Gregory 2017; Jenkins 2008; Mallozzi 2021; Roca-Royes 2011; and Tahko 2012.

We can think of our process of imaginatively assessing the relevant counterfactuals as involving the performance, not of ordinary causal manipulations, but of *imaginative interventions*. In imaginative intervention, we
imagine changing a variable (in the worldly sense discussed above) and
imaginatively simulate what would result. I imaginatively remove the bush
and simulate the resultant path of the rock. While "imaginative intervention" may *sound* novel and fancy, ultimately, imaginative interventions are
just thought experiments, in which we "work through the implications of
scenarios" (Gendler 2010, 1–2).[18] If so, we assess interventionist counterfactuals by running thought experiments.

Now, if imagination is the primary mode of epistemic access to counterfactuals, how good are the causal interventionist's and the grounding
interventionist's chances of knowledge (or justification, or whatever) of
causation and grounding, respectively? Williamson notes that our ability
to handle mundane counterfactuals might not extend equally well to all
reaches of modal space: "[W]e may well be more reliable in evaluating
counterfactuals whose antecedents involve small departures from the
actual world than in evaluating those whose antecedents involve much
larger departures. We may be correspondingly more reliable in evaluating
the possibility of everyday scenarios than of 'far-out' ones, and extra
caution may be called for in the latter case" (2007b, 164). The more
familiar the imagined scenario, the more reliable imagination will be as
a source of modal information; the less familiar, the less confidence we
should have in its deliverances.[19] Williamson therefore speaks approvingly
of those philosophers who have comparatively low confidence in their
"radically strange" imaginative exercises (164).[20]

If Williamson is right, then his epistemology of counterfactuals makes
the epistemic credentials of causal interventionism rather a mixed bag.
That's because causal interventionists demand the assessment of both
relatively mundane counterfactuals and relatively strange ones, and modal
imagination is a better guide to the former than to the latter.[21] The
epistemic value of the imagination in a particular context depends largely

[18] On the role of imagination in thought experiments, see also Arcangeli 2010 and Meynell
2014 and 2018.

[19] Similarly, Nichols points out that it's less clear that we can trust the verdicts of imagination about absolute possibility and necessity, as compared with local risk and opportunity
(2006, 253).

[20] Some conceive of metaphysics as an imaginative endeavor. For instance, Godfrey-Smith
(2012) and Paul (2012) characterize metaphysics as model building, which involves imagination. A picture like this may require us to rethink the epistemic aims of metaphysics. For
example, McSweeney (forthcoming) argues that metaphysics is essentially imaginative and
defends its value relative to the epistemic aim of understanding.

[21] This makes sense evolutionarily, in that, as Nichols points out, "the connection between
imagination and modal judgment presumably earned its keep by facilitating nomological
modal judgments" (2006, 246).

on how the imagination is constrained in that context.[22] It is because
the imagination is "radically informed and disciplined" by experience
that it is, on Williamson's view, plausibly reliable in the evaluation of
mundane counterfactuals concerning things like rock trajectories—that
is, in situations where folk physics is adequate for predictive purposes; it
is because imagination lacks adequate constraint in less mundane cases
that it is not obviously reliable in those cases.[23] The upshot is that modal
imagination has highly restricted adequacy conditions. When it comes to
strange enough counternomics, ordinary experience doesn't adequately
prepare the imagination, and assessing them requires us to stretch our
imaginative capacities beyond their adequacy conditions.

What happens then? Recall the idea that our imaginative simulations
of counterfactual scenarios are thought experiments. We can compare
the epistemic constraints on those thought experiments with those on
real-life scientific experiments: "In the case of actual experiments, the
theory-relevant evidence generally takes the form of data concerning the
behavior of the physical world under specific conditions; in the case of
thought experiments, the theory-relevant evidence generally takes the form
of intuitions (or predictions) concerning such behavior" (Gendler 2010, 2).
That is, in cases where empirical evidence cannot inform or constrain
imaginative simulations, imagination frequently calls on antecedent
intuitions. I will suppose that intuitions are "gut-feeling" judgments. Now,
these moves are admittedly quick. Intuitions have been characterized in a
number of ways.[24] Moreover, the network of relations among intuitions,
thought experiments, imagination, science, and non-science is undoubtedly
complex and deserves a deeper treatment than I can give here (see, for
instance, Levy and Godfrey-Smith 2019). On the definitional matter, I'm
just stipulating. On the role of intuitions in thought experiments, I believe
a natural characterization of what it is for a judgment to be made "from
the gut" is for it to be made without significant guidance from experience,
among other forms of evidence and constraint (such as logical constraint,
discussed further below). We lack such guidance in pervasive, weird
metaphysical cases. Thus, we rely on intuition when thinking through such
cases.

By invoking intuitions, causal interventionism invokes one of the primary epistemic resources of modal rationalism in a way that diminishes
the appeal of the view. While intuitive judgments are potentially valuable in
contexts of discovery, in contexts of justification, they are epistemically suspect for a number of familiar reasons. Some experimental evidence points

---

[22] On the notion of epistemic constraint, its role and significance, see Bryant 2021.

[23] There are exceptions, however. For instance, imagination sometimes does poorly in
seemingly mundane cases, such as cases where we attempt to imaginatively predict our own
responses to situations (Maibom 2016).

[24] Booth and Rowbottom 2014; Cappelen 2012; Deutsch 2015; Devitt 2015; Dorr 2010;
Gendler 2010; Nicoli 2016; and Weinberg 2016.

to their cultural variation, and some suggests they are strongly vulnerable to cognitive bias.[25] Moreover, science has a track record of repeatedly overturning commonsense metaphysical intuitions (Shtulman and Harrington 2016), including even the strongest modal intuitions, such as the intuitions "that non-Euclidean geometry is impossible as a model of physical space, that it is impossible that there not be deterministic causation, [and] that non-absolute time is impossible" (Ladyman and Ross 2007, 16). Since surprise is a measure of scientific success (French and Murphy 2021), we might even think that counterintuitiveness is *characteristic* of scientific discovery. These points cast serious doubt on the evidential weight of intuitions. Independently of these sorts of arguments, however, I believe that in many contexts—metaphysics included—there is little reason to take intuitions to be even defeasibly evidential in the first place. At the far reaches of modal space, where experience leaves imagination blind and counterfactual evaluation must invoke intuition, the causal interventionist's epistemology is rendered ineffectually rationalist.

As for grounding interventionism, it fares worse than its causal cousin when coupled with Williamson's epistemology of counterfactuals. In the causal case, imagination operates against a relatively rosy epistemological backdrop. We have (*pace* Hume) a great deal of empirically based causal knowledge. As Woodward stresses (2003, 34), many causal dependencies are evidenced by actual experimentation. Prior experience of causal patterns reliably enables prediction.[26] We also appear to have a hardwired capacity to identify instances of causation that "emerges early in development, and in some cases is remarkably fast and efficient" (Woodward 2003, 29). So the causal interventionist can capitalize on a great deal of prior working knowledge of causation.

By contrast, in the grounding case the epistemological backdrop is less auspicious. The sorts of grounding relations typically at issue in metaphysics are distinctively metaphysical, composing a level of metaphysical structure that is not directly empirically discoverable, to which we have only indirect epistemic access. Neither prior experience nor empirical experimentation informs judgments about, for instance, abstract objects like Singleton Socrates or nonempirical matters like the goodness of an action. Neither should we hold our collective breath for studies in developmental psychology to show that we excel at identifying instances of grounding, since grounding is tied to practices of abstract metaphysical explanation rather than to the sphere of action and decision-making like

[25] On their cultural variability, see Beebe and Undercoffer 2016; Machery et al. 2004; Li et al. 2018; Nichols, Stich, and Weinberg 2003; and Weinberg, Nichols, and Stich 2001; on their vulnerability to cognitive bias, see Andow 2016; Schwitzgebel and Cushman 2012; Swain, Alexander, and Weinberg 2008; and Wheatley and Haidt 2005.

[26] Jansson (2018) likewise highlights how a posteriori knowledge of local causal matters constrains judgments of the aptness of causal models.

its causal cousin. With grounding, we just don't have the epistemic traction we have with causation.

The fact is that the metaphysics of grounding gets murky and perplexing, fast. Some grounding interventions are "radically strange," as Williamson put it. With countermetaphysicals, experience constrains the imagination even less than it does with counternomics—and leaves it even more reliant on intuitions that we have no good reason to believe are reliable or evidential. For that reason, an imagination-based epistemology of counterfactuals renders grounding interventionism epistemically impoverished, and grounding interventionists must either defend the permissibility of stretching our imaginative resources beyond their adequacy conditions or point to some other mode of epistemic access to the relevant modal truths.

4.2. Structural Equation Models

Perhaps would-be grounding interventionists can benefit from an alternate (potentially complementary) tack, in which they co-opt formal tools that have been used fruitfully to model causal relations. In this vein, Schaffer claims that "the causal discovery algorithms associated with structural equation models furnish as precise and well-understood an epistemology as one could hope for" (2016, 67). Since those models are not inherently causal, Schaffer (2016) and Alastair Wilson (2018a and 2018b) are optimistic about the prospects of structural equation models to illuminate features of grounding structure and to reveal first-order grounding facts. Schaffer is careful to emphasize that the models are not a "magical panacea" but rather the best available formalism (2016, 61).

In essence, structural equation models comprise variables representing independent and dependent conditions (that is, causes and effects; grounds and grounded entities or facts), and structural equations that say what the value of dependent variables will be given certain values for the independent ones. Modelers then say "what actually happens" (Schaffer 2016, 62), by assigning values to the independent variables. The models then spit out values for the dependent variables, from which we read off causal or grounding claims.

Schaffer acknowledges various complicating factors here. First, as we have seen, it is controversial how best to read token relations off causal models—and by extension grounding models—in problem cases such as those involving preemption (65). In particular, some argue that structural equation models must distinguish between default and deviant variables, corresponding to expected and surprising events, respectively.[27] In response, Blanchard and Schaffer (2017) argue that the distinction

---

[27] See for instance Menzies (2007), Hitchcock (2007), and Hall (2007).

encodes a cognitive bias that influences causal judgment but that shouldn't be incorporated into models of causation itself.

Second, it is also a matter of debate how to handle the problem of under-determination. As Schaffer explains, there can be multiple apt models of a situation, and they can disagree over causation. In such cases, it's not clear which causal claims we should commit to or why. While we might relativize causal claims to particular models, doing so eliminates the metaphysical objectivity we might have hoped for (Schaffer 2016, 68).

Finally, Schaffer acknowledges that like interventionism itself, structural equation models are also circular. That's because the division of variables into independent and dependent conditions and the parent-child asymmetry of the structural equations are built into the models (66). At any rate, it is clear that structural equation models don't make all substantive questions and difficulties disappear; on the contrary, they come with their own deep and difficult choice points.

Let us suppose for argument's sake that, in time, these issues will be satisfactorily resolved. Other prospective problems still remain. For instance, Koslicki (2016) presents a number of reasons to doubt that structural equation models apply equally well to grounding and to causation. Among other things, she argues that prototypical cases of grounding like the determinate/determinable relation are problem cases for structural equation models because they are structurally similar to cases of massive causal preemption. For instance, Koslicki considers Schaffer's own example of the shirt's being maroon grounding the shirt's being red. She points out that the example is a case in which wiggling the grounds need not wiggle the grounded, because supposing the shirt's color changes from maroon to crimson, "the shirt continues to be red, only in a different way" (2016, 107). So we have a case of grounding that is analogous to a case of massive causal preemption, in that the grounded can be brought about by multiple grounds, each of which can individually constitute a full ground and obtains only if the others don't obtain. Koslicki remarks: "At most, then, we are dealing with a situation in which a supposedly clear case of grounding is comparable to a problematic case of causation, one which has led to headaches for extant theories of causation including, by Schaffer's own admission, the structural equation model of causation" (2016, 108). If Koslicki is right that structural equation models render problematic erstwhile unproblematic cases of grounding, then we might doubt that structural equation models are really the key to a satisfactory grounding interventionist epistemology. In fact, from these and other concerns relating to the extension of structural equation models to grounding (such as those in Jansson 2018), one might draw the conclusion that far from being a beneficial component of a satisfactory epistemology of grounding, the interventionist framework makes theories of ground *worse off* epistemically than they would be otherwise. This is a stronger conclusion than I currently wish to defend, but I flag it as a live possibility.

At any rate, suppose again for the sake of argument that interventionists can adequately resolve this concern by developing a novel approach to preemption cases.[28] If they were to do so, could we then say that structural equation models imbue grounding interventionism with adequate epistemological resources? I believe not.

To my mind, a central factor to consider in evaluating the potential of structural equation models to flesh out the grounding interventionist's epistemological story is that we don't just want to model causation and grounding, we want to model them well. It's clear that we need good reason to be confident of what we put into our models—including, among other things, the functions that purportedly relate the variables—before we can justifiably be confident of what the models spit out. This much is uncontroversial. Indeed, Schaffer acknowledges the point explicitly: "I am not trying to show that merely by adopting the structural equations formalism, one gets the right answers to grounding questions for free. On the contrary: to get the right answers to grounding questions one has to put the right structural equations into the model, which encode the form and direction of dependency" (2016, 77). Likewise, one of Schaffer's aptness conditions for grounding models requires that the counterfactuals encoded in the model's equations be true (2016, 75). So the need for true (or justified, or known, or otherwise epistemically well-founded) starting counterfactuals is clear and acknowledged. But this immediately raises an important and more foundational epistemological question. Why should we think *those* counterfactuals are true (or justified, or known, and so on)? Grounding theorists may fill in this more foundational epistemological blank as they like. Yet the presence of such a blank shows that structural equation models can only supplement the grounding interventionist's epistemology. We need independent reasons for believing or accepting the counterfactuals we use to set up our structural equation models. So structural equation models cannot form the basis of an independently adequate epistemology of interventionist counterfactuals, nor are they intended to. Rather, they must complement some further and more foundational epistemic resource, in virtue of which we can be assured that we're setting up the relevant models well. The epistemic credentials of causal and grounding interventionism will then largely hang on the reliability of that resource.

4.3. *Theoretical Constraint*

One possibility is that certain theoretical constraints could provide the needed epistemic resource. I have discussed the nature and importance of such constraints elsewhere (Bryant 2021), but the general idea is simple and familiar: holding fixed certain background claims restricts the sorts

---

[28] For instance, by taking Alastair Wilson's approach (2018a and 2018b) to such cases (see my footnote 13 above).

of further claims we can make. In the interventionist context, one might hope that background theory can appropriately constrain counterfactual assessment. Three main candidates immediately suggest themselves: background science, background logic, and background metaphysics.

First, let's consider whether science can adequately constrain the assessment of interventionist counterfactuals. Here, we might take inspiration from certain causal interventionists. For instance, in their manipulationist account of causation, Menzies and Price appeal to artificial simulations to make sense of how we can justify causal claims about unmanipulable events. Take the claim that some earthquake was caused by friction between continental plates. Menzies and Price argue: "We can make such causal claims because we believe that there is another situation that models the circumstances surrounding the earthquake in the essential respects and does support a means-end relation between an appropriate pair of events. The paradigm example of such a situation would be that created by seismologists in their artificial simulations of the movement of continental plates" (1993, 197). The simulation informs judgments about the relevant counterfactuals because it adequately models the mechanics of earthquakes. When artificial simulations are founded on a rich body of data and have a track record of predictive success, they can significantly aid counterfactual reasoning.

That's fine for the physical possibilities, but matters get trickier when it comes to counternomics. Woodward is cognizant of the epistemological worries that arise from his move toward conceptual or logical possibility. He remarks: "It is arguable that as we make the relevant notion of 'possible intervention' more and more permissive, so that it includes contra-nomic possibilities and so on, we reach a point at which this notion and the counterfactuals in which it figures become so unclear that we can no longer use them to illuminate … causal claims" (2009, 256). That's because it is unclear what the proposed intervention would involve and how to determine what would result from it (2009, 257). If Woodward is correct, then perhaps counternomics might be thought to take us beyond the "natural range of application" of causal interventionism (2009, 256).

Woodward suggests, however, that, at least in some cases, elements of well-confirmed scientific theories constrain our judgment with regard to physical impossibilities. Recall the example of the moon's gravitational attraction and its effect on the tides. Woodward suggests: "Although it may be true that any actual physical process that changes the position of the moon will also directly influence the tides, Newtonian theory and familiar rules about the composition of forces tell us how to subtract out any direct influence from such a process so that we can calculate just what the effect of, say, doubling of the moon's orbit (and no other changes) would be on the tides, even though it also may be true that there is no way of actually realizing this effect alone" (2003, 131). That is, the appropriate physical theory can help us to establish the right kind of modularity in our model of the intervention and its consequences. Woodward continues: "Newtonian theory itself delivers a determinate answer to questions about what would happen to the tides under an intervention that doubles the moon's orbit, and this is enough for counterfactual claims about what would happen under such interventions to be legitimate and to allow us to assess their truth" (2003, 131). So science can constrain our assessments of at least some counternomics.

Does this approach give causal interventionism adequate epistemic footing? The example works because it involves isolating variables that wouldn't normally be isolable *in an otherwise familiar* possible world; it's less clear that science can guide inferences about worlds where the physical laws differ more significantly from those of the actual world. At any rate, when causal interventionism invokes (as it inevitably does) counterfactuals with merely logically or conceptually possible antecedents, science doesn't obviously help. So the appeal to scientific models and background theory as a means of answering questions about counternomic scenarios may go some way to allaying concerns about the epistemic credentials of causal interventionism, but it won't provide a completely satisfying story.

As for grounding interventionism, scientific models and background theory are likewise powerless to constrain our reasoning about certain paradigmatic metaphysical cases.[29] For instance, science has no clear bearing on what would happen to Singleton Socrates had Socrates not existed or to the good had God desired differently. Accordingly, while the framework of interventionism does possess a moderate glow of scientific respectability (owing in part to its intimate ties with causal modeling), it does not impart that same glow to the metaphysics of ground. That is to say, at the risk of bursting certain bubbles, if causal interventionism has reasonably good naturalistic credentials, theories of ground don't necessarily improve their own naturalistic standing just by co-opting interventionist language and resources.

While science doesn't appear to bear on the standard metaphysical cases, it might be thought that a special class of semiempirical grounding claims can be drawn from science and usefully modeled within the interventionist framework. While it may not be obvious at first glance, science does have some relevance to questions of ground (Bryant 2018), which is evidenced by other sorts of example. For instance, suppose that being an electron grounds having negative charge (Audi 2012, 117). Suppose also that x is an electron. To test this grounding claim, the grounding interventionist would have us assess the following counterfactual: if an intervention

---

[29] Jansson (2018) argues, similarly, that while our assessments of the aptness of causal models are constrained by local, a posteriori theories of causal mechanisms and processes, there is no analogous a posteriori constraint on our judgments of the aptness of grounding models. While I agree with the general sentiment, I suggest below that empirical and scientific background theory provides partial epistemic constraint in some cases of grounding.

were to remove the property of being an electron from x, then x would no longer have negative charge. Now, science does bear on the assessment of this counterfactual, by furnishing us with requisite background information about the characteristic properties of electrons. Science also tells us that other sorts of particles can be negatively charged. Metaphysics rears its head, however, when we ask whether x might have been one of those other sorts of particles. So scientific background theory may help to constrain our assessments of some such grounding counterfactuals, but murky metaphysical questions quickly intrude.

We may also wonder what proportion of grounding counterfactuals will be amenable to scientific constraint. As I noted above, grounding theorists commonly posit grounding relations among abstract, nonempirical relata, where scientific models and background theory are not clearly relevant. At any rate, as we have seen, the epistemology gets a lot murkier when we come to far out counterfactuals such as countermetaphysicals. As I noted in the case of causal interventionism, when we assess certain modally remote counterfactuals, the door is open for scientifically unmoored intuitions to sneak into modal judgment. The greater the evidential role those intuitions play, the more suspect the epistemology of grounding interventionism will be.

To the extent that grounding interventionists wish to reason about counterfactuals to which scientific background theory offers little guidance, those interventionists would do well to invoke further constraints. For instance, one might wonder whether logic can constrain the assessment of grounding counterfactuals. Indeed it can—and this is relatively straightforward in certain cases. For instance, so long as P and Q aren't necessarily true statements, wiggle P and you wiggle P∧Q. Even in more modally remote cases, where we must consider counterlogicals, our reasoning can be well constrained by clear formal frameworks for reasoning in the face of contradictions. This shows that it's not modal remoteness per se that is the most epistemically relevant factor but how well our epistemic resources constrain counterfactual assessment. At any rate, the results of interventions that follow as a straightforward matter of logic are one thing; the results of interventions in meatier metaphysical matters are another. Does wiggling the part wiggle the whole, the brain state the mental state, the determinate the determinable, the truthmaker the truth, the natural properties the moral properties ... ? Our theories concerning such matters are subject to logical constraints just like any other theories, but logic radically underdetermines the answers to these questions and thus does not constitute an adequately robust constraint of its own accord (see Bryant 2020). I suggest that the straightforward cases in which logic adequately constrains the assessment of grounding counterfactuals don't constitute a particularly large swath of the sorts of counterfactuals that theorists of ground are normally interested in.

Perhaps a more substantive form of constraint can come from background metaphysical theory. Once again, there are relatively straightforward cases of this. If we hold fixed a metaphysics according to which sets supervene on their members, this metaphysics has clear implications for what happens when we wiggle Socrates. If we hold fixed a metaphysics according to which God's will uniquely determines the good, this metaphysics has clear implications for what happens when we wiggle God's will. Note that the imagination isn't invoked in these cases; all that's needed is an understanding of the relevant metaphysical principles and relations, as well as some basic logical capacities.

Notice, however, that we need to know a fair bit about the relevant dependence relations before we can perform the relevant counterfactual assessments—we need to know that sets *supervene* on such-and-such and that God's will *uniquely determines* so-and-so.[30] So it's not clear—at least from these initial paradigm cases—to what extent this approach fosters the discovery of new information about hierarchical structure. What *is* clear is that appeal to metaphysical constraint makes grounding interventionism an exercise in determining what follows from our antecedent metaphysical commitments, not a direct interrogation of objective grounding structure. Some might think that's a perfectly acceptable place to situate theories of ground in the epistemic scene and a perfectly accurate characterization of what grounding theorists are actually up to. But for those grounding theorists with loftier epistemic aims, this may be an unacceptable limitation of the approach.

It's also worth emphasizing that what gets held fixed as the metaphysical background theory is relatively open—perhaps *too* open for us to be assured that we're engaging effectively in a truth-seeking activity. While there is relative consensus about many matters in science (which is, of course, complemented by much substantive disagreement, for example about matters of theoretical interpretation and unification), there is comparatively far less consensus on matters metaphysical (which isn't to say there is no such consensus). Most things are up for grabs in metaphysics, including even foundational assumptions and basic conceptual matters. So in many cases how one fixes the metaphysical background will depend on one's metaphysical proclivities and allegiances. This makes grounding interventionism no more factional than the rest of metaphysics, but it does somewhat quash any latent hope that the interventionist framework might lend *increased* objectivity to theories of ground.

---

[30] If grounding critics like Jessica M. Wilson (2014) and Koslicki (2015) are right, in having such knowledge we have a finer-grained understanding of the dependence at issue than we do by positing a grounding relation.

5. Conclusion

The aim of this essay has been to consider the prospects for an adequately formulated and epistemologically well-founded grounding analog of causal interventionism. I have considered several formulations of grounding interventionism, in which grounding relations are (non-reductively) cashed out in terms of possible interventions on variables representing grounding relata. A grounding intervention on one variable with respect to another changes the value of the one in such a way that if any change occurs to the other, it occurs in virtue of the change in the value of the one. We have seen that such interventions should be understood in worldly terms, as adding something to or deleting something from the roster of entities, or making some fact obtain or fail to obtain.

After considering candidate formulations of the view, I turned to the evaluation of its epistemic credentials. This involved considering how well imagination, structural equation models, and background theory constrain our assessments of interventionist counterfactuals. I argued that causal interventionism and grounding interventionism both demand that we stretch our imaginative capacities beyond their adequacy conditions when they ask us to assess certain modally remote counterfactuals that neither experience nor other forms of evidence and constraint adequately prepare us to assess. In such cases, imagination relies on unchecked intuition. Moreover, I pointed out that structural equation models merely formalize causal and grounding assumptions that require independent justification. Finally, I argued that while certain forms of background theory can help constrain the assessment of some causal and grounding counterfactuals, our epistemic grip weakens relatively quickly. In the trickier cases, counterfactual reasoning again invokes unfettered intuitions. Just how satisfied we should be with these epistemological options depends on the proportion of causal and grounding counterfactuals whose assessment is robustly constrained relative to those whose assessment isn't. In my view, the available epistemological options for causal interventionism and grounding interventionism are insufficiently powerful relative to the full spectrum of cases philosophers tend to be interested in—*especially* so for grounding. Therefore, grounding interventionism requires firmer epistemological foundations if it is to be a viable and attractive theoretical alternative.

Acknowledgments

I thank Al Wilson, Nick Emmerson, Noelia Iranzo Ribera, the EIDOS research group, and two anonymous referees for remarkably helpful feedback on a draft of the essay. For helpful discussion, I also thank the audience at my presentation of this work at the *New Directions in Metaphilosophy* symposium at the University of Kent in 2021.

248 AMANDA BRYANT

References

Andow, J. 2016. "Reliable But Not Home Free? What Framing Effects Mean for Moral Intuition." *Philosophical Psychology* 6: 1–8.

Arcangeli, M. 2010. "Imagination in Thought Experimentation: Sketching a Cognitive Approach to Thought Experiments." In *Model-Based Reasoning in Science and Technology*, edited by L. Magnani, W. Carnielli, and C. Pizzi, 571–87. Dordrecht: Springer.

Audi, P. 2012. "A Clarification and Defense of the Notion of Grounding." In *Metaphysical Grounding: Understanding the Structure of Reality*, edited by F. Correia and B. Schnieder, 101–21. Cambridge: Cambridge University Press.

Beebe, J. R., and R. Undercoffer. 2016. "Individual and Cross-Cultural Differences in Semantic Intuitions: New Experimental Findings." *Journal of Cognition and Culture* 16, nos. 3–4: 322–57.

Bennett, K. 2011. "By Our Bootstraps." *Philosophical Perspectives* 25, no. 1: 27–41.

Bernstein, S. 2016. "Grounding Is Not Causation." *Philosophical Perspectives* 30, no. 1: 21–38.

Blanchard, T., and J. Schaffer. 2017. "Cause Without Default." In *Making a Difference*, edited by H. Beebee, C. Hitchcock, and H. Price, 175–214. Oxford: Oxford University Press.

Booth, A. R., and D. P. Rowbottom (eds.). 2014. *Intuitions*. Oxford: Oxford University Press.

Bryant, A. 2018. "Naturalizing Grounding: How Theories of Ground Can Engage Science." *Philosophy Compass* 13: e12489.

Bryant, A. 2020. "Keep the Chickens Cooped: The Epistemic Inadequacy of Free Range Metaphysics." *Synthese* 197: 1867–87.

Bryant, A. 2021. "Epistemic Infrastructure for a Scientific Metaphysics." *Grazer Philosophische Studien* 98: 27–49.

Byrne, R. 2007. *The Rational Imagination*. Cambridge, Mass.: MIT Press.

Cappelen, H. 2012. *Philosophy Without Intuitions*. Oxford: Oxford University Press.

Casullo, A. 2012. "Counterfactuals and Modal Knowledge." In *Essays on A Priori Knowledge and Justification*, 251–70. New York: Oxford University Press.

Correia, F. 2014. "Logical Grounds." *Review of Symbolic Logic* 7, no. 1: 31–59.

Dasgupta, S. 2014a. "On the Plurality of Grounds." *Philosophers' Imprint* 14: 1–28.

Dasgupta, S. 2014b. "The Possibility of Physicalism." *Journal of Philosophy* 111, nos. 9–10: 557–92.

Dasgupta, S. 2016. "Metaphysical Rationalism." *Nous* 50, no. 2: 379–418.

Dasgupta, S. 2017. "Constitutive Explanation." *Philosophical Issues* 17, no. 1: 74–97.

deRosset, L. 2010. "Getting Priority Straight." *Philosophical Studies* 149, no. 1: 73–97.

Deutsch, M. 2015. *The Myth of the Intuitive: Experimental Philosophy and Philosophical Method.* Cambridge, Mass.: MIT Press.

Devitt, M. 2015. "Relying on Intuitions: Where Cappelen and Deutsch Go Wrong." *Inquiry* 58, nos. 7–8: 669–99.

Dorr, C. 2010. Review of *Every Thing Must Go: Metaphysics Naturalized. Notre Dame Philosophical Review.* https://ndpr.nd.edu/news/24377-every-thing-must-go-metaphysics-naturalized/

Fine, K. 2012. "Guide to Ground." In *Metaphysical Grounding*, edited by F. Correia and B. Schnieder, 37–80. Cambridge: Cambridge University Press.

French, S., and A. Murphy 2021. "The Value of Surprise in Science." *Erkenntnis.*

Gendler, T. 2010. *Intuition, Imagination, and Philosophical Methodology.* Oxford: Oxford University Press.

Glazier, M. 2020. "Explanation." In *The Routledge Handbook of Metaphysical Grounding*, edited by M. Raven, 121–32. New York: Routledge.

Godfrey-Smith, P. 2012. "Metaphysics and the Philosophical Imagination." *Philosophical Studies* 160: 97–113.

Gregory, D. 2017. "Counterfactual Reasoning and Knowledge of Possibilities." *Philosophical Studies* 174, no. 4: 821–35.

Hall, N. 2007. "Structural Equations and Causation." *Philosophical Studies* 132: 109–36.

Hitchcock, C. 2007. "Prevention, Preemption, and the Principle of Sufficient Reason." *Philosophical Review* 116: 495–532.

Hitchcock, C., and J. Woodward. 2003. "Explanatory Generalizations, Part II: Plumbing Explanatory Depth." *Nous* 37, no. 2: 181–99.

Hoerl, C., T. McCormack, and S. Beck (eds.). 2011. *Understanding Counterfactuals, Understanding Causation: Issues in Philosophy and Psychology.* Oxford: Oxford University Press.

Ichikawa, J. 2011. "Quantifiers, Knowledge, and Counterfactuals." *Philosophy and Phenomenological Research* 82, no. 2: 287–313.

Jansson, L. 2018. "When Are Structural Equation Models Apt? Causation Versus Grounding." In *Explanation Beyond Causation: Philosophical Perspectives on Non-Causal Explanations*, edited by A. Reutlinger and J. Saatsi, 250–66. Oxford: Oxford University Press.

Jenkins, C. 2008. "Modal Knowledge, Counterfactual Knowledge and the Role of Experience." *Philosophical Quarterly* 58, no. 223: 693–701.

Koslicki, K. 2015. "The Coarse-Grainedness of Grounding." In *Oxford Studies in Metaphysics, Volume 9*, edited by K. Bennett and D. Zimmerman, 306–44. Oxford: Oxford University Press.

Koslicki, K. 2016. "Where Grounding and Causation Part Ways: Comments on Schaffer." *Philosophical Studies* 173: 101–12.

Kroedel, T. 2012. "Counterfactuals and the Epistemology of Modality." *Philosophers' Imprint* 12, no. 12: 1–14.

Kroedel, T. 2017. "Modal Knowledge, Evolution, and Counterfactuals." In *Modal Epistemology After Rationalism*, edited by R. Fischer and F. Leon, 179–95. Cham: Springer.

Ladyman, J., and D. Ross, with D. Spurrett and J. Collier. 2007. *Every Thing Must Go: Metaphysics Naturalized*. Oxford: Oxford University Press.

Leuenberger, S. 2014. "Grounding and Necessity." *Inquiry: An Interdisciplinary Journal of Philosophy* 57, no. 2: 151–74.

Levy, A., and P. Godfrey-Smith (eds.). 2019. *The Scientific Imagination*. Oxford: Oxford University Press.

Li, J., L. Longgen, E. Chalmers, and J. Snedeker. 2018. "What Is in a Name? The Development of Cross-Cultural Differences in Referential Intuitions." *Cognition* 171: 108–11.

Machery, E., R. Mallon, S. Nichols, and S. Stich. 2004. "Semantics, Cross-Cultural Style." *Cognition* 92, no. 3: B1–B12.

Maibom, H. 2016. "Knowing Me, Knowing You: Failure to Forecast and the Empathic Imagination." In *Knowledge Through Imagination*, edited by A. Kind and P. Kung, 185–206. New York: Oxford University Press.

Mallozzi, A. 2021. "Superexplanations for Counterfactual Knowledge." *Philosophical Studies* 178, no. 4: 1315–37.

Mandel, D., D. Hilton, and P. Catellani (eds.). 2005. *The Psychology of Counterfactual Thinking*. London: Routledge.

Maurin, A.-S. 2019. "Grounding and Metaphysical Explanation: It's Complicated." *Philosophical Studies* 176, no. 6: 1573–94.

McSweeney, M. Forthcoming. "Metaphysics as Essentially Imaginative and Aiming at Understanding." *American Philosophical Quarterly.*

Meek, C., and C. Glymour. 1994. "Conditioning and Intervening." *British Journal for the Philosophy of Science* 45, no. 4: 1001–21.

Menzies, P. 2007. "Causation in Context." In *Causation, Physics, and the Constitution of Reality: Russell's Republic Revisited*, edited by H. Price and R. Corry, 191–223. Oxford: Oxford University Press.

Menzies, P., and H. Price. 1993. "Causation as a Secondary Quality." *British Journal for the Philosophy of Science* 44, no. 2: 187–203.

Meynell, L. 2014. "Imagination and Insight: A New Account of the Content of Thought Experiments." *Synthese* 191, no. 17: 4149–68.

Maynell, L. 2018. "Images and Imagination in Thought Experiments." In *The Routledge Companion to Thought Experiments*, edited by M. Stuart, Y. Fehige, and J. R. Brown, 498–511. London: Routledge.

Nichols, S. 2006. *The Architecture of the Imagination: New Essays on Pretence, Possibility, and Fiction*. Oxford: Oxford University Press.

Nichols, S., S. Stich, and J. Weinberg. 2003. "Metaskepticism: Meditations in Ethnoepistemology." In *The Skeptics*, edited by S. Luper, 227–47. Burlington: Ashgate.

Nicoli, S. M. 2016. *The Role of Intuitions in Philosophical Methodology*. London: Palgrave Macmillan.

Paul, L. A. 2009. "Counterfactual Theories." In *The Oxford Handbook of Causation*, edited by H. Beebee, C. Hitchcock, and P. Menzies, 158–84. Oxford: Oxford University Press.

Paul, L. A. 2012. "Metaphysics as Modeling: The Handmaiden's Tale." *Philosophical Studies* 160: 1–29.

Pearl, J. 2000. *Causality: Models, Reasoning, and Inference*. New York: Cambridge University Press.

Raven, M. 2015. "Ground." *Philosophy Compass* 10, no. 5: 322–33.

Roca-Royes, S. 2011. "Modal Knowledge and Counterfactual Knowledge." *Logique et analyse* 54, no. 216: 537–52.

Roca-Royes, S. 2017. "Similarity and Possibility: An Epistemology of De Re Possibility for Concrete Entities." In *Modal Epistemology After Rationalism*, edited by F. Leon and R. Fischer, 221–45. Cham: Springer.

Rosen, G. 2010. "Metaphysical Dependence: Grounding and Reduction." In *Modality: Metaphysics, Logic, and Epistemology*, edited by R. Hale and A. Hoffman, 109–36. New York: Oxford University Press.

Schaffer, J. 2009. "On What Grounds What." In *Metametaphysics: New Essays on the Foundations of Ontology*, edited by D. Manley, D. Chalmers, and R. Wasserman, 347–83. Oxford: Oxford University Press.

Schaffer, J. 2016. "Grounding in the Image of Causation." *Philosophical Studies* 173: 49–100.

Schulz, M. 2017. *Counterfactuals and Probability*. Oxford: Oxford University Press.

Schwitzgebel, E., and F. Cushman. 2012. "Expertise in Moral Reasoning? Order Effects on Moral Judgment in Professional Philosophers and Non-Philosophers." *Mind and Language* 27, no. 2: 135–53.

Shtulman, A., and K. Harrington. 2016. "Tensions Between Science and Intuition Across the Lifespan." *Topics in Cognitive Science* 8: 118–37.

Skiles, A. 2015. "Against Grounding Necessitarianism." *Erkenntnis* 80, no. 4: 717–51.

Spirtes, P., C. Glymour, and R. Scheines. 2000. *Causation, Prediction and Search*. Cambridge, Mass.: MIT Press.

Swain, S., J. Alexander, and J. Weinberg. 2008. "The Instability of Philosophical Intuitions: Running Hot and Cold on Truetemp." *Philosophy and Phenomenological Research* 76, no. 1: 138–55.

Tahko, T. 2012. "Counterfactuals and Modal Epistemology." *Grazer Philosophische Studien* 86, no. 1: 93–115.

Thompson, N. 2016. "Grounding and Metaphysical Explanation." *Proceedings of the Aristotelian Society* 116, no. 3: 395–402.

Trogdon, K. 2013. "Grounding: Necessary or Contingent?" *Pacific Philosophical Quarterly* 94, no. 4: 465–85.

Wang, J. 2020. "Cause." In *The Routledge Handbook of Metaphysical Grounding*, edited by M. Raven, 300–311. New York: Routledge.

Weinberg, J. 2016. "Intuitions." In *The Oxford Handbook of Philosophical Methodology*, edited by H. Cappelen, T. Gendler, and J. P. Hawthorne, 287–308. Oxford: Oxford University Press.

Weinberg, J., S. Nichols, and S. Stich. 2001. "Normativity and Epistemic Intuitions." *Philosophical Topics* 29, nos. 1–2: 429–60.

Wheatley, T., and J. Haidt. 2005. "Hypnotic Disgust Makes Moral Judgments More Severe." *Psychological Science* 16, no. 10: 780–84.

Williamson, T. 2007a. "Philosophical Knowledge and Knowledge of Counterfactuals." *Grazer Philosophische Studien* 74, no. 1: 89–123.

Williamson, T. 2007b. *The Philosophy of Philosophy*. Oxford: Blackwell.

Wilson, A. 2021. "Counterpossible Reasoning in Physics." *Philosophy of Science* 88, no. 5: 1113–24.

Wilson, A. 2018a. "Grounding Entails Counterpossible Non-Triviality." *Philosophy and Phenomenological Research* 96, no. 3: 716–28.

Wilson, A. 2018b. "Metaphysical Causation." *Nous* 52: 723–51.

Wilson, J. M. n.d. "On the Notion of Diachronic Emergence."

Wilson, J. M. 2014. "No Work for a Theory of Grounding." *Inquiry* 57, nos. 5–6: 535–79.

Woodward, J. 1997. "Explanation, Invariance, and Intervention." *Philosophy of Science* 64: S26–S41.

Woodward, J. 2000. "Explanation and Invariance in the Special Sciences." *British Journal for the Philosophy of Science* 51, no.2: 197–254.

Woodward, J. 2003. *Making Things Happen: A Theory of Causal Explanation*. Oxford: Oxford University Press.

Woodward, J. 2009. "Agency and Interventionist Theories." In *The Oxford Handbook of Causation*, edited by H. Beebee, C. Hitchcock, and P. Menzies, 234–63. Oxford: Oxford University Press.

Woodward, J., and C. Hitchcock. 2003. "Explanatory Generalizations, Part I: A Counterfactual Account." *Nous* 37, no. 1: 1–24.

CHAPTER 12

IMPOSSIBLE WORLDS AND THE SAFETY
OF PHILOSOPHICAL BELIEFS

ZACK GARRETT AND ZACHARIAH WRUBLEWSKI

1. Introduction

When considering the necessary conditions on knowledge, there is intuitive appeal in accepting conditions that properly connect our beliefs to the truth of their objects. In large part, modal conditions on knowledge, such as the sensitivity and safety conditions, are motivated by the aim of ensuring that knowledge maintains this connection. Further, given some well-known problems with the sensitivity condition, the safety condition seems to be more plausible for this purpose. But, the safety condition on knowledge faces problems with maintaining this connection in specific cases—cases in which the relevant beliefs are necessarily true.

In this essay, we show that the problems for the safety condition arise because analyses involving the condition have only included possible worlds in the evaluation of safe beliefs. Further, we argue that including *impossible* worlds in these analyses enables the safety condition to avoid the problems mentioned above. Next, we offer and defend an account of impossible worlds, and the inclusion of impossible worlds in safety conditions. Lastly, we outline and consider what we believe are potentially substantive ramifications for philosophical knowledge: namely, that making such a move would mean that we should be skeptics about many potential instances of philosophical knowledge.

Examining Philosophy Itself. Edited by Yafeng Shan.
Chapters and book compilation © 2023 Metaphilosophy LLC and John Wiley & Sons Ltd.
Published 2023 by John Wiley & Sons Ltd.

2. Safety and Triviality

2.1. Sensitivity and Safety

Given that the focus of our project is modal conditions on knowledge, it's prudent to start our discussion with a brief history of the most prominently discussed and supported modal criteria. Generally speaking, modal conditions on knowledge are meant to provide resources for epistemological theories to ensure that if one's belief amounts to knowledge, it properly tracks the truths related to the belief. In *Philosophical Investigations*, Robert Nozick argues for this connection straightforwardly, supporting the necessity of the *sensitivity* condition to the concept of knowledge. He formulates the sensitivity condition as follows:

> *Sensitivity:* If p weren't true and S were to use M to arrive at a belief whether (or not) p, then S wouldn't believe, via M, that p. (1983, 179)

Importantly, Nozick intends the conditional expressed in *Sensitivity* to be a subjunctive conditional. When understood in terms of a possible-worlds locution, satisfying *Sensitivity* requires it be the case that in the nearby possible worlds in which p is false and S uses M to arrive at a belief whether (or not) p, S doesn't believe, via M, that p.

The sensitivity condition as outlined above faces several well-known challenges.[1] But, Nozick's aim in attempting to formulate such a condition seems amicable. Intuitively, if a belief amounts to knowledge, it should track the relevant truths.

In order to account for this aim while avoiding the problems identified for the sensitivity condition, many theorists opt for a similar, but importantly different, condition on knowledge: the safety condition. An early formulation of this condition by Ernest Sosa goes as follows:

> *Sosa (SF):* If S were to believe that p, then p would be true. (1999, 141–53)

As formulated by Sosa, this condition does not include reference to the method by which S comes to believe p. As many commentators subsequently accepting safety think this is an important feature of any such criterion, we can modify this original definition to include such a link:

> *Sosa (SF*):* If S were to believe p via M, then p would be true.

As in *Sensitivity*, the conditional expressed here is meant to be a subjunctive conditional. Using a possible-worlds analysis, the basic idea would be

---

[1] For some discussion of general problems for sensitivity, see Vogel 1987; Sosa 1999; Kripke 2011; and the critical essays in Luper-Foy 1987.

as follows: in order for a belief to be safe, it must be the case that in the nearby possible worlds in which S believes p via M, p is true. Not only does this formulation avoid the problems for the sensitivity condition, it also (purports to) maintain the "truth-tracking" phenomenon that modal conditions are meant to ensure.

2.2. Safety and Necessity

As mentioned above, the sensitivity condition faces several well-known objections, and so in this essay we largely leave out discussions of the sensitivity condition and narrow our focus on the problems such beliefs pose for the safety condition. The problems that ultimately plague safety conditions on knowledge stem from the triviality associated with specific kinds of counterfactuals—in particular, *counterpossibles* and counterfactuals with necessarily true consequents.

A counterpossible is a counterfactual conditional in which the antecedent is necessarily false. The following are examples of counterpossibles:

1. If Hobbes had (secretly) squared the circle, all sick children in the mountains of South America at the time would have cared.
2. If Hobbes had (secretly) squared the circle, all sick children in the mountains of South America at the time would not have cared.[2]

Given that it's necessarily false that Hobbes squared the circle (and, more so, secretly!), the antecedent of both conditionals is necessarily false. Or, in a possible-worlds analysis, there are no possible worlds in which the antecedent is true. Accordingly, it seems, both of the conditionals (as well as all other counterpossibles) are *trivially true*.[3]

Similarly, counterfactual conditionals with necessarily true consequents face problems with triviality. For example, consider the following counterfactuals:

3. If Tokyo were the capital of Spain, then $2 + 2 = 4$.
4. If I were to wear a red shirt tomorrow, then $2 + 2 = 4$.

When analyzing (3) in terms of possible worlds, here's how the analysis goes. In order to determine whether this conditional is true, we look at the closest possible worlds in which Tokyo is the capital of Spain. While it's not exactly clear which of these worlds would be closer to the actual

---

[2] Both of these counterpossibles are described in detail in Nolan 1997, 554.

[3] David Lewis refers to these as *vacuously* true. While there may be some important distinctions between triviality and vacuity made by some philosophers, none of these differences or distinctions will matter to the argument at hand.

world than others—for example, is the world in which Spain takes control of Japan after World War II and moves the Spanish capital to Tokyo closer to the actual world than the world in which Spain colonizes Japan during the Sengoku period and relocates the Spanish capital to Tokyo (then called Edo)? It's not clear. But, this doesn't matter when considering the truth of such conditionals. Given that $2 + 2 = 4$ is necessarily true (that is, true in all possible worlds), we know that in both of these worlds, $2 + 2 = 4$. Because of this, we know that both (3) and (4) are trivially true. Furthermore, when we look at *any* possible world, we know that in this world $2 + 2 = 4$. Accordingly, conditionals with $2 + 2 = 4$ (or any other necessary truth) as a consequent are trivially true.

While potentially problematic for theories of counterfactuals generally, the trivial truth of the sorts of counterfactuals detailed above in possible-worlds analyses presents special problems for modal conditions on knowledge—specifically for our current discussion, the safety condition. Counterfactuals with necessarily true consequents cause the following problem for the safety condition, which we call the "Triviality Problem": the triviality involved in the truth of such counterfactuals undermines one of the central aims of the safety condition on knowledge—ensuring that beliefs which satisfy the safety condition track the relevant truths involved.

To see why this is, consider a case in which the relevant belief under scrutiny is a belief about something that is necessarily true. As formulated above, a general safety condition is as follows: If S were to believe p via M, then p would be true. Further, in the kind of case currently under consideration, p is necessarily true. This means that all possible worlds where S believes p via M are worlds in which p is true. Because p is true in every possible world, it *could* be that S's belief that p is safe, even when M is an epistemologically problematic methodology. The safety of such beliefs undermines what is supposed to be a crucial motivation for modal conditions on knowledge, generally: that they ensure some sort of connection between the relevant belief, the method of coming to that belief, and the truth of that belief.

Generally speaking, most theories of counterfactuals and counterpossibles suggest that we should consider only possible worlds when evaluating their truth-values. Because of this, such theories entail that counterpossibles and counterfactuals with necessarily true consequents are trivially true. But, opening up these theories to allow impossible worlds into the fold would allow for varying analyses of the truth-values of counterpossibles and counterfactuals with necessarily true consequents. To see how this works, consider the following examples from earlier:

1. If Hobbes had (secretly) squared the circle, all sick children in the mountains of South America at the time would have cared.
2. If Hobbes had (secretly) squared the circle, all sick children in the mountains of South America at the time would not have cared.

3. If Tokyo were the capital of Spain, then $2 + 2 = 4$.
4. If I were to wear a red shirt tomorrow, then $2 + 2 = 4$.

Earlier, we argued that if we consider only possible worlds in the scope of the relevant counterfactuals and counterpossibles, (1) and (2) are trivially true because there are no possible worlds in which Hobbes squares the circle, and (3) and (4) are trivially true because every possible world, regardless of antecedent conditions, would be one in which $2 + 2 = 4$ is true. But, if we incorporate impossible worlds in our analyses of the relevant conditionals, *none of* (1), (2), (3), or (4) is trivially true. In the case of examples (1) and (2), the inclusion of impossible worlds in which Hobbes *does* square the circle would mean we would have to look at the closest impossible worlds in which this happens to see whether or not all sick children in the mountains of South America at the time care about this development. If they do care, then (1) is true, while (2) is false; if they don't care, then (1) is false, while (2) is true. Whichever ends up being the case, clearly neither conditional is *trivially* true. Similarly, for (3) and (4), we would have to look at the closest worlds (possible or impossible) in which Tokyo is the capital of Spain and in which I wear a red shirt tomorrow, respectively. If $2 + 2 = 4$ in the closest world in which Tokyo is the capital of Spain, then (3) is true; if not, and $2 + 2 \neq 4$ (that is, the closest world considered is an *impossible* world), then (3) is false. And, if $2 + 2 = 4$ in the closest world in which I wear a red shirt tomorrow, then (4) is true; if not, and $2 + 2 \neq 4$, then (4) is false. Regardless of what the truth of the conditionals in (3) and (4) ends up being, clearly neither conditional is *trivially* true.

One way that theorists have attempted to defend the safety condition from the Triviality Problem *without* including impossible worlds is to argue for a "basis-relative" modification of the view. To see how this might go, consider Duncan Pritchard's version of the safety condition:

Pritchard (P-SF): S's belief is safe iff in most nearby possible worlds in which S continues to form her belief about the target proposition in the same way as in the actual world, and in all very close near-by possible worlds in which S continues to form her belief about the target proposition in the same way as the actual world, her belief continues to be true. (2009, 34)

This condition, as expressed, doesn't quite address the triviality problem as such. But, Pritchard does suggest a way in which such an account might be extended to address the Triviality Problem:

The way safety theorists like myself respond to this [the Triviality Problem] is to say that once we shift to a basis-relative formulation of safety ... then our focus should not be on the particular proposition believed in the actual world, but rather on the doxastic output of the basis in the actual world instead. This means that while there is, of course, no close possible world where one falsely believes the necessary proposition that one actually believes, the kind of haphazard basis described above will lead to lots of false beliefs in close possible worlds (just not false beliefs in the proposition actually believed). As such it will be an unsafe basis. (2020, 209–10)

To summarize the strategy exemplified by Pritchard's discussion above, a basis-relative version of the safety condition holds that merely considering the relevant beliefs themselves is only part of the correct full analysis. In order for a belief to be safe, some argue, the method or basis used to form the belief must be such that it would not lead the agent to false beliefs in close possible worlds.[4]

This type of modification appears in many popular contemporary accounts of the safety condition, such as the following example of Timothy Williamson's formulation:

Williamson (W-SF): If one knows, one could not easily have been wrong in a similar case. (2000, 147)

The short idea inherent in such an approach is this: in cases involving the potential problematic types of beliefs (that is, beliefs that are necessarily true), we should not merely look at the beliefs in question in nearby possible worlds; we should also be looking at the basis for the belief in order to determine whether the basis itself is a safe basis. In Pritchard's terms, we should look to see if one is "lucky" in having a true belief in the case; in Williamson's terms, we should look to see if one "could easily have been wrong" in the relevant case. If the belief is formed on a safe basis (that is, if one was not lucky or could not easily have been wrong, and so on) and is otherwise safe, then the belief is safe. If one or the other of these conditions is not met, then the belief is unsafe.

This sort of modification *does* help the safety theorist with some of the relevant potential counterexamples to the condition. For example, consider the following case and suppose that Goldbach's Conjecture is true:

Coin-basis: Arnold formulates his belief that Goldbach's Conjecture (henceforth "G") is true on the basis of a coin flip. In coming to the belief, Arnold uses the following method: "If this coin lands on heads, I will believe G. If it lands on tails, I will believe not-G." Arnold flips the coin, the coin lands heads up, and, as a result, Arnold believes G.

---

[4] For more discussion of and objections to Pritchard's solution to the Triviality Problem, see Miščević 2007; Bernecker 2010; Melchior 2017; and Melchior 2021.

In this example, a non-basis-relative safety condition that doesn't include impossible worlds would struggle with the Triviality Problem because there are no close possible worlds in which G is false. So, according to such a condition, the belief would be safe. But, a basis-relative safety condition can avoid this conclusion because there *are* close possible worlds in which the basis of belief (the coin flip) would lead Arnold to false beliefs—all of the nearby possible worlds in which the coin lands tails up!

While this does save the safety condition from the Triviality Problem in certain cases, it does not do so in *all* cases. Consider a very similar example:

Coin-basis*: Arnold formulates his belief that G on the basis of a coin flip. In coming to the belief, Arnold uses the following method: "If this coin lands on heads or tails, I will believe G. If not, I will not form a belief." Also, suppose that Arnold will use *only* this method when considering whether or not to believe G, and will reliably use this method when confronted with the question of whether or not G. Arnold flips the coin, the coin lands heads up, and, as a result, Arnold believes G.

In this case, the belief-formation method is very similar to that of the first case. But, importantly, *this* method would never lead Arnold to a false belief. Further, Arnold would not *luckily* come to his belief—he would not be lucky to have a true belief (as he will form the belief G in almost all nearby possible worlds), nor would he be lucky to avoid forming a false belief, given that in the odd event that the coin does not land heads or tails up, Arnold will not form a belief at all. Similarly, it's not the case that Arnold *could easily be wrong* in his belief. There is no nearby false belief he would form on the basis of this method (as he employs the methodology only to form a belief about whether or not G), nor is there a similar methodology that Arnold might use to come to some false belief (as he uses this specific methodology reliably and only when considering whether or not G). Intuitively, this seems to be just as bad a method for forming the relevant belief as was the method in *Coin-basis*.[5] It's cases like these that remain a problem for safety conditions that merely range over possible worlds. And while the problematic cases are certainly fewer for these basis-relative safety conditions, the fact that there are problem cases at all—that is, that there are cases in which a belief like Arnold's is safe—continues to be a problem for basis-relative safety conditions that do not include impossible worlds.

---

[5] According to Williamson, the idea of "not easily being wrong" involves looking not just at possible worlds in which an agent might use a particular methodology but also at different methodologies that are in some sense "close." While this response might seem to avoid the problem exemplified by *Coin-basis**, the viability of this strategy is contentious. Unfortunately, we do not have the requisite space to fully treat this issue here. For more on this type of response from Williamson, see Williamson 2009, 325–28. For more on the potential problems with such a solution, see Hirvela 2019 and Zhao 2021.

Before moving on, we should say one more thing about the potential for using impossible worlds when considering the safety condition; in order to adequately consider the possibility of adding impossible worlds to the mix (without yet conceding that we *should* add impossible worlds), we have to consider (and alter) our understanding of the safety conditional and what it should mean to satisfy this conditional. When outlining safety conditions, historically safety theorists have suggested that what's important for safe beliefs is that the safety condition is not falsified—that is, that "if S believes p via M, then p" is not false. This idea lurks in the background of formulations of the condition like, for example, the condition argued for by Williamson—in the idea that one should not easily be wrong in holding safe beliefs. Importantly, safety theorists have also written as if the important part about satisfying the safety condition is that the conditional is true—such as in Sosa's initial formulation of safety. Until now, only worlds that are possible (that is, worlds that obey classical logic and, subsequently, are such that there are no real contradictions) have been considered—meaning, we haven't had to settle the issue of whether it's more important that the safety conditional not be falsified or that the safety conditional be true. But, now that impossible worlds may be added to the mix (as we argue), we *do* have to consider the matter—given that real contradictions may exist in impossible worlds. We suggest that what is important to safety is that the consequent of the safety conditional is true only (rather than both true and false) when the relevant belief is that p is true only. This is because understanding the conditional in this way achieves *both* of our epistemic goals—it ensures that in these cases we have the relevant true beliefs, while simultaneously avoiding relevant false beliefs. For example, in a world where S believes p, and p is both true and false, S has a false belief, falling short of the second epistemic goal. But, in a world where S believes p, and p is true only, S meets both the goal to have true beliefs and the goal to avoid false ones.

For the reasons outlined above, it seems that including impossible worlds in the scope over which safety-related conditionals range may help with the Triviality Problem (specifically considering beliefs that are necessarily true). If the necessary truth relevant to the belief *could be false* in some impossible world, and impossible worlds are included in the worlds we consider when evaluating safety, then these problematic beliefs would not be safe—they would be safe only when the nearby worlds considered are ones where the consequent is true and would be unsafe when the nearby worlds are ones in which the consequent is false. Thus, the central aim of modal conditions on knowledge like the safety condition—that of ensuring that our beliefs are properly connected to the truth—could be salvaged by such an analysis.

In "Sensitivity, Safety, and Impossible Worlds" (2021), Guido Melchior argues that the specifics of an impossible-worlds account will cause problems for using impossible worlds in analyses of the safety condition.[6] In broad strokes, Melchior's argument is as follows: A plausible constraint on the closeness of impossible worlds makes it the case that including impossible worlds will not change whether or not a given belief is safe. To kick off this argument, Melchior considers the Strangeness of Impossibility Condition (SIC).

> *SIC:* Any possible world is more similar (nearer) to the actual world than any impossible world. (Nolan 1997, 550)

If SIC is true, then clearly this is a problem for the impossible-worlds analysis of the safety condition because it would mean that each world we're investigating, if it really is a nearby world, will be a possible world. So, the evaluations of counterfactuals with necessarily true consequents would be *unchanged*, even if impossible worlds are included in the scope of the worlds considered when evaluating such conditionals.

The other option Melchior considers is the case in which SIC is false. In short, he argues that SIC's falsity would entail that some impossible worlds are closer than some possible worlds and thus could potentially alter the evaluations of the conditionals. But, Melchior contends that we should accept SIC because accounts that reject SIC face problems with conditionals with contingent antecedents and consequents. The basic idea is this: If we reject SIC, then the potential closeness of impossible worlds will lead to counterintuitive results when we consider "normal" counterfactuals (that is, non-counterpossibles, and counterfactuals without necessarily true consequents). In light of these potential problems, Melchior concludes that we should accept SIC.

While Melchior does well to outline the general landscape, there's something further that should be said about SIC and its relation to the safety condition: not only would one have to reject SIC in order to save the safety condition, one would also have to *radically* reject SIC. One way to reject SIC would be to hold that there is *some* impossible world that may be closer to the actual world than some far-out, deeply odd possible world. Call this the *weak rejection of SIC*.

If one weakly rejects SIC, this still wouldn't be enough to salvage the safety condition in the face of the Triviality Problem. Because the safety condition only considers worlds near the actual world in which the antecedent is true, the addition of one far-out impossible world to the mix would never change the evaluation. In other words, if rejecting SIC is just a matter of accepting that one or two impossible worlds are closer than some extremely distant possible world, then these worlds won't be close enough to the actual world to change the evaluation of the conditional.

---

[6] Melchior further argues that the sensitivity condition escapes the Triviality Problem, and so we should accept a sensitivity condition on knowledge rather than a safety condition.

According to the *radical rejection of SIC*, not only is some impossible world closer to the actual world than some extremely distant possible world, *many* impossible worlds are closer to the actual world than *many* possible worlds. Further, this radical rejection of SIC is necessary for salvaging the safety condition because the only way in which an impossible-worlds analysis would differ from a traditional possible-worlds analysis of the same conditional is if the impossible worlds were both close enough and plentiful enough to change some safety evaluations. In what follows, we argue that we *should* radically reject SIC and, thus, contra Melchior, an impossible-worlds analysis of the safety condition is viable.

3. Impossible Worlds, Closeness, and SIC

3.1. Starting Assumptions

Before discussing our objections to SIC, we should elucidate our basic assumptions about impossible worlds. To begin, we follow Graham Priest in treating impossible worlds as ones that obey a different logic from one another.[7] "One might wonder, therefore, what makes a world impossible. Answer: an impossible world is one where the laws of logic are different from those of the actual world (in the way that a physically impossible world is a world where the laws of physics are different from those of the actual world)" (2014, xxiii). Treating impossible worlds as worlds with different logical laws is intuitively appealing. As Priest mentions, doing so mirrors our understanding of physically impossible worlds. Another benefit is that this definition subsumes many other definitions. For example, the view that Francesco Berto and Mark Jago call "contradiction-realizers" claims that impossible worlds are ones where sentences of the form φ and $\sim \varphi$ both hold (2019, 32). A world that realizes a contradiction would, however, be one that obeys logical laws different from those the actual world obeys.[8]

As for what counts as a world, it is clear that we must accept some ersatz theory. For reasons described by Berto and Jago, realist theories struggle to handle impossible worlds (2019, 44–47). Berto and Jago argue for an ersatz theory on the grounds that it is the only way to accommodate impossible worlds, which prove to be incredibly useful philosophical tools. Ersatz theories of worlds treat worlds as maximally consistent sets of sentences.[9] A set of sentences is maximally consistent if, for any sentence φ, exactly one of

---

[7] Sandgren and Tanaka (2020) argue that there are two kinds of logically impossible worlds. Our set of impossible worlds is a subset of theirs, and so if our argument works here, then it works under their account as well.

[8] We are assuming that the actual world obeys classical logic.

[9] The view described here is linguistic ersatzism. Instead of using sentences, one could use combinations of objects and universals—that is to say, states of affairs. We do not intend to take a stand on the metaphysical status of the components of worlds. For our purposes here it will not matter if worlds are sets of sentences or sets of states of affairs.

φ or ∼ φ is a member of the set. Since we are making use of impossible worlds, we can drop the "consistent" part of this definition. The definition of a world, then, would be a maximal set of sentences—a set of sentences for which at least one of φ or ∼ φ is a member. One may even remove the maximal requirement. If the correct logic in a world *n* allows for truth-value gaps, then there may be some φ and ∼ φ such that neither is a member of *n*. There could still be some constraints on which sets of sentences count as worlds. For example, in the next few paragraphs we argue that worlds are constrained by the meanings of the words that appear in the sentences that are their members.

Impossible worlds are not without controversy, and some may reject our approach to safety on the grounds that impossible worlds come with too much baggage. We feel that other philosophers like Daniel Nolan (1997) and Berto and Jago (2019) do a good job of defending the use of impossible worlds, but here we will briefly handle one objection that we feel has not received adequate treatment yet. Some reject the use of impossible worlds because they undermine compositionality. Impossible worlds appear to allow synonymous sentences to receive different truth-values. This would mean that the words that compose the sentences do not determine the meanings of the sentences. For example, since impossible worlds can include contradictions, we can have a man, Winston, for whom it is true that he is a bachelor and false that he is an unmarried man. Since "bachelor" is synonymous with "unmarried man," it would appear that two synonymous sentences receive different truth-values, and hence their truth-values cannot be a product of the components that make up the sentences. For many, the loss of compositionality is too costly.[10]

Luckily, we do not have to give up compositionality. Impossible worlds are not real metaphysical entities like David Lewis's concrete possible worlds. Ersatz theories of worlds often treat them as linguistic entities, like sentences or sets of sentences. As linguistic entities, impossible worlds are constrained by what language can sensibly describe—more specifically, they're constrained by analytic entailment. A sentence φ analytically entails ψ iff ψ follows from φ by virtue of the meanings of the words in φ and ψ. Amie Thomasson describes analytic entailment as follows: "It is in part constitutive of the meaning of 'house' that all houses are buildings, so that the truth of 'X bought a house' is sufficient for the truth of 'X bought a building': if we know the truth of the first, the meanings of the terms, and have reasoning abilities, we can infer the truth of the second claim on that basis alone" (2007, 28). "Winston bought a house" analytically entails "Winston bought a building." The former cannot be true when the latter is false, but this isn't because of the logical structures of the sentences. Instead, the entailment comes from the meanings of "house"

---

[10] This is because it is normally thought that a necessary condition for a language to be learnable is that the meanings of sentences are determined by the meanings of their parts.

and "building." Because worlds in an ersatz theory are linguistic entities, they will make use of words like "house" and "building." They will be constrained by analytic entailments.

Something's being water analytically entails its being H_2O. So, a world could contain the sentence "Water is not H_2O," but it must also contain "Water is H_2O."[11] If one were to claim that a world could include the former without the latter, then one simply is not using the word "water." Consider the people on Hilary Putnam's Twin Earth. When they say that water is XYZ and not H_2O, they are using a homophone of "water," not the word "water." "[I]n the sense in which it is used on Earth, the sense of water$_E$, what the Twin Earthians call 'water' simply isn't water" (Putnam 1974, 285). A world containing the sentence "Water is not H_2O" but not its negation would be like Twin Earth—the sense of "water" is different. The worlds, both possible and impossible, that we are describing in this essay, however, are composed of sentences that get their meanings from the meanings of the words in the actual world, not from a Twin Earth world. So, whenever "water" appears in a sentence that is a member of a world, it means "H_2O." In every world, "Water is H_2O" is true. Worlds that allow for contradictions, however, may also include the sentence "Water is not H_2O." Such a world would contain both "Water is H_2O" and its negation.

To summarize this point, if worlds (possible or impossible) are linguistic entities, they must be closed under analytic entailment. The only viable accounts of impossible worlds treat them as linguistic entities, and so they must be closed under analytic entailment. Given analytic entailment, the world where Winston is a bachelor and not a bachelor is one where he is an unmarried man and a married man. Therefore, "Winston is a bachelor" is both true and false, and "Winston is an unmarried man" is also both true and false. The meanings of the sentences are being determined by their components, and so compositionality is saved. In his recent attack on the use of impossible worlds, Williamson writes: "[I]f we want to take impossibilities seriously, why exclude the impossibility in which A but not B is true, where those sentences are in fact synonymous?" (Williamson 2020, 344). The answer to Williamson's question is that such worlds are not meaningful descriptions, since they fail to follow through on some analytic entailment.

Even with a solution to potential compositionality problems in hand, some still might wonder whether, and why, we ought to incorporate impossible worlds into our consideration of the safety condition given that impossible worlds are, well, *impossible*. That is, one might think that the fact that impossible worlds could never be realized, or that we could never have counterparts in impossible worlds, or, relatedly, that the safety condition was initially conceived of as relying on a subjective conditional (which

---

[11] For every instance of something that is water, it must also be H_2O. So, the waters that are not H_2O must also be H_2O (that is, it is both true and false that they are H_2O) for the analytical entailment to be preserved.

by definition considers only possible worlds) is intuitive evidence against the idea of considering impossible worlds in this way. But, these concerns miss one of the central ideas of the account of impossible worlds we've laid out—that these "worlds" are merely useful tools (on our account, tools composed of sets of sentences) with which we can potentially get a better understanding of how well our beliefs track the relevant truths involved in a variety of situations and scenarios. These tools themselves need not include realizable worlds, as on many accounts of possible worlds the relevant worlds are also not realizable (because they are, for example, physically impossible, epistemically impossible, and so forth). In addition, impossible worlds, according to our account, are not radically different from the actual world, so it's not clear that we *couldn't* have counterparts in them. It seems that what matters most is whether or not the worlds are *close*, rather than that they are realizable, and so on.

3.2. Worlds with Different Laws

There is a strong intuition that worlds with different laws are by default very dissimilar from the actual world (and thus our beliefs in these worlds might not affect the safety of our beliefs in the actual world). This intuition isn't wholly wrong. "Similar" is context sensitive (see, e.g., Nolan 1997, 551). We make use of counterfactuals every day to consider how things might have gone if some mundane fact about ordinary objects had been different. For example, "What would have happened if I had drunk water instead of coffee this morning?" and "If Janet had been vaccinated, she wouldn't have ended up in the hospital" are examples of such counterfactuals. In the context of such "everyday" counterfactuals, differences in laws should make worlds more dissimilar. Our concern in everyday counter-factuals is what would happen with different non-modal facts but the same laws. Consider how a chess player pondering what would have happened had she made a different move will consider only sequences that follow the rules of chess she was using. Consider also the kind of counterfactual described by Kit Fine. "If Nixon had pressed the button, there would have been a nuclear holocaust" should be true. Fine claims that it is false on Lewis's original account of counterfactuals because there is a world where a small miracle stops the signal from the button to the bomb (1975, 452). Lewis alters his account to weight law differences more heavily, thereby "pushing away" worlds with small violations of physical laws (1979, 472).

Importantly, weighting differences in laws more heavily in the context of everyday counterfactuals removes one of Melchior's primary concerns with rejecting SIC. He was concerned that rejecting SIC would give us the wrong truth-values for counterfactuals, but because "similar" is context sensitive, SIC can be true in the context of everyday counterfactuals and false in the context of safety.

Though we do weight law differences more heavily in the context of everyday counterfactuals, we should not in the context of safety. With everyday counterfactuals, we do not care about how things would go if the natural laws were different. With safety, we do care, since, were the laws different, some of our beliefs might be false even when we formed them in the same way that we did in the actual world. It would be epistemically problematic if we formed a belief in some law on the basis of an experiment and would have believed the same thing via the same basis in a world where that law is false. That is to say, if a world is similar enough to the actual world that our evidence remains the same and our belief is false, that would indicate that there is a problem with our belief-forming method. A belief that is safe according to a view that does not weight law differences more heavily is better than one that is safe merely because worlds with different laws are treated as too dissimilar to consider.

Not all differences in laws will have a large impact on the world. Consider the debate about Humean supervenience in the philosophy of science. Humean supervenience claims that "the whole truth about a world like ours supervenes on the spatiotemporal distribution of local qualities" (Lewis 1994, 473). A number of counterexamples to Humean supervenience have emerged. Consider the following example from Michael Tooley:

> Suppose that there are ten different kinds of fundamental particles. So, there are fifty-five possible kinds of two-particle interactions. Suppose that fifty-four of these kinds have been studied and fifty-four laws have been discovered. The interaction of X and Y particles have not been studied because conditions are such that they never will interact. Nevertheless, it seems that it might be a law that, when X particles and Y particles interact, P occurs. Similarly it might be a law that when X and Y particles interact, Q occurs. There seems to be nothing about the local matters of particular fact in this world that fixes which of these generalizations is a law (1977, 669).

In Tooley's example we have two putative laws, and nothing about the particles themselves seems to count in favor of either of the laws. So, if the laws were to change, there would be no discernible changes in the local matters—in the non-modal facts. This would be problematic for theories of Humean supervenience. For our purposes here, Tooley's example gives us a case where differences in laws do not require differences in the non-modal local facts of the world. Two worlds with different laws need not differ with regard to other facts, contrary to the intuition that differences in laws make worlds significantly dissimilar.[12]

---

[12] For staunch Humeans, note that for our purposes here we only need it to be the case that there could be some difference in law without a *drastic* difference in the non-modal local facts. To get this, one could tweak Tooley's case to allow for some small local difference between a world with one law and a world with the other. Since X and Y particles never actually interact, a minor change to X particles between the worlds need not cause drastic changes to the other fifty-four kinds of two-particle interactions.

Now, imagine that we had entitled this essay "Mission: Impossible Worlds." Such a difference would require changes to various non-modal facts about the world, such as our personalities and the prospects for the essay's publication. Each of these non-modal differences would bring with them other changes both to the history of the world prior to this essay and to the future of the world after the essay. Differences between worlds with regard to non-modal facts about ordinary objects will often require a substantial number of other differences. We are involved in enough chaotic systems in our daily lives that even seemingly mundane differences between worlds can have significant effects. We have argued already that differences in laws do not necessitate significant other differences. So, we could have a world with different laws—different modal facts—without much difference from the actual world with regard to non-modal facts. We could also have a world with drastically different non-modal facts but the same laws as the actual world. For the purposes of safety, the world with minor differences in laws is more similar to the actual world than the world with significant non-modal differences.

The intuition that differences in laws are more significant than others can be explained by the fact that many law differences *are* very impactful. Were the gravitational constant different, the world would be a drastically different place. This is not because we are changing a law but instead because altering the gravitational constant would require significant changes to the non-modal facts of the world.

3.3. An Argument Against SIC

Once we've acknowledged that law differences should not be weighted more heavily than other differences, rejecting SIC is simple. A world with different physical laws need not be too different from the actual world. To find a similar phenomenon among logically impossible worlds, we need only find logics that preserve large swaths of classical logic. Luckily logicians have given us a nice set of such logics.

Imagine a world just like the actual world except that it obeys the logic of paradox; let's call this world p. All of the atomic sentences in p get the same values that they do in the actual world.[13] According to the truth-tables (see Priest 1979, 226–27) for the logic of paradox, all negations, conjunctions, disjunctions, and so forth get the same values as they do in the actual world, assuming that these sentences do not contain modal operators.[14] This means that p does not actually contain any contradictions. Since it

[13] Because the logic of paradox treats contradictory values as designated, inferences that would lead to explosion are blocked. A world where the logic of paradox is true would be impossible, but it need not be a world where everything is both true and false.

[14] In the logic of paradox, the truth-functional logical operators output classical values when the inputs are classical.

is governed by the logic of paradox, contradictions are possible but need not actually happen. Of course, there are some notable differences. For example, true contradictions are possible in p. Everything else is the same. The world works like the actual world. This essay still gets written. Joe Biden still wins the 2020 election. Alpha Centauri is still four light-years away from Earth.

Compare p to the world described earlier where the title of this essay is "Mission: Impossible Worlds." Let's call this possible world z. Here are each world's differences from the actual world (hereafter "@"):

Differences from @	z	p
Logic	None	Allows contradictions, invalidates MP, MT, DS, and so on
Non-modal facts	Moderate differences	None
Physical laws	None	None
Modal facts	Different counterfactuals	Possible contradictions

As we have already mentioned, there will be modal differences between p and @. But, there will also be modal differences between z and @. If we are using an S5 modal logic, in which the accessibility relation between worlds is an equivalence relation, then what is possible in @ will be possible in z, and what is necessary in @ will be necessary in z. World z will have different nearby possible worlds, however, and so some counterfactuals in z will receive truth-values different from those they do in @. Since the possible worlds near p will be physically and metaphysically identical to the possible worlds near @, unlike z, these same counterfactuals will get the same value in p that they do in @.[15]

The big differences between @ and z concern non-modal facts. Differences in the title of this essay require differences in our personalities, which require additional physical differences between @ and z. Seemingly minor differences in the physical world can have drastic effects on the truth-values of other non-modal facts due to the chaotic nature of many physical systems.

How about the differences in the logic? World z has the same logic as @, but p does not. We have argued that they should not be weighted significantly more heavily than other differences, but what exactly are the differences here? Of course, the possibility of assigning both truth-values to a sentence is a difference. We should be wary, however, of double counting. The fact that the logic of paradox allows a sentence to be assigned both the true and the false values can be construed as the modal fact that true contradictions are possible. Other differences in the logics include the loss of

---

[15] Note that we are considering these modal differences because some beliefs we have are modal, and so we need to know about the modal features of nearby worlds.

modus ponens, disjunctive syllogism, and *modus tollens* as valid inferences. These can also be construed as modal differences. *Modus ponens* puts a constraint on what is possible. A world that obeys classical logic is one that could not have been such that $\{\varphi \rightarrow \psi, \varphi\}$ are true and ψ is false. A world that obeys the logic of paradox is one that could have been such that $\{\varphi \rightarrow \psi, \varphi\}$ both get designated values and ψ is false.

Ultimately, many of the modal differences are identical to the differences in the logic, so they should not be counted twice. World z diverges from @ with regard to both modal and non-modal propositions, while p only diverges from @ when it comes to modal propositions. More things are possible in p, but $\Diamond\varphi$'s being true in p doesn't entail that φ is true in p. One may think that invalidating *modus ponens* would lead to substantial differences in the non-modal facts between p and z. But, remember that not all differences in laws require substantial non-modal differences. The possibility of a counterexample to *modus ponens* does not require that one is actual. In all close worlds, every instance of $\{\varphi \rightarrow \psi, \varphi\}$ may be accompanied by ψ. There is just some distant possible world where $\{\varphi \rightarrow \psi, \varphi\}$ are true and ψ is not. Note also that a world where contradictions are possible does not have to be a world where contradictions are realized. A world where the logic of paradox is correct needs only a distant possible world where a contradiction is realized.

Since, in the context of safety, we should not weight differences in laws more heavily than other differences, the moderate non-modal differences between z and @ are weighted similarly to the modal differences between p and @. It is not clear that p is closer to @ than z is, but it is also not clear that z is closer than p is. So, p will be closer to @ than many possible worlds with differences more significant than a change to the title of this essay.

The existence of a single impossible world that is closer to @ than some possible world is enough for the weak rejection of SIC, but it is not enough to show that impossible worlds can play a role in safety. We need to show also that there are sufficiently many impossible worlds that are close enough to @ to affect the safety of our beliefs. That is to say, we need to establish the radical rejection of SIC.

To get the radical rejection of SIC, take the set of close possible worlds. For each world, u, in the set, consider an impossible world u' that is just like u except that the correct logic in u' is the logic of paradox. As we saw, a world that merely differs from @ with respect to its logic is relatively close. So, each u' is relatively close to the u from which it is generated. Since those parent worlds are close to @, the generated impossible worlds are also somewhat close. They will be closer to @ than many possible worlds with more significant differences in non-modal facts than u. Many of these close impossible worlds will be relevant in evaluating the safety of our beliefs about necessary truths.

4. Philosophical Beliefs

If there can be close impossible worlds, then we can properly evaluate the safety of our beliefs in necessary truths, even in the cases where our coming to our belief was not lucky. Returning to *Coin-basis**, suppose that we include worlds where intuitionistic logic is correct in our evaluation of the safety of Arnold's belief. The worlds under consideration here are ones where excluded middle is not always true and where double negation is invalid. In intuitionistic worlds where G has not been proven, it is neither true nor false. Whether or not Arnold's belief is safe will turn, in part, on what he would believe in these worlds and whether they are close enough to the actual world. We hold that Arnold's belief is not safe. After all, intuitionistic logic does not change the truth-values of most propositions about the world. The fact that some mathematical propositions are neither true nor false does not lead to absurdities like $2 + 2 = 5$. With the exception of unproven mathematical propositions and various modal facts about, for example, double negation, not much else is changed. Many possible worlds with different non-modal facts about ordinary objects will be more distant than these merely intuitionistic worlds. These worlds are close, Arnold flips his coin in them, and he comes to believe that G. Unfortunately for Arnold, his belief is not true in the intuitionistic worlds, and so it is not safe.

This analysis of safety is not restricted just to mathematical beliefs. It finds its primary usefulness when analyzing philosophical beliefs. For the remainder of this essay we consider philosophical beliefs that, if true, would be necessarily true. There are two main ways that philosophical beliefs could come out safe. First, our belief-forming methods could be such that they "push away" impossible worlds where the belief is false. Second, the belief could be such that its not being true is sufficient to make the world too dissimilar from @ to play a role in safety.

The efficacy of philosophical methodologies is a topic of much discourse in metaphilosophical circles. Some of the central controversies focus on the viability of abduction and the evidentiary status of intuitions. Interestingly, the efficacy of these methodologies will have an effect on the safety of philosophical beliefs on an account that includes impossible worlds. First, we consider intuitions and the safety of philosophical beliefs that are arrived at by intuition. After this, we consider abduction and the safety of philosophical beliefs arrived at on its basis.

Though philosophers make use of deductive and inductive arguments, the bottom-level premises of our arguments are usually supported only by abduction or intuition. Herman Cappelen (2012, 112) treats this role of being a bottom-level justification as a central feature of intuitions. Though Cappelen thinks that it is a feature of intuitions that they play this role, he also argues that philosophers don't actually make much use of intuitions. What we are going to treat as intuitions, here, are the basic premises of arguments that are not supported by deduction, induction, or abduction, whether they receive the name "intuition" or not. Our targets are the starting assumptions that come from reflections on or graspings of the meanings of concepts, whether immediate or formed through a mediate process. Unless our premises reduce to logical truths, at some point the support for them must connect to the world, and when it does, the support for the premises must come from either empirical data or our understandings of the concepts involved. Our understandings or graspings of the concepts are the intuitions we are targeting.

We do, to some extent, weigh in on the debates about the efficacy of intuitions, but only insofar as we consider whether these methods are safety conducive with regard to philosophical beliefs. We are not concerned with the general reliability of intuitions. We proceed by considering a particular philosophical belief—the belief that classical logic is the correct logic—and assume that this is a true belief. That is to say, we assume that the logic that is correct in the actual world is classical logic. For example, worlds where sentences get values other than true or false, where *modus ponens* is invalid, and where excluded middle is not a tautology are all impossible.

Without keeping fixed the facts about belief formation, there are many close worlds where classical logic is not the correct logic. Consider the u' worlds that were used to show that SIC is false. Many of those worlds are close enough that they factor into evaluations of safety. Suppose that someone believes that classical logic is the correct logic by means of intuitions. They think about excluded middle and intuit that it must always be true. In order for this person's belief to be safe, it must be the case that in the u' worlds their intuitions would have given them a different belief.

Now, the close impossible worlds where the logic of paradox is correct are spatiotemporal matches for @, and so our intuitions about the correct logic will not change from what they are in @. There are numerous accounts of intuitions, but for almost all of them it is the case that having different intuitions requires having different brain chemistry. If one's brain chemistry is exactly the same in @ and in p, then φ cannot seem true to one in @ and false to one in p. There are, however, views of intuitions that would entail that changing the logic of a world would require changing our brain chemistry. If intuitions give us direct access to truths, then a world where the correct logic is the logic of paradox would be one where our intuitions (and brain states) are different. Ethical intuitionism is such a view. Ethical intuitionism holds that ethical properties are real and that they can be known non-deductively. In the context of logic, Kurt Gödel has a view like this (see Parsons 1995, 62). He claims that mathematical intuitions are direct perceptions and need no further justification. Such views, however, are extremely controversial. We do not intend to take a stand on the nature of intuitions here, but if intuitions are direct in the way that Gödel, for example, claims they are, then we stand a better chance of getting safe beliefs. After all, changing the relevant concept should change our perception of it. As mentioned above, however, such a view is controversial, and so pinning one's hopes for safe philosophical beliefs on these kinds of intuitionism is dubious.[16]

Abduction does not fare much better. Suppose someone believes that classical logic is correct on the basis of abduction. As Williamson puts it, "Classical semantics and logic are vastly superior to the alternatives in simplicity, power, past success, and integration with theories in other domains" (2002, 186).

If we look at the many close impossible worlds where the logic of paradox is correct, the theoretical virtues of classical logic are unchanged. It fits the evidence we have in those worlds, it is simpler than the logic of paradox, and it is more powerful. So, if, in @, abduction was the basis of our belief that classical logic is correct, then it should give us the same belief in *p*.

The problem for both intuitions and abduction is that they sometimes do not track the relevant truths. In the case of intuitions, they will only track differences in truth-value across worlds if a difference in the truth-value requires the kinds of changes to our experiences that would result in a *proper* change in intuition. As for abduction, changing which theory is correct doesn't have to impact the theoretical virtues of that theory, as the example above shows. With so many close impossible worlds, a failure of tracking can lead to unsafe beliefs.

So far we have looked only at one philosophical belief—the belief that classical logic is the correct logic. This belief, whether it is arrived at via intuition or abduction, is not safe. Other philosophical beliefs could fare better. There are two ways this can happen. First, the impossible worlds where the belief is false may all be distant from @. Second, intuitions or abduction may do a better job in some domains of philosophy than they do in others.

Let's consider the belief that phenomenal zombies are possible and assume for the sake of argument that it's true. Assuming that S5 is the correct modal logic, if the belief about phenomenal zombies is true, then it is necessarily true. This is because it is a belief that zombies are possible, and $\Diamond\varphi$ entails $\Box\Diamond\varphi$ in S5. In the situation where the belief is false, there is no world containing a phenomenal zombie. Would an actual believer in the possibility of phenomenal zombies have a safe belief? Let's consider the reasons that people actually believe zombies are possible. The basic version of the argument for the possibility of zombies is the argument from conceivability.

P1. Phenomenal zombies are conceivable.
P2. Everything that is conceivable is possible.
C. Phenomenal zombies are possible.

---

[16] Note that these kinds of intuitionism are not intuitionistic logic.

Many object that it is unclear that zombies are conceivable. In defense of the conceivability of zombies, David Chalmers argues like this: "I confess that the logical possibility of zombies seems equally obvious to me. A zombie is just something physically identical to me, but which has no conscious experience—all is dark inside. While this is probably empirically impossible, it certainly seems that a coherent situation is described; I can discern no contradiction in the description. In some ways an assertion of this logical possibility comes down to a brute intuition" (1996, 96). Many nonphysicalists may find that their own arguments against physicalism ultimately rest on this kind of brute intuition that there is no logical contradiction in the existence of zombies.

Should we expect that these intuitions about the conceivability of zombies would change if zombies were impossible? We think not. Consider the non-modal facts about a world where zombies are impossible. Such a world could be physically identical to @. World @ may be a world where physicalism is false but be a world that lacks zombies. All qualia in @ and nearby worlds may be the result of physical processes. So, in the world where zombies are impossible, our brains would work in the same way as they do in @ and we would come to the same intuitions. But, in a world where zombies are impossible, our beliefs about their possibility would remain the same.

Are the worlds where zombies are impossible close to worlds where they are possible? One feature of zombies is that they function indistinguishably from non-zombies. The only required difference between a zombie-possible world and a zombie-impossible world is that in one of them the physical facts do not determine the mental facts. It may still be the case that in both worlds the physical and the mental facts are the same. Accordingly, these two worlds can be *extremely* similar to each other. Since the impossible worlds where zombies are impossible are close and our intuitions would not change in them, a belief that zombies are possible on the basis of intuition is not safe.

There are numerous philosophical beliefs that can be evaluated using impossible worlds in an account of safety. For each of them, we need to consider how different the world would be were the belief false, and whether or not certain philosophical methodologies would work better than they do in the cases described above.

Of course, philosophers don't always use intuitions or abduction. Some areas of philosophy are more empirically based than others. For example, were someone to come to a belief that the world is not gunky on the basis of an empirically supported physical theory, then the belief may very well be safe. Were the belief false, then the observations that led to the empirically supported physical theory would change. Alternatively, were someone to come to a philosophical belief through pure deduction using only inferences that are valid or quasi-valid in reasonable logics, then that belief has a good chance of being safe.[17] Unfortunately the project of evaluating various philosophical beliefs will have to be left for a different time. Here are some interesting avenues for discussion:

- The belief that utilitarianism is true.
- The belief that properties are tropes.
- The belief that indiscernibles are identical.
- The belief that the world is gunky.

One might worry that a substantial number of philosophical beliefs will turn out to be unsafe. But, even if we cannot get safe philosophical beliefs in many domains by aiming for knowledge, we could still make philosophical progress by acquiring *safer* beliefs (by employing more empirical methodologies) or by aiming for rational belief or reflective equilibrium, as various metaphilosophers have advocated (see Beebee 2018).

5. Conclusion

Accounts of safety that do not include impossible worlds have problems with beliefs in necessary truths. Adding impossible words to an account of safety allows us to give a more interesting and adequate account of the safety of beliefs in necessary truths. Because impossible worlds can be extremely similar to world @, to know whether or not a belief is safe we need to consider what beliefs one would form in these close impossible worlds. Many philosophical beliefs are such that we would still believe them in close worlds *where we are wrong*. At best, this is epistemically troubling; at worst, it supports a deep metaphilosophical skepticism.

Acknowledgments

Special thanks to Reina Hayaki and Adam Thompson for reading and providing helpful comments on early drafts of this essay, as well as to the anonymous reviewers for *Metaphilosophy*, whose comments and suggestions helped strengthen the piece.

References

Beebee, Helen. 2018. "Philosophical Scepticism and the Aims of Philosophy." *Proceedings of the Aristotelian Society* 118, no. 1: 1–24.
Bernecker, Sven. 2020. "Against Global Method Safety." *Synthese* 197, no. 12: 5101–16.

[17] A quasi-valid inference is one that would be valid were we to restrict the premises to sentences that receive classical values. See Priest 1979, 232.

Berto, Francesco, and Mark Jago. 2019. *Impossible Worlds*. Oxford: Oxford University Press.

Cappelen, Herman. 2012. *Philosophy Without Intuitions*. Oxford: Oxford University Press.

Chalmers, David J. 1996. *The Conscious Mind: In Search of a Fundamental Theory*. Oxford: Oxford University Press.

Fine, Kit. 1975. "Critical Notice." *Mind* 84, no. 335: 451–58.

Hirvela, Jaako. 2019. "Global Safety: How to Deal with Necessary Truths." *Synthese* 196, no. 3: 1167–86.

Kripke, Saul A. 2011. "Nozick on Knowledge." In *Philosophical Troubles: Collected Papers, Volume 1*, 162–264. Oxford: Oxford University Press.

Lewis, David. 1979. "Counterfactual Dependence and Time's Arrow." *Noûs* 13, no. 4: 455–76.

Lewis, David. 1994. "Humean Supervenience Debugged." *Mind* 103, no. 412: 473–90.

Luper-Foy, Steven, editor. 1987. *The Possibility of Knowledge: Nozick and His Critics*. Lanham, Md.: Rowman and Littlefield.

Melchior, Guido. 2017. "Epistemic Luck and Logical Necessities: Armchair Luck Revisited." *Thought Experiments Between Nature and Society: A Festschrift for Nenad Miščević*, edited by Bojan Borstner and Smiljana Gartner, 137–50. Cambridge, Mass.: Cambridge Scholars.

Melchior, Guido. 2021. "Sensitivity, Safety, and Impossible Worlds." *Philosophical Studies* 178, no. 33: 713–29.

Miščević, Nenad. 2007. "Armchair Luck: Apriority, Intellection and Epistemic Luck." *Acta Analytica* 22, no. 1: 48–73.

Nolan, Daniel. 1997. "Impossible Worlds: A Modest Approach." *Notre Dame Journal of Formal Logic* 38, no. 4: 535–72.

Nozick, Robert. 1983. *Philosophical Explanations*. Cambridge, Mass.: Harvard University Press.

Parsons, Charles. 1995. "Platonism and Mathematical Intuition in Kurt Gödel's Thought." *Bulletin of Symbolic Logic* 1, no. 1: 44–74.

Priest, Graham. 1979. "The Logic of Paradox." *Journal of Philosophical Logic* 8, no. 1: 219–41.

Priest, Graham. 2014. *One: Being an Investigation into the Unity of Reality and of Its Parts, Including the Singular Object Which Is Nothingness*. Oxford: Oxford University Press.

Pritchard, Duncan. 2009. "Safety-Based Epistemology: Whither Now?" *Journal of Philosophical Research* 34: 33–45.

Pritchard, Duncan. 2020. "Anti-Risk Virtue Epistemology." In *Virtue Theoretic Epistemology*, edited by Christoph Kelp and John Greco, 203–24. Cambridge: Cambridge University Press.

Putnam, Hilary. 1974. "Meaning and Reference." *Journal of Philosophy* 70, no. 19: 699–711.

Sandgren, Alexander, and Koji Tanaka. 2020. "Two Kinds of Logical Impossibility." *Noûs* 54, no. 4: 795–806.

Sosa, Ernest. 1999. "How to Defeat Opposition to Moore." *Philosophical Perspectives* 13: 141–53.

Thomasson, Amie. 2007. *Ordinary Objects.* Oxford: Oxford University Press.

Tooley, Michael. 1977. "The Nature of Laws." *Canadian Journal of Philosophy* 7, no. 4: 667–98.

Vogel, Jonathan. 1987. "Tracking, Closure, and Inductive Knowledge." In *The Possibility of Knowledge: Nozick and His Critics*, edited by Steven Luper-Foy, 197–215. Lanham, Md.: Rowman and Littlefield.

Williamson, Timothy. 2000. *Knowledge and Its Limits.* Oxford: Oxford University Press.

Williamson, Timothy. 2002. *Vagueness.* London: Routledge.

Williamson, Timothy. 2009. "Reply to John Hawthorne and Maria Lasonen-Aarnio." In *Williamson on Knowledge*, edited by Patrick Greenough and Duncan Pritchard, 313–29. Oxford: Oxford University Press.

Williamson, Timothy. 2020. *Suppose and Tell: The Semantics and Heuristics of Conditionals.* Oxford: Oxford University Press.

Zhao, Bin. 2021. "A Dilemma for Globalized Safety." *Acta Analytica.* doi:10.1007/s12136-021-00478-w. Accessed December 30, 2021.

INDEX

Examining Philosophy Itself. Edited by Yafeng Shan.
Chapters and book compilation © 2023 Metaphilosophy LLC and John Wiley & Sons Ltd.
Published 2023 by John Wiley & Sons Ltd.